In a Strange Room

Modernist Literature & Culture

Kevin J. H. Dettmar & Mark Wollaeger, Series Editors

In a Strange Room

Modernism's Corpses and Mortal Obligation

David Sherman

OXFORD
UNIVERSITY PRESS

OXFORD
UNIVERSITY PRESS

Oxford University Press is a department of the University of
Oxford. It furthers the University's objective of excellence in research,
scholarship, and education by publishing worldwide.

Oxford   New York
Auckland   Cape Town   Dar es Salaam   Hong Kong   Karachi
Kuala Lumpur   Madrid   Melbourne   Mexico City   Nairobi
New Delhi   Shanghai   Taipei   Toronto

With offices in
Argentina   Austria   Brazil   Chile   Czech Republic   France   Greece
Guatemala   Hungary   Italy   Japan   Poland   Portugal   Singapore
South Korea   Switzerland   Thailand   Turkey   Ukraine   Vietnam

Oxford is a registered trademark of Oxford University Press
in the UK and certain other countries.

Published in the United States of America by
Oxford University Press
198 Madison Avenue, New York, NY 10016

© Oxford University Press 2014

Library of Congress Cataloging-in-Publication Data
Sherman, David, 1971–
In a Strange Room: Modernism's Corpses and Mortal Obligation / David Sherman.
   pages cm. — (Modernist Literature & Culture ; 23)
Includes bibliographical references and index.
ISBN 978-0-19-933388-2 (acid-free paper)   1. Modernism (Literature)
2. Death in literature.   I. Title.
PN56.M54S55 2014
809'.9112—dc23

9 8 7 6 5 4 3 2 1
Printed in the United States of America
on acid-free paper

For my parents, in friendship and love—
first teachers,
first readers,
first storytellers.

Contents

Series Editors' Foreword

In 1927, trying to give a sympathetic reader—his father, Homer—a way into his *Cantos*, Ezra Pound announced as one of the poem's three subjects, "Live man goes down into world of Dead." It's an experience that, as David Sherman amply demonstrates, had become both more infrequent and more symbolically charged during the reign of literary modernism—and at the same time, an experience that poets and novelists sought to render, if not vital, at least vivid once again.

In a Strange Room: Modernism's Corpses and Mortal Obligation seeks to re-sensitize contemporary readers to the unsettled position of the corpse in modernist writing: the way it vacillates, in a phrase Sherman adapts from Sarah Cole's book in this series, "between the enchantment and disenchantment of violence." Sherman articulates modernism here as "the emergence of an ethical body of thought about the renovation of mortal obligation in a time of death's modernization," as well as "an archive for understanding who and what modern people became, as political, ethical, and erotic subjects." Scholars have long argued that the twentieth century witnessed a technologizing and sanitizing of traditional ways of death; in 1904 Leopold Bloom, trying to make small talk in the coach on the way to Paddy Dignam's funeral, scandalizes the party by blithely mapping the logic of efficiency onto the mortal obligation of burying the dead.

And if modern subjects felt disconnected from the death of loved ones who, a generation or two earlier, would have died at home rather than quarantined off in hospitals, how much more so the deaths of half a million British soldiers in continental Europe, who never came home? "Graves generate graves which generate further graves, all of which generate the nation," Sherman observes—a logic that, to retain its power, must remain occluded. For this reason, the poetry of Wilfred

Owen represents a potent threat, for the corpses in his poetry "remain arbitrary, meaning nothing. This demanded a new set of poetic techniques responsive to a powerful nationalist rhetoric intent on making them mean everything." In this context, Sherman unearths a metonymic and synecdochal logic at work—one body standing in for many—best exemplified in Britain's Tomb of the Unknown Warrior.

The book moves via twinned authors: Wilfred Owen and the Virginia Woolf of *Jacob's Room*, on WWI; James Joyce and William Faulkner, on the modernist "burial plot"; T. S. Eliot and Djuna Barnes, on the queer erotics of modern death; W. C. Williams and Wallace Stevens, on the potential—if not the actual—ability of modernist writing to reorient modern people's relationship to the dead, to render them "agents of their own ethical capacities in relation to the dead." Even when the logic of these pairings seems clear on the face of it, the work Sherman does with them and through them is fresh and unexpected. Examining the role of corpses in *As I Lay Dying* and the "Hades" chapter of *Ulysses*, for instance, Sherman writes that "Faulkner makes burying the dead hard, after Joyce risks making it easy." In Faulkner, he argues, "The corpse can be buried, but not contained. Faulkner insists that we are still a part of its death because it cannot bury itself."

Happily, the chapter Sherman acknowledges as his riskiest also pays the greatest dividend. In his ingenious reading, the sex-averse *Waste Land* and the sex-soaked *Nightwood* flower from the same queer root; in the writing of Eliot and Barnes, "sex and death radicalize each other in ways that put familiar social forms and identities at risk." Much has been written about the disavowed queer sexuality of *The Waste Land*, of course; Sherman argues that in completing its project, *Nightwood* "refuses broad principles of social inclusion and reform for the radical possibility of death itself, death without norms, and the ethical force mobilized by mortality to disorient the homogenization and alienation of death in a normative order."

The writing of *In a Strange Room* is confident and fluent, the work of someone widely and deeply read in the primary and secondary sources. Though a thoroughly scholarly study, at times it seems less like an analysis than a philosophical, and even lyrical, meditation.

We're pleased to publish *In a Strange Room* in the Modernist Literature & Culture series, and to bring it to you.

Kevin J. H. Dettmar & Mark Wollaeger

Acknowledgments

I am grateful for the intellectual solidarity of many friends in the lively academic world of Brandeis University. I am particularly thankful for the insightful comments and generous encouragement that Caren Irr and Ulka Anjaria offered over several years. Paul Morrison gave robust, incisive readings of particularly difficult aspects of this book. Laura Quinney, with patience, helped untangle one of its most recalcitrant knots. John Plotz, William Flesch, Dawn Skorczewski, and John Burt have clarified my ideas and offered sustaining friendship. Jon Sudholt and Marg Carkeet shared their formidable talents for research. A grant from the dean's office at Brandeis supported a final stage of the manuscript's preparation.

Others beyond Brandeis have also been crucial interlocutors. Karen Bishop's rigorous commitment to modern literature involving corpses has been a model and inspiration for this work. Lewis Kirshner escorted me with finesse through the thickets of Lacan's thought. And John Paul Riquelme offered invigorating perspectives on how to engage modernist scholarship with these ideas.

At Oxford University Press, Mark Wollaeger and Kevin Dettmar supported this project with generosity and imagination. Brendan O'Neill's editorial care nourished the manuscript in innumerable ways. Two anonymous readers for Oxford University Press, to whom I am especially obliged, gave a tremendously helpful set of suggestions, clarifications, and challenges—many of which I must continue to respond to in future work. I hope that I have begun to learn from their critical precision and scholarly grace. An earlier version of a section of chapter two was published as "Burial Plots, Inoperative Community, and Faulkner's

As I Lay Dying" in *Theory@Buffalo* 11 (2007), and I am grateful for permission to republish it.

Holly Fritz, my most honest broker and the best teacher I know, has helped me understand from beginning to end how ideas about literature can matter. More than I can tell, I have been able to do this work because she shares her life with mine.

List of Abbreviations

AILD   Faulkner, William. *As I Lay Dying*. New York: Vintage International, 1990.

TWL   Eliot, T. S. *The Waste Land*. *Collected Poems 1909–1962*. New York: Harcourt Brace, 1963.

CPF v. 1   Owen, Wilfred. *The Complete Poems and Fragments*. Vol. 1. Edited by Jon Stallworthy. London: Chatto & Windus, The Hogarth Press, and Oxford University Press, 1983.

EP   Lacan, Jacques. *The Ethics of Psychoanalysis*. Translated by Dennis Porter. Edited by Jacques Alain-Miller. New York: W. W. Norton, 1992.

IC   Nancy, Jean-Luc. *The Inoperative Community*.Translated by Peter Connor, Lisa Garbus, Michael Holland, and Simona Sawhney. Edited by Peter Connor. Minneapolis: University of Minnesota Press, 1991.

JR   Woolf, Virginia. *Jacob's Room*. London: Penguin, 1992.

N   Barnes, Djuna. *Nightwood: The Original Version and Related Drafts*. Edited by Cheryl J. Plumb. Normal, IL: Dalkey Archive Press, 1995.

U   Joyce, James. *Ulysses*. Edited by Hans Walter Gabler. New York: Vintage, 1993.

Introduction

Toward the Modernist Corpse

Just as life had been strange a few minutes before, so death was now as strange.

—Virginia Woolf, "The Death of the Moth"

My death ship lost its way...

—Franz Kafka, "The Hunter Gracchus"

The house of modernism has many strange rooms; those I pass through in this book hold its corpses. The preternatural beauty of modernist writing about the dead arose from an uneasy desire to know what it could still mean, in the twentieth century, to be alive to the dead bodies in one's midst, to actively care for them, to claim them in acts of obligation. If death is always strange, it was particularly strange in the modernized West in the first part of the twentieth century. Modernist attempts to make sense of the death practices of the time themselves became an important set of death practices, a set of potent symbolic acts involved in the care and signification of corpses.[1] When the young Marcel, in Proust's *Within a Budding Grove*, arrives at the hotel in Malbec where he is to pass the summer, he is overwhelmed by an uncanny sense of mortal fragility—his own, but mingled with that of those to whom he will one day bear a unique responsibility: "Perhaps this fear that I had—and that is shared by so many others—of sleeping in a strange room [*une chambre inconnue*], perhaps this fear is only the most humble, obscure, organic, almost unconscious form of that great and desperate resistance put up by the things that constitute the better part of our present life towards our mentally acknowledging the possibility of a future in which they are to have no part; a resistance which was at the root of the horror that I had so often been made to feel by the thought that my parents would die some day...; a resistance which was also at the root of the difficulty that I found in imagining my own death."[2] Marcel's new room is made strange not just by the intimations of mortality he finds within the fact of its difference, but by the quiet resistance to this difference embodied in the people and things that find themselves mortal within it. Marcel's attunement to this resistance of the dead to their mere passing, an attunement to their insistence on making the world strange in their mortal wake, is what I seek to describe in modernism. At stake is an understanding of modernism as the emergence of an ethical body of thought about the renovation of mortal obligation in a time of death's modernization. In one of his most lyrically brooding passages in *As I Lay Dying*, Faulkner has Darl think about his dying mother, Addie, whom he will soon help transport as a corpse across Mississippi for burial. It is in the very ways that his night-thoughts break apart that they open up new possibilities for thinking about what the deaths of others require of us:

> In a strange room you must empty yourself for sleep. And before you are emptied for sleep, what are you. And when you are emptied for sleep, you are not. And when you are filled with sleep, you never were. I dont know what I am. I dont know if I am or not. Jewel knows he is, because he does not know that he does not know whether he is or not. He cannot empty himself for sleep because he is not what he is and he is what he is not. Beyond the unlamped wall I can hear the rain shaping the wagon that is ours, the load that is no longer theirs that felled and sawed it nor yet theirs that bought it and which is not ours either, lie on our wagon though it does, since only the wind and the rain shape it only to Jewel and me, that are not asleep. And since sleep is is-not and rain and wind are *was*, it is not. Yet the wagon *is*, because when the wagon is *was*, Addie Bundren will not be. And Jewel *is*, so Addie Bundren must be. And then I must be, or I could not empty myself for sleep in a strange room. And so if I am not emptied yet, I am *is*.
>
> How often have I lain beneath rain on a strange roof, thinking of home.[3]

I discuss this passage in detail in Chapter Two, but I turn to it now because it gropes at the edge of coherence around questions of knowledge, possession, and being toward Addie's dying, an event beyond the questions and answers available in these categories. Addie's corpse—modernism's most familiar one precisely for its powers of defamiliarization—lies throughout the novel at the limits of narrative order, where in its condition of extremity and estrangement it offers the possibility of the corpse meaning more than it was supposed to in an aggressively moderniz-ing culture. Darl's memories of rain on a strange roof far from home are a medita-tion on the social displacement and aesthetic return of the dead.

Modernism's corpses, in their enigma of displacement and return, need attend-ing. Dying, like birthing and the labors of living, has in recent centuries been mod-ernized into conditions that would have been unfathomable to those in premodern worlds. If the simple (and banal) fact of our mortality is, as it were, immortal, the social organization of mortality and the demands of the dead bodies it leaves for us are alarmingly protean, shifting in modern cultures even between generations. The self's relation to its mortality, and to the mortality of others, is no less socially and politically complex, no less fraught with social currents of imagination and desire, than its relation to its own and others' sexuality (and, as modernism will rediscover, these relations are profoundly involved with one another). Adorno, reducing the metaphysics of death to the social situation of particular people dying, reminds us that "death comes within the scope of history"; with a simi-lar, if uncharacteristic, historicism, Freud acknowledges during the First World War that "we are unable to maintain our former attitude towards death, and have not yet found a new one."[4] Dying, and the corpse produced by dying, is not one single knowable thing: a man dies, Yeats writes, yet "Many times he died, / Many times rose again." The West has re-made its dying in many ways, a fact that Yeats, at the end of this poem, does not find disorienting but expressive of our will to power: "He knows death to the bone—/ Man has created death."[5] By many socio-logical and historical accounts, the modernization of dying and corpse disposal has fashioned death into remarkably strange forms, an inhabitant of increasingly strange rooms, but the vivid account of this sea change given by literary mod-ernism has not been fully appreciated. In this book, I approach Anglo-American modernism as an archive for understanding who and what modern people—as political, ethical, and erotic subjects—became through the modernization of their death practices. Modernist engagements with the dying and dead bodies of its time, engagements that demanded astonishing innovations of literary technique, expressed anxieties about modern death that still trouble the West and are a reason so many continue to read modernism with urgency. Modernism was there when the West's corpses fell far from its familiar knowledge and care, and it began the work of reimagining its ethical capacities around the dead, its mortal obligations.

I hope to show that the social reorganization of mortality in the early twentieth century did its part to precipitate modernism's aesthetic crises and renewals, and that its radical explorations of literary form grasped the new political relations and pressures around the dead, the era's new thanatopolitics. Edward Said has characterized modernism as "an aesthetic and ideological phenomenon in response to the crisis of what could be called *filiation*—linear, biologically grounded process, that which ties children to their parents."[6] I argue that modernism also responds to the crisis of filiation across mortal lines, to the era's depletion of symbolic exchange and binding between the living and dead. In this analysis, I build on Alan Friedman's work in *Fictional Death and the Modernist Enterprise*, where he describes the "epistemological and religious incertitude [that] help explain modernism's turn from stable rituals associated with Victorian dying," a turn by which "fictional death became attenuated, denied, or horrific: initiatory or evaded rather than climactic."[7] Friedman's insistence that we recognize modernist death as a representational problem[8] informs my approach toward modernist representations of mortal obligation. Some of the highest political and ethical stakes of the modernist literary imagination are elaborated through its corpses, which emerged in those years as a flashpoint for tensions between ritual action and scientific knowledge, communal tradition and market calculation, lay authority and the authority of technical specialists. Literary scholars have not paid sustained attention to modernism as a response to the shifting ways people died and handled each other's corpses, I suspect for the unfamiliarity of mortuary practices, or deathways, as a political concern: if there is such a politics, it comes to us filtered through ancient ethical intuitions and does not immediately involve the same freedoms and rights as other social issues long at the center of literary scholarship. The dead are obscure in the ways they affect the contours of power, even if those who wield power are not always subtle in their administration of the dead. But attention—in my approach, a historically responsive philosophical attention—to the materiality of the dead, and to the dead as material culture, opens modernism to a set of productive questions about relations among literature, death practices, and ethical desire in an increasingly secular and industrial age. In what symbolic, as well as geographical, locations do the dead dwell in modern cultures, and with what filiations and affiliations? How does modernism work through, construct, and reconstruct those symbolic locations and affiliations? How has the modernization of dying and corpse disposal refashioned the obligation to another's dying and dead body, and how has modernism rearticulated this obligation? If modernism has in recent years been read as a discourse of profound mourning, of a culturally saturating grief in times of traumatic violence and degradation, how might we also read it as a discourse of mortal obligation? These questions return, by different paths, to modernism's negotiation between ancient ethical intuitions about corpses and the twentieth century's new regime for their efficient, medical administration and hygienic disposal. In other words, they return to the impulse in Pound's question in "Coda": "O My Songs, / Why do you look so eagerly and so curiously into people's faces, / Will you find your lost dead among them?"[9] A rhetorical question, but answerable: modernism does find its lost dead, and in surprising ways. Just as philosophy has long been called a preparation for death, so too is literature, which takes up the ethical and existential work of philosophy with the images, rhetorical figures, poetics, and plots we need for working through our relation to the dead in an age of this relation's extreme attenuation, abstraction, and mediation. It is inevitable, says Freud, "that we should seek in the world of fiction, in literature and in the theatre compensation for what has been lost in life. There we still find people who know how to die."[10] And who know how to retain those who die as a part of our lifeworlds. "When culture is dead, the risk of thought is to encounter death as something alive, as light-particles refracted in the glass cases of a corpse museum," writes Stathis Gourgouris. This risk of encountering death as it is still alive, and as it involves responsibilities that crucially shape us, is what modernism undertakes.[11]

In this study, I speculate that if the human is traditionally conceived as that which intentionally disposes of its dead, then the modern is that period in which the human is no longer certain about its ability to do so or the meaning of doing so. Modernism helps its readers feel anxious about this uncertainty; the premise of this study is that the modern subject needed—and needs—this anxiety for his or her well-being. As an aestheticized anxiety about the integrity of the era's deathways, modernism reveals the corpse as a site of ideological recalcitrance and disorientation, a vestigial thing only awkwardly available for modern processes of rationalization, secularization, marketization, governmental regulation, and so on; it is, actually or potentially, "that compelling, raw, insolent thing in the morgue's full sunlight."[12] In this cultural insolence, the corpse means both more and less than what it is supposed to mean, so that the circulation of corpses shares a compelling strangeness, a marginal quotient of charisma, with the circulation of literary texts. Literary forms die, to be tended by the likes of humanities scholars, and literature itself is a potent practice for resolving the ideological impasses that generate its culture's anxieties about death practices. "Literature *follows* great social changes—. . . it always 'comes after.' To come after, however, does not mean to repeat ('reflect') what already exists, but the exact opposite: to *resolve* the problems set by history. For every transformation carries with it a quantity of ethical impediments, perceptual confusions, ideological contradictions. It involves, in short, a *symbolic overload* that risks rendering social cohesion precarious, and individual existence wearisome."[13] Modernism arrived after the symbolic overloading, or chaotic resignifying, of the dead, whose traditional religious meanings lingered even as these bodies entered the increasingly complex technological, scientific, economic, and governmental processes of their secularization. As social contradictions, these bodies solicited new literary forms capable of working through their tensions as they carried them with something like proper care. If "history is how the secular world attends to its dead," as Saidiya Hartman shows, literature is how the secular world manages the tensions at the heart of this attending and seeks to understand the obligations that motivate it.[14] This imaginative writing at its strongest finds a modern idiom for acknowledging the distinctive and extraordinary experience of intimate, attentive contact with the dead, an ultimate encounter with the enigma of embodiment: "Corpses *show me* what I permanently thrust aside in order to live.... There, I am at the border of my condition as a living being"; "The corpse, smelling now of excrement and rot, pushes ever nearer, smearing with its messy touch the lines that make of me a someone and not a something."[15]

We are still learning to read modernism's corpses. What this literature has to tell us, beyond the fact that the corpse is an ideological problem for the ethical thought and feeling of its time, is that there is an aspect of modern self-making that seeks to renovate obligations to the dead by establishing some compelling way to reckon the worth of their bodies within their new contexts. This reckoning is what death practices have always done, but in the twentieth century these practices unravelled, thinned out, and came under strange new auspices (as I discuss in detail below). The strangeness of modernism's aesthetic power has to do with the ambivalence, anxiety, and nostalgia of this reckoning of the dead as an aspect of modernization, a set of social processes largely hostile to them. It may be that modernity's freedoms require hostility to the terrible authority of the dead, but the experience of these freedoms, these texts tell us, is inextricable from the task of self-forging in an ethical trial. The modern self is hungry for ethical meaning, with all its uncertainty and threat to autonomy, as well as for freedom. The dead are a task by which the living give their freedom a sense that it is worth struggling for. Mortuary practices are a significant way for a community to conceptualize justice and bind itself to a desire for it. As Vincent Brown demonstrates, articulating obligations to the dead helps communities find the political resources to survive: "None of the practices that make up political history are givens: belonging must be articulated, authority constituted, inheritance disputed, communal morality acknowledged, territory claimed, and memory revised. In these activities, the dead not only provide a focus for continuity—they are an inspiration for change. In the struggle to shape the future the dead do not necessarily have the last word, but they have always had a voice."[16] Even in times that aggressively orient themselves toward the future and its promise of new freedoms, obligations to the bodies and voices of the dead help constitute the ethical meaning of political aspiration.

Modernism traces the fragile, ambiguous role of the corpse and discerns the voices of the nearly obsolete dead in an increasingly secular struggle for ethical self-formation. I develop different facets of this argument in the following chapters by working through poetry and fiction by Wilfred Owen, Virginia Woolf, James Joyce, William Faulkner, T. S. Eliot, and Djuna Barnes, as well as giving brief attention in a coda to poems by William Carlos Williams and Wallace Stevens. These writers put the modern corpse, in its semiotic volatility, at the center of modernism's fundamentally double itinerary: to both make literature radically new and recuperate its abandoned possibilities, to express the unruly energies of the living and shape them to the legacies they have reclaimed and that have retained their claims over them. The twentieth century's social reorganization of mortality has at stake, these writers show us, the ethical capacity to exceed the determining logics of capital and state power in relations to the dead, an excess I call its mortal obligations. Modernism's neglected struggle is to imagine a form of life, in terms that break with traditional religious ways of imagining it, that keeps the dead and their bodies at least a hair's breadth apart from the scientific objectification, cultural disenchantment, bureaucratic expansion, and economic calculation and abstraction that defined the modernization of the West. This book is an attempt to conceptualize, in critical terms, the life of the dead that modernism imagined in its new aesthetic forms.

I develop the concept of mortal obligation throughout this book, and I suspect that the way that each chapter fails to conceptualize it comprehensively reveals something about this concept's basic opacity. Others' deaths demand something of us, and every attempt to definitively identify what this is, how it works, and what it does to its recipient fails to account for some aspect of what lies behind the force of this demand: the ambiguities of identity and agency in proximity to another's dying, anxiety about the repose and well-being of the dead, the struggle to narrate one's reckoning with time and loss, the ambivalence between secular and religious (or literal and figurative) discourses around death, some simultaneously charismatic and abject quality of the corpse, the combination of dread and longing toward whatever remains of the dead one. Corpses, unable to say what they need from us, are nevertheless eloquent in their need. In the most pragmatic and logistical sense, bodily remains simply require respectful care and disposal. I try, however, to understand how this fully intelligible demand is the manifestation of an unintelligible aspect of the self that knows its mortality through its involvement in the mortality of others, and how this involvement, as a part of one's obligation to the dead, loses its communicable forms as dying and corpses are rationalized and sequestered. The demands of the dead are strange, and make modernization strange. Toward the beginning of *The Notebooks of Malte Laurids Brigge*, Rilke has Malte describe the disruption caused by his grandfather's long dying in nearly all the rooms of his house:

> Christopher Detlov's death was alive now, had already been living at Ulsgaard for many, many days, talked with everyone, made demands. Demanded to be carried, demanded the blue room, demanded the small salon, demanded the great banquet-hall. Demanded the dogs, demanded that people laugh, talk, play, stop talking, and all at the same time. Demanded to see friends, women, and people who had died, and demanded to die itself: demanded. Demanded and screamed.[17]

This is an age, Rilke suggests, in which a death must scream its demands to be heard. As I hope to show, the heightened demands of reading modernism have to do with the new forms that these demands of the dying and dead take in modernizing cultures.

The concept of mortal obligation that I develop in this book derives from the paradox that the modernized corpse was (and is) both more and less demanding than those that came before it: it was a simultaneously high- and low-maintenance thing, but in a way that had never before been the case. On the one hand, it lay for the first time at a complicated intersection of medical institutions and procedures, industrial processes, governmental bureaucracies, legal codes, and commercial exchanges; on the other, it involved dramatically less ritualization, physical contact with family and friends, and community attention than in the past. It demanded both high expertise among a wide range of technical specialists and virtually no traditional knowledge or cultural competence among laypeople—precisely the reverse of premodern worlds. The modernized dead were financially expensive but ritualistically and symbolically cheap; the value of the former was supplanting the values of the latter. I think the peculiarity of this reversal helps explain both the excitement and awkwardness of Roger Fry's observations, in his 1935 letter that Woolf includes in her biography of him, about the philosopher J. M. E. McTaggart's funeral.

> And while the Bach Chorale was being played the coffin moved by hidden mechanism through the doors into?—How odd that this up to date, hygienic, scientific machine-made and machine-worked disposal of the body is ten times more impressive, more really symbolic than that age-long consecrated business of earth-to-earth—with the ugliness of the big

hole—so unsuggestive of the infinities which surround us... Whereas this with its slow silent movement through doors into the unknown is really dramatic and a perfect symbol of the inevitable mechanism of things and the futility of our protests against its irresistible force.[18]

Fry's unsentimental transformation of a mechanized process into the very source of symbolic richness embraces, with a rare willfulness, the new situation of the twentieth-century corpse. It is the object of intricate attention not from mourning family and friends but from both a literal and a bureaucratic machinery run by strangers. Meanwhile, friends and families watch. And pay. Or have their insurance companies pay. The modernist writers I examine consider Fry's pleasure in the depersonalized futility of this death practice to be as flawed a response to this situation as an uncritical sentimentality or nostalgia for traditional death practices, and in their writing imagine alternative ways to renovate the ethical dimension of modernized death. Mortal obligation, the ethical response to the dead that I describe in modernism, was a response not just to their new cultural poverty but to the obfuscation of this poverty that Fry refuses to acknowledge. The writers I discuss in this book resist this obfuscation and explore new ethical possibilities for undertaking noninstrumental commitments to the dead from within this cultural impoverishment, in full knowledge of it.

This approach to modernism as a response to the combination of technological abundance and symbolic dearth of dying and dead bodies is relevant to critical approaches involving mourning and trauma, but it is distinct from them. While having the corpse of another is important for mourning—and its absence can be traumatizing—the heart of mortal obligation is an ethical desire for the corpse's proper care for its own sake, as an instance of the symbolic integrity of a culture's material practices, not for the sake of the emotional well-being of the living. The obligation to tend to corpses extends to strangers, for whom we may have little grief, because their corpses have an order of cultural meaning distinct from mourning (as the next section discusses). There is an extremely rich body of scholarship that discerns modernism's profoundly elegiac functions, describes its labor of mourning in an age of social upheaval and mass state violence, and theorizes the nature of modern trauma. This study has profoundly benefited from that work.[19] But this book is not primarily about how modernism represents working through loss and grief. Rather, it is about managing a presence—an ethically significant bodily presence that has become much stranger in the early years of the twentieth century—and about how this strangeness reveals an impasse or contradiction in the cultural logic of the West's modernization.

Corpse, Language, Ethics

If human death is a many-historied thing, materialized and signified in astonishingly diverse ways across times and places, there nevertheless seems to be a basic ethical impulse toward the dead that cuts across the historical changes we know. The corpse inhabits two temporalities, its specific moment in all its vicissitudes as well as a *longue durée*, a span that extends much further back than our most ancient historical records, in fact preceding what we even mean by history. The corpse is strange in part because it draws its meaning from both temporal frames.[20] Tending to corpses is a primordial aspect of the human, a manifestation of Michael Serres's dramatic claim that "a certain number of contemporary actions, behaviors, or thoughts repeat, almost without change, extremely archaic modes of thought or behavior. We are ancient in most of our actions and thoughts."[21] Even if we contest this claim in almost every other instance, we should take the longevity of corpse disposal in human behavior seriously. Many have, across several disciplines. Archaeologists claim that Neanderthal humans ritually buried their dead—the pollen preserved in the earth around the corpse of Shanidar IV in a cave in Kurdish Iraq has been interpreted as evidence of a flower ritual from approximately sixty thousand years ago—and nearly all agree that ritual burial was common among upper paleolithic humans ten to forty thousand years ago.[22] These are periods— *in the tens of thousands of years*—that collapse even our best critical historicism, let alone the categories "modern" and "traditional." To acknowledge that we buried the dead so remotely, even before we undertook agriculture, is to acknowledge that intentional, ritual disposal of these bodies has been a uniquely pervasive element of human worlds—or equally as pervasive as language.[23] Humans signify; humans tend to each other's corpses. "Humanity is not a species (*Homo sapiens* is a species)," Robert Harrison asserts; "it is a way of being mortal and relating to the dead. To be human means above all to bury."[24] Jacque Lynn Foltyn claims that "ceremonial burial coincides with the beginning of human social and aesthetic life," emphasizing corpse disposal as the origin of aesthetic practices: "Mesolithic and neanderthal humans painted their dead and buried crowns, ornaments, flowers, and pots of body paint in their graves."[25] Malinowski influentially claimed, "Of all the sources of religion, the supreme and final crisis of life—death—is of the greatest importance." This is similar to Durkheim's suggestion that "the first rites were funeral rites...and the first alters were graves." And Pascal Boyer argues that religion is at its evolutionary roots a response to corpses. He specifies this assertion is distinct from the claim that religion is a response to knowledge of one's own potential to die, which is an abstraction of or derivation from the corpses in one's midst.²⁶ This sense of the elementality of corpse-tending to human world-making informed Giambattista Vico's claim, in his speculative anthropology *The New Science*, that burial is one of three universal institutions, along with marriage and religion, and that it is the one that produces human place: "By long residence and burial of their dead [early humans] came to found and divide the first dominions of the earth, whose lords were called giants, a Greek word meaning 'sons of the earth,' i.e., descendants of those who have been buried"; "by the graves of their buried dead the giants showed their dominion over the lands, and Roman law called for burial of the dead in a proper place to make it religious. With truth they could pronounce those heroic phrases: we are sons of the earth, we are born from these oaks." He also reminds us that "*humanitas* in Latin comes first and properly from *humando*, burying," because "humanity had its origin in *humare*, to bury."²⁷ In his philosophical anthropology, Emmanuel Levinas considers this mortal engagement our primary humanizing fact: "What I am here saying might appear to be a pious thought, but I am persuaded that around the death of my neighbor is manifested what I call the humanity of man."²⁸

Humans tend to each other's corpses; humans signify. To say that we, in some essential sense, tend to our dead is to say that we invest corpses with meaning, involve them in our collective symbolic formations,²⁹ yet it also suggests, more radically, that the symbolization of the dead is inseparable from the symbolic faculty itself as a kind of ground for every cultural signification. In this view, the concept of culture without significance attached to mortal remains would be incoherent.³⁰ Harrison argues that the dead constitute the cultural realm as such: "As *Homo sapiens* we are born of our biological parents. As human beings we are born of the dead—of the regional ground they occupy, of the languages they inhabited, of the worlds they brought into being, of the many institutional, legal, cultural, and psychological legacies that, through us, connect them to the unborn."³¹ "Children, / Still weaving budded aureoles, / Will speak our speech and never know," agrees the speaker in Stevens's "A Postcard from the Volcano," and after writing his poem on the beach early in *Ulysses*, Stephen registers this same saturating legacy: "Dead breaths I living breathe, tread dead dust, devour a urinous offal from all the dead."³² These thoughts—that worlds of human matter and meaning are made in and from the remains of the dead—are akin to Lacan's claim that the burial mark is a paradigm for all language: "The first symbol in which we recognize humanity in its vestigial traces is the sepulture, and the intermediary of death can be recognized in every relation in which man comes to the life of his history."³³ Lacan's structuralist intuition that marking corpse remains is the threshold of the symbolic, an inauguration of all differential systems of meaning, implies that naming is a quintessentially mortal act. In *Antigone*, he writes, "the fact that it is man who invented the sepulchre is evoked" because "the register of being of someone who was identified by a name has to be preserved by funeral rites.... The unique value involved is essentially that of language. Outside of language it is inconceivable"(*EP* 279). Language is structurally inextricable from attention to the corpse, the primordial catalyst of signification; this is along the lines of Gillian Rose's insight that death "is the demarcation between physical nature and signification."[34] The corpse catalyzes the sign. As Harrison writes, "It is not for nothing that the Greek word for 'sign,' *sema*, is also the word for 'grave.' For the Greeks the grave marker was not just one sign among others. It was a sign that signified the source of signification itself, since it 'stood for' what it 'stood in'—the ground of burial as such."[35]

But if this is the case, what does tending the dead have to do with ethics? If such behavior is as prehistoric and pervasive as making tools and signs, why mystify it with rhetorics of virtue, obligation, responsibility, moral codes? If corpse disposal has to do with everything, it means nothing in particular for our moral lives; it is an uncontroversial anthropological fact. It is universal, and so uninteresting. Or we might say it is an ethical absolute, and so the absolute diffusion of ethics: human care for the dead becomes too typical to be an interesting ethical problem.[36] In fact, I suspect this is how most of us experience the death practices around us: as emotionally and socially significant but not as ethically demanding, as a test of emotional resilience rather than of our morality or virtue. Nor, in our grief, would we wish for a sense of ethical ambiguity or complexity in our death rituals. So why the association of tending to the dead with ethics, above and beyond its association with emotional therapeutics, sociality, aesthetics, hygiene, religious and ethnic tradition, and so on? If an ethical capacity or performance is more than a name for a complex combination of these others—which I think it is—why do the dead hold our ethicality, our goodness, at stake? We can put this question another way, in terms of Michael Rosen's philosophical investigation into duties to corpses: "What good thing would be produced and continue to exist if the last sentient being in the universe were to treat the corpse of the next-to-last one with dignity?"[37] If the corpse is not a person with rights, and neither is there a utilitarian justification for its unique forms of care, what justifies treating the corpse with dignity, even reverence? The difficulty of this question assumes that we, following Nietzsche, were to purge ourselves of God's shadow: "If God is not there to hear, why express respect?"[38] To whom do we express respect when we care for the dead? Can we have meaningful duties when no one in particular benefits from them, when they are not duties to a being that can benefit?

Rosen does not consider the duty to treat the dead with dignity as an expression of humanism, since this duty does not benefit another being with intrinsic human value or answer to some teleology beyond itself.[39] Yet it is a duty anyway; the duty theorist, who "has...no further reply...must simply appeal to the conviction that, nonetheless, the expression of respect would remain a duty, even if there is no one else to perceive it."[40] This line of thought helps us recognize the tautology of our obligation to corpses: they hold our ethicality, our goodness, at stake because that is what they do. We are faced with a kind of ethical circularity or redundancy, a proposition like *Tending to the dead is what ethics is*, or a premise that the duty to the corpse is inseparable from the very idea of ethical duty, according to which what is necessary becomes what is good, or what is becomes what ought to be, and vice-versa. To open up this tautology—to ask why there is an ethical dimension to deathways, why the corpse speaks to us in the imperative—is to ask for a cause when there is not so much a cause as a correlation, in the same way that it is fruitless to ask what causes language to be meaningful. (That is what makes it language.) A relation to a corpse is constituted by responsibility—by a nonreciprocal, asymmetrical, and nonrational duty. What this means in practical terms varies. Most dramatically, it means the responsibility to retrieve, transport, protect, wash, arrange, dress, ritualize, dispose, identify, and commemorate a dead body. Less dramatically, it means the responsibility simply to acknowledge the body in speech and attitude, to witness it, to refrain from exploiting or abusing it, to not be indifferent to its presence and condition, to arrange for others to tend to it, to pay others to do so. To say that a relation to a corpse by definition involves some degree of obligation is to acknowledge it as a threshold of what is intelligible as an experience of ethicality, just as Lacan and others acknowledge it as a threshold of signification.

At this threshold that precedes the familiar logics of humanist respect for rights or utilitarianism, duties to the corpse, Rosen writes,

> are principally symbolic: they require us to act in ways that *express* respect. And I am not put off by the thought that it may well be that we are being asked to express respect when there is no one else there to become aware of that expression. Our duty to respect the dignity of humanity is—on this I agree with Kant—fundamentally a duty toward ourselves. By which I mean, not that we are benefited when we observe our duties, but that our duties are so deep a part of us that we could not be the people that we are without having them. In failing to respect the humanity of others we actually undermine humanity in ourselves.[41]

Corpses are worthy of our dignity to the extent that our identity is constituted by our use of symbols. The corpse is where culture, as a realm of both symbolic action and obligation, finds an initial set of forms and practices to articulate itself, and so a point where ethical and signifying acts have not yet been differentiated. We might say this is the point where every meaning has an ethical valence and weight because it means that a responsibility is being fulfilled. This dynamic is circular. A corpse means, among humans, and what it means is that we are obliged to tend it; we are obliged to do so because it is meaningful. Freud speculates that "what came into existence beside the dead body of the loved one was not only the doctrine of the soul, the belief in immortality and a powerful source of man's sense of guilt, but also the earliest ethical commandments. The first and most important prohibition made by the awakening conscience was: 'Thou shalt not kill.'"[42] Freud imagines that the dead, in their native eloquence, create the ethical agents that tend to them; this relation is not the result of a judgment but an inauguration of ethical subjects capable of making such judgments, wherever they may lead. Levinas imagines a similar inaugural power in the corpse, an ethical force grounded in nothing but itself and manifested as guilt: "What is signified by the advent of conscience, and even the first spark of spirit, if not the discovery of corpses beside me and my horror of existing by assassination?"[43]

Levinas, in fact, is a primary thinker of this kind of groundless but grounding circularity in our ethical capacities, which he conceptualizes as the primordial quality of our obligation to the other, before any decision or intention, a being-for-the-other deep at the heart of being a self. Throughout his phenomenological descriptions of subjectivity's constitution in its irrepressible venturing toward the other in responsibility, Levinas insists that ethics is first philosophy, an order of human truth that precedes epistemology and ontology because it is in this arduous responsibility for the other that we achieve our singularity as persons. Our ethical relation to the other is what organizes us as discrete selves, which will always carry traces of their implication in an alterity that precedes them. The other, for Levinas, is quintessentially that presence before us in naked vulnerability, the face exposed before ours in a radical alterity that we acknowledge as irreducible to our projects and desires. The other comes before the self, is there as its terrible and unfathomable interruption, and so is the measure of its transcendence of or dislocation from its own being. That we are rarely conscious of others in such a manner is not the point, in Levinas's thought; this excessive response to the other is a condition, a capacity, that precedes our conscious intentions and active decisions, which are derived from this originary and passive being-for-the-other. Those who are dying and the bodies of the dead solicit us in this way, because "the human consists precisely in opening itself to the death of the other, in being preoc-cupied with his death."[44] "Death," Levinas writes elsewhere, "is *present* only in the Other, and only in him does it summon me urgently to my final essence, to my responsibility," a concept of self-emergence always already in relation to another's mortality.[45] Levinas describes this self-emergence as a function of an "obligation not to leave the other alone in the face of death," because this obligation is that which "summons me, demands me, claims me: as if the invisible death faced by the other...were 'my business.'"[46] At the limits of his thought, Levinas seeks "an other relation with the death of the other," one that registers our implication and participation in it: "In the guiltiness of the survivor, the death of the other [*l'autre*] is my affair. *My* death is my *part* in the death of the other, and in my death I die the death that is my fault."[47] This essential nonindifference, or existential expo-sure, to another's dying—an event which "awakens [us] to the other"— defines our relation to the corpse.[48] In his commentary on Hegel's *Phenomenology of Spirit*, Levinas emphasizes how "there exists an ethics proper to the family that, on the basis of its terrestrial mortality, relates to the subterranean world and consists of burying the dead. It is here that the relationship with death is inscribed, or more precisely, with the dead *one*."[49] The corpse, even as it inscribes our relation with mortality, has no way to make us take care of it, yet we do, because it cannot take care of itself. If we do not, this is a fact with an immediately ethical meaning. I dis-cuss Levinas, along with Lacan, most extensively in Chapter Three, which focuses on the erotics of this relation to another's mortality.

When Vico vividly imagines the consequences of not taking care of corpses, he sees the beginning of the end of social cohesion, and from this perspective our death practices are valuable for what they avoid as much as for what they fulfill. The sheer fragility of our responsibility to the dead, who in their abject exposure have no agency with which to compel it, is in stark contrast to the catastrophic consequences of their neglect. To realize, Vico writes,

> what a great principle of humanity burial is, imagine a feral state in which human bodies remain unburied on the surface of the earth as food for crows and dogs. Certainly this bestial custom will be accompanied by uncultivated fields and uninhabited cities. Men will go about like swine eat-ing the acorns found amidst the putrefaction of their dead. And so with good reason burials were characterized by the sublime phrase "compacts of the human race" (*foedera generis humani*), and with less grandeur were described by Tacitus as "fellowships of humanity" (*humanitatis commercia*). Furthermore, it is an opinion in which all gentile nations have certainly

concurred, that the souls of the unburied remain restless on the earth and go wandering about their bodies, and consequently that they do not die with their bodies but are immortal.[50]

At stake in corpse disposal, for Vico, is the purging of the bestial from the human; it is our most dramatic principle for the exclusions that mark our species as something apart. He intuits the dramatic nature of corpse disposal as such a principle because there is always a possibility of sliding back, of our corpses being left lying about like those of animals, not just vacated of meaning but taking on the specific meanings of corruption and disgrace. This possibility has seized the modern literary imagination. The dying and dead bodies strewn about in novels such as Cormac McCarthy's *Blood Meridian*, José Saramago's *Blindness*, Albert Camus's *The Plague*, as well as any number of twentieth-century novels about its wars and concentration camps—all of which exacerbate the challenges to systematic corpse disposal in their precedent mass-death novel, Daniel Defoe's *A Journal of the Plague Year*[51]—are novels, finally, about the human struggling with more or less success against Vico's "feral state." The failure of these worlds' death practices index their failure as human worlds. Camus's narrator refers, sardonically, to this struggle as the dead pile up in the quarantined city: "The next of kin were asked to sign the register of burials, which showed the distinction that can be made between men and, for example, dogs; men's deaths are checked and entered up."[52]

However, if Vico insists that we maintain burial "so that the world should not again become a bestial wilderness," twentieth-century writers seem to know that this bestiality can also be a product of modern political design, not a reversion to wilderness but an expression of conflict at its most elaborate socialization, an entirely cultural phenomenon.[53] Conrad signals the complexity of such a failure in death practices—through which the human produces the animality that it abhors—near the beginning of *Heart of Darkness*. On his way upriver, Marlow stops at a forced labor camp where prisoners are building a railway. Disturbed by the sight, he moves away, into a grove of trees.

> My purpose was to stroll into the shade for a moment; but no sooner within than it seemed to me I had stepped into the gloomy circle of some Inferno.... Black shapes crouched, lay, sat, between the trees leaning against the trunks, clinging to the earth, half coming out, half effaced within the dim light, in all the attitudes of pain, abandonment, and despair. Another mine on the cliff went off, followed by a slight shudder of the soil under my

feet. The work was going on. The work! And this was the place where some of the helpers had withdrawn to die.

They were dying slowly—it was very clear. They were not enemies, they were not criminals, they were nothing earthly now,—nothing but black shadows of disease and starvation, lying confusedly in the greenish gloom.... Near the same tree two more bundles of acute angles sat with their legs drawn up. One, with his chin propped on his knees, stared at nothing, in an intolerable and appalling manner: his brother phantom rested its forehead, as if overcome with a great weariness; and all about others were scattered in every pose of contorted collapse, as in some picture of a massacre or a pestilence. While I stood horror-struck, one of these creatures rose to his hands and knees, and went off on all-fours toward the river to drink. He lapped out of his hand, then sat up in the sunlight, crossing his shins in front of him, and after a time let his woolly head fall on his breastbone.[54]

These are dying and dead who cannot die, even if their bodies perish, because this is not human death. Conrad captures the acute, or surplus, malevolence underwriting this imperial project within which the dying not only fall under the threshold of human meaning, but, in their weakness, cannot raise the others dying with them above this threshold either.[55] This strategy of dehumanization in death is Primo Levi's concern in describing, in the essay "Useless Violence," the "at once stupid and symbolic violence" of the concentration camps, where "iniquitous use...was made (not sporadically but with method) of the human body as an object, an anonymous thing belonging to no one, to be disposed of in an arbitrary manner.... This cruelty, typical and devoid of apparent purpose but highly symbolic, was extended, precisely because symbolic, to human remains after death: those remains which every civilization, beginning with remotest prehistory, has respected, honored, and sometimes feared. The treatment to which they were subjected in the Lagers was intended to declare that these were not human remains but indifferent brute matter, in the best of cases good for some industrial use."[56] The antiquity or atavism involved in this offense is part of its power; Conrad saturates a world, or a population, in a modern version of Sappho's still-resonant curse: "When you lie dead there will be no memory of you, / No one missing you afterward, for you have no part / in the roses of Piéria. Unnoticed in the house of Hades / too, you'll wander, flittering after fading corpses."[57] The greatest complexity of Conrad's scene lies in the fact that it is not some simple reversion to animality by force of nature, which Vico seems to fear, but a carefully designed

and enforced degradation at the heart of a very modern project of colonial industrialization. These monstrous deaths are specifically cultural events, intended to be
what they are by those in authority. Such corpses have been produced throughout
modernity's most brutal episodes, and any concept of a counter-modernity that
resists its forms of domination must include at its core the project of tending to the
corpses abandoned in its wake.[58]

The Corpse and Ethical Monopoly

Conrad shows in a modern guise what Sophocles reveals with devastating clarity in
Antigone: that the ethics of deathways is inseparable from the complexities of political administration. Attending our dead is never an act of transcendent obligation,
free from issues of social organization and hierarchy, which is to say that a death
obligation can never exist entirely for its own sake and on its own terms. Like the
aesthetic charge of literature, the ethical charge of our care of the dead mingles with
its more worldly uses, overdetermined by the social and political dynamics around
it, through and against which it defines itself. As ambiguous combinations of the
ethical and political, in which a reverential care for and political leveraging of the
corpse can inhabit the same social practices, care for the dead exemplifies the politics of ethics itself, the more or less subtle contests over who can become an agent
of one's own ethical capacities. Corpses are crucial in the politics of subject formation, in the social distribution and recognition of ethical agency, of the means one
has to claim oneself as a consequential ethical agent. Groups and institutions with
authority over corpses—the ecclesiastical, governmental, medical, private-sector,
or other agents of a culture's death practices—have immense power, then, over who
can achieve a sense of self and a social articulation of self ethically robust enough
to undertake fundamental existential obligations.[59] (We will see how what we call
the modernization of death consists in large part of the relative recalibration of
these various social players' authority over corpses.) Care of the dead is an ethical
practice toward the dead; at the same time, control of the dead is a manifestation
and consolidation of power among the living, with enormous economic consequences.[60] These various facets of deathways are inextricable. Sophocles realized
this a long time ago: Antigone's refusal to abide by Creon's prohibition against burying Polyneices is both a political and ethical act, so that her pursuit of divine justice
for her brother is inseparable from her subversion of Creon's regime.

By acknowledging this fairly straightforward fact—that the particular practices
toward the dead that we count as ethical are legitimated, and even organized, by

those with social power, and that these practices in turn are crucial for legitimating a social order—I am not claiming that we can reduce the intensity and strangeness of our mortal obligations to social and political relations among the living. Our death practices are not merely self-interested politics by other means. The fact that a monopoly, or even partial authority, over corpses creates formidable social power does not negate the uniquely, intensely disturbing power of the dead over our sense of self, and part of this power comes from a corpse's ability to disrupt a purely social determination of self and our negotiations within the social realm. This is a power of another order and along a different axis, the estranging force of existential alterity on one's claims to identity. It is this power that I approach with the concept of mortal obligation. Blanchot shares this intuition that the abject, errant form of the corpse may have a strangeness that cannot be recruited by the social or its operations of power. Reminiscent of the fiction and poetry at the heart of this study, he imagines the way the corpse can displace us from the map of the given, an irrational principle in the organization of bodies in space.

> What we call mortal remains escapes common categories. Something is there before us which is not really the living person, nor is it any reality at all. It is neither the same as the person who was alive, nor is it another person, nor is it anything else. What is there, with the absolute calm of something that has found its place, does not, however, succeed in being convincingly here. Death suspends the relation to place, even though the deceased rests heavily in his spot as if upon the only basis that is left him. To be precise, this basis lacks, the place is missing, the corpse is not in its place. Where is it? It is not here, and yet it is not anywhere else. Nowhere? But then nowhere is here. The cadaverous presence establishes a relation between here and nowhere.[61]

The corpse introduces the elsewhere, or nowhere, into here, yet this quality of the corpse's alterity or excess is inseparable from the highly circumscribed social situations in which one can encounter its effect. In modernism's death rooms, Blanchot and Levinas must acknowledge Foucault and his meditations on power, just as he cannot ignore their insights into the sheer strangeness of the corpse to political rationality and social identity. (Chapter One discusses Foucault's thought in relation to the state's management of corpses.) Our challenge in approaching modernism's investigation of emerging forms of dying and corpse disposal is in conceptualizing the corpse as an overdetermined manifestation of both a trans-historical obligation, with something like our fundamental humanness at stake, and as a set of historically specific and local ideological and institutional arrangements.

The corpse is a significant thing for the way it is implicated in both, able to play one against the other, a unique compromise formation between obligations within a political economy and obligations where this economy falls to paradox, in which power is held by bodies in their absolute vulnerability and passivity.

If, as I am arguing, there is in modernizing societies a strangeness of relation to the dead that cannot be recruited by what already organizes the social realm—alongside many aspects of this relation that can—such strangeness is what modernism frequently seeks to recruit for its emerging literary forms. This writing helps us imagine a less restricted zone for our ethical agency toward the dead, an intensification of that axis of relation. The literary—and the aesthetic more broadly—acts as a third term between the ethics and politics of deathways, a public and social act of imagining, or rehearsing, the mortal obligations that readers may not be able to perform otherwise. In his highly regarded story "Odour of Chrysanthemums" (1914), D. H. Lawrence describes a remarkable encounter between a woman and the corpse of her husband, who has just been killed in a coal mine and brought back to their home. The story is first a portrait of the hardships of workers' lives, but its narrative energy is primarily organized around Elizabeth's encounter with her husband's corpse. She struggles to respond to it, to properly claim it, to become the subject of her ethical capacities toward its alarming presence. If we are to approach the social conflict in the story's background, we must do so in the context of the uncanny unreadability of his corpse, which complicates any available calculus of social power with an irrational element that cannot be reduced to it. For Jonathan Strauss, elaborating Kristeva, corpses are irrational in their abjection, the way that they "have faces and eye-sockets that seem to stare. They look as if they were able to return our gaze, although we know they cannot, and with their resemblance to people, it is difficult not to imagine that cadavers retain some sort of consciousness as they rot into the dirt, offering the image of a thinking that defies both death and the limits of the subject."[62] The question taken up by the modernist literary imagination is if this deep strangeness that marks the limit of the subject has anything to do with how social power works.

Lawrence makes the corpse encounter an event of basic disorientation of self, an estrangement in who and what the subject is. Elizabeth's husband's body is not an object she can know, as a subject: "She saw him, how utterly inviolable he lay in himself. She had nothing to do with him. She could not accept it. Stooping, she laid her hand on him in claim. He was still warm, for the mine was hot where he had died.... Elizabeth embraced the body of her husband, with cheek and lips. She seemed to be listening, inquiring, trying to get some connection. But she could not. She was driven away. He was impregnable."[63] Lawrence anticipates Blanchot's thought that "the corpse appears in the strangeness of its solitude as that which has disdainfully withdrawn from us."[64] Elizabeth's husband's alien presence, beyond her claiming, is not something she can simply know or have; it is not a term in a relation in which she confirms her position as subject. Yet it animates her subjectivity as a dynamic thing, startling her into a new possibility of self-relation: "She looked at his face, and she turned her own face to the wall. For his look was other than hers, his way was not her way. She had denied him what he was—she saw it now. She had refused him as himself.—And this had been her life, and his life.—She was grateful to death, which restored the truth. And she knew she was not dead."[65] The sense of knowledge, or restored truth, that Lawrence seeks to produce through the corpse is startling because it combines estrangement with intimacy, so that the corpse's forbidding alterity is known with a kind of sensuous immediacy. The effect involves both pleasure and pain, desire and revulsion. The idea of truth or knowledge at stake in contact with the corpse is one which does not fit in any phenomenological category, as if another's death or dead body could only be an experience for a subject in intense contradiction with itself. "In [the corpse], death is not an absolute or an epistemological premise on which anything can be grounded with certainty: too bad for abstract individuality, for subjects, and for the modern, democratic polis that they permit."[66] Lawrence rehearses this ambiguity, or uncertain grounding, of the affective and ethical entangling of the living with their dead. At the end of the story, Elizabeth and her mother-in-law finish preparing the corpse.

> She was almost ashamed to handle him; what right had she or anyone to lay hands on him; but her touch was humble on his body. It was hard work to clothe him. He was so heavy and inert. A terrible dread gripped her all the while: that he could be so heavy and utterly inert, unresponsive, apart. The horror of the distance between them was almost too much for her—it was an infinite gap she must look across.
>
> At last it was finished. They covered him with a sheet and left him lying, with his face bound. And she fastened the door of the little parlour, lest the children should see what was lying there. Then, with peace sunk heavy on her heart, she went about making tidy the kitchen. She knew she submitted to life, which was her immediate master. But from death, her ultimate master, she winced with fear and shame.[67]

What nature of authority does Lawrence imagine with this corpse? What manner of mastery and submission unfolds here? This corpse is involved in the work of an ironic interpellation, or a re-interpellation of the subject in and through what we might call existential dissonance: as a materialization of infinite distance and embodiment of negation, the corpse estranges Elizabeth from herself, in guilt and shame, in order to deliver whatever is left of her to herself once again, as a problem or question about death. Strauss's elegant formulation of such a transaction conceptualizes the abjection of the corpse as source of self-reckoning: "The swollen body of the dead does not wait patiently elsewhere for me to die. It is not another. It is I, since the corpse is always already here, none other than this body that is mine, this body that will survive me, that I think of as subordinate but that will remain after I last close my eyes. It is the remnant that comes from before, that persists after, and on which I inscribe myself, like words in a book."[68] The political consequences, or recalibration of social authority, in this self-inscription through the death of the other—which is also the death of the self—is Lawrence's concern. Just as Elizabeth's husband's corpse cannot be authoritatively claimed, as it is somehow both too inert and too endlessly receding for her grasp, so is her experience of self an experience of incommensurability, of something painfully beyond grasp. This irony is Lawrence's idea of political rupture at the level of the symbolic formation of selves. It is a political consequence of abjection, which is not only a violence against self-possession but an evocation of the self's most arduous ethical capacities and their disruption of social relations. We cannot be commanded to be who we are simply by and among the living, because the dead will twist this commandment askew; the angle of this skewing is the angle of mortal obligation, an aspect of the self irreducible to social power.

In "Washing the Corpse," written in 1907, Rilke tests the intelligibility of this ethical skewing, and of the phenomenology of mortal obligation, with images of a transaction at the limits of both politics and ethics. The poem imagines the corpse in an almost erotic lucidity that marks its peculiar mode of power, an ability to transform the silence around it into an open, absolute demand, and to transform those around it into subjects of this demand.

> They had, for a while, grown used to him. But after
> they lit the kitchen lamp and in the dark
> it began to burn, restlessly, the stranger
> was altogether strange. They washed his neck,
>
> and since they knew nothing about his life
> they lied till they produced another one,
> as they kept washing. One of them had to cough,
> and while she coughed she left the vinegar sponge,

dripping, upon his face. The other stood
and rested for a minute. A few drops fell
from the stiff scrub-brush, as his horrible
contorted hand was trying to make the whole
room aware that he no longer thirsted.

And he did let them know. With a short cough,
as if embarrassed, they both began to work
more hurriedly now, so that across
the mute, patterned wallpaper their thick

shadows reeled and staggered as if bound
in a net; till they had finished washing him.
The night, in the uncurtained window-frame,
was pitiless. And one without a name
lay clean and naked there, and gave commands.[69]

This is not an exploration of grief or mourning but of inarticulate imperative forces emanating from the materiality of an anonymous corpse. By referring to these forces as commands (or laws—Rilke's word is *Gesetze*), Rilke suppresses their essential tautological quality. These are not commands to wash, exactly, because the women are willing to wash the corpse already, but rather commands to listen to its commands, to heed its commanding eloquence, imperatives fulfilled in the acknowledgment of their articulation. Many modernists attempted to relearn the neutered eloquence of the corpse, to heed its command even when it collapses into ethical tautology, into nothing more (but nothing less) than an obligation to be obligated. Modernism suggests that modern thought must find its way into this tautology before working its way out. The disquieting, impalpable, and baffling energy of this body, reflected in the unnerving blankness of the uncurtained night, is for Rilke the feeling of an ethical tautology without an unfolding, obligation without the possibility of enactment or realization. Rilke seeks to give this tautological relation to the corpse its own reality, to think the simultaneously absolute and empty command of the corpse, a kind of limit or vanishing point for modern ethicality, as potent. Later, Blanchot will more explicitly invoke the potency of this tautology: "The cadaver is its own image. It no longer entertains any relation with this world, where it still appears, except that of an image, an obscure possibility, a shadow ever present behind the living form which now, far from separating itself from this form, transforms it entirely into shadow. The corpse is a reflection becoming master of the life it reflects."[70]

Lawrence, Rilke, and Blanchot share a peculiarly modern way of thinking about these dead bodies as immensely but only vaguely powerful, masters over the living but not toward any particular end, an intransitive mastery through something like a charismatic field of presence within which the living feel some obscure aspect of themselves warp and strain. In their violent stillness, the corpses that these writers imagine are powerful, even if this power of the modernized dead is at most (or at least) a power to refuse the uses that the living would put them to. Their portion, as Michael Rosen suggests, is not utility but dignity—not for the sake of the dead, who cannot experience it, nor for the sake of the living, even if they might vicariously appreciate this dignity, but for the sake of the basic symbolic integrity of the culture that converts species life and mortality into collective existential purpose and history.[71]

There are many ways to frame the politics of death and dead bodies, including the racial and class politics of burial grounds (necrogeographic mapping),[72] medical and legal definitions of death, the economic power of the funeral industry, the legal status of posthumous rights and interests,[73] the governmental regulation of corpse disposal, inheritance laws, state disappearances and torture, euthanasia, the cultural and identity politics of particular death practices, repatriation, and so on. In this book I read modernism without attaching it, hard and fast, to any particular opinions about these interrelated issues.[74] What modernist writing has to offer that is most unique and consequential are concepts of mortal obligation, concepts that depend on the possibility of hearing in a modern idiom the tautological command of corpses in a world that instrumentalizes them. In other words, modernism is, in part, a historically responsive philosophical discourse about the nature of ethics and subjectivity in a context of rapidly changing death practices. Chapter One (on Owen and Woolf) does discuss this inquiry in explicitly political terms, in relation to the wartime state and repatriation of the dead; but Chapters Two (on Joyce and Faulkner) and Three (on Eliot and Barnes) examine this possibility of hearing the corpse's imperative otherwise, in terms of the monetization of time and of the ethics of desire, which I examine at a theoretical removal from the details of social and political history. Louis-Vincent Thomas, in an anthropological description of funeral rites, claims that "in traditional societies, [a] notable belief is that the corpse is simultaneously alive and dead. It no longer has a voice, but in its fashion it speaks."[75] Rilke, Lawrence, and the others I discuss in this book reimagine this speaking as a command that can still be heard. For these writers, the modernization of the corpse does not entail its muteness.

Modernized Corpses

On the one hand, the very phrase "modernized corpses" invites a sentimental or nostalgic lament that we should treat with suspicion. No doubt my own thought in these pages hovers over this nostalgic abyss more than I know, and no doubt a nostalgia for premodern death practices is itself an entrenched part of our most deceptive ideologies about death and authenticity. Any notion of modernizing the dead, by the very organizing tension of its terms, is bound to provoke some combination of anxiety and outrage, just as it evokes some lurking ideal of a more authentic and replete premodern way of dying and corpse disposal. This is the feeling that Faulkner mythologizes in *Absalom, Absalom!*, when he has Mr. Compson describe earlier generations as "simpler and therefore, integer for integer, larger, more heroic and the figures therefore more heroic too, not dwarfed and involved but distinct, uncomplex who had the gift of loving once or dying once instead of being diffused and scattered creatures drawn blindly limb from limb from a grab bag and assembled, author and victim too of a thousand homicides and a thousand copulations and divorcements."[76] Death (like life), once unified, became dispersed, scattered.[77] Death is a central protagonist of modern myths about modernity's own corruption. Take, as exemplary, Charles Péguy's prewar meditation "We Are Defeated," which, as a Catholic rewriting of something like Marx's "A Ruthless Critique of Everything Existing," is a total condemnation of the modern, culminating vaguely with its death practices: "The modern world debases....It debases the state; it debases man. It debases love; it debases woman. It debases the race; it debases the child. It debases the nation; it debases the family. It even debases...what is perhaps most difficult in the world to debase, because this is something which has in itself, as in its texture, a particular kind of dignity, like a singular incapacity for degradation: it debases death."[78] The clash in this thought between death, as a singularly inviolable thing, and modernity, as a principle of universal violation, can be heard more subtly throughout Philippe Ariès's pioneering, influential historical work on Western deathways. His story of death's modernization is a story of its relative deficiency and alienation. In past centuries, the living and the dead were not strangers: "The spectacle of the dead, whose bones were always being washed up to the surface of the cemeteries, as was the skull in *Hamlet*, made no more impression upon the living than did the idea of their own death. They were as familiar with the dead as they were familiarized with the idea of their own death." But this familiarity, or familial closeness, has vanished in an age "where death is so frightful that we dare not utter its name."[79] Modern thought constructs the natural death from which it is alienated again and again, so that this death that is less than it once was is itself an object of mourning.[80] In a book that impressed Ariès early in his research, Geoffrey Gorer laments that in the twentieth century "natural death became more and more smothered in prudery," effectively replacing sex as a taboo (which, he implies, had returned to its natural state).[81] Something in modern thought needs premodern death to have a consummate, organic wholeness. Max Weber's 1918 speech "Science as Vocation" invokes the way "Abraham, or some peasant of the past, died 'old and satiated with life' because he stood in the organic cycle of life; because his life, in terms of its meaning and on the eve of his days, had given to him what life had to offer; because for him there remained no puzzles he might wish to solve; and therefore he could have 'enough' of life."[82] People, it became possible to think, used to fulfill their lives by dying in ways we no longer can. These thoughts of a natural death in the past are also utopian thoughts. Fredric Jameson's critique of capitalist social formations, in which existential terror is a symptom of social fragmentation, quietly translates images of a communal past into the future:

> In future societies people will still grow old and die, but the Pascalian wager of Marxism lies elsewhere, namely in the idea that death in a fragmented and individualized society is far more frightening and anxiety-laden than in a genuine community, in which dying is something that happens to the group more intensely than it happens to the individual subject. The hypothesis is that time will be no less structurally empty, or to use a current version, presence will be no less of a structural and ontological illusion, in a future communal social life, but rather that this particular "fundamental revelation of the nothingness of existence" will have lost its sharpness and pain and be of less consequence.[83]

In a way of thinking that has been established for a long time, modern death is deficient, debased, smothered, an acute sign of our alienation; we know all this because, in contrast, premodern death is natural, genuinely communal, and accompanied by a "simple acceptance" that "bespeaks a familiarity with death, a relationship that will remain constant throughout the ages," that is, until its sequestration in the twentieth century: "Death was always public. Hence the profound significance of Pascal's remark that one dies alone, for at that time one was never physically alone at the moment of death. Today his statement has lost its impact, for one has a very good chance of literally dying alone, in a hospital room."[84] While this kind of thought shares an impulse with significant critiques of modernity, the nostalgia it depends upon makes it precisely the sort of floating theme or proto-narrative—to use Jameson's term, the sort of *ideologeme*[85]—that can distort our reading of modernism with notions of death as the alibi of a lost individual authenticity (even if this takes the form of individuals being authentic together, as a group). In showing the strangeness of death's modernization, modernist fiction and poetry at their most penetrating are not nostalgic for an imagined repletion in past deathways in which one achieved one's self by having an authentic death, but explore radically new possibilities for a death ethics made possible by the unusual conditions of the present.[86] We still need to learn these possibilities.

On the one hand, we risk this nostalgia, but on the other, the modernization of corpses has been a consequential phenomenon that has confused ethical agency and collective meaning in the context of death. Even if nostalgia for preindustrial death practices, or even pre-twentieth-century death practices, is part and parcel of an exhausted ideology of individual authenticity, the modernization of the dead matters immensely. Death, always subject to history and always strange, became strange in new ways around the turn of the twentieth century. It became socially and physically private, commercial, and a primarily medical concern. It shed more and more of its religious trappings. It became increasingly regulated by state bureaucracies. Lawyers and doctors, instead of clergy and family, shepherded the dying through their deaths. People increasingly died in hospitals and other neutral social spaces instead of homes. Corpses were less frequently kept or viewed in homes. Corpses were cremated and embalmed. Corpses were buried further away from the living, in newly established cemeteries outside cities. Corpses were handled by (male) strangers, professionals and technical experts that the dead had likely never known, instead of (female) family, neighbors, and local layers-out.[87] Corpses became more like things to be managed than people to be tended. In this shift from relations between persons toward relations between persons and things, from I-Thou to I-it, corpses became more obscure as a field for ethical action and value. This book is about the way modernism sought to complicate the I-Thou-It categories around the dead.

We can examine these cultural changes in more detail. Although there was "a deep chasm between the cultural norms relating to death and loss in 1851 and 1951," many signs of the changes that created this chasm first appeared in the nineteenth century.[88] By 1850, it was common in England for doctors to manage dying, to have the funeral arranged by a commercial undertaker and other entrepreneurs able to "mass-produce funerals for anyone prepared to pay," to bury the corpse in a cemetery rather than a churchyard, and to have the death recorded by the state. Wealthy Victorian families in particular began to avoid physical contact with corpses by

employing professional nurses to wash and dress them.[89] British corpses also fell
under a more demanding legal regime. The fifteen Burial Acts that Parliament
passed between 1852 and 1906—along with the Cemeteries Clauses Act of 1847,
the Public Health (Interments) Act of 1879, and the Cremation Act of 1902—made
arrangements for corpse disposal difficult for lay people: "The intricate network
of these statutes with their many overlapping and amending provisions produced
a complexity of burial authorities, a complexity of burial areas and a complexity
of burial laws."[90] Enacted toward the beginning of this intensified legal oversight,
the Metropolitan Interments Act of 1850 prohibited further burials in London's
notoriously overcrowded graveyards, creating new physical distance between the
living and dead; while the living urbanized, the dead became ex-urban in cemeteries.[91] This sense of death's increasing remoteness was also demographic: between
1870 and 1928, the death rate in England and Wales fell from 21.8 per thousand
to 11.7. "Within half a century death began to be perceived as the monopoly of
the elderly and society's preoccupation with death receded"; in contrast to those
living in the nineteenth century, "English people living in the twentieth century
could choose to try to ignore death."[92] There was a similar "mortality revolu-
tion" in the United States, as infant mortality dropped from 125 out of 1000 at
the end of the nineteenth century to 50 out of 1000 in 1940, and as mortality for
adults aged 25–34 reduced by approximately two-thirds over the same years.[93] In
England, many of these social and geographical changes de-emphasized the role
of the church, which was in the process of losing its approximately thousand-year
monopoly on the spaces and rites of death in the British Isles. Laws enacted by
Parliament throughout the 1850s created Burial Boards, new municipal agencies
able to raise funds through taxation to establish cemeteries and close overcrowded
churchyards.[94] These cemeteries displaced churches as centers of burial throughout England, "sometimes in a matter of less than a decade. It took just seven years
for the General Cemetery in Northampton, for example, to establish its position
as the main location for burial in the town."[95] Clergy were not required for these
cemetery burials. Nor, after 1880, were burials at churches required to be Anglican;
the Burial Law Amendment of 1880 "allowed Nonconformist ministers to conduct
funerals in Anglican churchyards, without an obligation to use Anglican rites, but
also permitted burials without any religious service."[96] Parliament's 1902 legaliza-
tion of cremation, a practice with no church precedent and largely promoted by
intellectual and scientific communities, was associated with secularization and
further weakened the church's control of corpses: the "tight schedules, industrial
hardware, and functional buildings" involved in cremation "seemed to suit a society increasingly inclined to keep death at a distance. Its simplicity appealed to

a modern age which reacted against elaborate Victorian funeral display."[97] There were thirteen crematoria in England in 1914 and fifty-four by 1939. Although only a tiny fraction of corpses were cremated in these years—3.5 percent by 1939—a widely perceived foundation was being laid for a later consensus in England that cremation was an efficient, sanitary, and respectful form of disposal. By 1968, 50 percent of corpses were cremated, and 71% by 2000, so that England was the first industrialized nation to have the majority of its corpses cremated.[98] The first crematory in the United States opened in 1876, accompanied, as in England, by a robust discourse on hygiene (with an anti-immigrant subtext) and efficiency.[99] However, cremation remained less popular than embalmed burial in the United States; in 1920, only thirteen thousand corpses—less than 1 percent—were cremated, which increased to 40.62 percent by 2010.[100]

At the forefront of both embalming and cremation, undertakers—renaming themselves "funeral directors"— created vast new professional associations and aggressively promoted embalming in particular as a specialized procedure within their exclusive purview: "Embalming was the lifeblood of the American funeral industry from the beginning of the twentieth century," the procedure that enabled funeral directors to become "the primary mediators between the living and the dead from the moment of death to the final disposition."[101] In the United States, the National Funeral Directors' Association was formed in 1882; by 1900, it had nearly four thousand members and had secured legislation in twenty-five states that required specialized licensing for embalming. They had ample work: "By 1920, almost all dead bodies were embalmed, not just those intended for transport."[102] Formaldehyde, discovered in 1893 and available at affordable prices by the turn of the century, replaced arsenic and other deadly chemicals that had been used previously. In 1914, a battery-powered pump for injecting embalming chemicals was introduced, only to be supplanted in the 1930s by an electric injection machine.[103] These procedures, with this equipment, helped establish the conditions in which "funeral men—and most, though not all, were men in this period—took the dead out of the hands of living relations and performed all the necessary, increasingly complicated, and for many Americans, deeply unpleasant tasks associated with the death of a loved one."[104] The results were corpses with new smells, textures, and appearances that, by the 1920s, found themselves primarily in new, confusing spaces—funeral homes—which combined business practices, religious activity, corpse preparation, and family living.[105] While embalming had first become widely practiced in the United States during the Civil War, when it was widely advertised and desired by dead soldiers' families, it was still an unregulated and frequently unreliable practice, often inspiring discomfort and suspicion in a public that would not fully embrace embalming for many years.[106] In addition to this shift in corpse preservation, US funeral services between 1880 and 1920 generally became shorter as sermons and solemn music were eliminated; attendance at funerals slowly came to assume "secular meanings associated with a transient sense of obligation" rather than a defining one.[107] (Bearing news of this future back to the Nebraska prairie, Carl in Cather's 1913 *O Pioneers!* reports that "off there in the cities there are thousands of rolling stones like me. We are all alike; we have no ties, we know nobody, we own nothing. When one of us dies, they scarcely know where to bury him. Our landlady and the delicatessan man are our mourners, and we leave nothing behind us but a frock-coat and a fiddle, or an easel, or a typewriter, or whatever tool we got our living by.")[108] At the same time, funerals became dramatically more expensive, increasing in cost by as much as 250 percent because of cemetery costs, florists, livery stables, mausoleum companies, and industrial insurance premiums, as well as funeral directors.[109] The period between 1910 and 1920 was also when the automotive hearse replaced the horse-drawn one in the United States.[110] (So that Faulkner has the protagonist of his story "Beyond," a man who has recently died but can still wander through the world of the living, notice the line of cars outside his house and complain, " 'Damn that Pettigrew! I told him, in the presence of witnesses when I signed my will, that I would not be hauled feet first through Jefferson at forty miles an hour. That he couldn't find me a decent pair of horses.")[111] The era's corpses were at the center of increasingly elaborate technological processes and a politically influential commercial industry that mediated expressions of dignity and respect through market transactions.

Meanwhile, hospitals modernized into something like the institutions they are today, shifting from sick houses for the indigent or those without family to medical centers that based admittance on diagnosis—so much so that there were even early critics, anticipating the arguments of later decades, "contending that the patient was in danger of being reduced to his or her diagnosis—to a discrete biopathological phenomenon."[112] There were 2 hospitals in the United States in 1800 (in Philadelphia and New York), 120 in 1873, and over 6,000 in the 1920s. By then the hospital had clearly "emerged as the center of advanced medical practice" to such an extent that few substantial towns lacked a community hospital.[113] After the turn of the century, for the first time, the middle class went in large numbers to hospitals for treatment and to die, in large part because hospitals enabled antiseptic surgery and now had diagnostic laboratories and sophisticated medical equipment not available elsewhere (e.g., the X-ray and electrocardiogram).[114] Rosenberg observes, "If the hospital had been medicalized, the medical profession had been hospitalized in the years between 1800 and 1920."[115] By the end of this process, the consequence was that "in the first half of the twentieth century, medical professionals rapidly assumed the power to define death, to record the pathological details of its appearance in once-living bodies, and to control the living bodies surrounding the dying, often lonely, patient."[116] Hospitals, whose administrators formed an active international professional association in 1899, were increasingly institutions of complex bureaucracies oriented toward a cash marketplace and managed according to principles of efficiency learned from factories and the military.[117] (Rilke evokes this association in *The Notebooks of Malte Laurids Brigge*, when Malte reflects on the Hôtel-Dieu in Paris: "Now there are 559 beds to die in. Like a factory, of course. With a production so enormous, each individual death is not made very carefully; but that isn't important. It's the quantity that counts.")[118] This modernization of the hospital directly affected death practices, not just because "death in the hospital is no longer the occasion of a ritual ceremony, over which the dying person presides amidst his assembled relatives and friends," but because of the enormous increase in autopsies among corpses that found themselves in hospital morgues.[119] Anatomy, or dissection, "expanded the technical repertoire and proficiency of medicine...To the public, the anatomist, and by extension all physicians, demonstrated mastery over the welter of emotions, beliefs, and regulations associated with death and the dead, and wielded shocking powers."[120] Prominent physicians and the American Medical Association (AMA) regularly called for more autopsies to be performed, and if this was a call for a better understanding of the causes of death it was also a practice that made the corpse a newly scientific, impersonal, and even instrumental object. Eighty-six percent of corpses at the Mayo Clinic had autopsies in 1925, 84 percent at Johns Hopkins in 1924, 80 percent at St. Agnes in Baltimore in 1925, 56 percent at Mt. Sinai in New York in 1922, and Philadelphia General Hospital's rate increased from 12.5 percent in 1916 to 51.3 percent in 1922.[121] In 1927, the AMA required that teaching hospitals perform autopsies on a minimum percentage of their corpses and that residents had frequent opportunities to participate.[122] Dissection, a fraught issue throughout the nineteenth century—there were at least twenty "anatomy riots" against medical schools that dissected corpses in the United States between 1765 and 1884—was becoming an acceptable part of everyday death.[123] As Frederick Smith, a doctor in Marion, Ohio (population thirty-four thousand), observed in 1927 in a boast about increasing his autopsy rate outside of any urban center, "I am certain that the public is not as much opposed to necropsies as physicians generally believe. It appears that the laity is more appreciative of the need of autopsies than is the medical profession itself....I feel certain...that autopsies of not less than 20 per cent of all our dead could be made for the mere asking."[124] They asked. (William Carlos Williams's doctor-narrator certainly does in the story "Jean Beicke": "Listen, I said, I want to ask you something. Do you think she'd let us do an autopsy on Jean if she dies? I hate to speak to her of such a thing now but to tell you the truth, we've worked hard on that poor child and we don't exactly know what is the trouble.... Would you take it up with her for me, if—of course—she dies.")[125] And this asking became political advocacy. In the same year, Howard Karsner argued that "civil laws should be adjusted to recognize the need for more frequent and more complete autopsies.... The law should assume that the autopsy is an essential procedure and that it will be performed in all cases of death, from either 'natural' or accidental causes.... The consent should be given by the state rather than the individual, granting to the latter the privilege of withdrawing consent only for good and sufficient reasons." He concludes with an absolute standard for the corpse's medicalization: "The duty of the physician to himself and to society is to have a postmortem examination of the body of every patient who dies while under his care."[126] As early as 1895, Walter Suiter promoted to the AMA this kind of governmental involvement in the standardization and medicalization of US death practices: "A general regulation of the disposal of dead bodies is believed to be most urgently demanded...[W]ithout doubt the potent influence of this great organization may be secured to bring about the enactment of laws with uniformity of requirement, covering the preparation for burial, cremation and transportation of all dead bodies. These laws should have an intra-State, inter-State and international character, and I beg to remark that the Association could not at the present time lend its powerful aid to a project of vaster or more salutary importance to the public weal."[127] Falling death rates, hospitalization, professional funeral directing with related death entrepreneurship, embalming, the idea of cremation, medical autopsy, cemetery and secular burial, and the legal regulation of corpses combined as never before around the turn of the twentieth century to change dying and corpse disposal in England and the United States. While some of these changes had appeared in the mid- and late nineteenth century, they gathered into a cohesive network of mutually justifying practices that saturated modern social spheres only later, in the early twentieth century. During this period, these formerly distinct aspects of death's modernization became largely inextricable, each element legally, financially, and socially entailing the others. Heavily industrial societies, it turned out, could make good use of their corpses. These uses were simultaneously scientific, commercial, and bureaucratic. The corpse became a significant part of how the modern world tried to rationalize itself, that is, to replace traditional ends with quantifiable and efficient means that, as they broke down ways of life into their smallest component parts, could become ends unto themselves. As Joseph

Roach argues, "modernity itself might be understood as a new way of handling (and thinking about) the dead."[128]

The rationalization of human dying and its remains was reflected in what came to be most emphatically claimed as consequential knowledge about death: statistics. The early nineteenth century saw an explosion in statistical descriptions of Victorian life, probabilistic ways of thinking about events, and insurance. In England, the Statistical Society of London was founded in 1834 and began its journal in 1837; more important, the government's Office of the Registrar General was established in 1839 to oversee "the compulsory notification of deaths. These statistics were collated and presented with information on births and marriages in an abstract annually laid before Parliament. This counting of the dead by the state was the beginning of a process that would eventually re-create dealing with death as a municipal and medical function, increasingly hidden from the general population."[129] What earlier had been a sporadic use of the life table became systematic with William Farr's English Life Table No. 1, published in 1843, the first to "incorporate the death rate, and also the first to apply mathematical concepts of probability to patterns of death in an entire nation."[130] Farr, the superintendent of statistics in the General Registrar Office and author of *A Statistical Account of the British Empire* (1837), meditated on the strangeness of the knowledge he was producing about the future of any given one hundred thousand people born alive in 1841:

> The toil of the labourer, the wear and tear of the artisan, the struggles and drains of the intellect, and more than all of these, the natural falling off of vitality reduces the numbers to 9,398 by the age of eighty. Here we may pause for a moment. It would formerly have been considered a rash prediction in so uncertain a matter as human life to pretend to assert that about 9000 of the children born in 1841 would be alive in 1921; such an announcement would have been received with as much incredulity as Halley's prediction of the return of a comet after the lapse of 77 years. What knew Halley of the vast realms of aether in which the comet disappeared? Upon what grounds did he expect its re-appearance from the distant regions of the heavens? Halley believed in the constancy of the laws of nature; hence he ventured from the parts of the comet's course to calculate the time in which the whole would be described; and it will shortly be proved that the experience of a century has verified quite as remarkable a prediction of the duration of human generations, so that, although we little know the labours, the privations, the happiness or misery, the calms or tempests, which are prepared for the next generation of Englishmen, we entertain little doubt that

9000 of 100,000 of them will be found alive at the distant Census in 1921. After the age of 80 the observations grow uncertain; but if we admit our accuracy, 1140 will be alive at the age of 90; 16 will be centenerians; and of the 100,000 one man and one woman—like the lingering barks in an innumerable convoy will reach their distant haven in 105 years and die in 1945.[131]

Dying, translated by demographic thought into mortality rates, became calculable, predictable, and representable in the "smooth geometric curves" at the center of an "actuarial vision of human existence."[132] While the concept of probability meant little in 1800, when it was still thought that understanding individual deaths consisted of knowing their individual causes, by 1900 "those very causes of death were described as probabilistic in nature."[133] This quantification of dying across populations was one of the crucial forms of its rationalization.

In these years of death's reconceptualization, when "the nature of 'mortality' was endlessly and meticulously broken down into finer and finer divisions" and "measured through ever more complex instruments," it also became insurable, accessible in a new way to marketplace logic—that is, it became a new kind of commodity.[134] By the end of the nineteenth century, insurance had become a pervasive form or structure of sociality, "an organizing schema of management and rationality capable of being realized in any and every kind of provident institution." By the time of modernism, "no one [was] any longer in doubt that provident institutions must conform to the rationality of insurance."[135] At the founding meeting of the Actuarial Society of America in 1889, during a series of toasts to the insurance industry, a Mr. Barker of Pennsylvania Mutual is recorded in the meeting minutes making relevant calculations:

> The population of this country is to-day in excess of sixty millions. Allowing five persons to a family, which I believe is pretty nearly the average, it gives about twelve million, five hundred thousand families. Out of each family there certainly ought to be two members who are insurable; that would give twenty-five million of insurable people in the United States to-day. Let us examine the statistics and find out how many we have insured. There are less than two million five hundred thousand, I think, out of that possible twenty-five million who are insured to-day in the United States. I think, gentlemen, it is well to look forward to the possibilities of increase in the business. [Applause.][136]

As an existential and religious logic of mortal time was obscured by the same abstract economic logic that was used to calculate the value of other commodities, obligations around the dying of others changed. Deaths and acts of obligation to the dead were quantified and made exchangeable in the market. Just as the corpse became a newly rationalized, secularized, and scientific object in the hands of technical experts, so was death increasingly conceived in the actuarial terms that would occlude the presence of the dead, in their arduous and demanding singularity, from modern cultures. These were the historical conditions out of which modernism emerged to explore ethical capacities in the context of others' deaths.

We can further interpret the meaning of this cultural sea change. Broadly speaking, it disarticulated the cultural authority—the symbolic resonance, affective force, moral weight—of the West's corpses. The deritualization of dying and corpse disposal left the corpse symbolically bereft. Corpses came to lack the strong cultural practices that would integrate them with other symbolizations of the body; these practices (as we will see in Chapter One, in terms of the Tomb of the Unknown Warrior) are fundamentally figurative, rhetorical: "Funeral rites can shift the drama of dying from the plane of the real to that of the imaginary (by displacements and metonymy, symbols and metaphors), and it is in this that their efficacy resides."[137] Good deaths are good rhetoric, the source of symbolic richness; literal death veers toward abjection. Thomas describes the symbolically depleted state of the dead in a wide range of practical details:

> Modern life, especially in an urban milieu, entails multiple mutations that are probably irreversible on the level of ritual, and perhaps disquieting for the psychic equilibrium of one's contemporaries. Many practices are simplified or omitted: The wake is impossible at the hospital or in tiny apartments; condolences and corteges are practically eliminated. Consider, for example, today's laying out of the dead: For the impurity of former times, the pretext of hygiene is substituted; for respect for the corpse as subject, obsession with or horror of the corpse as object; for family deference, the anonymity of an indifferent wage. In the same way, the signs of mourning have fallen into disuse—society has passed from "mourning clothes in twenty-four hours" to twenty-four hours of mourning!—and it is unseemly to show one's sorrow. People care less and less about the deceased, who sink into the anonymity of the forgotten; fewer and fewer masses are said for the repose of their souls, while the scattering of ashes eliminates the only possible physical support for a cult of the dead. If, at least on the imaginary plane, rites once primarily concerned the deceased, today they primarily concern the survivors. Thus, to take only one example, the new Roman Catholic ritual of anointing the sick tends to deritualize and desacralize death itself

as an essential mutation. It is truly the disappearance of death, considered
as a passage, that is witnessed by others.[138]

These conditions, pervasive now, emerged during modernism. Over the twentieth century, deaths were reduced "to an individual event with an individual
cause," in each instance so severely contained "in a specific medical explanation"
able to be compiled in actuarial tables that they could not be integrated with
"either the cycle of generations or with broader moral issues concerning the relation between human beings and inorganic nature."[139] Because the passage from
life to death and the body that made the journey were invested with diminished
symbolic power—because there was so much less for this passage and its passenger to mean—the dead lost relevance in modern lifeworlds. (I discuss the
role of corpses in conceptualizing liminality, as the condition of this passage,
in Chapter Two.) The dead, as a group, suffered the social death that had previously been reserved for the most unfortunate among the living. Their depar-
tures had fewer determinate arrivals, and the destinations of these arrivals were
increasingly marginalized on the symbolic maps of the living. To the extent that
modern people felt—and feel—a powerful symbolic apparatus around mortality, it was and is a largely individualized one: "the conscience collective" around
the dead has become "a series of atomized *consciences individuelles*. Now the
individual, the individual being-in-the-world, is facing death and suffering all
on his or her own."[140] If a secular age, as Charles Taylor has written, is one in
which "the depths which were previously located in the cosmos, the enchanted
world, are now more readily placed within," a critical element of this interiorization of "the rich symbolism of the enchanted world" has been the privatization
of the meaning of death.[141] (And so, after hearing of his friend Percival's death,
Bernard, in Woolf's *The Waves*, wanders into an art museum, where he becomes
aware of this depletion: "Behold then, the blue madonna streaked with tears.
This is my funeral service. We have no ceremonies, only private dirges and no
conclusions, only violent sensations, each separate.")[142] As Thomas suggests, we
might suspect that this deritualization of death was the precondition for the
corpse ever to assume the power of abjection over the individual psyche that
many now attribute to it; the power of this abjection could then be understood
as its surrogate, ironic re-enchantment, the corpse-effect that came to fascinate
modern consciousness in lieu of earlier meanings. Only the ritually, symbolically abandoned corpse is abject. Because in modernity every corpse is always
already to some degree abandoned, on the verge of public meaninglessness, the
ethical task, according to the modernist imagination, is to devise something like

its symbolic refuge. This is hard to do because such a refuge, to be effective, needs to be collective. The deep mythological strain of modernism responds to the collective dimension of this need.

Largely stripped of its ritual charisma and no longer thoroughly integrated into a larger symbolic economy, the modernized corpse has been assimilated into its culture in primarily economic terms, as a kind of commodity or recipient of commodities. Modern death practices are fundamentally structured by commercial transactions. This commodified or commercialized structure of exchange around mortuary practices is important because it has replaced the corpse's significance in symbolic exchange, in which the dead are not passive. Modernization in the West, as a process of commodification, has excluded the dead from symbolic circulation so that "they are no longer beings with a full role to play, worthy partners in exchange." "This is the fundamental fact that separates us from the primitives: exchange does not stop when life comes to an end" in premodern lifeworlds.[143] The dead, cash poor after their property has been redistributed, traditionally traffic in symbolic capital, as a part of social relations that make no sense within a cash nexus. Modernity is when it is difficult to even acknowledge that "death (like the body, like the natural event) is a *social relation*,... its definition is social."[144] In a wide-ranging anthropological survey, Elias Canetti describes traditional conceptions of the dead and living "as a double crowd, whose component parts continually interact." In nearly every culture "is found the conception of the *invisible dead*. It is tempting to call it humanity's oldest conception.... [T]he action of the dead upon the living has been an essential part of life itself."[145] Yet modernity occludes this sphere of interaction and represses the traditional, cross-cultural sense that, as Harrison explains, "the dead are not content to reside in our genes alone, for genes are not *worlds*, and the dead seek above all to share our worlds."[146] The idea of symbolic exchange accomplished through death practices involves the more or less ritualized interactions across mortal lines in which the dead are bearers of social value, agents with interests and rights, and partners in the circulation of symbolic capital, that is, status and prestige. The reciprocity between the living and dead constitute the social identities and worth of both. They negotiate their mutual obligations. The dead participate in, and are at the root of, the economy of meanings that makes merely biological life culturally purposeful. Canetti writes, "Some people believe that the crowd of the dead is the reservoir from which the souls of the newborn are taken. Thus it depends on them whether the women have children or not. Sometimes the spirits come as clouds and bring rain; they can also withhold the plants and animals which serve as food; and they can fetch new victims for themselves among the living."[147] (As an evocation of such an economy, near the end of Book III of *Paterson*, Williams includes a long description of how Ibibio women rescue the corpse of a relative killed in battle: "They lay him on a bed made of fresh leaves. Then they cut young branches from a sacred tree and wave the bough over the genital organs of the warrior to extract the spirit of fertility of men into the leaves.")[148] The modernized corpse has become nearly inert in these currents of existential exchange.[149]

In an elegant meditation on the economy of the dead, John Berger conceptualizes these dynamics as a fundamental ontology, an elemental foundation of being:

> The dead surround the living. The living are the core of the dead. In this core are the dimensions of time and space. What surrounds the core is timelessness.... Between the core and its surroundings there are exchanges.... Having lived, the dead can never be inert.... The memory of the dead existing in timelessness may be thought of as a form of imagination concerning the possible. This imagination is close to (resides in) God; but I do not know how.... How do the living live with the dead? Until the dehumanization of society by capitalism, all the living awaited the experience of the dead. It was their ultimate future. By themselves the living were incomplete. Thus living and dead were interdependent. Always. Only a uniquely modern form of egoism has broken with this interdependence. With disastrous results for the living, who now think of the dead as the *eliminated*.[150]

This interdependence, through which the living create relations to possibility and the divine, is for Berger grounded in the imagination; modernism is an attempt to reimagine the eliminated dead, even if this is made artistically severe by being an attempt to reimagine them precisely as that which modernity has eliminated, within the processes of that elimination. In their return, no matter how ambivalent, reciprocal exchange and obligation can continue. This dynamic with the dead, following Berger's thought, is the exchange that enables modernism's new aesthetic possibilities. (Chapter Two addresses symbolic exchange and the dead in terms of narrative transactions and Chapter Three in terms of poetic lineage, filiation, and influence.) Dying and disposal are, traditionally, processes of initiation that establish these dynamics, initiatory rites that, as Baudrillard writes, establish "an exchange...where there had been only a brute fact: they [i.e., the dead] pass from natural, aleatory and irreversible death to a death that is *given* and *received*, and that is therefore reversible in the social exchange, 'soluble' in exchange."[151] It has been a recurring speculation that this giving and receiving of mortality is the secret of aesthetic experience, akin to Stevens's suggestion in "Sunday Morning" that "death is the mother of beauty."[152] Following Baudrillard's thought, we might say that the dead and living are in an exchange in the sense that they profoundly complicate one another's temporality, interweaving finitude with commemoration, lineage, and aesthetic pleasure. The dead give the time of the living density, recursivity, rhythm, and narrative shape, and vice-versa, so that the pronounced thematics of time in so much modernist writing can be seen as an attempt to recuperate exchange across mortal lines.[153] The ritual, initiatory establishment of death in its symbolic solubility, or exchangeability, was traditionally supported by a material apparatus and infrastructure that gave it weight in the world. "At one time the most significant objects—monuments, memorials, churches, mausoleums, walls, ramparts, gates—were those that mediated between life and death. These paradigmatic objects were not inside the frame of symbolic exchange, the good life and the city. They were also not outside the frame, as were death, the bad and contingency. Instead, these mediating objects *were* the frame itself.... These design and architectural objects were not representations like painting and sculpture. One side of them was truly symbolic, but the other eminently practical."[154] These objects are no longer paradigmatic because the market, as the dominant modern paradigm for exchange, has made them obsolete, along with the dead they mediated with the living.

This symbolic solubility of death, given and received across mortal lines, demanded complex, interactive categories for who lives and who does not. This complexity, Baudrillard argues, has not survived in modern societies:

> Every other culture says that death begins before death, that life goes on after life, and it is impossible to distinguish life from death. Against the representation which sees in one the *term* of the other, we must try to see the radical *indeterminacy* of life and death, and the impossibility of their autonomy in the symbolic order. Death is not due payment [*échéance*], it is a nuance of life; or, life is a nuance of death. But our modern idea of death is controlled by a very different system of representations: that of the machine and the function. A machine either works or it does not. Thus the biological machine is either dead or alive. The symbolic order is ignorant of this digital abstraction. And even biology acknowledges that we start dying at birth, but this remains with the category of a functional definition. It is quite another thing to say that death articulates life, is exchanged with life and is the apogee of life: for then it becomes absurd to make life a process which expires with death, and more absurd still to make death equivalent to a deficit.[155]

To say that the living die with the dead and the dead live with the living—Eliot's first principle in "Little Gidding," discussed in Chapter Three—is to say that the dead are a part of the living's mobility and possibility, that which gives a figurative, nonliteral dimension to human being. The dead are a principle of rhetorical and temporal complexity, of the meanings and narratives that are worth struggling over. The alarming rhetorical and temporal complexity of modernist poetry and fiction seeks to compensate for the symbolic dearth around the dead in modernizing cultures.

Chapter Descriptions

The following three chapters and coda each juxtapose two authors who I find to be addressing similar concerns about the modernization of dying and corpse disposal. Each chapter addresses a distinct aspect of this sea change, moving from the state's increased power over the bodies and spaces of the dead, through the effects of time's monetization on death practices, to the erotic dimension of mortal obligation. The comparative structure within each chapter allows the articulation of different strategies for representing each phenomenon, and in each chapter these distinct strategies have varying degrees of tension and compatibility. In other words, as I go on I present distinct conversations within modernism about how far the literary imagination can or should go in renovating obligations to the dead in the context of their modernization.

Chapter One, on Owen and Woolf, examines Owen's war poetry, which he wrote shortly before dying in battle, in relation to her postwar novel *Jacob's Room* (1922) and later fiction. The First World War was a threshold for the modernization of Western deathways, particularly in Europe. Similar to shifts in the United States in the 1860s, but more extensive, the war caused a breakdown in the traditional organization of mortality and instigated new governmental techniques for managing the burial of the dead. The emergency amplification of state power over its corpses inaugurated what Agamben has called a "thanatopolitics" that elaborated the biopolitics at the center of Foucault's theories of state power over the biological life of its subjects. This amplification extended to the representation of the war dead in the official war painting of the time, which I discuss as a background for Owen and Woolf. I argue that these two writers represent this thanatopolitics of the modern state as an appropriation of ethical capacities toward the dead. I focus in particular on the rhetorical structure of synecdoche, or one for many, which the British state incarnated in its crucial memorial innovation after the war, the Tomb of the Unknown Warrior. The state's use of this single, anonymous corpse to stand for a multitude of displaced and irrecoverable corpses gave it a potent hold over the ethical desires of its citizens. Owen and Woolf contest this synecdochic logic in their representations of the dead in order to imagine alternative forms of mortal obligation and public, collective mourning that would not accrue to state power.

Shifting from the spatial politics of death practices, Chapter Two focuses on the modern corpse's temporality. I analyze the "Hades" chapter of Joyce's *Ulysses* (1922), along with several related sections of the novel, and Faulkner's *As I Lay Dying* (1930). These "burial plots," narratives organized by the problem of an unburied corpse, revisit the vital imperative to bury the dead in ancient Greek and Hebrew literatures (Faulkner takes his title from Agamemnon's line in Book 11 of the *Odyssey*, the epic that also guides Joyce). These fictions stage the difficulty of plotting the liminal time between bodily perishing and ritualized burial, the act that grants cultural intelligibility and value to a death in most Western traditions. The status of this social pause, during which the unburied corpse traditionally interrupts the time of the living with its demand for care, is increasingly fragile in a modernity organized by linear, efficient, homogenous time quantified in terms of economic exchange value. Joyce and Faulkner make the problem of burial plotting, as a vestigial temporality, central to the modern experience of ethical agency. In addition to narrative theorists (Peter Brooks, Roland Barthes) and theorists of liminality in the social sciences (Victor Turner, Pierre Bourdieu), this chapter considers Jean-Luc Nancy's concept of community as a group formed around its members' mortality. Faulkner's novel, in particular, animates the complexity of Nancy's ideas about the shared, transitive nature of dying as a critical response to its modern depersonalization and atomization. Joyce's and Faulkner's complex narrative practices are a struggle with time in its rationalized forms, attempts to make time accommodate the dead in their slowness.

Chapter Three, the most speculative chapter, focuses on the erotic register of mortal obligation in Eliot's *The Waste Land* (1922) and Barnes's *Nightwood* (1936), which Eliot originally edited, published, and influentially introduced. I read *The Waste Land* as a frustrated attempt to secure a symbolic location for the dead in modern lifeworlds by refashioning erotic desire. Eliot's dead, I argue, fall within a queer libidinal circuit, which becomes a circuit of mortal obligation that resists their social sequestration. His radical experiments with poetic form are necessary to accommodate this queering of mortal obligation, in which an ethical response to the mortality of the other is figured as illicit desire. In *Nightwood*, a tour de force of post-decadent fiction, Barnes radicalizes queer desire as an experience of one's implication in another's mortality. Her antic, spellbinding rhetoric, which still eludes established critical terms, brings this ethical binding to representational impasse. I argue that Eliot and Barnes disagree about the possibility of reintegrating the dead with integrity into their modernizing social worlds, and in this disagreement anticipate a debate within queer studies about the assimilability of queerness into a heteronormative mainstream. The theoretical terms of this conversation come from Levinas and Lacan, who investigate, from different angles, ethical responsiveness to another's mortality as a catalyst for erotic desire. This chapter extends Lee Edelman's important arguments about the socially radical, unassimilable nature of queerness in *No Future: Queer Theory and the Death Drive* (2004) into ideas about the radical nature of mortal obligation.

The book's coda addresses an interconnected set of poems by Williams and Stevens with competing visions for the possibilities of twentieth-century mortuary practices, with a focus on Williams's 1917 "Tract," a guide to modern burial, and Stevens's 1947 elegy "The Owl in the Sarcophagus." Bracketing the era at either end, they thematically and chronologically frame the problem of death's designification in the modern world. Williams's pragmatic, pedagogical response contrasts with Stevens's resignation to the impossibility of reconciling to the abstraction and alienation of the dead in the final years of modernism. These poems return us to a debate about the failure of modernism to establish the conditions for ethically refashioning—for rehumanizing—modernity. I take Williams's side in this debate, even if his side means nothing without Stevens's insights: modernism, in my view, identifies real possibilities for a modern ethics of death that many people have successfully cultivated during the twentieth century. The ritual, aesthetic, and technological creativity on behalf of the Western dead in recent decades has a crucial origin in early twentieth-century literary explorations of how we die and obligate ourselves to those who die among us.

1. The State's Unending Vigil: Owen's and Woolf's Unknown Warrior

---

We are on the verge over here of serious trouble about the number of bodies lying out still unburied on the Somme battlefields. The soldiers returning wounded or on leave to England are complaining bitterly about it and the War Office has already received letters on the matter. There is every reason to expect that the question may be raised in Parliament any day and I do not see what defence the Government could offer for the neglect of the Army in the Field in this connection.

—letter from Fabian Ware, founder of the Imperial War Graves Commission, June 1917

I am anxious that there should be equality for all, and that the right which is inalienable to every man, the right to do as he likes with his own dead, should not be taken away. Relatives should... treat their own loved ones in their own distinctive way, and I hope the House of Commons will hesitate long before it allows the right to be taken away or any interference with it. The dead are certainly not the property of the State or of any particular regiment; the dead belong to their own relatives.

—Sir James Remnant in a speech to the House of Commons in 1920

The three years between Fabian Ware's anxious letter about the state's neglect of the war dead and Sir James Remnant's indignant speech to the House of Commons about the state's excessive control over these dead was a period of unprecedented ambiguity in questions of sovereignty over British corpses. During the First World War, "death...had many stage-managers.... Acceptable levels of death and appropriate responses were negotiated between the state, various interest groups (such as the medical profession and funeral directors) and the bereaved. The First World War was to dramatically rearrange the theatre of death."[1] The process by which the British government, in particular, negotiated this ambiguity and clarified its role in the theater of death, a process of political amplification, was a crucial element of what made the war a threshold in the modernization of the Western dead. The amplification of the state's role in tending to the dead, which "questioned certainties concerning ownership of the corpse," "meant that families across Britain were confronted with the dispossession of the dead."[2] The tension between too little governmental attention to the dead and too much—between corpses abandoned on the battlefield and the state's systematic management of them to the exclusion of relatives and other agents—had at its center a set of vexed political and ethical questions about who has the right to claim a corpse and what it means to do so. These questions, which became so acute during the war, had a precedent in modern British political history. It is possible to hear in debates about sovereignty over the war dead echoes of the conflict over the 1832 Anatomy Act, controversial legislation that nationalized the unclaimed dead in poor houses and work houses for dissection in anatomy schools.[3] Like this debate over the right of the state to distribute the unclaimed corpses of the poor to a professionalizing medical field, debates over whether the war dead should be repatriated, photographed, or allowed individualized grave markers had at stake the role of the modern state in the ethical obligation to tend to the dead. This was more than a legal or procedural question. Through official British war painting, Wilfred Owen's war poetry, and Virginia Woolf's *Jacob's Room*, we can interpret debates about the war dead as fundamental investigations into the way social power was negotiated through corpses and the state's use of this power over its living subjects. Such a mass of war dead was a problem the British state had never encountered before, and it did so by asserting itself as the mediating principle between its subjects and their corpses. This mediation was made possible in part by an astonishing innovation in its rhetoric of memorialization, and the political possibilities of this rhetorical innovation are what Owen and Woolf reveal.

In this chapter, I consider Owen's and Woolf's insights into how modern states accrue power over the living through the dead. I examine official war painting to initiate this exploration. At stake in the contest for control over the bodies of the dead is the ability to shape ethical roles and feelings related to the primordial desire to tend to one's dead. This power becomes obvious in wartime, when a state produces a need among its subjects that only it can satisfy. It produces the corpses that those at home desperately long to see, touch, and ritually tend to. If the wartime state is primarily interested in injuring and killing its enemies as a way to win a war, it also acquires tremendous leverage—a kind of emotional or ethical capital—over its own subjects by producing the dead bodies of its own soldiers.[4] Early in the war, British officials established a policy against repatriation. The government buried soldiers abroad where they died, and civilians were prohibited from repatriating the corpses of their relatives, because those who could not afford the expense would be disadvantaged compared to those who could.[5] Although this policy provoked initial protest, the public largely acquiesced; with very few exceptions, the British war dead remained where they died. The most significant exception was the anonymous soldier exhumed in 1920, two years after the war's end, and converted into the Unknown Warrior, the synecdochic object of mourning for each and all of those with dead far from home.

In this analysis of the relation between the modern state and the corpse, a relation brought to a critical intensity by war, I hope to conceptualize the psychic life of corpse power, the way that identities and affiliations are forged through the rendering and material circulation of corpses. Several observers have acknowledged that corpses matter a great deal to the stability of political institutions and as a way to gather political charisma. It is a fundamental anthropological insight. Maurice Bloch and Jonathan Parry examine "the relationship between mortuary beliefs and practices and the legitimation of the social order and its authority structure." They argue that a social order is legitimated by an authority's ability to symbolically convert death into another form of life, to transform "the dead into a transcendent and eternal force.... In these instances the social group is anchored, not just by political power, but by some of the deepest emotions, beliefs and fears of people everywhere. Society is made both emotionally and intellectually unassailable by means of that alchemy which transforms death into fertility. This fertility is represented as a gift made by those in authority which they bestow by their blessings."[6] I want to extend this claim—that death increases the power of the authority that can make it fertile—into one about another kind of political alchemy that takes place when the corpse is missing or distant, a political alchemy based on a symbolic transaction between the wartime state and those with ethical desire for war's absent corpses. Elaborating Bloch and Parry, Lawrence Taylor claims that "any symbolic statement which succeeds in framing and defining the experience of death as part of some larger and compelling order (structurally or by association) not only makes sense of death, it also invests that larger order with a kind of ultimate reality...derived from the deep emotional power and resonance of the experience of death."[7] As we will see, the Tomb of the Unknown Warrior invested the state with a potent ethical reality, or authority, that had previously been outside its domain.

In the same years, Owen, Woolf, and several official war painters discovered distinct aesthetic forms that articulated some of the consequences of investing the charisma of the dead with the state. They developed insights into the strategies and techniques that the state needed to realize itself as an irrefutable ontological fact, the sedimentation that Foucault considers in his discussions of governmentality. Foucault writes that "the state is at once that which exists, but which does not yet exist enough.... The art of government must therefore fix its rules and rationalize its way of doing things by taking as its objective the bringing into being of what the state should be. What government has to do must be identified with what the state should be. Governmental *ratio* is what will enable a given state to arrive at its maximum being in a considered, reasoned, and calculated way."[8] Owen, Woolf, and war painters intuit the role of the war corpse in governmental *ratio*, in producing the reality effect of the wartime and postwar state. During the First World War, the British state discovered ways to absorb its soldiers' deaths into a proof of its own reality, and the dynamics of this political alchemy inform Owen's and Woolf's innovations in writing about the war.

Corpsescapes

We can start with an alarming question: what if we were to tell the history of the war through its corpses? The question echoes Vincent Brown's broad challenge: "What might reading politics through the social and cultural history of the dead mean for our general understanding of history—the way we think, write, and read about the past?"[9] And Hemingway proposes something along these lines about the war specifically in "A Natural History of the Dead": "It has always seemed to me that the war has been omitted as a field for the observation of the naturalist.... Can we not hope to furnish the reader with a few rational and interesting facts about the dead?"[10] Such a corpse history of the war would not be of lives that ended, but the stories that begin at death and unfold as the impossible project of managing nine or ten million military dead across large sections of Europe, an average of 1,459 Russian, 1,303 German, 890 French, and 457 British soldiers each day.[11] What if, just for a moment, we took these corpses as the protagonists of the war and their burials as its major plot? Or, to focus just on the approximately 772,000 British military dead:[12] what if we told the story of Great Britain at war as the story of thousands of designated searchers scouring battlefields, finding and identifying corpses, burying them, erecting markers over them, registering burial sites, and photographing the graves for families? As a coda, the story could include the postwar government-subsidized family pilgrimages to the war cemeteries in France and Belgium.[13] This account of the war—essentially the plot of Philip Longworth's *The Unending Vigil*, a history of the Commonwealth War Graves Commission, an organization which I discuss below—would be about the complexities of administering a population of bodies with no subjectivity but immense power to shape the subjectivities of the civilians back home in mourning for them. In Hemingway's words, "Let us therefore see what inspiration we may derive from the dead."[14]

In *Postcards from the Trenches*, Allyson Booth coins the term "corpsescapes" to describe the "disturbing susceptibility of [dead] bodies to becoming indistinguishable from the landscape of mud and objects through which they moved" in trench warfare at its most extreme: "Trench soldiers in the Great War inhabited worlds constructed, literally, of corpses. Dead men at the front blended with the mud and duckboard landscape, emerging through the surface of the ground and through the dirt floors of dugouts.... Live soldiers found themselves buried in falling dirt while shells disinterred their dead companions from shallow graves."[15] In his memoir, Edmund Blunden writes that "the whole zone was a corpse, and the mud itself mortified."[16] William Clarke explains a similar phenomenon: "Seeing so many corpses became just another sight. Often when you moved in the trenches you trod and slipped on rotting flesh."[17] Or slept with it: "I remember after one show rolling a dead German off a bed in a dugout and going to sleep with him beside me on the floor."[18] Even when not within sight or reach, the dead still made their presence known. "The stench of rotten flesh was over everything, hardly suppressed by the chloride of lime sprinkled on particularly offensive sites.... You could smell the front lines miles before you could see it."[19] Similarly, in a letter to his mother, Owen writes, "I have not seen any dead. I have done worse. In the dank air I have *perceived* it, and in the darkness, *felt*."[20] The pervasiveness of the dead even extended, in particularly alarming moments, to soldiers' own bodies, suddenly revealed as pre-corpses: in the "great battles of attrition of 1916–17 mass graves were dug in advance of major offensives. Singing columns of soldiers fell grimly silent as they marched by these gaping pits en route to the front-line trenches."[21] The ubiquitous dead and the soon-to-be dead shared space indiscriminately.

While the dead have become an indistinguishable part of almost the entire terrestrial world—in a fundamental sense, most of the world is a corpsescape—the theater of war is unique for being obviously so, in its failures to absorb the dead into other cultural and biological forms, that is, into graves, monuments, ritual acts, soil, vegetation, and other structures of meaning and matter. The war dead frequently exceeded these available forms and remained in the abject form of corpses, a form in and for grotesque dissolution. These unburied dead pervade fiction, memoir, and poetry about the war, and this writing frequently has as its uneasy subtext attempts to convert the dead into something else, into anything besides the rotting bodies they were. By both necessity and accident, these were often conversions into forms of everyday utility, of oddly useful objects or materials, and especially as landmarks in a terrain that had been made barren of anything else. Soldiers used corpses to navigate their corpsescapes. The strangeness of this function, its hint of morbid irony, is that it finds soldiers mapping the ground with the bodies they have failed to bury within it, the ground of the living literally mapped by the deaths it is supposed to have absorbed. In his autobiography, Stuart Cloete describes this function of the dead at the Somme: "Everything was active, only the dead in their thousands lay still. I had seen dead before but this was a new experience. There were more dead lying about than could be buried. It was new to have the mummified body of a German officer used as a landmark, a rendezvous for guides—a golden-haired young man who was sitting up, desiccated, in a beautiful state of preservation, a kind of mummy."[22] With this mummified rendezvous point, we veer toward the kind of irony that Owen brought to a high pitch in his poetry: the war dead's extended enlistment in the war, sometimes for the other side. Arthur Graeme West, a private killed by a sniper in 1917, captured this merging of corpse and landscape in "The Night Patrol," a poem published posthumously with his diaries. The last half of the poem registers both the intimate, ubiquitous proximity of the dead at the front and their unlikely capacity to orient the living:

> The rustling stubble and the early grass,
> The slimy pools—the dead men stank through all,
> Pungent and sharp; as bodies loomed before,
> And as we passed, they stank: then dulled away
> To that vague foeter, all encompassing,
> Infecting earth and air. They lay, all clothed,
> Each in some new and piteous attitude
> That we well marked to guide us back: as he,
> Outside our wire, that lay on his back and crossed
> His legs Crusader-wise; I smiled at that,
> And thought on Elia and his Temple Church.
> From him, at quarter left, lay a small corpse,
> Down in a hollow, huddled as in bed,
> That one of us put his hand on unawares.

Next was a bunch of half a dozen men
All blown to bits, an archipelago
Of corrupt fragments, vexing to us three,
Who had no light to see by, save the flares.
On such a trail, so lit, for ninety yards
We crawled on belly and elbows, till we saw,
Instead of lumpish dead before our eyes,
The stakes and crosslines of the German wire.
We lay in shelter of the last dead man,
Ourselves as dead, and heard their shovels ring
Turning the earth, then talk and cough at times.
A sentry fired and a machine-gun spat;
They shot a flare above us, when it fell
And spluttered out in the pools of No Man's Land,
We turned and crawled past the remembered dead:
Past him and him, and them and him, until,
For he lay some way apart, we caught the scent
Of the Crusader and slid past his legs,
And through the wire and home, and got our rum.[23]

West's poem, in all its prosaic matter-of-factness, is about soldiers calibrating their physical contact with and emotional responsiveness to the landscape's corpses: they are everywhere among these dead but must construct apartness from them as well, must avoid accidentally laying a hand on them (or through them, as in the passage below) if they are to retain their sense that being alive is a distinction with a difference. Following Mary Douglas's *Purity and Danger: An Analysis of Concepts of Pollution and Taboo*, Eric Leed writes that "war experience is nothing if not a transgression of categories.... [W]ar offered numerous occasions for the shattering of distinctions that were central to orderly thought, communicable experience, and normal human relations. Much of the bewilderment, stupefaction, or sense of growing strangeness to which combatants testified can be attributed to those realities of war that broke down what Mary Douglas calls 'our cherished classifications.'"[24] In the extremity that West describes in his poem, the dead were useful as a kind of ontological limit point for defining the unstable category of the living as well as a geographic device for marking their movements. The dead were everywhere at the front, and were everywhere re-enlisted as a trope in writing about the front, aesthetically orienting this emerging body of writing just as they had geographically oriented the soldiers in the desolation of the trenches and No Man's Land.

The problem, ultimately, was burying the dead in this unprecedented mass, when "the individuality of death [was] buried under literally millions of corpses."[25] Bodies were obliterated, lost, disinterred by explosions, unidentifiable; over five hundred thousand British war dead were never found or identified.[26] Stuart Cloete, whose autobiography I quoted above, shows how this chaotic mass became a defining element of the war's phenomenology and arguably the crucial representational challenge in writing for those at home. I quote another description of his at length, about Serre as well as the Somme, because it is among the saddest and most disturbing of any I have read, and so a vivid example of how difficult this calibration of physical and emotional contact with the war's corpses was. Cultures undergo this calibration all the time—the precise organization of relations between living and dead bodies is a significant part of what culture is for—but war throws these relations into chaos.

> The sun swelled up the dead with gas and often turned them blue, almost navy blue. Then, when the gas escaped from their bodies, they dried up like mummies and were frozen in their death positions. There was even a man bandaging himself who had been killed by a shell fragment as he unrolled the bandage. There were sitting bodies, kneeling bodies, bodies in almost every position, though naturally most of them lay on their bellies or their backs. The crows had pecked out the eyes of some and rats lived on bodies that lay in the abandoned dugouts or half buried in the crumbled trenches....
>
> Burial was impossible. In ordinary warfare the bodies went down with the limbers who brought up the rations. But then there were seldom more than three or four in a day. Now there were hundreds, thousands, not merely ours, but German as well. And where we fought several times over the same ground, bodies became incorporated in the materials of the trenches themselves. In one place we had to dig through corpses of the Frenchmen who had been killed and buried in 1915. These bodies were putrid, of the consistency of Camembert cheese. I once fell and put my hand right through the belly of a man. It was days before I got the smell out of my nails. I remember wondering if I could get blood poisoning and thinking it would be ironic to have survived so much and then be killed by a long-dead Frenchman.
>
> The only previous experience I had had of rotting bodies had been at Serre, where, as a battalion we dealt with the best part of a thousand dead who came to pieces in our hands. As you lifted a body by its arms and legs

they detached themselves from the torso, and this was not the worst thing. Each body was covered inches deep with a black fur of flies which flew up into your face, into your mouth, eyes and nostrils, as you approached. The bodies crawled with maggots. There had been a disaster here. An attack by green, badly led troops who had had too big a rum ration—some of them had not even fixed their bayonets—against a strong position where the wire was still uncut. They hung like washing on the barbs. Like scarecrows which scared no crows since they were edible. The birds disputed the bodies with us. This was a job for all ranks. No one could expect the men to handle these bodies unless the officers did their share. We worked with sandbags on our hands, stopping every now and then to puke.[27]

Cloete suggests another possibility of strategic outnumbering and infiltration, not by an opposing army but by corpses; in moments like these, the strategic question is not which military is winning a battle, but whether the living as such are holding the line against the dead. This kind of realignment in hostilities organizes the most disturbing moment in Herbert Read's "Kneeshaw Goes to War":

> He started when he heard them cry "Dig in!"
> He had to think and couldn't for a while...
> Then he seized a pick from the nearest man
> And clawed passionately upon the churned earth.
> With satisfaction his pick
> Cleft the skull of a buried man.
> Kneeshaw tugged the clinging pick,
> Saw its burden and shrieked.[28]

He shrieks against the ambiguously polluting effect of his own act. In war, "corpses collapse the distinction between ally and enemy and confuse the boundary between life and death. This pair of attributes... subvert the very structure of war."[29] As such a subversion, these corpses demanded a process of narrative working through and sense-making. Without such a process, the bodies fell between the categories of enemy and ally, just as they fell between the categories of an impersonal environmental or elemental presence (like mud, rats, lice, cold) and the human. They were a unique problem, the remains of a human population become its own mute and alien population under human governance. Governing the dead, in this situation, meant getting them into the ground as quickly as possible, but this process cost more than it ever had before.

This process was difficult in part because the ground itself, subject to the war's violence, was an unreliable element for stabilizing the relative positions of the dead and living. Under mortar fire, any ground at the front could either have its corpses disinterred or become a sudden burial ground for the living. In his war diary, West describes this fundamental confusion in the structure of burial practices, how the entire project of disposing of the dead was made incoherent by the way the living could be put in their place. In one attack, he writes, "we lost six men by burying and ten others wounded or suffering from shell-shock....It exploded, and a cloud of black reek went up—in the communication trench again. You went down it; two men were buried, perhaps more you were told, certainly two. The trench was a mere undulation of newly-turned earth, under it somewhere lay two men more. You dug furiously. No sign. Perhaps you were standing on a couple of men now, pressing the life out of them, on their faces or chests."[30] The task of burial was overshadowed by the task of unburial.[31] Patrick MacGill, who after being wounded published his account of fighting with the London Irish Rifles in 1916, has his readers pause to consider the scope of live burial in a trench at Loos. The Munster Fusiliers "had been in there for eight days, and the big German guns were active all the time. In one place the trench was filled in for a distance of three hundred yards. Think of what that means. Two hundred men manned the deep, cold alley dug in the clay. The shells fell all round the spot, the parados swooped forward, the parapet dropped back, they were jaws which devoured men. The soldiers went in there, into a grave that closed like a trap. None could escape. When we reopened the trench, we reopened a grave and took out the dead."[32] Burial, as a basic death practice, was contorted throughout the war into the burial of the living and unburial of the dead. Sometimes the living simply disappeared into the mud, never to be reclaimed. Lord Boyd-Orr describes the Somme in the winter of 1916–1917: "The area between the reserve trench and the front line was much pitted with deep shell holes which filled up with liquid mud after rain. As there was no communication trench we had to go up and down at night on narrow duckboards....It was an ordeal for men carrying sixty pounds of equipment plus the mud on their clothes. If they slipped off the duckboard on to the mud in the dark, they were liable to stumble into a shell hole, and with the weight of their equipment sink like a stone to the bottom where rescue was impossible. On one pitch black night we lost forty men drowned in shell holes."[33] Burial was thwarted not just by the sheer number of corpses but by a fundamental disarticulation of its elemental conditions. In a poem about this disturbance, Mary Borden brings the mud's grotesque, engulfing appetite alive:

> This is the hymn of mud—the obscene, the filthy, the putrid,
> The vast liquid grave of our armies.

It has drowned our men.

Its monstrous distended belly reeks with the undigested dead. . . .

The mute enormous mouth of the mud has closed over them.[34]

The dead cannot be buried because the earth that would receive them as they ought to be received, arranged and marked, has already subjected them to a monstrous process of effacement and decomposition. It became the state's project to recreate the conditions and take up the task of human burial.

The Imperial War Graves Commission

The British state took on many new powers at the outset of the war in an expansion that "impinged upon virtually all areas of domesticity and communal life."[35] The Defence of the Realm Act (DORA), established on August 8, 1914, gave the state new authority to regulate speech, personal behavior, communications, and industry. Like most other belligerent nations, the British government quickly took control of railways, mines, and shipyards in a general centralization of the economy.[36] The strangest of the state's new enterprises was the jurisdiction it assumed over male bodies and the corpses so many of them would become. "During the war manpower shortages meant that men's bodies became more unequivocally the property of the state. Conscription took away men's right to refuse to transfer ownership of their bodies to an institution in which the risk of being slaughtered was immeasurably increased. Furthermore, it promised them the ugliest death possible, and an equally unseemly burial."[37] These burials became the state's task on May 10, 1917, when, after years of political resistance and bureaucratic delay, Parliament created the Imperial War Graves Commission to oversee all British and Commonwealth military dead. (Its name would be changed in 1960 to the Commonwealth War Graves Commission, which continues as its name today.) The first organization of its type, in charge of all the nation's military dead and dedicated solely to this charge, the Commission was empowered to procure land for cemeteries, create memorials, exhume and re-bury British and Commonwealth corpses, and maintain records of graves.[38] It took over this task from the French government, which in 1915 had agreed to finance military cemeteries for Allied soldiers.[39] The Commission was immediately overwhelmed. The logistical difficulty of organizing the unburied or unofficially buried dead so far exceeded the Commission's capacities that it found itself in 1917, and for nearly a generation following the war, in astonishing arrears. The mathematics of the exponentially increasing difference between the Commission's powers and its responsibilities—the ever-widening gap between the number of corpses officially buried by the Commission and those produced by the war's violence and depri- vation—was unforgiving, as if its burials generated more unburied corpses in a grotesque modernization of one of Xeno's paradoxes. In fact, the Commission was already behind from the beginning: in April, just before its official creation, "arrangements had been made to acquire sixty burial grounds in France, but six times that number awaited requisition....Even with the good will of everyone concerned the wheels of bureaucracy never moved fast enough."[40] The numerical gap between the administered, organized dead and those still at large increased until the end of the war in November 1918. The number was staggering. According to the Commission's own estimates, there were "over half a million graves and more than 1,200 cemeteries in France and Belgium alone for which they must take responsibility. In all, over the world, there were to be 580,000 identified and 180,000 unidentified graves, and 530,000 men whose graves were not known."[41] The challenge was one of not only managing quantity but ordering chaos: grave registration workers "found headstones in places where there were no bodies" and "they found a number of bodies buried under only one headstone. Graves were numbered, but there was no list matching numbers with names. They had to be detectives as much as searchers. Relationships with the families of the deceased were often fraught."[42] By 1918, in addition to millions of known and unknown dead in war zones, there were thousands of improvised cemeteries in northern France and Flanders. Many of these lacked clear boundaries, were dif- ficult to locate, or had been damaged by fighting.[43] In the early 1920s, four thou- sand headstones were being sent from England to France each week, and by 1934, at the Somme alone, the Commission had buried and marked 150,000 British and Commonwealth dead in 242 cemeteries.[44] While statistics about war dead often sound like numbers of living people who have ceased to exist, from the per- spective of the Commission these numbers represented an existing population of bodies awaiting—below and above ground, identifiable and anonymous—careful governmental attention. Such a project was unprecedented in Europe, although Drew Gilpin Faust documents a similar expansion of the federal government in the United States during the Civil War. During those years, she writes, "national cemeteries, pensions, and records that preserved names and identities involved a dramatically new understanding of the relationship of the citizen and the state."[45] Fifty years later, the British state assumed an even more total administration of the war dead, to the increasing exclusion of its private citizens. That it actually had significant, even if not nearly complete, success in this administration marked a decisive change in authority over the bodies of the dead.

This change was registered by the public in various, ambivalent ways. Similar to earlier protests against the prohibition of repatriation, there was protest in response to the Commission's decision, which was ultimately approved by the House of Commons, to use uniform headstones throughout its cemeteries. In January 1918, the Commission issued a statement of principles about its regulation of memorials and the uniformity of military graves:

> If memorials were allowed to be erected in the War Cemeteries according to the preference, taste and means of relatives and friends, the result would be that costly monuments put up by the well-to-do over their dead would contrast unkindly with those humbler ones which would be all that poorer folk could afford. Thus, the inspiring memory of the common sacrifice made by all ranks would lose the regularity and orderliness most becoming to the resting places of soldiers, who fought and fell side by side, and would, in the end, grow to be ill-assorted collections of individual monuments. Thus the governing consideration which has influenced the Commission's decision is that those who have given their lives are members of one family, and children of one mother who owes to all an equal tribute of gratitude and affection, and that, in death, all, from General to Private, of whatever race or creed, should receive equal honor under a memorial which should be the common symbol of their comradeship and of the cause for which they died.[46]

Despite this rhetoric of equality and kinship, "bereaved families all over the country began to claim that they had prior rights over their dead loved ones."[47] An article in *The Times* argued that this was "bureaucratic tyranny and nothing else....It is equally repugnant to British feeling that even in death the family should surrender all rights over the individual to the state, and that private memorials should therefore be prohibited."[48] Yet such criticisms were exceptions to a widespread acquiescence to the Commission and the state's new role in burial obligations. It seemed to be understood that this was an enterprise on behalf of the properly British corpse, that is, an enterprise to make these corpses mean something by meaning Britishness, to both saturate them with national meaning and embody the nation in them. German corpses and bones, often alongside British, were removed. In his 1929 reflection on the war, Henry Williamson wrote, "The bones of the slain may lie side by side at peace in wartime, but in peacetime they are religiously separated into nations again, each to its place: the British to the white gardens 'that are forever England', and the others to—the Labyrinthe."[49] This counterintuitive thought, that the dead from opposing nations are acceptable company during a war but not after, reveals the importance of these bodies in the long-term construction of national identity. They had to be recruited by the nation once again, as the dead. The Commission's work was not just hygienic but highly symbolic, to order the disordered meanings of soldiers' remains. Elaine Scarry's point that "in war the damage inflicted on bodies is unalterable, whereas the symbolic claims or issues change with great ease" helps explain the distinctiveness of the Commission's task: to shore up this grotesque, scattered mayhem of bodies as the basis of the state's claims to ethical authority and ontological depth.[50] Scarry brings to vivid light the referential fragility of the war corpse that was at the heart of the Commission's project:

> There is nothing in the interior of what had been a boy's face, nothing in the open interior of what had been a torso, that makes the wound North Korean, German, Argentinian, Israeli. Though a moment before he was blown apart he himself had a national identity that was Chinese, British, American, or Russian, the exposed bones and lungs and blood do not now fall into the shape of five yellow stars on a red field, nor into the configuration of the union jack, nor the stars and stripes, nor the hammer and sickle; nor is there written there the first lines of some national hymn, though he might have, up to a moment ago, been steadily singing it. Only alive did he sing: that is, only alive did he determine and control the referential direction of his own embodied person and presence.... Does this dead boy's body "belong" to his side, the side "for which" he died, or does it "belong" to the side "for which" someone killed him, the side that "took" him? That it belongs to both or neither makes manifest the nonreferential character of the dead body that will become operative in war's aftermath, a nonreferentiality that rather than eliminating all referential activity instead gives it a frightening freedom of referential activity, one whose direction is no longer limited and controlled by the original contexts of personhood and motive, thus increasing the directions in which at the end of the war it can now move.[51]

The public's misgivings about ceding control of their dead to the state ultimately deferred to this larger imperative, the willing of their corpses, en masse, to national meaning, to a reliable referentiality. Families that gave up their sons once, when alive, agreed to do so again, after their sons died, in exchange for the participation of these bodies in a compelling, collective symbology. Those who did not agree had no recourse: this was the unalterable fate of all the British war dead.

Official War Art, Corpses, and "That Absence around Which Real Anxiety is Knit"

The state's work with corpses abroad had to be symbolically robust enough to compensate for their absence at home. The difference in contact with the dead in the two domains was stark. "The extremely restricted space within which trench warfare was fought simultaneously ensured that Great War soldiers would live with the corpses of their friends and that British civilians would not see dead soldiers. Soldiers buried their dead and then encountered them again...but British policy dictated that the civilian bereaved would never have anything to bury. Soldiers inhabited a world of corpses; British civilians experienced the death of their soldiers as corpselessness."[52] The state's radically new monopoly of the corpses that mattered most during these years, along with corpselessness at home, was the subtle but crucial ideological context in which Owen and Woolf wrote. As we will see, their writing explored the new wartime relations between the state and the dead as "the British government used regulations to wipe the home front clean of corpses."[53] These new relations also generated striking responses in the visual arts. We need to understand that this absence of material corpses was compensated for by a careful set of representations of the dead in official and unofficial propaganda, images and descriptions that rendered these bodies to the homefront as belonging to the state, and that rendered the state as the referent of these bodies. Images of corpses were censored but also produced, withheld by the state even as it projected them in its own image. It was this dialectic between the inaccessible and accessible corpse, the withheld and delivered bodies of the dead, that structured the ethical formation of mourning subjects at home. If corpses were "that absence around which real anxiety [was] knit," in Pierre Macherey's phrase about how literary production contains its culture's negative images, they were also made present by the government in ways that converted the energy of this anxiety into an affective attachment to the nation and its state apparatus.[54] We can read for both these absences and reappearances of the dead in official discourse. Owen's and Woolf's writings are important for the ways they register this ideological sleight-of-hand with corpses.

Images of British corpses, like other bad war news, were censored by the government. DORA provided for strict control of publications, and the government's press bureau monitored dispatches, issued news releases, and instructed newspaper editors on how to treat current issues and events. The bureau banned all news correspondents from the front until May 1915 and official photographers from the front until 1916, when a mere sixteen were allowed throughout the entire theater of war.[55] In addition, for the first time in its history the British government organized a publicity campaign to increase its support at home and abroad by founding the War Propaganda Bureau in August 1914 under Charles F. G. Masterman.[56] The bureau, located at Wellington House, sponsored nationalist sentiment in litera- ture, film, painting, photography, stage performances, postcards, pamphlets, and the like. By 1916, it reported the worldwide distribution of seven million books, speeches and pamphlets; by 1917, it was distributing over four thousand war pho- tographs weekly.[57] Wellington House was overhauled to become the Department of Information under John Buchan in February 1917. By the time it was further upgraded to a ministry under Lord Beaverbrook in February 1918, there was hardly a public medium in British culture that had not been used for propaganda.[58] The war's dead British bodies were the absent center of this rampant pro-war dis- course, and we can track this absence throughout it. Yet we are not merely reading the negative when it comes to the war's corpses: if government officials considered images of British corpses too volatile or harmful to morale to be circulated, it nev- ertheless knew that something had to be brought back to the homefront. After prohibiting repatriation and cancelling images of the dead, the government and its allies in the press and culture industry also became responsible for supplying surrogate dead bodies (by early 1916, illustrated newspapers were offering cash to soldiers for "authentic" front-line sketches.)[59] These surrogates, which were in various media and provided differing degrees of apparent proximity to corpses, culminated with the dramatic return of the anonymous corpse that would become the Unknown Warrior in 1920.

The official, government-supported war art of these years was at the center of conflicts over representing the war dead, and these officially appointed artists con- tinually troubled the criteria for defining acceptable images. Following French, German, and Australian initiatives, in summer 1916 Masterman began contracting artists to go to the front to produce pictures that could supplement the very lim- ited number of official war photographs available back home.[60] This art emerged at a time when visual images of the war were almost entirely carefully edited newspa- per photographs and illustrations, nearly free of British death or mortal wounds.[61] The illustrators on Fleet Street, who drew the war without having seen it, often rendered ludicrous scenes: in one edition of the *Illustrated London News* a picture showed soldiers in No Man's Land carrying camouflaged "portable trenches" and another showed a patrol making their way across a nighttime battlefield by follow- ing lines of suspended bottles with candles in them.[62] Therefore, the art of those who actually spent time at the front was a response not only to the war as the artists saw it but also to a tightly controlled and confused imagistic repertoire of the war as represented at home. Yet this art from the front, because it was officially sponsored and subject to censorship, was also implicated in the imperatives of an elaborate propaganda campaign. The British cultural imagination, particularly in its newspapers and illustrated weeklies but also in its more ambitious art, was having difficulty visualizing its dead soldiers. They frequently appeared in entirely fraudulent, fairy tale-like scenes, such as "The Great Sacrifice" printed in *The Graphic* of London on December 25, 1914 (figure 1.1). With this sensibility, journalists such as W. Beach Thomas claimed about the British soldier corpse that "even as he lies in the field he looks more quietly faithful, more simply steadfast than others."[63] But for the most part corpses did not appear through official channels or in mainstream periodicals at all.[64] In the beginning of the Battle of the Somme, on July 15, 1916, *The Illustrated London News* published a drawing by Albert Forestier of the British army's "big push" against the Germans (figure 1.2). This was the most brutal phase of the Somme, but nearly every man in this vast battleground landscape lives and moves, so that even the holes in the ground, the trenches, are full of vigorously active bodies. "No one would guess, from this anodyne picture, that the British army suffered 60,000 casualties on the first day of the attack. Nor is there any sign of the barbed-wire entanglements which made the advance across No Man's Land so treacherous. The caption attached to Forestier's drawing claimed that only the 'remnants' of the German wire had 'here and there escaped destruction by the preliminary bombardment'. But the reality was that, despite its intensity, the initial shelling had failed to clear the way for the infantry."[65] Most widely published illustrations purporting to capture the action at the front were similarly euphemistic, holding suggestions of conflict but keeping actual enemies and casualties outside their frames. A special 1918 number, edited by Charles Holme of *The Studio* (a popular arts magazine that at the beginning of the war had promoted the war effort among artists) was dedicated to "The War Depicted by Distinguished British Artists" without a single dead body—and only two or three wounded ones—in its ninety-eight pages. This pictorial withholding of the dead correlated to the state's material withholding of them.

In many cases, official war artists brought the British dead inside their frames metonymically, as not-quite-present or -presentable, as an inferred or included exclusion. Muirhead Bone, the first artist officially contracted by Masterman, went to northern France in August 1916, at the height of the Battle of the Somme, and by October had produced about 150 drawings in charcoal, pencil, watercolor, and ink. This work was collected and published in monthly segments throughout 1916 and 1917 as the periodical *The Western Front* with a circulation of thirty thousand

Figure 1.1 *The Great Sacrifice*, published in *The Graphic*, December 25, 1914.

Figure 1.2 Albert Forestier, war illustration, published in *The Illustrated London News*, July 15, 1916.

across Britain and the United States under the imprint of *Country Life* magazine to mask its government sponsorship; these pictures also circulated in prominent exhibitions and were reprinted in a book.[66] In this formidable collection of drawings, Bone combines a distinctive architectural precision with a sense of panoramic sweep to render devastated landscapes, towns in ruins, columns of marching soldiers, and complex industrial activities such as shipbuilding and munitions fabrication. But only a few of these pictures acknowledge dying and dead bodies, and these do so only obliquely. The implication that British soldiers died is simultaneously evoked and dismissed in "On the Somme: In the Old No Man's Land" (figure 1.3), in which Bone draws a few irregular grave markers, but with a caption (written by journalist Charles E. Montague) that makes them French: "The foreground was won last July by the Manchesters. They found in No Man's Land the bodies of many Frenchmen killed in earlier fighting, and buried them beside their own dead. Not all the bodies could be identified: Some of the crosses shown in the drawing bear such inscriptions as 'In honoured Memory of Two Unknown French Soldiers, buried here.'"[67] He draws more grave markers of the unknown dead in "Inconnu" (figure 1.4), but the visual detachment and remote neutrality of these drawings transformed these dead into impersonal landscape, from the unknown into those without identities to be known. The viewer's relation to these dead is heavily buffered, mediated. In "A Soldiers' Cemetery at Lihons" (figure 1.5), Bone locates the dead, according to Montague's caption, in "graves marked by rough

Figure 1.3 Muirhead Bone, *On the Somme: In the Old No Man's Land*. © 2013 Artists Rights Society (ARS), New York / DACS, London

Figure 1.4 Muirhead Bone, *Inconnu*. © IWM (Art.IWM REPRO 000684 60)

Figure 1.5 Muirhead Bone, *A Soldier's Cemetery at Lihons.* © 2013 Artists Rights Society (ARS), New York / DACS, London

crosses or by the rifle or steel helmet of the dead man" where "shell-fire has disturbed many of the graves."[68] While this seems to represent the vulnerability of the war dead, the picture's implicit message, directed to the homefront, was more reassuring: despite everything, the British dead ultimately remained secure in their graves, a claim that was not the case for countless soldiers confronted after mortar fire once again with the comrades they had buried. The sense of some hovering, quasi-religious force that guarded British corpses where they fell more explicitly animated "A Via Dolorosa: Mouquet Farm" (figure 1.6). The caption reads: "The little white heap of ruins on the sky-line marks the site of the famous farm. The slope up which our men fought their way to it is marked with improvised memorials to a few of those who fell on the way. A similar series of these tragic and noble finger-posts points the way up from the valley of the Ancre to the heights of Thiepval. It is to be hoped that monuments so uniquely eloquent as these Stations of the Cross of soldierly self-sacrifice may not be suffered to disappear."[69] When they refer to soldiers' corpses at all, Bone's widely viewed drawings imply that they are problems that have largely been resolved out of their materiality into greater questions of national, spiritual salvation. Bone's metonymic displacement of the dead into their symbols helped make this a war imaginable without the blasted, rotting bodies that the state found too volatile for the homefront. While admired

Figure 1.6 Muirhead Bone, *A Via Dolorosa: Mouquet Farm.* © IWM (Art.IWM REPRO 000684 55)

by Wellington House, these pictures were dismissed by soldiers: Owen himself wrote home about them on January 19, 1917, that "those 'Somme Pictures' are the laughing stock of the army—like the trenches on exhibition in Kensington."[70]

By 1917, officials overseeing the war artists had explicitly prohibited "the depiction of corpses in official films, photographs and artworks," though "token injuries such as bandaged head wounds or arms in a sling—preferably clean—were acceptable."[71] Of course, officially painted corpses could be German, a ready displacement for homefront death-thoughts. William Orpen's *Dead Germans in a Trench* (figure 1.7), first shown in May 1918, combined anti-German sentiment with the darkly thrilling realism-effect of abandoned war corpses.[72] The painting echoed popular illustrations of dead Germans, such as Frédéric de Harren's of Germans "annihilated by shell-fire" at Passchendaele (drawn "from material supplied by an eye-witness") in *The Illustrated London News* of December 8, 1917 (figure 1.8). The culture was working out its feelings toward these distant, but vitally important corpses however it could, with swerves of attention that could seem panicked and strange. Both fake and real British dead appeared before massive audiences in the 1916 propaganda film *The Battle of the Somme*. First screened in August while the battle it depicted was still underway, the film was viewed by hundreds of thousands in its first week and eventually seen by approximately twenty million people.[73] It is an astonishing film. While much of it is clearly staged to contrive

Figure 1.7 William Orpen, *Dead Germans in a Trench.* © IWM (Art.IWM ART 2955)

cheerful impressions of the front, it also portrays genuinely startling moments of
soldiers in their exposure to the elements, violence, and their own fatigue. As well
as its infamous over-the-top sequence early in the film, in which two British soldiers pretend to die as they rush from a fake trench, it also contains a two-minute
sequence that shows corpses littered across the ground. This sequence starts with
a disheveled German soldier in a pit, shifts to a dead British officer barely visible in the weeds near the corpse of his dog in the foreground, presents images of
other bodies in deathly stillness, and ends with a scene of British soldiers digging

Figure 1.8 Frédéric de Harren, war illustration, published in *The Illustrated London News*, 8 December 1917.

mass graves for long rows of corpses. *The Battle of the Somme* was criticized and admired for this sequence as well as for its fraudulent one, because the war's absent corpses were at the center of both fascination and abhorrence. Official war painters were negotiating the visibility of the dead, not just in the context of this important film but in the context of hysterical accounts of German industrial use of soldier corpses. In spring 1917, stories began to emerge in the British press about a German "conversion factory" (or "Kadaververwertungsanstalt") that processed German and Allied corpses into lubricating oils, soap, and a food supplement for pigs. *The Times* ran stories in April and a pamphlet, *A Corpse Conversion Factory*, apparently from the Department of Information, appeared soon after. Parliament discussed the issue. While *The Times* soon questioned the veracity of this story, the idea of such horrific abuses seized the public's imagination; it spoke to the deep, distorting anxiety at the homefront about the bodies that had fallen from their care. The story was a complete fabrication, but it was an important element of the mood confronting the artists sent to represent soldiers' bodies at the front.[74] Siegfried Sassoon refers to it in "The Tombstone Makers": "I told him with a sympathetic grin, / That Germans boil dead soldiers down for fat; / And he was horrified. 'What shameful sin! / 'O sir, that Christian souls would come to that!' "[75]

Several painters sought techniques for figuring the living's sense of obligation to the dead in the war's extremity, an obscure or intangible relation at the limits of both ethical possibility and visual representation. William Orpen, who became an

Figure 1.9 William Orpen, *A Highlander Passing a Grave.* © IWM (Art.IWM ART 2995)

official artist in January 1917 with permission and resources for an extended tour of France, depicts a kind of transaction between a living and dead soldier in his *A Highlander Passing a Grave* (figure 1.9).[76] The soldier, striding by himself into the rich blue of an immense and uninterrupted sky, is a figure for individual worth in the context of the military's homogenous mass, a quiet claim for singularity that he shares with the buried comrade in the grave he acknowledges. The painting captures the wish for differentiation in the context of mass death. In his c.1918 *A Death Among the Wounded in the Snow* (figure 1.10), Orpen paints and draws a soldier

Figure 1.10 William Orpen, *A Death Among the Wounded in the Snow.* © IWM (Art.IWM ART 2985)

apparently just at the moment of his death on a stretcher, surrounded by grieving comrades. The corpse is literally exposed but figuratively circumscribed in two ways, by the soldiers wrapped about him in a line that moves toward the viewer, and by the arching brushstrokes of sky bent over him in a kind of atmospheric blanketing. Both techniques combine into a subtle, multidimensional geometry of enclosure. William Roberts, who joined the Royal Field Artillery as a gunner in 1916 and made art in this capacity before he was officially commissioned in April 1918, painted *British Military Cemetery* that summer (figure 1.11).[77] If Orpen's *Highlander* renders a death's claim to specificity, Roberts's scene abstracts burial acts and the bodies at the center of them into repeatable elements of an efficient system. The distant, skewed, overhead perspective further articulates the awkward impersonality of this labor. Yet—and this is the painting's point—this labor is rationalized, within the sphere of the state's logistical competence. When Roberts returns to such a scene in 1919, in *Burying the Dead after a Battle* (figure 1.12), the evocation of a rational state system for the dead gives way to the more intimate scene of a single burial in which this geometry has been absorbed into each mourner's rigid, angular body, so that the group of these bodies is arranged as an elaborately

Figure 1.11 William Roberts, *British Military Cemetery*. The Estate of John David Roberts. By Permission of the William Roberts Society.

connected microsystem around this single grave. It is the state's systematic burial processes inscribed in particular soldiers' bodies. The corpse is nearly invisible, not so much effaced as assimilated into the system around it. This assimilation of the dead into an abstract geometry is a form of care to the extent that it precludes their wholesale abandonment. Harold Williamson's striking 1918 chalk and water-color picture *Stretcher-bearers* (figure 1.13) renders both this care and this abandonment as equal, undecidable conditions of the war corpse. One body—perhaps still alive, but corpselike, a pre-corpse—rises above the ground as another sinks into the mud, and these figures are bound as the dialectical possibilities of one another. At the front, each tended, buried corpse contained within it the defining possibility of its abandonment. Williamson, who fought extensively at the front with the King's Royal Rifle Corps and was wounded twice, elaborated this dialectic in April 1918 in *A German Attack on a Wet Morning* (figure 1.14).[78] The neglected, sprawling corpse in the foreground is under the gaze of the wounded soldier, the only other figure not watching the distant line of advancing Germans. The wounded soldier's look downward is not the acknowledgement given by Orpen's vigorous Highlander under a lush sky but an expression of panic under the sun's near eclipse. If it evokes Nicolas Poussin's *Landscape with a Man Killed by a Snake*, with its man fleeing from the sight of death, it does so by exploring the ambiguity

Figure 1.12 William Roberts, *Burying the Dead after a Battle*. The Estate of John David Roberts. By Permission of the William Roberts Society.

of such a flight, since it is not clear if the injured soldier is turning toward or away from the corpse. He is doing both at once. "What is most dreadful about the dead body is its immobility, its becoming a mere thing," T. J. Clark writes in a meditation on Poussin's painting, and we can add with reference to Williamson's that the corpse's dreadful, immobile thingliness is even more dreadful if no one can see it, if it is an abandoned thing.[79] This painting's punch line is that that the wounded soldier, the only figure with a face, is Williamson himself: it is the war painter's task, the painting tells us, to look at the dead no one at the homefront sees, and the fact that the soldier's wound is in his hand suggests the cost—the psychic pain, the aesthetic confusion, the ethical anxiety—of performing this manual task.[80]

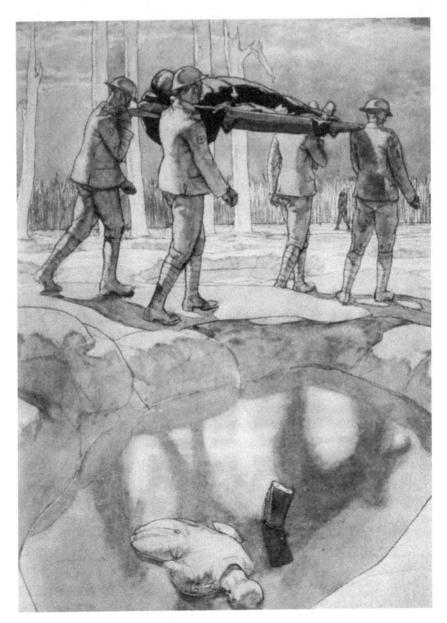

Figure 1.13 Harold Williamson, *Stretcher-bearers*. The Estate of Harold Williamson. By Permission of the Estate of Harold Williamson.

We can examine a few more of the officially rendered corpses that, in their increasing abandonment, tested the social and political limits of artistic representation at home. These limits were relaxed in 1919, but corpses strewn about battlefields remained difficult subject matter, caught in the ideological wake of earlier

Figure 1.14 Harold Williamson, *A German Attack on a Wet Morning*. The Estate of Harold Williamson. By Permission of the Estate of Harold Williamson.

propaganda. Orpen makes the central corpse difficult to discern in his 1917 pencil drawing *A Trench, Beaumont Hamel* (figure 1.15). It is nearly camouflaged, so that the viewer's sudden recognition that he or she has been looking at it without seeing it creates a suspicion that others could be anywhere, imperceptibly saturating the landscape.[81] They were. Paul Nash—an officer in France in early 1917, who was sent home with an injury from an accident and then appointed official artist in October—creates the same sense of camouflaged saturation in his 1918 *After the Battle* (figure 1.16).[82] This wasteland holds four corpses, by my count, in varying degrees of indifference and obscurity, and it is the sheer incidental quality of their role in the composition—we can look for them or not, it makes no difference, nothing becomes clearer if we do—that articulates their abandonment. (Unsurprisingly, this painting was not published in the 1918 issue of *British Artists at the Front*, a continuation of Bone's *The Western Front*, dedicated to Nash's work.) Paul's younger brother John Nash, who was sent to the front in June 1917 and appointed war artist in 1918, began work on *Over the Top* (figure 1.17) soon thereafter.[83] *Over the Top* is a scene of vivid, inevitable slaughter in progress. The living will soon join, are in the process of joining, the dead face down in the snow, and the dead have not yet achieved their stillness. It could not be shown until 1919.[84]

Figure 1.15 William Orpen, *A Trench, Beaumont Hamel.* © IWM (Art.IWM ART 2393)

Yet it is C. R. W. Nevinson's work that most forcefully directs the homefront's gaze to the brutality of such dying, even to the point of official censorship. Nevinson, a prominent British futurist aligned with Marinetti before the war, well known in the London art world, was first commissioned in summer 1917. His "Dante-esque" *Harvest of Battle* (figure 1.18), first shown in 1919, was criticized for, among other things, being too realistic, and it was not included in a 1918 issue of *British Artists at the Front* showcasing his art.[85] The foregrounded corpse, in rigor mortis, is bent back to look at the viewer, watching us watching it. From its preliminary stages, this painting caused Nevinson official trouble: "Sketching, for what would later be painted up into *Shell Holes* and *Harvest of Battle* was done in and around Passchendaele and this earned him a reprimand, from a Major Lee, of Intelligence F, that would get him sent home. He arrived in London in the first week of August [1917]...and was replaced at the Front by Eric Kennington."[86] Nevinson fell into deeper trouble after his return with another corpse painting, *Paths of Glory* (figure 1.19). Originally titled *Dead Men* in November 1917 when Major Lee first flagged it as a problem, the painting was the object of Nevinson's dispute with censors for months.[87] (Another painting of his, *A Group of Soldiers*—all of them

Figure 1.16 Paul Nash, *After the Battle*. © IWM (Art.IWM ART 2706)

Figure 1.17 John Nash, *Over the Top*. © IWM (Art.IWM ART 1656)

Figure 1.18   C. R. W. Nevinson, *Harvest of Battle.* © IWM (Art.IWM ART 1921)

Figure 1.19   C. R. W. Nevinson, *Paths of Glory.* © IWM (Art.IWM ART 518)

alive—had nearly been censored but finally allowed in fall 1917.) Although *Paths of Glory* had been definitively, unambiguously banned in a letter from Alfred Yockney dated December 20, 1917, Nevinson exhibited it at the Leicester Galleries the following March—but with a large "Censored" sign posted across the bodies (figure 1.20).[88] The press was intrigued; a March 16 article in the *London Mail* asked, "What is hidden by that patch?"[89] In this gesture, putting the war's corpses under visible erasure, Nevinson found a startling form for representing the absence of literal, physical corpses from the homefront. They were not simply absent but banned from presence, and making the force of this ban palpable was a way to approach the dead themselves, who remained within its sphere.

Nevinson's *Paths of Glory*, seen without obstruction, actually tells us something significant about dead bodies. They are merely matter. Nevinson paints the sensuous poverty of their inert, unmeaning materiality. These two dead soldiers are troubling because they have become things without humanist value, anonymous objects scattered among others. They are simply piles of organic matter at rest, a repletion of tissue, and will remain so. How does Nevinson create this effect? He is able, somehow, to actually paint the *weight* of these bodies pressing

Figure 1.20   C. R. W. Nevinson, *Paths of Glory*, published in *Daily Mail* March 2, 1918.

into the earth and slightly down the slope, to paint the feel of their blank and inanimate downwardness. They have the heaviness of stones and scrap metal, and like these they are mindless of their heaviness, which merely happens. The strangeness of visually experiencing this physical sensation of mindless human weight disarms the viewer in many ways, but there is one way in particular that is relevant to Owen's war poetry. It is the disorientation that happens when one suddenly perceives the brute physicality of signs, when written letters and words are reduced to the humility of the ink marks that they actually are, with their minute weight pressing down on paper. So with Nevinson's corpses: they lie across the earth like marks fallen from the symbolic into the material, the physical remains of metaphysical meanings. It is a portrait of collapsed textuality, a cultural script falling apart. Nevinson's painting poses the question of what should be done with these awkward, disordered material fragments, these deflated ink marks from texts that used to mean something. He is asking if anyone is capable of attaching new sounds and referents to these suddenly arbitrary marks that still aspire to the condition of signs.

Owen and the Arbitrary Sign

Owen joined the Artists' Rifles on October 21, 1915, at the age of twenty-two. He began officer training in March 1916, and was commissioned to the Manchester Regiment in June. He commanded a platoon at the Somme's front the following January. In March 1917 he suffered a concussion from a fall that left him briefly in a military hospital, but he found himself in hostilities again by mid-April. In May he was diagnosed with shell shock and hospitalized again. During this second hospitalization, at Craiglockhart War Hospital near Edinburgh in the summer and fall of 1917, he became friends with Siegfried Sassoon, who had a profound influence on his poetry. After many years of writing primarily under the enthusiastic influence of Keats, Owen was provoked by Sassoon into a new idiom and tone that more persuasively responded to his war experience. He returned to France as lieutenant in winter 1917, and by June 1918 he had rejoined the Manchester Regiment. After several periods of relative inaction, he returned to battle at the very end of the war, in September and October. He was killed near Ors, in the north of France, on November 4, one week before the Armistice; news of his death reached his mother, in Shrewsbury, on Armistice Day itself, amid the town's celebrations. He was buried by the War Graves Commission in the Ors military cemetery.[90] He had published only five poems in his lifetime, while seven more appeared in Edith

Sitwell's 1919 *Wheels* anthology. Sassoon edited and published a small collection of Owen's poetry in 1920, and Blunden edited a larger one in 1931: "This means that Owen's poems came to the notice of the public not as gestures of *protest* but as part of a larger structure of *bereavement*."[91] One way to understand this extended process of bereavement is as a process of reckoning with the arbitrary, unmeaning quality of the war's corpses. Owen's poetry was useful to a mourning nation in the years following the war in part because it represented the displaced, mediated, increasingly complex relation of the war dead to those at home. His poetry was about how these dead bodies fell out of and into meaning, how they returned and did not return to the cultural scripts devised for them.

The speaker in "The Unreturning" describes, in its opening stanzas, a condition in which the dead are beyond summoning even to simple forms of contact:

> Suddenly night crushed out the day and hurled
> Her remnants over cloud-peaks, thunder-walled.
> Then fell a stillness such as harks appalled
> When far-gone dead return upon the world.
>
> There watched I for the Dead; but no ghost woke.
> Each one whom Life exiled I named and called.
> But they were all too far, or dumbed, or thralled,
> And never one fared back to me or spoke. (*CPF* v. 1 107)

Owen imagines the dead as a silence within silence, and this sense of double negation, of an emptiness within an emptiness, complicates their absence. The presence of these dead cannot fill an absence but only amplify it. While he began this poem before the war, Owen finished it in 1917 or 1918, when it became a way to describe the proliferating absences of the dead and the proliferating ways that the dead could be absent in the theater of war. Santanu Das observes that, "unlike in Barbusse's *Under Fire* or Sassoon's *Counter-Attack And Other Poems* (the two war books that Owen most admired), the corpse is almost absent in Owen's poetry, reduced to metonymies ('hopes lay strewn') and synecdoches ('piteous mouths that coughed')." [92] This representational absence is significant because it reflects a real one, not among soldiers but among those at home awaiting them. Owen condenses this inaccessibility into a prohibition at the end of "Greater Love," directed toward civilians: "Weep, you may weep, for you may touch them not" (*CPF* v. 1 166).[93] Owen frames this inaccessibility as an undecidable proposition, as the dead's acute either/or, in "Asleep." After describing a soldier die in his sleep—a sleep within sleep, similar to an idea of silence within silence, another step in an ongoing withdrawal from the grasp of the living—the speaker asks:

> Whether his deeper sleep lie shaded by the shaking
> Of great wings, and the thoughts that hung the stars,
> High-pillowed on calm pillows of God's making,
> Above these clouds, these rains, these sleets of lead,
> And these winds' scimitars,
> – Or whether yet his thin and sodden head
> Confuses more and more with the low mould,
> His hair being one with the grey grass
> Of finished fields, and wire-scrags rusty-old,
> Who knows? Who hopes? Who troubles? Let it pass! (*CPF* v. 1 152)

This corpse is either sign or thing, a figure containing eternity or a mound of tissue fertilizing soil. Like Nevinson's corpses in *Paths of Glory*, this corpse is reduced to the raw, unmeaning materiality on which even the most expressive cultural symbols depend. In Sarah Cole's terms, the corpse vacillates between the enchantment and disenchantment of violence: "There is magic in death. But there is also emptiness and finality in death. . . . Historically, it has been war that most powerfully calls forth these dichotomized understandings of violent death: as a sign and precipitator of sublimity (in a person, community, or nation) or, conversely, as a sign and precipitator of total degeneration and waste."[94] To leave the reader, in the wake of great violence, suspended between the possibilities of corpse as sublime meaning and corpse as waste matter is to ask the reader to suspend the therapeutic work of mourning for an absent person or personality and to take up a more fundamental task, to tend a body without personhood. While mourning is certainly facilitated by tending to the dead body, the body itself is a fact beyond possession by the mourner; it is a demand of another sort, beyond the demand to experience emotions. The severely wounded soldier who speaks in "A Terre (being the philosophy of many soldiers)" desires this shift. He is not interested in civilian grief, which will fade, or in compassion for his new disabilities, which has already faded, but in the physical fact of bodies in the ground, which will remain.

> Certainly flowers have the easiest time on earth.
> "I shall be one with nature, herb, and stone,"
> Shelley would tell me. Shelley would be stunned:
> The dullest Tommy hugs that fancy now.
> "Pushing up the daisies" is their creed, you know.

To grain, then, go my fat, to buds my sap,

For all the usefulness there is in soap.

D'you think the Boche will ever stew man-soup?

Some day, no doubt, if...

                   Friend, be very sure

I shall be better off with plants that share

More peacably the meadow and the shower.

Soft rains will touch me,—as they could touch me once,

And nothing but the sun shall make me ware.

Your guns may crash around me. I'll not hear;

Or, if I wince, I shall not know I wince. (*CPF* v. 1 178)

In several passages, Owen thinks about the recalcitrant materiality of the war corpse as its primary meaning. He offers the radical suggestion that the dead are dead bodies, and that these bodies mean merely themselves, as lifeless tautologies that retain their integrity in the context of the state's propaganda and fraudulent claims of soldiers' sacrificial glory in dying. He develops a poetics of the war corpse's disenchantment as a response to the aesthetic dynamic that Cole describes: "Enchantment, understood as a form of generative violence, underlies nearly all military violence....In the peculiar conditions of war, violent death is transformed into something positive, communal, perhaps even sacred."[95] This transformation happens in large part through the bodies that war leaves scattered about its fields and trenches. In Owen's poetry, these bodies do not aspire to enchant themselves, or to be enchanted by others, into powerful signs or aesthetic satisfactions—nearly all of which had been appropriated to justify and prolong the war's violence.

Examples of this exploitative appropriation are still striking. Arthur Radclyffe Dugmore, a prominent wildlife painter and photographer who became a captain at the Somme, published in 1918 an account of his experiences in battle. His nationalist invocation of the dead went beyond the familiar call not to let them have died in vain; he provokes concern for the well-being of the very corpses in the ground, now quasi-hostages of the enemy: "From a sentimental point of view we feel very deeply having to yield ground that was won at such a terrible cost in lives and energy... Apart from the actual material loss there is the terrible thought that the graves of our poor Dead are desecrated by the very presence of the Hun. At least we had hoped that the bodies of those who made the Great Sacrifice for the cause of Right might have been allowed to rest undisturbed in their simple graves. But such apparently was not to be, and we can only pray that the time is not far distant when the Hun and all he stands for shall be driven forever from the soil of France and Belgium." He concludes his exhortation by suggesting that these bodies hold, in the sheer pathos of their condition, the homefront accountable for continued contributions to the war: "We owe nothing less than this to our heroic Dead, and we should never dare look on the little White Crosses that mark their last resting places if we failed in this sacred obligation."[96] Rupert Brooke famously gives this concept of the corpse's embodiment of the nation—this sense that the nation is at stake in its corpses—in "The Soldier," published in 1915 and widely circulated for several years: "If I should die, think only this of me: / That there's some corner of a foreign field / That is forever England."[97] Brooke imagines a corpse that is simultaneously repatriated home and colonizing abroad, a hyper-fulfillment of nationalist possibilities. As Patrick Deer observes about this poem, "only in death, it seems, can the soldier's body merge with the nation."[98] For comic effect, Woolf exaggerates the idea of this merging in *Mrs. Dalloway* with Lady Bruton, whom "one could not figure…even in death parted from the earth or roaming territories over which, in some spiritual shape, the Union Jack had ceased to fly. To be not English even among the dead—no, no! Impossible!"[99] The war's corpses were so widely, predictably subject to nationalist rhetoric that E. M. Forster's 1922 satire, "Our Graves in Gallipoli," can refer to it even then as a stock line in political speeches of the day. He stages a conversation between two of the war dead:

> [FIRST GRAVE]: We are important again upon the earth. Each morning men mention us.
>
> [SECOND GRAVE]: Yes, after seven years' silence.
>
> [FIRST GRAVE]: Every day some eminent public man now refers to the "sanctity of our graves in Gallipoli."
>
> [SECOND GRAVE]: Why do the eminent men speak of "our" graves, as if they were themselves dead? It is we, not they, who lie on Achi Baba.[100]

They go on to discuss the possibility of future wars resulting from the state's use of its war corpses as ciphers for its essential being, the principle of the state's sacralization:

> [FIRST GRAVE]:…it is well for a nation that would be great to scatter its graves all over the world. Graves in Ireland, graves in Iraq, Russia, Persia, India, each with its inscription from the Bible or Rupert Brooke. When England thinks fit, she can launch an expedition to protect the sanctity of her graves, and can follow that by another expedition to protect the sanctity of the additional graves…. England cannot spare a penny for anything except for her heroes' graves.[101]

Graves generate graves which generate further graves, all of which generate the nation. This fatal logic is what prompts Owen, despite his personal admiration for Brooke, to imagine the dead as irretrievably beyond the grasp of such nationalist instrumentality in "With an Identity Disc," in which the speaker hopes his identity will fade from public view after death: "Let my death be memoried on this disc. / Wear it, sweet friend. Inscribe no date nor deed. / But let thy heartbeat kiss it night and day, / Until the name grow vague and wear away" (*CPF* v. 1 96). It is a desire to exhaust the meaning of a military death without coercing others to die.

Up to a certain point, Owen's corpses resist the symbolic apparatus of the war effort. But even if this is a claim to something like the integrity of the dead, it is small solace. Many of Owen's speakers still wish something could be done to bring the corpses before them to symbolic life. "Futility" (quoted here in its entirety) laments the poverty of the corpse reduced to its literal, absolute facticity, and the impotence of those around it.

> Move him into the sun—
> Gently its touch awoke him once,
> At home, whispering of fields half-sown.
> Always it woke him, even in France,
> Until this morning and this snow.
> If anything might rouse him now,
> The kind old sun will know.
>
> Think how it wakes the seeds –
> Woke once the clays of a cold star.
> Are limbs, so dear achieved, are sides
> Full-nerved, still warm, too hard to stir?
> Was it for this the clay grew tall?
> – O what made fatuous sunbeams toil
> To break earth's sleep at all? (*CPF* v. 1 158)

Rhetoric, like the sun, is a force that brings inanimate matter to life, to meaning; the desire in this poem is for a field of discursive energy able to saturate and animate the dead bodies left cold on the battlefield. But the poem's more interesting task is to explore what it means for this desire to be frustrated, to examine the failures and impasses of this discursive project around the dead. In this exploration, the poem anticipates the third section of Read's "My Company," written a few years later, in which the speaker describes the frustrated reanimation of a corpse that is too dangerous to retrieve: "A man of mine / lies on the wire; / And he will rot / And first his lips / The worms will eat. // It is not thus I would have him kissed, / But with the warm passionate lips / Of his comrade here."[102] The war's corpses inevitably signified such failures; the last stanza of Owen's "Exposure" holds us in a prolonged moment of one.

> Tonight, this frost will fasten on this mud and us,
> Shrivelling many hands, puckering foreheads crisp.
> The burying party, picks and shovels in shaking grasp,
> Pause over half-known faces. All their eyes are ice,
> But nothing happens. (*CPF* v. 1 186)

This nothing that happens among the war's corpses is a stark revision, or depletion, of the astonishing rhetorical power of earlier war elegies. The final lines of Whitman's "Vigil Strange I Kept on the Field One Night" displays this linguistic machinery with such clarity that it is worth going to the other side of the Atlantic to read it. Whitman collapses the distinction between rhetorical address to the dead and their physical burial in a seamless elegiac performative:

> My comrade I wrapt in his blanket, envelp'd well his form,
> Folded the blanket well, tucking it carefully over head and carefully under feet,
> And there and then and bathed by the rising sun, my son in his grave, in his rude-dug grave I deposited,
> Ending my vigil strange with that, vigil of night and battle-field dim,
> Vigil for boy of responding kisses, (never again on earth responding,)
> Vigil for comrade swiftly slain, vigil I never forget, how as day brighten'd
> I rose from the chill ground and folded my soldier well in his blanket,
> And buried him where he fell.[103]

The body is deposited in this rude-dug poem just as it is in its rude-dug grave, wrapped in a poetic voice just as in his blanket, all in the illumination of the rising sun, a figure for the rhetorical energy that Owen's icy corpsescapes lack. Whitman's poem, in this performative care, moves line by line toward the eradication of the corpse's contingency in the field of meaning. To bury, for the speaker, is to banish the arbitrary quality of the dead: he "buried him where he fell" because this transforms the ground into human place and correlates the corpse with its mark, the thing with its sign. As Robert Harrison reminds us (and as I discuss in the introduction), "it is not for nothing that the Greek word for 'sign,' *sema*, is also the word for 'grave.' For the Greeks the grave marker was not just one sign among others. It was a sign that signified the source of signification itself, since it 'stood for' what it 'stood in'—the ground of burial as such."[104] Whitman's eloquent gathering of poetic language, ground, and corpse into the same act is what breaks down in Owen's poetry. His corpses remain arbitrary, meaning nothing. This demanded a new set of poetic techniques responsive to a powerful nationalist rhetoric intent on making corpses mean everything.

Owen and the Synecdochic War Corpse

Owen's insistence on the unmeaning contingency of the war corpse was a distinctive stance at the time, but not enough for a robust and memorable ideological critique of the state's use of the dead. He goes beyond this set of questions in many of his most powerful poems, those that established him, for generations to come, as the preeminent soldier poet of the First World War and the model for what a modern soldier poet sounds like. These other poems explore not the stripped-down materiality of the dead but the way they take on the specific meaning of sacrifice. He reveals, in this interrogation, the synecdochic logic of the war corpse in the state's grasp. In fact, his poems seem preternaturally aware of the synecdochic capacities of the war dead that would not be fully exploited by the state until after his own death. "The Parable of the Old Man and the Young" is based on the story of the binding of Isaac in Genesis 22.

> So Abram rose, and clave the wood, and went,
> And took the fire with him, and a knife.
> And as they sojourned both of them together,
> Isaac the first-born spake and said, My Father,
> Behold the preparations, fire and iron,
> But where the lamb for this burnt-offering?
> Then Abram bound the youth with belts and straps,
> And builded parapets and trenches there,
> And stretchèd forth the knife to slay his son.
> When lo! an Angel called him out of heaven,
> Saying, Lay not thy hand upon the lad,
> Neither do anything to him, thy son.
> Behold! Caught in a thicket by its thorns,
> A Ram. Offer the Ram of Pride instead.
>
> But the old man would not so, but slew his son,
> And half the seed of Europe, one by one. (*CPF* v. 1 174)

In the poem's final lines, this slaughter becomes both singular and multiple; the victim is one and many, or many within one. This condensation, in which the singular one bleeds synecdochically for the European whole, occurs because metaphor fails. The available ram is not substituted for Isaac; synecdoche trumps metaphorical substitution. This tropological tension between synecdoche and metaphor, condensation and substitution, is the tension between two ways of accounting for or acknowledging war deaths, based on either multiplicity or singularity. The triumph of synecdoche as a tropological structure is the triumph of an instrumental totalization as a political structure, that is, of a structure that gathers all the dead into one that can be used by the state.[105] In an earlier poem, "The One Remains," Owen begins exploring this logic of the one that gathers the many. The poem ends with a pre-political synecdochic desire:

> And as for those long known and worshipped long,
> But now, alas! no longer, and the song
> Of voices that have said 'Adieu, we part,'
> Their reminiscences would cease my heart,
> Except I still hoped find, some time, some place,
> All beauty, once for ever, in one face. (*CPF* v. 1 103)

It is Owen's new insight in "Parable" that this synecdochic structure lends itself to officially sponsored slaughter as well as to beauty.

Owen's imaginative exploration of the synecdochic capacities of the war dead continues more emphatically in "The Show," which he wrote after fighting at the Somme. This poem knows more than it says about both the temptation and the ethical price of collapsing a totality of deaths within a single, chosen one:

> We have fallen in the dreams the ever-living
> Breathe on the tarnished mirror of the world,
> And then smooth out with ivory hands and sigh.
>   W. B. Yeats

> My soul looked down from a vague height, with Death,
> As unremembering how I rose or why,
> And saw a sad land, weak with sweats of dearth,
> Grey, cratered like the moon with hollow woe,
> And pitted with great pocks and scabs of plagues.

> Across its beard, that horror of harsh wire,
> There moved thin caterpillars, slowly uncoiled.
> It seemed they pushed themselves to be as plugs
> Of ditches, where they writhed and shrivelled, killed.

By them had slimy paths been trailed and scraped
Round myriad warts that might be little hills.

From gloom's last dregs these long-strung creatures crept,
And vanished out of dawn down hidden holes.

(And smell came up from those foul openings
As out of mouths, or deep wounds deepening.)

On dithering feet upgathered, more and more,
Brown strings, toward strings of grey, with bristling spines,
All migrants from green fields, intent on mire.

Those that were grey, of more abundant spawns,
Ramped on the rest and ate them and were eaten.
I saw their bitten backs curve, loop, and straighten,
I watched those agonies curl, lift, and flatten.

Whereat, in terror what that sight might mean,
I reeled and shivered earthward like a feather.

And Death fell with me, like a deepening moan.
And He, picking a manner of worm, which half had hid
Its bruises in the earth, but crawled no further,
Showed me its feet, the feet of many men,
And the fresh-severed head of it, my head. (*CPF* v. 1 155–156)

The peculiarity of the poem—its hallucinatory dislocation and bizarre life forms—is the peculiarity of a world in which the corpse is a problem that cannot be solved by burial. We might imagine, through Owen's refracted corpse imagery, a world that does not bury its dead because there is no point in doing so, no faith that either the dead or the living will be served by such a gesture, and no place to bury the dead since the earth itself is a corpse. These disarticulations of death from decay and of the earth from burial ground become the speaker's disarticulation, or removal, from his own locatable selfhood and subject position. He is both witness and victim to this violence, spatially and temporally beyond his own fatal participation in the scene, as if the personification of death has replaced his own personhood and mortality. In devising a voice that speaks from neither life nor death, but from a kind of ontological neutrality or existential bracketing, Owen provides the poetic correlative of an unburied body, neither alive nor complete in its death.

The synecdochic collapse of many into Isaac at the end of "Parable" repeats in the last few lines of "The Show," this time from the perspective of the speaker himself: "And He, picking a manner of worm, which half had hid / Its bruises in the earth, but crawled no further, / Showed me its feet, the feet of many men, / And the fresh-severed head of it, my head." The speaker perceives his own corpse as both specifically his and communally shared, a momentarily common body designated to hold the collectively unidentified dead. This final synecdoche, in which the speaker is both himself and the whole of the dead, obliquely returns to the pervasive imagery of the earlier part of the poem, in which the quasi-human creatures swarm across the battlefield's encompassing body. The final image organizes and stabilizes this earlier, disconcerting juxtaposition of dehumanized swarm and humanized ground, multiplicity and unity; the speaker, working through these hallucinatory scenes, finally gathers the many and the one together in a single rhetorical structure. It is the drama of the poem to realize, through struggle, synecdoche as a mode of perception, just as it is the purpose of "Parable" to prioritize synecdoche over metaphor. The parts that are sacrificed to and for the whole—Isaac, the speaker in "The Show," the corpse-battlefield this speaker describes—are bodies that can die more than once and, by assuming the deaths of many, instrumentalize, for the state's interest, the rhetorical malleability of the war corpse in the organization of mourning.

Owen intensifies the consequences of this tropological economy of many gathered in and around one, of the fractional one taking on the burden for the whole, in "Dulce et Decorum Est," one of his best-known poems (also written in fall 1917). The first verse paragraph describes an anonymous, insensible mass of soldiers designated simply as a "we," "men," "many," "all":

> Bent double, like old beggars under sacks,
> Knock-kneed, coughing like hags, we cursed through sludge,
> Till on the haunting flares we turned our backs
> And towards our distant rest began to trudge.
> Men marched asleep. Many had lost their boots
> But limped on, blood-shod. All went lame; all blind;
> Drunk with fatigue; deaf even to the hoots
> Of tired, outstripped Five-Nines that dropped behind. (*CPF* v. 1 144)

As if too exhausted to individuate itself, or as if this suffering were most significant as a collective experience, the soldier's voice is absorbed into the sensations of the group, in which no particular person suffers because everyone does. It is a momentary abstraction of the subjective location of a suffering that nevertheless retains its sensory vividness. The speaker tries to sustain this collective subject position—we, men, many, all—but fails in the last, fragmentary sentence of the paragraph that swallows the grammatical subject altogether. In the following lines, during an attack, their dying is reorganized among differentiated subjects, almost as if this differentiation were a part of the attack or a precondition for dying:

> GAS! GAS! Quick, boys!—An ecstasy of fumbling,
> Fitting the clumsy helmets just in time;
> But someone still was yelling out and stumbling
> And flound'ring like a man in fire or lime...
> Dim, through the misty panes and thick green light,
> As under a green sea, I saw him drowning.
>
> In all my dreams, before my helpless sight,
> He plunges at me, guttering, choking, drowning. (ibid.)

From the initial collective, one is individualized to die, and his death solicits the individualization of the speaker himself, who emerges from the "we" as an "I" only at this moment of pained witnessing. The consolidation of this singular subject in response to the dying other suggests an alternative to synecdoche and the multiplicity of sacrifice it entails. It is the possibility of substitution. "Before all my helpless sight, / He plunges at me": it is the sound of a self overwhelmed by the dying other, that finds its subject position in response to—in responsibility for—the other's dying, and that maintains this other's dying in the same ongoing present tense as the continuous present of consciousness. The rhetorical principle of this responsive condition, evoking the possibility of substitution, is metaphor. Owen stages the impossible ethical desire to die for the other, to summon the self as the sacrificial ram in the bush, as if the self could transcend its riveting to its own being and be for the being of another. As the speaker fails to do this—the principle of substitution is thwarted by the other soldier's solitary death within and for the group—he turns and solicits the subject position of the reader instead, directly addressing us in the well-known recrimination that has become virtually emblematic of the very idea of "war poetry" in modern literature:

> If in some smothering dreams you too could pace
> Behind the wagon that we flung him in,
> And watch the white eyes writhing in his face,
> His hanging face, like a devil's sick of sin;

> If you could hear, at every jolt, the blood
> Come gargling from the froth-corrupted lungs,
> Obscene as cancer, bitter as the cud
> Of vile, incurable sores on innocent tongues,—
> My friend, you would not tell with such high zest
> To children ardent for some desperate glory,
> The old Lie: Dulce et decorum est
> Pro patria mori. (ibid.)

The vehemence of this single, strained sentence is derived in part from its movement from a descriptive to normative function: the speaker seeks to transcend his described experience by exerting power over the social and ethical codes governing the civilian reader's relation to war. This address, in its unrelenting imagistic violence, positions us in an ambivalent relation to these codes, both in obedience to and in violation of them, simultaneously as liars complicit in war death and subjects privileged with the truth about such death. This doubled position—distant from the violence but mediately present, blind but forced to see, complicit but potentially absolved—precludes both our identification from the inside and sympathy from the outside of this experience, leaving us with no stable or determinate relation to the soldiers we witness. We can feel both anger and guilt about this death, irreconcilably. The aesthetic pleasure of the poem is in the precision of this ethical and political disorientation; we are precisely nowhere in this complex economy of sacrificial suffering, responsive witnessing, ideological complicity, and ethical revelation. As Jahan Ramazani writes, "Owen's work helps us to rethink the elegiac triad of mourning poet, mourning reader, and mourned victim, eerily suggesting that, even in war elegies, both poet and reader may partly create the victimization they mourn."[106] In this disorientation, what we are left with, finally, is a terrible awareness of the fragility of the human body in modern war. The fragility of this exposed life becomes, in death, the grotesque vulnerability of the corpse carted before us, a final burden we cannot understand or manage and which we know only through our failure to properly assume it.

Owen's poetry has long been read as a protest against reckless war policy and civilian ignorance of soldiers' suffering on the one hand, and as a part of the postwar mourning process (less protest than expression of grief) on the other. However, as we have seen, we can approach this poetry with elements from both concerns simultaneously, as a distinctive ideological critique of the political use to which the dead were put under the alibi of grieving for them. Owen lays bare the cognitive structures most available for imagining relations among the dead and between the dead and the living. In addition to his poems about the inaccessibility and recalcitrant materiality of war corpses, he wrote poems about their alarming synecdochic power, the way one could be made to die for and with many, and the way this rhetoric of multiplicity and totalization could be instrumentalized. I explore the nature of this instrumentalization below. If synecdoche emerges where metaphor fails in Owen's thought, it is to show us how the state can use the play between the corpse's singularity and totalization, its ways of being both one and many, to amplify its power over the living who desire to become ethical subjects in relation to the corpses they lack.

The Thanatopolitical State and The Unknown Warrior

As I have suggested, Owen imagined these corpses at a unique moment in the history of corpse disposal in Western war. The establishment of the Imperial War Graves Commission was, according to war historians Luc Capdevila and Daniele Voldman, part of a pervasive policy shift among belligerent nations according to which military personnel took nearly complete responsibility for the collection and burial of the dead. In earlier wars, local populations cleared the battlefields they were unfortunate enough to live by, or a combination of military and civilian authorities handled the job. "Up until 1914, as warfare for the most part involved moving around, armies which were extremely mobile did not always have time to deal with their dead."[107] Furthermore, battlefield casualties were no longer buried in communal pits or interred in ossuaries, bones jumbled together, as they had been for centuries, but were whenever possible given individually marked graves according to identification tags or other markers—a practice the United States had been among the first to implement in the 1860s—to the extent that "the individual treatment of each body" was "the key factor in the handling of the war dead." "Although there were national variations, a Western pattern for dealing with war dead became established around 1914–18. From this time on, the authorities took responsibility for bodies on the battlefield and extended to all who died in war the same military funeral rites which were imbued with the spirit of bourgeois funerals." Soldiers' deaths "became both public and individual during the First World War. The face, name, history and remains of each were known," or at least attempted to be known. By contrast, in the Franco-Prussian War (1870–1871), the French government buried 87,396 corpses "with most of the brave souls lying anonymously and scattered in ossuaries."[108]

This double shift, from civilian to military burial responsibilities and from anonymous communal graves on the battlefield to individually marked graves in a dedicated cemetery, was a response to a complex, even contradictory set of ideological imperatives. The military's intimate involvement in claiming, identifying, and burying the dead—a difficult exercise in both mass organization and individual identification—expressed the West's larger attempt to reconcile the depersonalizing economic efficiencies of modern industrial production with the individualistic ideology of liberal democracy. These horrific years of industrially structured, state-sponsored corpse production marked a radical change in the life of the Western war dead. They were for the first time both spread across large swaths of Europe and, in an unlikely democratization, granted their private spaces and identities. It was a vertiginous totalization in the context of liberalism's fierce claims to the subject's individual autonomy. Geoff Dyer meditates on this vertiginous quality of the war's violence: "Was there not, amidst all this grief, a faint shudder or shiver of excitement at the unimaginable vastness of it all? The war had set all kinds of records in terms of scale: the greatest bombardments ever seen, the biggest guns, shells and mines, the biggest mobilization, the greatest loss of life ('the million dead'). Was there not a faint glow of pride, an unavoidable undertow of semantic approval, in terming the war 'Great'?"[109] This disturbing thrill responds to both the vastness and the hallucinatory individuality of these deaths, which fell into a kind of endless repetition of the same. To bring to mind the quantity of dead—nine million soldiers and five million civilians among all European nations—is impossible; but to conceive of this unthinkable quantity together with the discrete, individuated identities it contained is impossible for its quality of paradox: so large, yet so singularized a population of corpses.[110] It is the cognitive complexity that informs Owen's synecdochic corpses, each one able to die as and for many.

This paradox was significant for the power of the states that administered it. The war's corpses, tended by the military apparatus that mobilized them while alive, were involved in the modern state's formation as a power—as Foucault has most prominently described it—over biological life as it occurs in both individual human bodies, in their distinct identities, and bodies *en masse*, as populations. "Right from the start, the state is both individualizing and totalitarian," that is, totalizing, governing over aggregates of life.[111] Foucault conceptualizes biopower as the collision between a government's regulatory, prescriptive machinery and species-life; it is "the set of mechanisms through which the basic biological features of the human species became the object of a political strategy, of a general strategy of power, or, in other words, how, starting from the eighteenth century, modern

Western societies took on board the fundamental biological fact that human beings are a species."[112] His genealogy of the verb *to govern* from the sixteenth century in France locates it not in terms of "a state, a territory, or a political structure" but of "people, individuals, or groups" in smaller or larger arrangements of their bodies.[113] The role of dead bodies in this complex government of living ones is not obvious, but it is a new question at stake in the First World War. In the first volume of *The History of Sexuality*, Foucault describes the historical shift in the sovereign's power from the right to kill to the cultivation and maintenance of life; it is a shift in the decisive instance of the sovereign's control from the power to take life from living bodies to the power to "ensure, sustain, and multiply" their energies and productive forces. Sex is the crucial linkage of this biologically focused sovereignty between individual bodies and populations.

> On the one hand, [sex] was tied to the disciplines of the body: the harnessing, intensification, and distribution of forces, the adjustment and economy of energies. On the other hand, it was applied to the regulation of populations, through all far-reaching effects of its activity. It fitted in both categories at once, giving rise to infinitesimal surveillances, permanent controls, extremely meticulous orderings of space, indeterminate medical or psychological examinations, to an entire micro-power concerned with the body. But it gave rise as well to comprehensive measures, statistical assessments, and interventions aimed at the entire social body or at groups taken as a whole. Sex was a means of access both to the life of the body and the life of the species.[114]

As the politicization of biological life, focused on sexuality, replaced that of death, focused on the body's mortality, the political status of the latter became ambiguous: death became the obstinate limit point for anatomo-power and biopower, the useless but inevitable element of a regime that sought, above all else, to bring "the living in the domain of value and utility."[115] In Foucault's scenario, in which the threat of killing is no longer the sovereign's ultimate basis for authority and dead bodies are not the exemplary referent of the sovereign's power, the mortality and remains of bodies disorient the logic of power: "Now it is over life, throughout its unfolding, that power establishes its dominion; death is power's limit, the moment that escapes it; death becomes the most secret aspect of existence, the most 'private.'"[116] Death, the body's de-politicization in a biopolitical regime, becomes the ungovernable element of embodied experience, the nondiscursive excess of power.

We can consider the administration of the dead in the First World War an attempt to correct this governmental lacuna. The body's mortality, the whispered implication of its sexuality, was subject in the states that elaborated their governmental techniques in the war to the same manner of surveillance, regulation, and disciplining at the level of the individual body, and it served as a similar axis for documenting and organizing populations. The corpse, far from exterior to biopower, came ironically to facilitate it by linking the individual and the mass in the state's administration of dying, burial, and commemoration. Management of its war corpses gave the British government access to the intimate ethical desires of its living subjects, a crucial part of their subject formation. To conceptualize the biopolitical function of the corpse, consider the following passage from *The History of Sexuality* volume 1, in which I have exchanged the word *sexuality* for *mortality* throughout:

> Mortality must not be described as a stubborn drive, by nature alien and of necessity disobedient to a power which exhausts itself trying to subdue it and often fails to control it entirely. It appears rather as an especially dense transfer point for relations of power: between men and women, young people and old people, parents and offspring, teachers and students, priests and laity, an administration and a population. Mortality is not the most intractable element in power relations, but rather one of those endowed with the greatest instrumentality: useful for the greatest number of maneuvers and capable of serving as a point of support, as a linchpin, for the most varied strategies.[117]

This changed wording is cogent and seems as if it were embedded in the original because mortality, like sexuality, is both biologically essential and politically negotiated, intimate and public, sacrosanct and instrumental. Power relations are configured differently around death than sex, but surely with no less intensity. The ironic capacities of this mode of power that both individualizes and totalizes biological life also involve the dead, the unhappy remainder of biopower, in its deployment. (In Chapter Three, following Barnes's *Nightwood*, I interpret this irony as a kind of social and ethical queerness.) Foucault himself, ambivalent about his own description of death, suggests this role of the body's mortality in its biopolitical administration. Modern war, he writes, is "no longer waged in the name of a sovereign who must be defended" but "waged on behalf of the existence of everyone"; paradoxically and inexorably, "it is as managers of life and survival, of bodies and the race, that so many regimes have been able to wage so many wars, causing so many men to be killed" in the twentieth century.[118] Foucault's theory of the politicization of living bodies has embedded within it thought about the politicization of dead bodies, which have a unique synecdochic capacity to link the individual and the population under the flag of the nation. We will see below what this looks like.

Others have further documented and theorized this strange combination of mass death and the cultivation of life in the context of the Great War.[119] J. M. Winter demonstrates through statistical analyses of the era's demographics that

> one of the central paradoxes of the war is that in the case of Britain, a conflict of unprecedented carnage created conditions—both political and economic—which accounted for a surprising and unplanned improvement in life expectancy among the civilian population. In France, some groups registered improvements; others did not. But on balance life expectancy among French civilians was about the same as it would have been had no war occurred.... Indeed, the success of the war effort in Britain and France to defend public health by defending living standards was, we shall argue, one of the prerequisites of military victory.[120]

For those fortunate enough to stay out of the trenches, "the surprising finding [is] that in 1916 and 1917, at ages above which men were likely to see active military service, that is, after ages 40–5, war-related mortality in Britain was either negligible or *negative*. In other words, the survival chances of older men in wartime Britain were actually greater than they would have been had the war never occurred."[121] The carnage in the trenches was accompanied in England, France, and Germany by robust pronatalism programs. The British Parliament passed the Notification of Births (Extension) Act in 1915 and the Maternal and Child Welfare Act in 1918, and established the Ministry of Health in 1919, which advocates had proposed as early as 1915 as a war measure.[122] Ironically, biopolitics expressed itself through death and the dead. The war's corpses were at the center of this unlikely expression of state power over life. In this sense, the political liabilities of life and death turned full circle, from the classical sovereign's power to "*take* life or *let* live," to a modern politicization of life—focused on sex—that reached impasse at death, and finally to the recuperation of death itself as a site for managing life as it is both individually embodied and as a population.[123] In a powerful investigation into Foucault's concept of biopolitics, Giorgio Agamben theorizes this full circle as the development of the modern state's thanatopolitics. He approaches the biopolitical significance of death as a function of the state's capacity to create political exceptions from legal rights protecting citizens. He argues throughout *Homo Sacer: Sovereign Power and Bare Life* that the aporia of such exceptions—the legally codified power to make exceptions from the law—is at the heart of the modern state, and that it leads to the negation of life in ever more subtle and ambiguous domains:

Along with the emergence of biopolitics, we can observe a displacement and gradual expansion beyond the limits of the decisions on bare life, in the state of exception, in which sovereignty consisted. If there is a line in every modern state marking the point at which the decision on life becomes a decision on death, and biopolitics can turn into thanatopolitics, this line no longer appears today as a stable border dividing two clearly distinct zones. This line is now in motion and gradually moving into areas other than that of political life, areas in which the sovereign is entering into an ever more intimate symbiosis with not only the jurist but also with the doctor, the scientist, the expert, and the priest.[124]

If the line between biopolitics and thanatopolitics collapsed, according to Agamben, in the concentration camps of the Second World War, we can perceive an earlier ambiguity in this line in the new governmental corpse-management programs of the First. Foucault's description of sex as the political linkage between the individuation of subjects and the administration of populations illuminates a similar linkage made possible for the state through dying and relations to the dead.

There was one corpse in particular during the era that had the capacity to be both one and many for the state, and in fact brought the national poetics of synecdoche to its apotheosis, although no one knew whose corpse it was. It became everyone's and everyone, in a grammar of possession that applied to both the living, as objective genitive, and the dead, as subjective. On Armistice Day, November 20, 1920, two years after the war's end, large crowds gathered in London and Paris to watch ceremonies that had never been performed before. In both cities, at the same time, the unidentifiable remains of soldiers that had been disinterred from French battlefields were carried for reburial to Westminster Abbey and the Arc de Triomphe.[125] The British soldier, transported in a coffin made with an oak from Hampton Court Palace, was welcomed by a symbolically significant group: "a thousand bereaved widows and mothers; a hundred nurses wounded or blinded in the war, a guard of honour made up of a hundred men who had won the Victoria Cross, fifty on each side of the nave. The highest-ranking commanders from the war were among the pallbearers: Haig, French and Trenchard. The king scattered earth from the soil of France on to the coffin."[126] The reburial, a dense articulation of nationalist meaning, involved "a riot of symbolism, for all the symbols present in the design of military cemeteries, and in the mythology which surrounded the fallen, were compressed into one ceremony."[127] While the device of the cenotaph, or empty tomb, had been used since antiquity to commemorate the lost dead, this was the first time that a random and anonymous body was asked, in its fragile materiality, to abstract itself into the nation's entire dead. On the day of the ceremony, a line of people a mile long and four deep waited outside Westminster Abbey, continued filing past the tomb at a rate of about seventy per minute until almost midnight, and came back in similar numbers for the rest of the week before the grave was sealed, for an estimated total of 1,250,000 people.[128] These visitors left tens of thousands of wreaths (although these were mostly left at the Cenotaph, down the street).[129] Almost two million copies of a special edition of the *Daily Mirror*, with photographic coverage of the Tomb, were sold the next day (a record); creative essays imagining the life of the unknown man appeared in *The Times*; and government officials admitted they had not expected such success for their public memorial.[130] Adrian Gregory comments that the *Daily Herald*, which had originally been hostile to the memorial, "was forced to take note of the genius of the symbolic power of the Tomb of the Unknown Warrior and the strength of popular reaction to it. 'As we stood there in silence while the muffled drums began to whisper, as it were a million miles away and grew and grew into the sound of a rushing wind, the stone atrocities faded, the vulgarity and bad taste were forgotten, the pomp and circumstance forgiven.' "[131]

Far more than the authorities had anticipated, the Tomb fulfilled the capacity of the British public to relate, as a mass, to their individual and specific losses: "The dead man who had set out without a name, a voice, or a face only a few hours before was being invested with a hundred thousand likenesses, and for those who could not resist a temptation to strip the symbol there was a possibility that one of the likenesses fitted."[132] An editorial in *The Times* described the simultaneously individualizing and collective nature of the ceremonies as "impersonal, or, more truly, they are personal to us all," while Masterman described the burial as simultaneously for "every boy's father, every woman's lover, every mother's son."[133] This was an embodiment of Foucault's "omnes et singulatim," each and all, in the heart of Westminster Abbey, what Thomas Laqueur calls in his description of the memorial "the corporeal 'distibutive singular term.' "[134] In a suggestive evocation of the rhetoric of paradox in "Burnt Norton," Sarah Cole writes that "the image of the unknown seemed to create a sense of balance, a point of contact between individuality and the enormity of the war ('the still point of the turning world,' as Eliot might have it), and this intersection of the deeply personal with the infinitely extended seemed to touch a real chord in post-war culture."[135] Like Eliot's paradoxes throughout *Four Quartets*, the Unknown Warrior was a productive paradox because it gathered the minute and immense into one figure able to reorient the postwar cultural landscape. Katherine Verdery, in her study of repatriation and reburial in a later era, writes that "reordering worlds of meaning" is "what is at stake in reburying the dead"; such civic and psychological reordering was precisely the project for the British public at this moment.[136] And not just for the British. Within a decade, the monument had been copied in almost every nation, victorious or defeated, that had fought in the war.[137] In fact, it became a diplomatic requirement for visiting dignitaries to honor Unknowns with wreaths and even medals; Charles Lindbergh followed this pattern by making his first acts after flying across the Atlantic in 1927 to put flowers at Unknowns' tombs in London, Paris, and Brussels.[138]

The reburied British soldier—unlike in other countries, he was officially called "Warrior" in deference to Britain's historically revered navy—was both one and many, the precisely appointed dead for each of a multitude of mourners. The accomplishment of this capacious meaning demonstrates Verdery's claim that "among the most important properties of bodies, especially dead ones, is their ambiguity, multivocality, or polysemy. Remains are concrete, yet protean; they do not have a single meaning but are open to many different readings"; in fact, it "is precisely its ambiguity, its capacity to evolve a variety of understandings" that "gives a dead body its symbolic effectiveness in politics."[139] In this case, the state discovered synecdoche, the one for all or for many, as the principle of its extraordinary monument. This structure of meaning reinforced the biopolitical imperative to both individualize and totalize its subjects, to govern through the body both discrete lives and a population. It seems impossible to find a more vivid example than this of the modern state's alchemical embodiment of the universal in the particular, of its formation of individual subjectivities across a population—in this case, through the private crucible of their public mourning. The Tomb of the Unknown Warrior, in other words, is more than a site for Benedict Anderson's nationalist imaginings, but the symbol of new relations among the claimed corpse, unclaimed corpses, those in mourning, and the state.[140] The tomb is a revelation of the political stakes of the modern subject's ancient ethical intuitions toward the dead—a revelation, in other words, of the utility of the corpse for the state's formation of subjects through the passions and energies of their mourning. In between the subject and the population lies, in this instance, the state's corpse, a presence that catalyzes the identities of all and each because it is itself without identity.

Owen's war poetry reveals the tropological structure of this binding facilitated by the tomb. Dyer notes "the mutual support of these two ostensibly opposed coordinates: the Unknown Soldier and the poet everyone knows."[141] In her brief discussion of Owen in "On Not Knowing Greek," Woolf acknowledges the difficulty of finding a poetic form to fit the times: "In the vast catastrophe of the European war our emotions had to be broken up for us, and put at an angle from us, before we could allow ourselves to feel them in poetry or fiction. The only poets who spoke to the purpose spoke in the sidelong, satiric manner of Wilfred Owen and Siegfried Sassoon. It was not possible for them to be direct without being clumsy; or to speak simply of emotion without being sentimental."[142] But it was the rhetorical complexity behind Owen's sidelong, satiric tone that captured the irony of the relation between the state's biopolitical project, linking each with all, and its mass of corpses, embodied in an anonymous one. Woolf, of course, even more radically refracts and estranges feelings for the dead, including the war dead, in her abrupt, bracketed death announcements in *To the Lighthouse*. In that novel's same chapter, "Time Passes," she associates this refraction with modern verse: "[Mr. Carmichael brought out a volume of poems that spring, which had an unexpected success. The war, people said, had revived their interest in poetry]."[143] Woolf's relation to this dyad, the dead soldier poet everyone knows and the unknown soldier everyone buried, is complex: in her postwar writing, she combines the dead body and anonymity in new ways to change the politics of mourning and death obligations.[144] In an important analysis, Bette London examines how Woolf restructures the postwar political imaginary by turning feelings from the Unknown Warrior toward the unknown (woman) poet, "Judith Shakespeare" of *A Room of One's Own*, an identity lost to literary history. "Woolf's spectacular fiction of this unknown poet's life might be heard to echo—indeed, to answer and improve—'the fanciful essays in which the life of the Unknown Warrior was re-created' in the newspapers of the time of the 1920 Armistice Day rites." London argues that "when Woolf enjoins her audience to 'let flowers fall upon the tomb of Aphra Behn'—in Westminster Abbey, no less—and dedicate themselves to bringing Shakespeare's sister (back) to life, she is evoking...the well-established rituals of collective mourning which she then displaces with her own idiosyncratic rites." [145] Woolf's writing, like Owen's, re-fashions nationalist structures of feeling about the dead. As I argue below, Woolf's crucial exploration of public anonymity begins with *Jacob's Room*, published in 1922. The point of the Unknown Warrior, of course, is that he must never be known. So with the remarkable narrator that Woolf invented for this novel, a voice for each and all, conscious everywhere but not located as a subject anywhere in particular.

Woolf and the Voice of the Unknown Narrator

Jacob's Room, Woolf's third novel, was her first recognizably experimental one. It is an anti-*Bildungsroman* about Jacob Flanders's passage into adulthood and death in the war told in disjointed, often lyrical or meditative fragments. His inner life remains more opaque, blocked to focalization, than most of the 160 or so other characters that intersect with him; he is known almost entirely from the outside, from the shreds of others' impressions and desires. We see him in spots of time: as a young child, son of a widowed mother, on the beach and collecting insects in the forest; taking the train to begin his studies at Cambridge; walking back to his undergraduate rooms in the echoing night; earnestly debating philosophy and literature with friends; and so on, through his post-college employment and romances in London and travels in Greece, until he disappears in the war, leaving the rest of us behind. Jacob's life does not accumulate so much as evoke an absent form and a desire for missing psychological presence. His interiority is continually under erasure, an inner life that is always already sacrificed to the war, a life we know as one that, in Geoff Dyer's phrase about the verb tense of photographs of departing soldiers and of soldiers in Owen's poetry (such as "The Send-Off"), is "*going to have died.*"[146]

The stylistic innovation of this rich and strange novel lies in its representation of the contingency lurking in ordered time and emptiness unfolding within structured space, or, as we might say, in the fragmentation of the subject's sequential logic and nodes of inhabitation or enclosure. There is little plot in *Jacob's Room*—in the sense of events unfolding into motivated lines of development and resolution—besides the plot of subjectivization itself, the drama of language entering into and falling out of particular subject positions. Following where the voice falls, into which suddenly available spheres of consciousness, is the novel's high drama. In narratological terms, it is the drama of shifting character focalization, the technique we have known since Austen and Flaubert of free indirect discourse across a cast of characters, but Woolf ungrounds it from the idea of "omniscience" in heterodiegetic and anonymous narration. The narrator of *Jacob's Room* who so promiscuously provides us with indirect access to so many character interiorities is a new creature in literary tradition, not a transcendental or omniscient presence from an absolute future but a narrative voice at the strange pitch of an illegible personhood, one scattered across different moments and in the interstices of realized people, diffused among them as something less than a self-objectifying subject. It, or she, speaks as a kind-of-person, flirting with the first-person perspective enough to suggest its everyday spatio-temporal logic, but withdrawing from it before it sediments; the voice takes the form of what Ronald Schleifer describes, in referring to a similar effect in *Mrs. Dalloway*, as "disembodiments…as vague as the subtle rhythms of experience, haunting not quite 'positively' the edges of things," and "whose anonymity…exists in the position of dispersal rather than a transcendental future."[147] In *Jacob's Room*, the narrator's authority is derived not from omniscience but from its agility with fragmentariness, contingency, and irony in the comings and goings of countless inner lives—aside from Jacob's.

This narrative voice is everyone's and everyone. Like the Unknown Warrior, it is without identity but a catalyst for every other identity, a mechanism for narrative individualization and totalization. This mechanism establishes a relation of sur-veillance in Woolf's thought, as in Foucault's. In chapter five, the narrating voice comes to a sudden, acute self-awareness while surveying an audience at the Royal Opera House. The music begins,

> then two thousand hearts in the semi-darkness remembered, anticipated, travelled dark labyrinths; and Clara Durrant said farewell to Jacob Flanders, and tasted the sweetness of death in effigy; and Mrs. Durrant, sitting behind her in the dark of the box, sighed her sharp sigh; and Mr. Wortley, shifting his position behind the Italian Ambassador's wife, thought that Brangäne was a trifle hoarse; and suspended in the gallery many feet above their heads, Edward Whittaker surreptitiously held a torch to his miniature score; and… and…
>
> In short, the observer is choked with observations. Only to prevent us from being submerged by chaos, nature and society between them have arranged a system of classification which is simplicity itself; stalls, boxes, amphitheatres, gallery. The moulds are filled nightly. There is no need to distinguish details. But the difficulty remains—one has to choose. For though I have no wish to be Queen of England—or only for a moment—I would willingly sit beside her; I would hear the Prime Minister's gossip; the countess whisper, and share her memories of halls and gardens; the massive fronts of the respectable conceal after all their secret code; or why so imper-meable? And then, doffing one's own headpiece, how strange to assume for a moment some one's—any one's—to be a man of valour who has ruled the Empire; to refer while Brangäne sings to the fragments of Sophocles, or see in a flash, as the shepherd pipes his tune, bridges and aqueducts. But no— we must choose. Never was there a harsher necessity! or one which entails greater pain, more certain disaster; for wherever I seat myself, I die in exile. Whittaker in his lodging-house; Lady Charles at the Manor. (*JR* 57)

Among these two thousand private, labyrinthine hearts, rationally ordered into a single public body, we hear a voice elegantly choking on interiority, inhabiting the linguistic subject position only to refute it and the social positions it constructs. This unpersoned or not-quite-personed speech hovers on the verge of each iden-tity but is bound to none. It overhears the interiorization of language but remains its exteriorized echo, refusing the exilic strangeness of a consciousness clinging to itself in the metaphysical and social apparatus of the first person. Yet this narrator, for the first time in the novel, suddenly speaks from the liminal areas around defined subjects with the "I," the ineradicable mark of subjectivity. Who speaks? What does this voice mean? What does it have to do, in Woolf's thought, with relations between each and all, the living and the dead?

As a loose analogue of the Unknown Warrior, the narrator's dispersed and fleeting survey of the social gallery of subjective life provides an instructive counterpoint to the Warrior's dense and stolid symbolism of the collective dead. This speaker remains nameless and liminal because it reaches the interior depths of each and all others, sounding the dimensions of life organized both as individual subjects and as a total population. We might imagine her as the Unknown Subject, an available and unmarked consciousness commemorating all those lost in the exile of their particular subjective enclosures. It is as if this were the voice of the dead mourning the isolate lives of the living. Two years after the state's use of its reclaimed corpse in Westminster Abbey to bind individual subjects, in their mourning, to the totality of the state, Woolf imagines an alternative subjectivity in the context of the dead. Reversing the silent embodiment of the soldier into her narrator's disembodied eloquence, Woolf imagines the use of the dead to unbind the subject from power, a contact with the dead that cuts against the state's logistical mediation and tropological distortion of them.

This unbinding of first-person consciousness from its subjectivizing authority occurs in the narrator's return, again and again, to images of graves and tombstones, from Christian churchyards to the old Roman burial ground above Jacob's childhood home to bones lying in the battlefield at Flanders. The novel's first few pages take us to the graveside of Jacob's father, where Jacob's mother focalizes:

> "Merchant of this city," the tombstone said; though why Betty Flanders had chosen so to call him when, as many still remembered, he had only sat behind an office window for three months, and before that had broken horses, ridden to hounds, farmed a few fields, and run a little wild—well, she had to call him something. An example for the boys.
>
> Had he, then, been nothing? An unanswerable question, since even if it weren't the habit of the undertaker to close the eyes, the light so soon goes out of them. At first, part of herself; now one of a company, he had merged in the grass, the sloping hillside, the thousand white stones, some slanting, others upright, the decayed wreaths, the crosses of green tin, the narrow

yellow paths, and the lilacs that drooped in April, with a scent like that of an invalid's bedroom, over the churchyard wall. Seabrook was now all that; and when, with her skirt hitched up, feeding the chickens, she heard the bell for service or funeral, that was Seabrook's voice—the voice of the dead. (*JR* 11)

Woolf quietly reverses the narrator's, and the war corpse's, synecdochic meaning; instead of encompassing many or all within itself, Seabrook's body dissolves into its surroundings. His disarticulation as a discrete figure and rearticulation as a spirit of the place—in other words, his function of making the place more rhetori-cally complex, instead of vice versa—is Woolf's image of a body, become mute, that seeks the symbolic locations where it can be voiced by some other expressive agent. Where do the modern dead, in their muteness, find their representative agents? And how did the war change this representation? This particular image of Seabrook's posthumous survival in the surrounding world, based on a met-onymic diffusion of a synecdochic capacity, anticipates Clarissa's philosophy in *Mrs. Dalloway*, her sense "that somehow in the streets of London, on the ebb and flow of things, here, there, she survived, Peter survived, lived in each other, she being part, she was positive, of the trees at home; of the house there, ugly, ram-bling all to bits and pieces as it was; part of people she had never met; being laid out like a mist, but it spread ever so far, her life, herself." It is her idea, as Peter Walsh remembers, of how "the unseen part of us, which spreads wide, the unseen part might survive, be recovered somehow attached to this person or that, or even haunting certain places after death...perhaps—perhaps."[148]

This metonymic dispersal, in both novels, of the posthumous self as a ghostly presence across a landscape, an obliquely signified remainder of a past conscious-ness, marks the beginning of an investigation. It is Woolf's investigation into the re-symbolization, or symbolic relocation, of the dead after so many failed to come home. It is the investigation into death's revised symbology that Owen begins in his startling figuration of mourning rites in "Anthem for Doomed Youth," which ends with a new set of signs for the dead.

> What candles may be held to speed them all?
>   Not in the hands of boys but in their eyes
> Shall shine the holy glimmers of goodbyes.
>   The pallor of girls' brows shall be their pall;
> Their flowers the tenderness of patient minds,
>   And each slow dusk a drawing-down of blinds. (*CPF* v. 1 99)

Like Woolf, Owen describes how the dead overdetermine the bodies and landscapes of the living. Although saturating, they are a fragile presence that demands new

tracking strategies. Owen's poem is about the absorption of collective mourning practices into the private body (like William Roberts's *Burying the Dead after a Battle*);
Jacob's Room is about cognitively remapping the war's corpses, and all corpses after
the war, at this new threshold of their modernization. In a striking passage from chapter nine, the dead pass through the British Museum, where Jacob has been reading:

> Stone lies solid over the British Museum, as bone lies cool over the visions
> and heat of the brain. Only here the brain is Plato's brain and Shakespeare's;
> the brain has made pots and statues, great bulls and little jewels, and crossed
> the river of death this way and that incessantly, seeking some new landing,
> now wrapping the body well for its long sleep; now laying a penny piece on
> the eyes; now turning the toes scrupulously to the East. Meanwhile, Plato
> continues his dialogue; in spite of the rain; in spite of cab whistles; in spite
> of the woman in the mews behind Great Ormond Street who has come
> home drunk and cries all night long, "Let me in!, Let me in!" (*JR* 94)

On the face of it, Woolf's poetic invocation of Shakespeare, myth, and antiquity
suggests that literature itself tends to the dead, or that it is to literature we return
when we want to remember how to tend the dead. It is an appealing thought
(which comes close to the premise of my entire study), but this passage does
more complex and ambivalent work in its description of an abstract, sovereign
force arranging and bearing London's dead bodies. It mirrors, in an aesthetic
of cognitive mapping, the sense of modern corpse disposal as the domain of a
large, impersonal agency, a mystified and abstract process that involved hired
strangers, esoteric technical expertise, complex financial transactions and insurance mechanisms, and an opaque bureaucratic machinery. If the unburied
war dead serve as landmarks for soldiers in No Man's Land, the dead at the
homefront are in search of familiar landmarks. Woolf develops images that, in
Jameson's description of cognitive mapping, bridge "a gap between phenomenological perception and a reality that transcends all individual thinking or experience."[149] If Jameson has described the aesthetic of cognitive mapping as a tactic
for politically empowering subjects of an incomprehensibly large and complex
global economic system, we can also describe it here as a tactic for asserting
one's ethical relevance to the dead in their increasing abstraction and distance,
an aesthetic recuperation of attenuated mortal obligations.[150] This mapping of
modern deathways and the routes of the dead continues a few pages later, now
in the daily traffic over Waterloo Bridge:

> Sometimes in the midst of carts and omnibuses a lorry will appear with
> great forest trees chained to it. Then, perhaps, a mason's van with newly

lettered tombstones recording how some one loved some one who is buried at Putney. Then the motor-car jerks forward, and the tombstones pass too quick for you to read more. All the time the stream of people never ceases passing from the Surrey side to the Strand; from the Strand to the Surrey side. (*JR* 97)

Jacob's Room's narrative cubism cuts and splices the elements of death across its pages both to foreclose the sacrificial, synecdochic meaning of the war dead that dominated the era and to engage the reader in the project of their remapping, as preface to obligation.[151]

The narrator's absorption of the corpse's synecdochic function within herself—her position as the Unknown that creates meaning for each and all—has as its correlate a second uncanny analogy. If the narrator fulfills the rhetorical function of the Unknown Warrior, Jacob, in his opacity and final absence, fulfills the function of the Cenotaph, the empty tomb for the war dead at the other end of Whitehall. Their nationalist symmetry—"the bodiless tomb out in Whitehall, the nameless body inside the Abbey"—also structures the two charged poles of Woolf's novel, Jacob and the narrator.[152] Karen Smythe first observed this quality in Jacob: "At the centre of the narrative frames of *Jacob's Room* is the absent addressee, Jacob himself.... If *Jacob's Room* is a fiction-elegy for Jacob (as well as 'an elegy for past youth and past summers'), the novel functions not as a consoling resurrection of the character's personality... but as a verbal cenotaph, or rather, ceno*graph*: it is an empty marker or tomb, since the body (the subject) lies elsewhere."[153] The novel ends with this architectural image of cenotaph-absence, a precise enclosure of nothing where Jacob used to live, a room now gone strange: "Listless is the air in an empty room, just swelling the curtain; the flowers in the jar shift. One fibre in the wicker arm-chair creaks, though no one sits there" (*JR* 155). His room, the "artifactual registration of his absence," "operates imagistically as an empty coffin."[154] Woolf inscribes the memorialization of the war dead occupying the heart of London into the structure of her novel, in both the precisely anonymous origin and receding primary object of its narrative discourse.[155]

Woolf begins imagining in *Jacob's Room* a condition of mind, some model or quality of self, that is not bound to its dead through the state. This is a voice that circulates without having been interpellated, and that stirs a desire for the dead to also circulate more freely, beyond processes of interpellation. This voice embodies a freedom in the experience of consciousness that no proper subject can know, a voice that is off-key at just the right tone to sound others' subjectivities, from the inside, as if sounding a suite of strange rooms. If, in Agamben's characterization, Foucault describes the processes that "bring the individual to objectify his own self, constituting himself as a subject and, at the same time, binding himself to a power of external control," Woolf imagines a condition of life other than those created by these processes, and suggests that this condition involves the uninterpellated dead.[156] This alternative condition is not necessarily an appealing possibility. In fact, it is this refusal to interpellate, to bring decisively into its narrative apparatus, the bracketed deaths of *To the Lighthouse* that makes them so distant and frustrating, so that we suffer the same disorientation as Lily: "Mrs. Ramsay dead; Andrew killed; Prue dead too—repeat it as she might, it roused no feeling in her."[157] But this disorientation, and the risk it carries for the subject's autonomy, can provoke the work of mortal obligation. This is the work that unites the symbolic and material dimensions of the dead, that materializes the corpse's symbolic value in forms that can be touched and put in rooms where people gather to help accomplish the death of the one before them. After the mass death of the war, the aesthetics of this obligation were painfully ambiguous, unfixed; it required immense imaginative work to recreate a sense of relevance and proximity to these corpses.[158] In a sailboat off the Scilly Isles, Jacob and his friend Timmy Durrant find themselves before an expressive horizon, as if it had been infused with the chaotic feelings of this cultural work:

> Imperceptibly the cottage smoke droops, has the look of a mourning emblem, a flag floating its caress over a grave. The gulls, making their broad flight and then riding at peace, seem to mark the grave.
>
> No doubt if this were Italy, Greece, or even the shores of Spain, sadness would be routed by strangeness and excitement and the nudge of a classical education. But the Cornish hills have stark chimneys standing on them; and, somehow or other, loveliness is infernally sad. Yes, the chimneys and the coast-guard stations and the little bays with the waves breaking unseen by any one make one remember the overpowering sorrow. And what can this sorrow be?
>
> It is brewed by the earth itself. It comes from the houses on the coast. We start transparent, and then the cloud thickens. All history backs our pane of glass. To escape is vain. (*JR* 39–40)

The native ground laments the bodies it does not hold. History, in the narrator's reverie, is the accumulation of these laments, a thickening and heaviness in the air, an ongoing and collective ethical frustration. The tropes that are discovered for articulating this frustrated desire for the missing dead, and that can also realize the dead in new forms, are the lifeblood of the state; re-troped they are its refutation.

Woolf briefly returns to the Cenotaph's enclosed absence in *Mrs. Dalloway*, her next novel. After his visit to Clarissa, Peter Walsh is passed on the street by a group of young uniformed men delivering a commemorative wreath to the memorial. The members of this procession "wore on them unmixed with sensual pleasure or daily preoccupations the solemnity of the wreath which they had fetched from Finsbury Pavement to the empty tomb. They had taken their vow. The traffic respected it; vans were stopped."[159] Woolf imagines the oblique, displaced presence of the Cenotaph's absent corpse in the mechanical impersonality of their procession:

> I can't keep up with them, Peter Walsh thought, as they marched up Whitehall, and sure enough, on they marched, past him, past every one, in their steady way, as if one will worked legs and arms uniformly, and life, with its varieties, its irreticences, had been laid under a pavement of monuments and wreaths and drugged into a stiff yet staring corpse by discipline. One had to respect it; one might laugh; but one had to respect it, he thought. (51)

If we do laugh at this scene, it is at the incommensurability between the nationalist assurance of this commemorative act and the void at the center of the Cenotaph. This incommensurability repeats the psychic fracture of the war's collective trauma and its legacy of an irresolvable desire for the absent dead. Or, if we do laugh, it may be at something else: at the possibility that these soldiers are bearing a wreath, in an intertextual gesture, for Jacob, the Cenotaph-character in Woolf's earlier novel. We might laugh at Woolf's subtle tribute to the absent corpse of her own earlier character because of the way she directs the irony of this commemorative desire at herself, at the impossible ambition of her own literary practice. Jacob's corpse can be rewritten, but not repatriated, even if Woolf wants us to take pleasure in the ambiguity of where the line between these two acts lies.

Woolf inaugurates the modernist possibilities of her fiction partly as an ethical response to the new politics of the era's corpses. She makes modernism work as a symbolic death practice in the way it reimagines the pervasive tropological relations among the dead in their different degrees of presence and absence in space. And, like Owen, she denaturalizes the synecdochic power of corpses in the rhetorical machinery of the state. But, unlike Owen's poetry, *Jacob's Room* begins a further inquiry, one that extends into the more general cultural effects of death's modernization: her writing begins to map the ways that dying and dead bodies at the homefront had become strange too. In the following chapter,

I further examine the role of this strangeness in modernist narrative innova-tions, in the way attention to corpses changed the temporal organization of modernist stories. Just as the places and spaces allocated to the dead were being contested in wartime burial and memorialization practices, so were their allo-cations in time.

2. Joyce, Faulkner, and the Modernist Burial Plot

...for I know that after you leave this place and the house of Hades

you will put back with your well-made ship to the island, Aiaia;

there at that time, my lord, I ask that you remember me,

and do not go and leave me behind, unwept, unburied,

when you leave, for fear I may become the gods' curse upon you;

but burn me there with all my armor that belongs to me,

and heap up a grave mound beside the beach of the gray sea,

for an unhappy man, so that those to come will know of me.

Do this for me, and on top of the grave mound plant the oar

with which I rowed when I was alive and among my companions.

— Homer, *The Odyssey*

Burial Plots

A burial plot is not simply a corpse's resting ground, but also its story, the arc of time between its perishing and final disposal.[1] Corpses, the ambiguous protagonists of these interstitial stories, organize plots which begin with a biological perishing and involve a search for ritual and hygienic care, marks of identification, and a secure state of rest that accomplish its death as a culturally intelligible event (although contemporary twists to this plot often involve autopsy, organ donation, medical training, and an alarming range of scientific experiments). "Human dying does *not* coincide with perishing," Robert Harrison argues against Heidegger: "To put it propositionally: *Dasein does not die until its remains are disposed of.*"[2] It is the lag of this crucial "until," this surprising hiatus or delay after a body stops living, this odd temporalization of the corpse's inanimate yet expectant presence, that is the ground for burial plots.[3] This period of unfolding cannot be collapsed or effaced as an undifferentiated block; we are not structuralists among the unburied dead. From an anthropological perspective, S. C. Humphreys argues that the social process of dying consists of a complex movement through time (although she does not consider this in terms of narrative or story form): "The process of dying, in its widest sense, stretches from the decision that a person is 'dying' . . . to the complete cessation of all social actions directed towards their remains, tomb, monument or other relics representing them." Along the way, the process includes "the transition from dying to being dead, the rituals surrounding removal of the corpse from the immediate proximity of the living (burial or other forms of disposal), and the transformation of the decaying cadaver into a stable material representation of the dead (mummy, skeleton, ashes, tomb, monument, ancestral tablet, etc.)"[4] Just as corpses alter the quality of space they inhabit, so do they reorganize time into a sequence of distinctive tasks and obligations. In this chapter, I am interested in how this sequence takes complex narrative forms as it accrues meaning and force. Although the corpse marks the end of the meaningful existential time that gives us the stories of the living, it nevertheless must pass through time of another order, must become a site of another narrativity that volatizes dead time into life. If, as Frank Kermode writes, we think of the "clock's tick-tock as a model of what we call plot, an organization that humanizes time by giving it form; and the interval between tock and tick [as] purely successive, disorganized time of the sort we need not humanize," then the burial plot emerges in the unmeaning blank time after our culturally dominant stories end, in the negative time of tock-tick when forms of life give way to a corpse-form.[5] Burial plots narrativize this interlude between a person's biological extinction and burial (or other form of disposal), an interlude that we can compare to other short microplots during which a community suspends its usual rules and behaviors: carnival, for instance, with its excesses and reversals; or the Jewish days of awe, between Rosh Hashanah and Yom Kippur, with their call to repent and ask forgiveness from those one has wronged. The hours or days that a corpse remains untended are, as Elpenor's spirit in Hades suggests in this chapter's epigraph, jagged, strained: the corpses waiting in our midst interrupt our principal plots about getting through life with their own about accomplishing their deaths.

Odysseus has no choice but to interrupt his journey home to complete Elpenor's corpse-story. Corpses have this power of narrative interruption and supplanting in the first place because their presence is a potent ethical demand, and in the second because those that have not been embalmed or frozen may be pungently rotting.[6] Corpse ethics, never far from hygiene, unfolds as narrative.

Corpses inhabit a complex, narratable temporality implicitly structured as demand because they are not inert objects in an unremarkable perduring, but only ambivalently objectifiable, both objects and subjects. They both are and are not the people we know, or knew; in the midst of their ritual and disposal processes, they are the quintessential liminal thing, and were at the heart of the anthropological conceptualization of liminality.[7] Heidegger calls the corpse not lifeless but "*unliving*," to mark a distinct category of the having-lived, because there is " 'still more' in his kind of being" than in something inanimately at hand for our use.[8] The ontological excess of this "still more," what Harrison calls the "charisma" of the corpse, derives from the aura of unfinished expectation that gives it a strange temporal traction, which is affecting in part for the way it is not entirely hospitable to the living.[9] "What 'object' is more other, more *unheimlich*, more charged in its obtrusive but fleeting presence, and what leaves a more indelible image when we chance upon it," Christopher Fynsk asks, evoking the corpse's unstable combination of the static and passing. The corpse, he writes, is a "material (non-) presence that is not quite of nature, no longer of the world and given in the absence of life," and so a thing that "presents the inassimilable other of spirit and meaning that has in fact always been there."[10] Fynsk is right—the corpse carries a potent otherness, felt as a rift in both nature and culture—but a burial plot is precisely the narrative response to this quality that seeks the corpse's psychological and social assimilation to the life-world it disrupts. A burial plot attempts to gather the temporal instability of the corpse into a coherent, transmissible form, to usher the corpse into its death: "A ritualised 'translation' of the dead into ancestors involves processes common to all ritual."[11] "A living person is, obviously, a member of a social group. So is a dead ancestor, since the dead provide the connection between various living people, as well as authority ('We must behave the way the ancestors wanted') and power (misfortune is often a result of offending the ancestors). Now the *passage* between these two stages is what the rituals emphasize and organize."[12] Narrative is among the most crucial of practices for bearing the dead to their postmortem social positions. Mere corpses become ancestors, the established dead, through ritualized disposal, and stories about corpse disposal are linguistic performances of this cultural process, allegories for the conversion of nature into culture. As it moves through narrative, just as it moves through its preparation for disposal, the uncanny or abject thingliness of the unburied corpse is converted into meanings we use to organize our social worlds; its awkward liminality is restructured as a story, the plot of which is our adequate perception of and response to its ethical demand for care.

Joyce, in *Ulysses*, and Faulkner, in *As I Lay Dying*, refashion this plot in response to the modernization of deathways in their midst. It is during these changes in deathways, as the charisma of the corpse is occluded, that what constitutes our "adequate" response to dying and dead bodies becomes ambiguous. The "Hades" chapter of *Ulysses*, along with its effects and correspondences elsewhere in the novel, and *As I Lay Dying* are modernist rewritings of traditional burial plots that explore the effects of this ambiguity, the fragility of the meaning of modern death practices. Both are fundamentally successful, or felicitous, burial plots that accomplish the task at hand, and in this sense differ from, say, Flannery O'Connor's story "You Can't Be Any Poorer than Dead" and Kafka's "The Hunter Gracchus," both of which are about failures to get bodies into the ground. Joyce and Faulkner, for all their stylistic differences, were similarly compelled by an ancient tradition of burial plots involving the scandal of an unburied corpse. Joyce's debt to antiquity is explicit, and Faulkner often explained his title as a translation of a line from *The Odyssey*, when the dead Agamemnon complains to Odysseus, in the same episode in Book XI in which he hears Elpenor's demand, that "As I lay dying, the woman with the dogs eyes would not close my eyes for me as I descended into Hades."[13] Beyond this episode in *The Odyssey*, the scandal of an unburied corpse motivates several ancient texts: the unburied stillbirths in the cursed Thebes of *Oedipus*, Polyneices's corpse in *Antigone*, the corpses of Hecuba's children in Euripedes's *Hecuba*, the bodies left for "delicate feasting / of dogs, of all birds" at the beginning of *The Iliad*, and the painful struggles over Patroclus's and Hektor's corpses in later chapters.[14] Joyce and Faulkner subject this tradition to audacious formal experiments able to render the ethical complexity of modern death.[15] Each makes the modernization of dying and corpse disposal an issue of temporality: our way of being in time, for both writers, organizes our relations to the dead.

Joyce and Two Versions of Delay

Few Joyce scholars pay sustained attention to "Hades," the sixth chapter of *Ulysses*, in which Bloom and others accompany the corpse of their friend Paddy Dignam through Dublin to Glasnevin Cemetery to hold his funeral service, yet this episode merits attention for the way it continues encounters with the dead from Joyce's early writing—in "The Sisters" and "The Dead," the first and last stories of *Dubliners*—through *Finnegans Wake*, and for the unique questions this chapter raises about narrating death obligations.[16] "Hades" is at the center of Joyce's long exploration of death practices and, as Pericles Lewis shows, evokes an extensive cultural history of these practices: "Bloom's trip to the underworld is just another weekday funeral, but at the same time it is Odysseus's encounter with the shades, Aeneas's confrontation with Cerebus, Dante's spiritual journey, and even the gravedigger scene in Hamlet."[17] The chapter begins at Dignam's house three days after his death as the carriages of the funeral party are about to leave, and ends with the dispersal of the funeral party along various cemetery paths after the burial. Dignam is, among other things, Joyce's figure for Elpenor, a pressing piece of unfinished narrative business that needs attention before the day's epic can continue. We never know him alive, although he appears in a satirical séance in "Cyclops" and phantasmagoric reanimation in "Circe," but we know he died unexpectedly of heart failure, leaving a wife and five young children. If the meaning of poor Dignam's life is not at issue—"Paddy Dignam...operates in the novel by his very anonymity and frailty; the only thing people remember about him is his drinking and a job he once had"—the ritualized response to his death is.[18]

There is little doubt, from the outset, that he will be competently buried. Yet "it is difficult in most cultures to locate the dead unambiguously in one place," Humphreys notices, and it is with this wariness that Ellman reminds us, "That the dead do not stay buried is, in fact, a theme of Joyce from the beginning to the end of his work; Finnegan is not the only corpse to be resurrected."[19] Talking with friends in the National Library, Stephen alludes to the words on Shakespeare's tombstone, which threaten "curst be he yt moves my bones" (*U* 9.1010).[20] Getting buried and staying buried are two different things, of course, but the latter relies on the efficacy of the former, and this efficacy relies on an intricate—or at least awkward—system of labor credit, since the dead can neither bury themselves nor bury their buriers. This is one social debt that is necessarily paid forward, with implications for narrative structure: no matter how many burials they include, burial plots cannot reach the end of their ethical accounting. There will always be some debit or credit remaining. At the cemetery, Bloom reflects on the way that burial acts are in a slippage of obligation through generations, begging repetition, with a value that unfurls in and as temporal sequence: "A fellow could live on his lonesome all his life. Yes he could. Still he'd have to get someone to sod him after he died though he could dig his own grave. We all do. Only man buries. No, ants too. First thing strikes anybody. Bury the dead. Say Robinson Crusoe was true to life. Well then Friday buried him. Every Friday buries a Thursday if you come to look at it" (*U*

6.807–6.812). This is a kind of minimal social contract against our isolation—bury another, get buried in turn[21]—leveraged on a labor to come, and as an accumulation of a burial credit it is a counter-thought to modernist obsessions with belatedness, as constitutive debt. (Joyce begins to develop this imagery with Stephen's theological panic in chapter three of *A Portrait of the Artist as a Young Man*: "At last he had understood: and human life lay around him, a plain of peace whereon antlike men laboured in brotherhood, their dead sleeping under quiet mounds.")[22] We bury others—and Dignam is in fact buried on a Thursday—because someone will do it for us, and this labor credit structures a meaning between generations in tension with anxieties of derivation. Joyce's burial plot will test the possibility of an ethical accrediting and creditorship as equally constitutive of the economics of modern identity as the debts of belatedness; burial, as an element of the social contract across generations as well as within them, longitudinally as well as latitudinally, gives the present a claim on the future by paying back the past's similar claim. And so Bloom's thought is a complex temporal defense against Molly's later derision of the funeral: "And they call that friendship killing and then burying one another" (*U* 18.1270–18.1271). If, as Ellman writes, Joyce's dead do not stay buried (in "Cyclops," Alf Bergan insists he has just seen Dignam talking with a friend on the street), at stake is the diachronic integrity of the social and its ongoing credit-economy of obligation (*U* 12.314). A world that cannot keep its corpses where it puts them cannot reproduce itself.[23]

The constitutive diachrony of this burial transaction across generations provides the macrostructure of the microplot of a corpse awaiting its burial. Any particular burial is an event in both latitudinal and longitudinal schemes, marking both the accomplishment of an individual death by its contemporaries and a link in a lineage of accomplished deaths, a line of acts that removes the human from natural processes for its place in cultural history. Each phenomenon, burial plotting and burial crediting, is realized in the play of time, through a constitutive delay that gives it meaning and force. There is something about this lag that produces both the corpse's ethical stakes, as its social weight and metaphysical truth, and the power of burial acts to bind generations in networks of historical endurance. In narratives, Barthes writes,

> expectation... becomes the basic condition for truth: truth, these narratives tell us, is what is *at the end* of expectation. This design brings narrative very close to the rite of initiation (a long path marked with pitfalls, obscurities, stops, suddenly comes out into the light); it implies a return to order, for expectation is a disorder: disorder is supplementary, it is what is forever

added on without solving anything, without finishing anything; order is complementary, it completes, fills up, saturates, and dismisses everything that risks adding on: truth is what completes, what closes.[24]

"Truth," here, is the work of time, and applied to our corpses it is the prolongation of their care before disposal. As Barthes suggests, this is the social time of ritual and initiation, time in which a member of a group passes liminally from one stage to another, thus the temporary disarticulation of social roles and affiliations. Bourdieu describes it as "quite the opposite of the inert gap of time, the time-lag, which the objectivist model makes of it....The temporal structure of practice functions here as a screen preventing totalization."[25] The delay before burial, affectively and symbolically charged, carries the existential uncertainty and social risk of all nontotalized initiatory processes, and the corpse that produces this temporal opening within a social structure is also asked to reproduce its closure.

I insist on the quality of social risk or rift in the unburied corpse as a function of its volatile temporality, its inhabitation of irreducible delay, because reading for time is so difficult in *Ulysses*. The novel notoriously collapses time in its dense system of simultaneous and interlocking parts, what Hugh Kenner calls the "hundreds of interpenetrating arches in this cathedral of metaphor."[26] It is a structuralist's nearly ideal novel, arguably an aesthetic inauguration of what later came to be known as structuralist thought. This sense of the novel's stance against time has a long critical history. Early on, in *Axel's Castle* (1931), Edmund Wilson writes that *Ulysses* is akin to "a set of Symbolistic poems," that "there is tremendous vitality in Joyce, but very little movement," and that "when we reread [*Ulysses*], we start in at any point, as if it were indeed something solid like a city which actually existed in space and which could be entered from any direction."[27] A few years later, David Daiches imagines Joyce's narrative aspirations for a totalizing sign: "If Joyce could coin one kaleidoscopic word with an infinite series of meanings, a word saying everything in one instant yet leaving its infinity of meanings reverberating and mingling in the mind, he would have reached his ideal."[28] Joseph Frank, elaborating these claims in his 1945 "Spatial Form in Modern Literature," argues that *Ulysses* is among works that "ideally intend the reader to apprehend their work spatially, in a moment of time, rather than as a sequence," and that Joyce in particular "proceeded on the assumption that a unified spatial apprehension of his work would ultimately be possible."[29] These early descriptions of the novel proved influential because they account for both Joyce's ability to compress an epic into a single day and his agility with unremitting textual correlation, potent qualities that allow us to read, for example, the schooner arriving from England with its three masts at the end of "Proteus" as an invocation of English imperialism, the Holy Trinity, crucifixion, Odysseus's return, Homer, and the narrative approach of Bloom himself, invocations which join related passages throughout the novel as a synchronic network.[30] It is narrative aspiring to the unifying force of Stephen's image of "time [as] one livid final flame," or of Bloom's idea about the chemist's temporal compression: "A lifetime in a night" (*U* 2.10, 5.474). Nor is the sentence-by-sentence representation of consciousness streaming past in chaotic fragments anything like a temporality of narrative delay and arrival. Joyce's stream is an ongoing present, as Franco Moretti suggests: "The great novelty of the stream of consciousness consists in its proceeding for pages and pages *without the slightest revelation*. It is the true world of prose: detailed, regular, rather banal....Parataxis offers a reliable, mechanical grid, where each present is at once followed by another—different, but no more important. No instant ever stands out from the others, unrepeatable..., to fix the meaning of the story once and for all."[31] The stream has velocity without narrative arc. The novel's various technical virtuosities tend toward time's spatialization and homogenization; there is little for expectation—and the sense of truth it produces—to feed on because the future has always already occurred throughout the past. So Bloom announces, "Coming events cast their shadows before," and the entire novel shadows itself (*U* 8.526).

Yet within this will-to-simultaneity of the novel's rhetorical architecture and ongoing present of interiority, there is, somehow, an unmistakable element of dynamic play and self-differentiation, an irruption of time that gives the novel its unique narrativity. "Hades" is one of its potent articulations. En route to the cemetery, Bloom imagines Dignam's corpse to be at risk, passing through the condition of unpredictability that constitutes diachrony:

> Bom! Upset. A coffin bumping out on to the road. Bust open. Paddy Dignam shot out and rolling over stiff in the dust in a brown habit too large for him. Red face: grey now. Mouth fallen open. Asking what's up now. Quite right to close it. Looks horrid open. Then the insides decompose quickly. Much better to close up all the orifices. Yes, also. With wax. The sphincter loose. Seal up all.
>
> —Dunphy's, Mr. Power announced as the carriage turned right.... But suppose now it did happen. Would he bleed if a nail say cut him in the knocking about? He would and he wouldn't, I suppose. Depends on where. The circulation stops. Still some might ooze out of an artery. It would be better to bury them in red: a dark red. (*U* 6.421–6.435)

In his analysis of those social practices "which, like rituals, derive some of their most important properties from the fact that they are 'detotalized' by their unfolding in succession," Bourdieu argues that "to reintroduce uncertainty is to reintroduce time, with its rhythm, its orientation and its irreversibility."[32] To have Bloom imagine this grotesque, accidental exposure of Dignam's corpse is to reintroduce its narrativity, to confirm it as a site where things can happen. Yet it also makes us not want anything to happen, associates diachrony with the grotesque, and provokes the desire for the detemporalized efficiency that Bloom himself advocates in the funeral carriage: "And another thing I often thought, is to have municipal tram lines like they have in Milan, you know. Run the line out to the cemetery gates and have special trams, hearse and carriage and all. Don't you see what I mean?" (*U* 6.405–6.408).[33] We do, because images of such efficient systems, as synchronic structures, pervade the novel, just as the novel itself behaves like one. Bloom's proposal for hearse trams removed from the delays and risks of city traffic is a proposal to assimilate the dead into the efficiency of a civic machine (even if Dublin, in actuality, was not nearly the kind of urban machine that such images suggest). Trams are its most regularizing mechanical element. Bloom describes the street in "Lestrygonians":

> Trams passed one another, ingoing, outgoing, clanging. Useless words. Things go on the same, day after day: squads of police marching out, back: trams in, out. Those two loonies mooching about. Dignam carted off. Mina Purefoy swollen belly on a bed groaning to have a child tugged out of her. One born every second somewhere. Other dying every second. Since I fed the birds five minutes. Three hundred kicked the bucket. Other three hundred born, washing the blood off, all are washed in the blood of the lamb, bawling maaaaaa.
>
> Cityful passing away, other cityful coming, passing away too: other coming on, passing on. Houses, lines of houses, streets, miles of pavements, piledup bricks, stones, changing hands. This owner, that. Landlord never dies they say. Other steps into his shoes when he gets notice to quit. They buy the place up with gold and still they have all the gold. Swindle in it somewhere. Piled up in cities, worn away age after age. Pyramids in sand. Built on bread and onions. Slaves Chinese wall. Babylon. Big stones left. Round towers. Rest rubble, sprawling suburbs, jerrybuilt. Kerwan's mushroom houses built of breeze. Shelter, for the night.
>
> No-one is anything. (*U* 8.476–8.493)

From the trams to the city to world history: Bloom's remarkable abstraction of discrete events into cumulative processes, and of discrete lives into replaceable biological and social functions, is alarming in almost the same way that the stoics' vision of the impersonal fluidity and fragility of everything we value might disarm us into selfless virtue. But if the stoics advocate transcendence of individual identity and self-interest for a larger state of harmony with the implicit justice of the universe, no matter our personal suffering, Bloom's vision offers nothing of the sort; in his image, there is nothing beyond the industrial processes to which we are subject, not a universal harmony but a political economy that sustains itself on the reproductive cycles of our flesh. Bloom envisions the absorption of death and the dead into the homogenizing systems of production, distribution, and disposal that Adorno later condemns: "For every person, with all his functions, society has a stand-in ready, to whom the former is in any case no more than an intrusive occupier of his workplace, a candidate for death. So the exchange of death is turned into that of the exchange of functionaries, and anything in the natural relationship to death that is not wholly absorbed into the social one is turned over to hygiene."[34] While in the funeral carriage, Bloom continues this inquiry into labor's redistribution: "A pointman's back straightened itself upright suddenly against a tramway standard by Mr Bloom's window. Couldn't they invent something automatic so that the wheel itself much handier? Well but that fellow would lose his job then? Well but the other fellow would get a job making the new invention?" (*U* 6.175–6.179). Joyce makes the arrangement of lives and deaths across an all-encompassing system of production a narrative problem. We are to think the slowness and instability of Dignam's corpse-time, the mortal diachrony that gives Dignam's burial a chance to gather meaning, along with its effacement, its collapse into the synchrony of an economic efficiency with no meaning beyond itself.[35]

It seems to be a paradox. If Bloom imagines Dignam's corpse at risk in the play of time, he also imagines its indifferent assimilation to a social and industrial machine. The latter, in fact, offers the surprising excitement of the self's urban vertigo ("No-one is anything"), a kind of sublime of modernization, a hallucinatory gathering of the totality of the modern's productive forces. The corpse, in its slowness, in the way it causes people throughout Dublin to pause their daily tasks and raise their hats in respect, is a noninstrumental interruption to the industrial machine, yet it evokes the overwhelming power of its totality. The plot of Dignam's burial is about the very possibility of such a plot, of an unassimilable hiatus from a social and narrative machine that reproduces itself as efficiently as possible. It is a plot plotting against itself, a narrative exploration of its own abstraction, returning again and again to the images of spatial interconnection, simultaneity, and repetition that efface the temporal dynamic of narrative. Bloom regards the gathering of horses and carriages at the cemetery: "Do they know what they cart out here every day? Must be twenty or thirty funerals every day. Then Mount Jerome for the protestants. Funerals all over the world everywhere every minute. Shovelling them under by the cartload doublequick. Thousands every hour. Too many in the world" (*U* 6.512–6.516). As a mass, the dead are not narratable but countable. For Mulligan, in medical training, they are not even that: "And what is death, he asked [Stephen], your mother's or yours or my own? You saw only your mother die. I see them pop off every day in the Mater and Richmond and cut up into tripes in the dissectionroom. It's a beastly thing and nothing else. It simply doesn't matter... To me it's all a mockery and beastly" (*U* 1.204–1.210). Joyce further insists on this brute, beastly fact of death in its submission to the logic of quantification with the cattle being taken to slaughter along Dignam's funeral route, which Bloom considers: "Thursday, of course. Tomorrow is killing day. Springers. Cuffe sold them about twentyseven quid each. For Liverpool probably. Roastbeef for old England. They buy up all the juicy ones. And then the fifth quarter lost: all that raw stuff, hide, hair, horns. Comes to a big thing in a year. Dead meat trade. Byproducts of the slaughterhouses for the tanneries, soap, margarine" (*U* 6.392–6.397). The idea of the dead meat trade, which seems like something Adorno should have named first, is an idea of a corpse's value that does not require the ritual passing of time to manifest. It is calculable in advance (allowing Bloom to muse about selling the dead: "Every man his price. Well preserved fat corpse, gentleman, epicure, invaluable for fruit garden. A bargain" (*U* 6.772–6.773). Throughout "Hades," Joyce tells us a story about the dead being extracted from their stories for a calculable, prestatistical state, and this kind of metastory has at issue the very possibility of burial plots, as a vestigial temporality, in modernity's abstractions of value and rationalizations of time. At the funeral ceremony, we see Bloom apply these modernized forms of experience to even the priest's religious rituals, ostensibly an exception to these forms but available for the same quantification:

> Holy water that was, I expect. Shaking sleep out of it. He must be fed up with that job, shaking that thing over all the corpses they trot up. What harm if he could see what he was shaking it over. Every mortal day a fresh batch: middleaged men, old women, children, women dead in childbirth, men with beards, baldheaded businessmen, consumptive girls with little sparrows' breasts. All the year round he prayed the same thing over them all and shook water on top of them: sleep. On Dignam now.
>
> —*In paradisum.*

Said he was going to paradise or is in paradise. Says that over everybody. Tiresome kind of a job. But he has to say something. (*U* 6.621–6.630)

This list of particular deaths means only that everyone dies, each death, in its disenchantment, too tedious to motivate the reorganization of repetition into a plot able to bear its meaning. Yet the energies of plot got us here, through Dublin to Glasnevin, in an irreducible span of time. It still seems to be a paradox, essentially between form and content: the episode's narrative diachrony, as the processual form of a burial's accomplishment, produces its nullifying rhetoric of the synchronic and atemporal. At the center of this paradox lies the modern corpse, an ungainly compromise formation between secular modernization and traditional religion, the stubborn delay within accelerating industrial processes gathering the power to collapse it into a repeatable element of a homogenous system. If Dublin in 1906 was not in fact such a highly industrial zone, Joyce by 1922 was able to use his Dublin effectively to investigate tensions between industrialization and mortal obligation.

Narrative Competence, Burial Competence

There is an old joke that can help us. A man is sent to prison. At his first meal in the mess hall, another prisoner stands up and says to the whole room, "Forty-two!" Everyone laughs, except for the new prisoner. A few minutes later, someone else stands up and shouts "A hundred and twenty-nine!" Everyone laughs again, and some of the men are laughing so hard they have to wipe tears from their eyes. The new prisoner asks the man sitting next to him what's going on. The man tells him, "Those are jokes. We've heard these jokes so many times that now we just give them numbers, and we all know the one someone's telling." This goes on for a while, prisoners standing up and saying numbers, with everyone bursting into laughter. Finally, across the room, a man stands up, looks around, and says "Six!" Nobody laughs, and there's an embarrassed silence. The new prisoner asks the man next to him why nobody laughed that time. He answers, "That guy, he just can't tell a joke."

It's funny because it imagines differences among performances, not of narrative but of its reduction and abstraction, as if saying a number were a recitation requiring a sense of timing and style. And it imagines that some people are so constitutionally inept at joke-telling that they cannot even tell a number. It is itself a metajoke, rehearsing the tension between narrative as an unfolding and as a collapsible summation in the difference between its form and content, just as Joyce does in "Hades." Bloom thinks through something analogous in "Sirens," not about jokes but about music:

> Numbers it is. All music when you come to think. Two multiplied by two divided by half is twice one. Vibrations: chords those are. One plus two plus six is seven. Do anything you like with figures juggling. Always find out this equal to that. Symmetry under a cemetery wall. He [Richie Goulding] doesn't see my mourning. Callous: all for his own gut. Musemathematics. And you think you're listening to the etherial. But suppose you said it like: Martha, seven times nine minus x is thirtyfive thousand. Fall quite flat. It's on account of the sounds it is.... Time makes the tune. (*U* 11.830–11.841)

The difference between a song's mathematical representation and its rendition in sound over time is like the difference between a polite conversation with Martha and one with an erotic charge (or the difference between Bloom's encounters with Mrs. Breen and Gerty McDowell). Time is the medium of pleasure and desire as well as ethical meaning, so that Peter Brooks's approach to narrative not with "theories of interpretation" but with "an 'erotics' of art" accounts first and foremost for its play in time.[36] We will explore the erotic complexity—the queerness—of mortal obligation in the next chapter, but it is already relevant to this basic fact about narrative delay. As Bloom realizes by analogy, and as the joke about the prisoners implies, narrative logic, according to Brooks,

> makes sense of succession and time, and... insists that mediation of the problem posed at the outset takes time: that the meaning dealt with by narrative, and thus perhaps narrative's raison d'être, is of and in time. Plot as it interests me is not a matter of typology or of fixed structures, but rather a structuring operation peculiar to those messages that are developed through temporal succession, the instrumental logic of a specific mode of human understanding. Plot, let us say in preliminary definition, is the logic and dynamic of narrative, and narrative itself a form of understanding and explanation.[37]

In particular, for Brooks, the time-spent of narrative is a strategy for understanding and explaining our dying: "Plot is the internal logic of the discourse of mortality," he writes, following Benjamin's claim that "death is the sanction of everything that the storyteller can tell."[38] If narrative has a mortal logic, it is not just because plots can end in deaths that retroactively shape them, and in some sense always imply this postmortem perspective, but because the dead actually make a claim on our time and on how we plot our time, a demand that they be given the slow social time they need to come to the fullness of their deaths. It is a demand, even, to make time drag. Bloom expects Dignam's funeral to be tedious: "Bore this funeral affair. O well, poor fellow, it's not his fault"; "Funeral be rather glum" (*U* 5.468–5.469, 5.505–5.506). If we no longer obligatorily offer sacrificial foods and libations to our dead in gestures of ancestor worship, we are still asked to sacrifice the efficient productivity or self-absorbed pleasure of our time for the integrity of their burial plots, which—Joyce tells us—the modern world narrates with increasing awkwardness and ambivalence. Just as the difference between a song and its math involves the vitality of pleasure and desire, so the difference between a corpse reduced to an indifferent repetition in a series and one accompanied through its plot involves the vitality, if not of pleasure, then of the recognition of a life's singular value and meaning. Brooks shows how plot is "the product of our refusal to allow temporality to be meaningless"; similarly, modern burial plots, to the extent that we can still construct them, refuse the meaninglessness of modern death.[39] The corpse matters to the living to the extent that it is given the needed time to pass through its liminality with dignity (hence "Dignam," c.f. *U* 10.4), and Joyce uses "Hades" to express anxiety about our pleasure in the impressive means emerging to collapse such interruptions to the time of the living. Yet Joyce also tells us that this pleasure is real, a fundamental part of being modern, and at the root of the strangeness of death's modernization.

Members of modern cultures are not necessarily competent at burying the dead (as O'Connor and Kafka show), or at least not necessarily sure about what genuine competence entails. Joyce's correlation between narrative and burial, in which the mortal logic of the former becomes the diachrony of the latter, also creates a correlation between narrative and burial competencies. The prisoner joke culminates with a guy who just cannot tell a joke; *Ulysses* is about this too, in Bloom, and about the risk of narrative incompetence more broadly. He botches his joke in the funeral carriage, on the way to bury Dignam:

> Mr Bloom began to speak with sudden eagerness to his companions' faces.
> —That's an awfully good one that's going the rounds about Reuben J and the son.
> —About the boatman? Mr Power asked.
> —Yes. Isn't it awfully good?
> —What is that? Mr Dedalus asked. I didn't hear it.
> —There was a girl in the case, Mr Bloom began, and he determined to send him to the Isle of Man out of harm's way but when they were both...
> —What? Mr Dedalus asked. That confirmed bloody hobbledehoy is it?

—Yes, Mr Bloom said. They were both on the way to the boat and he tried
to drown....
—Drown Barabbas! Mr Dedalus cried. I wish to Christ he did!
Mr Power sent a long laugh down his shaded nostrils.
—No, Mr Bloom said, the son himself....
Mr Cunningham thwarted his speech rudely:
—Reuben J and the son were piking it down the quay next the river on their
way to the Isle of Man boat and the young chiseller suddenly got loose
and over the wall with him into the Liffey. (U 6.262–6.280)

Cunningham manages the rest without him. From the beginning of his day, when
he admires *Matcham's Masterstroke* in the jakes, to the end, when he hears Stephen's
A Pisgah Sight of Palestine or *The Parable of the Plums* in his kitchen "tacitly appreciative of successful narrative," Bloom pays close attention to which stories do and
do not work (U 17.652–17.653). In a thinly veiled metaphor for masturbation, the
narrator of "Ithaca" describes Bloom's success in nightly self-narration, the only
reliable success he has: "It was one of his axioms that...some automatic relation to
himself of a narrative concerning himself or tranquil recollection of the past when
practised habitually before retiring for the night alleviated fatigue and produced as
a result sound repose and renovated vitality" (U 17.755–17.758). Joyce also gestures
toward a concern for narrative purchase in "Circe" when Bloom defends himself
against the charges of an angry, hallucinatory mob: "(*excitedly*) This is midsum-
mer madness, some ghastly joke again. By heaven, I am guiltless as the unsunned
snow! It was my brother Henry. He is my double. He lives in number 2 Dolphin's
Barn. Slander, the viper, has wrongfully accused me. Fellowcountrymen, *sgeul
I mbarr bata coisde gan capall*" (U 15.1768–15.1772). Bloom's Irish means, according to Gifford, "A tale in the top of a stick [a useless tale] is a horseless coach," and
we can hear this as a reminder of his joke's failure in the carriage that morning.[40]
He also recalls this attempt to tell Reuben J's story, and Simon Dedalus's joke after
Cunningham completes it, when he acknowledges Simon as someone who does
have narrative skills: "Reuben J's son must have swallowed a good bellyful of sew-
age. One and eightpence too much. Hhhhm. It's the droll way he comes out with
the things. Knows how to tell a story too" (U 8.52–8.55). "Jack Power could a tale
unfold: father a G man," he reflects soon after about another narrative superior,
and Joyce's use of this phrase to evoke the ghost in *Hamlet* 1.5 signals an initial connection between narrative competence and the dead (U 8.419–8.420). The ghost's
phrase recurs in "Circe," when Bloom's imaginary defense attorney argues on his
behalf: "If the accused could speak he could a tale unfold—one of the strangest

that have ever been narrated between the covers of a book" (*U* 15.951–15.953). But Bloom cannot unfold a tale, because he lacks the technique, and this lack implicates the burial task at hand in "Hades."

Speaking to Hamlet, the ghost of his father says:

> But that I am forbid
> To tell the secret of my prison-house,
> I could a tale unfold whose lightest word
> Would harrow up thy soul, freeze thy young blood,
> Make thy two eyes like stars start from their spheres,
> Thy knotty and combined locks to part
> And each particular hair to stand on end
> Like quills upon the fearful porpentine—
> But this eternal blazon must not be
> To ears of flesh and blood. List, list, O list,
> If thou didst ever thy dear father love—(*U* 1.5.13–1.5.23)

This fraught combination of narrative promise, denial, and demand—in which a tale first emerges through its unnarratability (or its unhearability, as if Claudius's poison were symbolically poised over a second victim's ear)—is useful to Joyce because it captures a sense of thwartedness and incommensurability in the narrative transactions between the living and dead.[41] This breakdown in community and communication between the living and dead is a fundamental aspect of modern identity and its affiliations, and it has narrative implications. We can tell stories of how the dead lived, but much less so the plots of their dying, of how they passed into death proper to become another kind of presence and authority in our social worlds, and of how by dying they complicated the temporality of the plots of the living. Shakespeare depicts the narrative power of the dead as a part of a transaction: the dead one tells a crucial story in return for a crucial promise (to exact revenge), and this idea of a transaction or exchange with the dead is precisely what modern thought occludes. The dead are inert in our symbolic economy; if we do something, such as exact revenge, in their name, it is not for their well-being but for our own, since the well-being of the dead is no longer a coherent concept. In his extensive reflections on the nature of symbolic exchange (which I also discuss in the introduction), Baudrillard addresses the social occlusion of the modern dead; he considers how, "to us, the dead have just passed away and no longer have anything to exchange. The dead are residual even before dying. At the end of a lifetime of accumulation, the dead are subtracted from the total in an economic operation. They do not become effigies: they serve entirely as alibis for the living and to their obvious superiority over the dead. This is a flat, one-dimensional death, the end of the biological journey."[42] Joyce's interest in narrative failure is also an interest in the failure of exchange with the dead, a transaction in narrative forms and acts. To the extent that the corpse must have a strong plot for its liminality if it is to achieve a legitimate and intelligible death, it requires our competence in the nexus of burial and narrative practices. When Dignam appears in "Circe," he repeats the exhortation from Hamlet's dead father: "Bloom, I am Paddy Dignam's spirit. List, list, O list!" (U 15.1218). He implies that he is on the verge of telling a story in exchange for some arduous demand on Bloom, the type of fatal demand that organizes *Hamlet*. In a concatenation of images and allusions, Joyce correlates narrative exchange and death obligation to explore the fragility of the dead in modern lifeworlds.

This fragility becomes the essential point. Despite Dignam's exhortation, Bloom does not in fact listen: he switches stories, swerving from revenge tragedy to a story of usurped identity, birthright, and blessing: "The voice is the voice of Esau," he responds (U 15.1220). This sudden turn to the story of Jacob's usurpation of his older brother's birthright and paternal blessing implicates narrative transactions with the dead, to whom the living owe burial plots, with the problem of one's right to birth and filiation. Bloom says he hears the voice of Esau; Esau's voice before Isaac in Genesis 27:34–38, after he realizes that he has been displaced by Jacob, is one of desperate lament: "'Bless me too, Father!... Have you not reserved a blessing for me?... Have you but one blessing, Father? Bless me too, Father!' And Esau wept aloud."[43] Joyce is doing considerably complex work by invoking Esau's lament against his usurpation as an element of the ghost's demand for recognition and exchange. He is narrating the failure of narrative relations across mortal lines not as a simple breakdown into silence but as an anxiety about usurpation and a contest over birthright, a contest over the right one can claim to inhabit one's contingent identity and being. If "Hades" is a burial plot testing the possibility of burial plots in an age of their reduction and abstraction, and *Ulysses* more broadly links a concern with narrative competence to competence in death practices, then we are faced with an exacerbating ethical tension between the living and the dead. We are faced with the problem of the contingency of who gets to be alive at all.

The Dead, the Never-Born, and the Precarious Legitimacy of the Living

Among many significant shifts in Joyce criticism since the New Critics, one of the subtlest but most philosophically consequential is a reconceptualization of how

Ulysses animates contingency. The novel's avalanching details have always made readers attentive to the aleatory nature of interpreting it, but the grounds of this aleatory experience have been remapped. Kenner, providing some of our earliest commentaries on Joyce, describes the novel's "aesthetics of delay," its scattering of unnoticeably related facts across hundreds of pages, as an unmasterable challenge that makes our interpretations a function of what we happen to be able to notice and remember in a given reading. For Kenner, we are necessarily inadequate detectives, able to track "one element now, one later, and leaving large orders of fact to be assembled late or another time or never."[44] The novel is so rich with interpretive possibilities but so far beyond our parsing as a complete system that we have in reading it "an experience comparable to that of experiencing the haphazardly evidential quality of life" with its exposure to the infinite complexity of the real.[45] More recently, Derek Attridge has acknowledged readerly performance as an element of the novel's randomness effect, but complicates this picture: the novel, he writes, is not an unmasterable system of meaningful correspondences but itself a randomness machine, a device for creating "outbreaks of coincidence that defy all predictability and programming."[46] In reading the novel, Attridge suggests, we rehearse our encounter not with the infinite complexity of the real but with its infinite randomness. The point of reading *Ulysses* is not to decode—even if inadequately—its inherent systems of meaning but to set into motion its numberless potential correspondences and associations across its overloaded pages, see which are actualized, and consider how we might come to care for those particular actualizations. "Rather than attempting to control the mass of fragmentary detail to *produce* meaning, Joyce's major texts *allow* meaning to arise out of that mass by the operation of chance," Attridge explains, and so "the opposition between the 'intended' and the 'accidental' begins to break down...: if Joyce intentionally builds a machine of such complexity that unforeseen connections are bound to arise when it comes into contact with a reader possessing equally complex systems of memory and information, we can't call them 'unintentional' in any straightforward sense of the word."[47] Attridge helps us conceptualize the novel as an exercise in methodical randomness, an environment intentionally designed for generating unpredictable connections among its elements; these connections are important because we must judge their value, and in doing so consider our commitments by which we give interpretive weight to one coincidence instead of another. *Ulysses* is about how we take responsibility for our interpretive commitments in the face of their contingency. We interpret the novel by usurping the other interpretations that could have been.[48]

Attridge's critical redescription is useful because Joyce suggests this quality of contingency and usurpation in how his characters experience the fact that they exist. If Joyce's dead do not stay buried, as Ellman notes, then neither do possible lives that were never lived rest quietly in his novel. In fact, he makes this quality of potential but unrealized being manifest in the presence of the dead, as an uncanny dimension of being with the dead. As we will see, it is an even more complex use of contingency in the context of death than that involved in the selection of the Unknown Warrior (Chapter One). Just after watching Dignam's coffin being lowered into the ground at Glasnevin Cemetery, Bloom silently half asks himself an unsettling question: "If we were all suddenly somebody else" (U 6.836). It is a preternaturally suggestive question at someone's gravesite, where a burial deposits a life's remains in its allotted, circumscribing spot so that it is, finally and unambiguously, itself without any possibility of alteration.[49] Yet he sounds like John Rawls, as if the veil of ignorance behind which one would arrange all social positions to be just also applied to the uncertain fate of the dead—since, as he has earlier reminded himself, you "never know who will touch you dead" (U 6.18). In fact, in this speculation about suddenly becoming otherwise Bloom is articulating a question that haunts the novel. It is not simply a question about the variability of social positions or identities but a question about the logical relation between possible and actual lives, about the contingency and necessity of those who (happen to) exist. How this contingency of the living is also a part of their relation to the dead is the question we have to work out. We have seen Bloom go through a thought complementary to this graveside speculation above—"No-one is anything," as he watches the trams—and Stephen poses a question resonant with Bloom's in "Proteus," as a couple passes him on the beach: "If I were suddenly naked here as I sit?" (U 3.390). These are moments of sudden and seemingly random self-alarm, in which the self questions its certifiability in the eyes of others and begins to question its ontological grounding. These moments carry a palpable sense that one could just as well not have existed—or not have existed as the self one happens to be—and that by coming into existence one has precluded other lives that could have been instead. Bloom takes stock of his aging in "Lestrygonians" with this sense that a given life may not have been given fully or exclusively: "I was happier then. Or was that I? Or am I now I?" (U 8.608). Stephen flirts with this question as a convenient escape from his debts: "Five months. Molecules all change. I am other I now. Other I got pound" (U 9.205–9.206). (Although Stephen generally resists this drift.) And Molly speculates about the contingency at the heart of identity by imagining the Prince of Wales, His Royal Highness, as her alternate origin: "H R H he was in Gibraltar the year I was born I bet he found lilies there too where he planted the tree he planted more than that in his time he might have planted me too if hed come a bit sooner then I wouldnt be here as I am" (U 18.500–18.503).[50]

Joyce shows us that thinking the identity of the self is to think the self otherwise and against itself, a fact crowded by its counterfactuals, just as Bloom's reflection on the street is a crowded one, a life entangled with the lives it does not actually live: "In Lionel Mark's antique saleshop window haughty Henry Lionel Leopold dear Henry Flower earnestly Mr Leopold Bloom" (*U* 11.1261–11.1262).[51] The narrator of "Ithaca" proposes that these entangled lives be traced along the lines of their hypothetical immiseration—"Reduce Bloom by cross multiplication or reverses in fortune"—and these scenarios, as knowable as they are nonexistent, arrive after a series of elaborations at the essential names of his contingency, "Everyman and Noman" (*U* 17.2008). The drama of Joyce's thinking is to make these hypotheticals an element of the actual, to weave what could have been into what is, as a way of naming the self's estrangement from itself.[52] Stephen recalls an alibi he hears to this effect in Paris—"Other fellow did it: other me"—and feels something like another me lingering even in his boots: "He counted the creases of rucked leather wherein another's foot had nested warm" (*U* 3.182, 3.447–3.448). One's life is another's (and another's and another's); this is the metaphysical resonance of Stephen's anxiety toward Mulligan at the end of "Telemachus," when his "voice, sweettoned and sustained, called to him from the sea. Turning the curve he waved his hand. It called again.... Usurper" (*U* 1.741–1.744). Each life usurps its actualization from infinite potential others, and can be usurped in turn.

A life is certainly made strange by intuitions of its alternate and usurped destinies, but Joyce has a particular agenda for this strangeness. It is a displaced reckoning with the lives that no longer exist, an experience of the dead refracted through the never-born. Joyce associates the two in several striking passages, and the effect is to make an intuition of one's contingency a way of experiencing one's implication with the dead, an oblique encounter with their ambiguous and increasingly attenuated presence. During his lesson in "Nestor," Stephen meditates on death as it relates to the problem of being in its hypothetical or counterfactual tenses: "Had Pyrrhus not fallen by a beldam's hand in Argos or Julius Caesar not been knifed to death. They are not to be thought away. Time has branded them and fettered they are lodged in the room of infinite possibilities they have ousted. But can those have been possible seeing that they never were? Or was that only possible which came to pass? Weave, weaver of the wind" (*U* 2.48–53). Stephen starts with an idea of death as the proof of a life's logical necessity—after being murdered, the possibility of Pyrrhus's and Caesar's lives are not to be thought away—but shifts to a question about the status of those infinite possible lives never lived. His questions attach two recalcitrant ontologies, the nonbeing of death and the counterfactual being of potential but unlived lives, as complementary complications of mere being. This strange affiliation of the dead and never-born pressures the living on both sides of their claim to life, and this is both a chronological (before birth, after death) and a logical outflanking (being as possible but not actualized, being as actualized but no longer possible). Joyce elaborates this double estrangement of the living in "Oxen," as Stephen holds forth to his friends:

> The aged sisters draw us into life: we wail, batten, sport, clip, clasp, sunder, dwindle, die: over us dead they bend. First, saved from waters of old Nile, among bulrushes, a bed of fasciated wattles: at last the cavity of a mountain, an occulted sepulchre amid the conclamation of the hillcat and the ossifrage. And as no man knows the ubicity of his tumulus nor to what processes we shall thereby be ushered nor whether to Tophet or to Edenville in the like way is all hidden when we would backward see from what region of remoteness the whatness of our whoness hath fetched his whenceness. (*U* 14.392–14.400)

Among the various symmetries between being born and dying—the old women who oversee births and deaths, the secluded niches where they happen—Stephen emphasizes the common uncertainty that lies just beyond them, the way these realms of unknowing mirror one another, as if death returned us to the same contingency from which we came. But why would this be the case? Stephen jokes about this equivalence earlier in the maternity ward—he has sworn himself to "obedience in the womb, chastity in the tomb but involuntary poverty all his days"—and the chapter's narrator invokes it as moral warning: "Therefore, everyman, look to that last end that is thy death and the dust that gripeth on every man that is born of woman for as he came naked forth from his mother's womb so naked shall he wend him at the last for to go as he came" (*U* 14.336–14.337; 14.107–14.110). Walking along the beach in "Proteus," Stephen plays with the physical sounds of this metaphysical rhyme: "His lips lipped and mouthed fleshless lips of air: mouth to her moomb. Oomb, allwombing tomb. His mouth moulded issuing breath, unspeeched: ooeeehah: roar of cataractic planets, globed, blazing, roaring wayawayawayawayaway" (*U* 3.401–3.404). His speech turns inchoate at these limit points of being and nonbeing, falling into the undifferentiated sounds that precede the language for distinguishing between the two, *womb* and *tomb*, which continue as echoes of each other. This correlation continues to echo in Beckett, who sounds it in *Texts for Nothing* IX: "Yes, I'd have a mother, I'd have a tomb, I wouldn't have come out here, one doesn't come out of here, here are my tomb and mother, it's all here this evening, I'm dead and getting born, without having ended, helpless to begin, that's my life."[53]

We should appreciate how bizarre this equivalence actually is, and how much this is the wild play of literature's speculative powers. We cannot parse Joyce's thematic interweaving of the contingent possibility of being before birth with the residual of being in death, two forms of existence in the shadows of actual life, with any familiar philosophical logic or by correlating it to some established aspect of his social context (even if the background of his imagining—which in itself explains nothing—demonstrably includes, for example, Aquinas as a philosophical source, and new technologies for recording the images and voices of the dead, as a cultural context). In his complex associations of the dead and never-born, Joyce takes us off a speculative cliff (which is why we read him). The never-born and dead are not absent in the same way, and they do not demand the same of the living: the lives that never came to be because ours did draw our attention to something like our constitutive luck or freedom, while the dead demand some combination of acknowledgment, remembrance, promise-keeping, and even dread or awe. At an emotional level, we might feel concern for the loneliness that we imagine the dead to suffer,[54] but we cannot quite imagine this sense of loss among the never-born because they never actualized any life to suffer in its being lost. If the constitutive luck or freedom implied by the contingency of being has been conceptualized by Judith Butler, with particular rigor, as the root of a politics of performative agency, then a sense of the presence of the dead has been conceptualized in a very different way, as the basis for the subject's familial obligations, religious beliefs, and, in a different register, a Benjaminian political critique of capitalism's homogenization of time. Why does Joyce bring such distinct itineraries, based on fundamentally different ontologies, so carefully together? It is as if Joyce sought to destabilize the identities of the dead with a sense of contingency while stabilizing the nonexistent with a kind of reversed and impossible remembrance. In this counterintuitive transference, evidence as much as anything else in Joyce's *oeuvre* of his precipitous adventures in thinking, Joyce is making death truly modern—not modernized, as a crude rejection of what came before, but actually new, responsive to the most surprising philosophical possibilities of his time in their reconfigurations of what was capable of being thought in the past. He is upsetting the traditional ontological and social categories that organize life and death, not by rejecting them but by rethinking them with scrupulous and fascinated attention from the ground up, so that the volatile energies of modernity's freedoms touch even the realm of the dead, as if Joyce wanted to imagine that the dead could also access these energies without being destroyed by them. Joyce's defamiliarization of death liberates it, in the first place, from religion—hence Bloom's running peanut-gallery demystification of Dignam's funeral service—and, in the second place, from a straightforward materialism that would reduce death and the dead to simple absence, to things becoming nothing. *Ulysses*'s dead are left in the same play of possibility and actuality that an infinity of possible lives are, so that Joyce seems to be saying that a genuinely modern sense of mortality finds it too strange for the doctrines of either religion or secularism, because the genuinely modern dead are the unfinished task of the living to actualize, to make real.[55] If the modernized dead are simply obsolete, the properly modern dead are an ethical and existential task for the living's aesthetic powers, a necessary fiction to replot with a new brilliance that can actualize them as a force and presence in the world.

In his speculations into the nature of these shadow ontologies, Joyce is posing a set of questions that are fundamental enough to remain with us today: can the modern world retell the stories of corpses, as they accrue to meaning, and of being-dead, as a positive condition that matters to the living? Can the dead themselves be genuinely modern, neither managed by religious habit or dogma nor subsumed in modern productive efficiencies, but an open task in an ethical struggle to acknowledge some alterity to the rationalization and instrumentalization of embodied being? Joyce satirizes the merely technological modernization of death with Bloom's clever schemes for corpses throughout "Hades": burying them standing to save room, selling them as fertilizer to gardeners, carrying them in reusable biers with sliding panels to save wood, taking them to cemeteries on municipal funeral trams, giving them telephones and clocks in their coffins, labeling their tombstones by professions, and recording their voices for graveside phonographs. Bloom is also a bit obtuse in his preoccupation with Dignam's insurance policy, that modern technology for financially rationalizing the contingencies of life and death. In these fantasies and preoccupations, Joyce plays with the sheer oddness of applying principles of innovation and rational progress to the dead, drawing on the sense that the corpse retains some degree of alterity to the processes of modernization that would bring its lurking antiquity up to date. He helps us see that the corpse, despite every innovation, is always already obsolete, a breach in progress and disjointing of time's sequential logic. Because of the dead, modernization cannot unfold its narrative of progress as seamlessly as it desires, but must awkwardly double-back in its plot toward some Elpenor-like presence it cannot quite account for. Even as the dead become objects of ever new technologies of preservation, transportation, and disposal, Joyce suggests they are estranged from these processes, just as they make them strange, a vivid reason why *"there is no such thing as a 'modern society' plain and simple; there are only societies more or less advanced in a continuum of modernization."*[56] The corpse, as a constitutive incompleteness of the modern and unfinishable task of modernization, raises the questions: can we still discern our mortal obligations? Can we articulate them? Can we fulfill them? Can we claim our dead? Stephen, feeling the contours of his mother's absence, thinks of her with a desperate image: "She was no more: the trembling skeleton of a twig burnt in the fire, an odour of rosewood and wetted ashes. She had saved him from being trampled underfoot and had gone, scarcely having been. A poor soul gone to heaven: and on a heath beneath winking stars a fox, red reek of rapine in his fur, with merciless bright eyes scraped in the earth, listened, scraped up the earth, listened, scraped and scraped" (*U* 2.144–2.150). He puts before us the thing in us that claws the earth for the corpses we fear we have abandoned.

Faulkner, the Corpse, and the Unsettling of the Secular

There are other, complementary fears about burial plotting at work in Faulkner's *As I Lay Dying*, and between Joyce and Faulkner we can discern a complex critique of the modernization of death based on an irreducible ethical desire to accord value to the dead in our economies of obligation. The two writers have different narrative strategies for doing this, or for animating our desire to do this. If Joyce works through several questions of the burial plot's fragility—the temptation to compress it and efface the dead in new narrative and industrial totalizations, anxieties about narrative incompetence in burial plotting, and an ontologically destabilizing affiliation of the dead with the never-born that invites us to approach the dead with new energies—Faulkner explores the burial plot's dangerous powers of expansion and excess, as if the moment that Bloom imagines Dignam's coffin falling off the carriage and opening on the street, which Joyce quickly forecloses, were amplified into an entire novel.[57] Published in 1930, *As I Lay Dying* is about a poor white Southern family's ordeal upon the death of its mother, Addie. Before dying, Addie makes her husband promise to bury her with her birth family in a distant cemetery.[58] It is a hot Mississippi summer at a time when few people have cars, before air conditioning and good roads, and when old bridges easily washed away in floods. Through delays and misadventures the burial journey becomes a trek of nine days, by the end of which the family's mule-drawn and vulture-shadowed carriage has offended most of the area. It is an extreme burial plot because it is so prolonged, as if the internal logic—a logic demanding timely, reliable closure as much as a detotalizing delay—had failed, not because of incompetence but because of an unremitting environmental hostility. Faulkner makes burying the dead hard, after Joyce risks making it easy. This difficulty is part of its meaning, so that Anse,

Addie's husband, seems to relish his obstacles. A neighbor describes his unlikely appreciation for a washed-out bridge: "He set there on the wagon, hunched up, blinking, listening to us tell about how quick the bridge went and how high the water was, and I be durn if he didn't act like he was proud of it, like he had made the river rise himself" (*AILD* 114). "Kind of pleased astonishment he looked, setting on the wagon in his Sunday pants, mumbling his mouth," another elaborates (*AILD* 123). Anse himself thinks of this challenge, as it forces the family beyond pragmatic sensibility and social etiquette, as an interpretable sign from God: "We drove all the rest of the day and got to Samson's at dust-dark and then that bridge was gone, too. They hadn't never see the river so high, and it not done raining yet. There was old men that hadn't never see nor hear of it being so in the memory of man. I am the chosen of the Lord, for who He loveth, so doeth He chastiseth" (*AILD* 111). And this theological interpretation of hardship, with its license to defy social custom, is what informs the preacher Whitfeld's thought as he tries to make his way to the Bundren house before Addie dies: "I heard that Tull's bridge was gone; I said 'Thanks, O Lord, O Mighty Ruler of all;' for by those dangers and difficulties which I should have to surmount I saw that He had not abandoned me; that my reception again into His holy peace and love would be the sweeter for it" (*AILD* 177–178). In lengthening the burial plot beyond all reason, until it threatens with its intolerable delays (and stench) to unravel the larger communal narrative (and hygienic standards) it interrupts, Faulkner suggests that the modern corpse is an opening in the secular that allows for the imaginative and emotional reconstruction of the divine.

The ancient burial plots that provided themes and models for Joyce and Faulkner all involve the gods, either in the rhetoric of human characters or as characters themselves, suggesting that burial obligations are an important way for imagining the divine, and a point at which concepts of the human are complicated by concepts of the divine.[59] Aphrodite and Apollo protect Hektor's body from Achilles's abuse, and Zeus finally influences Achilles to return Hektor to Priam. In Deuteronomy 34:5–6, as the Israelites approach the Promised Land, we read: "So Moses the servant of the LORD died there, in the land of Moab, at the command of the LORD. He buried him in the valley in the land of Moab, near Beth-peor; and no one knows his burial place to this day."[60] That God buries Moses is intended as a great honor; that nobody can visit his grave suggests, according to tradition, a rejection of idolatry, and that the Torah should instead be the destination of his survivors' pilgrimage. It is a kind of textual gravesite (one reminiscent of Oedipus's secret grave in *Oedipus at Colonus*). The relations among the living, the dead, and the divine become more obscure in *Antigone*, and they take an explicit twist in

Luke 9:57–60, as Jesus is gathering disciples: "To another he said, 'Follow me.' But he said, 'Lord, first let me go and bury my father.' But Jesus said to him, 'Let the dead bury their own dead; but as for you, go and proclaim the kingdom of God.'"[61] In this instance, when the divine does not impose, but rather nullifies our obligation to tend to the dead, we begin to anticipate the ethical ambivalence—if not confusion—of *As I Lay Dying*: Addie's family, transporting her corpse by mule cart for almost ten July days across rural Mississippi, is both obeying and outraging the gods. The elemental forces that function as the novel's articulation of the divine both aid the Bundrens and persecute them, making them suffer for their commitment to a divine law that they cannot fully discern.

Faulkner uses the burial plot as a hiatus in which the boundaries between the human and divine, secular and religious, are indeterminate, open for renegotiation. Death, especially in a time of its legal, medical, and economic transformations, puts these categories in play. Toward the beginning of the novel, an aging Dr. Peabody visits Addie, who is still barely alive. He tells us:

> I can remember how when I was young I believed death to be a phenomenon of the body; now I know it to be merely a function of the mind—and that of the minds of ones who suffer the bereavement. The nihilists say it is the end; the fundamentalists, the beginning; when in reality it is no more than a single tenant or family moving out of a tenement or a town. (*AILD* 43–44)

The first explicit point here—that a death is more than a body's biological extinction, that it needs the bereavement of the living to be death as such—becomes in the second sentence a more complicated positioning between religion and secularism, and a rejection of both these ways of thinking for his own exercise in metaphor-making. Yet it is not simply a metaphorical turn, not simply an exercise in figuring death: Dr. Peabody reproduces the tension between secularism and religion by creating a tension between the literal and the figurative, a tension created by the phrase "in reality it is no more than" with which he introduces his metaphor of the tenement and town. It is what we might call a "metaphorical realism," a self-conscious attempt to invest metaphor with the authority and value of the real, to supplant the real with our own analogies while simultaneously acknowledging their status as nonliteral. Death's unrepresentability requires such ambivalent gestures in a struggle for meaning within the neither/nor logic of the corpse's liminality, and we can understand this ambivalence as a tolerance for what Eric Sundquist describes as the absurdity of the corpse's liminality between what it is and what its analogies are: "What the book poignantly exposes is the precarious nature of

ritual expression, particularly that of funeral rituals, in which an absurd possibility—that the corpse of the person nonetheless *is* the person—is maintained not
because anyone believes it but because no one can immediately, emotionally deny
it."[62] The identities of the dead are a profound, and profoundly unstable, rhetorical
construction.[63] This unresolved combination of or collision between the literal and
figurative returns us to the ambiguous role of the divine in human death and the
obligations that attend it: we can consider Dr. Peabody's rhetoric as the unsettling
of thought that tries to translate the unreadability of the divine into the secular,
that tries to domesticate the alterity of the gods as we and others die. The interlude
during which a community converts a body's perishing into a culturally intelligible death through burial rituals is also a period in which our thought of finitude
itself is unsettled, oscillating between literality and metaphor, the secular and the
divine. The dead body challenges us to refigure our own finitude without effacing
it, to put it into circulation in a community's metaphorical economies.

Economies of the Corpse

> He [Priam]... lifted back the fair covering of his clothes-chest
> and from inside took out twelve robes surpassingly lovely
> and twelve mantles to be worn single, as many blankets,
> as many great white cloaks, also the same number of tunics.
> He weighed and carried out ten full talents of gold, and brought forth
> two shining tripods, and four cauldrons, and brought out a goblet
> of surpassing loveliness that the men of Thrace had given him
> when he went to them with a message, but now the old man spared not
> even this in his halls, so much was it his heart's desire
> to ransom back his beloved son.
>
> —Homer, *The Iliad*

As I Lay Dying has fifty-nine short chapters narrated by fifteen different characters. Deep in the middle of the work, Addie, who has died several days before,
gets her own chapter for the only time. Narrating from no locatable time or place,
one of the first things she tells us is: "I could just remember how my father used
to say that the reason for living was to get ready to stay dead a long time" (*AILD*
169). Her suggestion that death is not the cancellation of life but its purpose and
fulfillment, and that we might give death a duration with which to measure life,
is unsettling in the same way that Nietzsche's transvaluation in *The Gay Science*

is unsettling: "Let us beware of saying that death is opposed to life. The living is only a form of what is dead, and a very rare form."[64] But Faulkner complicates Nietzsche's ontological reversal with a question about what it might mean to "get ready" for death, about how and why one might prepare for it when the living are merely an aberration, even a mutation, of an almost entirely inorganic universe. What about living is a preparation for staying dead? What would it mean not to stay dead after death? What does it mean for a community to have its dead become either more or less than dead? And what arrangements between the religious and the secular, the metaphorical and the literal, can establish modern forms of value and meaning for the dead?

We can consider these questions about the terms by which we relate death and the dead to the living as economic questions—not just as the kind of financial question involved in Priam's bartering for Hektor's corpse, but as questions about the modernization of a community's various systems of equivalence and exchange. We might understand these two quotations as attempts to establish terms of equivalence between life and death, to overcome their incommensurability with some process of mutual valuation. The fact that Faulkner and Nietzsche so completely reverse the priority of life over death, assimilating the concept of death so radically to life that death actually replaces it (really, negating its own negation), reveals the volatility of the dead in our processes of equivalence and exchange. As I Lay Dying is fundamentally about this disruptive volatility of the dead, as well as the ethical importance of such disruptions to the narrative, symbolic, and financial systems by which the living make coherent psyches and communities. Addie's corpse is the novel's principle of narrative distortion, as Cash suggests: "The animal magnetism of the dead body makes the stress come slanting, so the seams and joints of a coffin are made on the bevel" (AILD 83). Faulkner makes narrative on the bevel, slantwise to the rationality of the modern, which excludes the dead from its calculations of value. The very fact of Addie's impossible chapter, narrated from beyond (or within, or toward) the grave, violates ontological boundaries as well as a diegetic boundary that structures the novel's narrative economy and maintains coherence. Addie's chapter is all the more striking a diegetic transgression because, as far as we know, we have not gone to Hades to retrieve her body; it is as if Hades has returned it to us until we properly tend to it. As a principle of simultaneously ontological and narrative distortion, Addie's corpse is, as Erin Edwards writes, "radically uncertain; it is known not through visual inspection but through anoptic penetration—a blind, often grotesque familarity with an ambient corporeality, which reformulates all corporeal and subjective possibilities in the novel."[65] This insight, that Addie's corpse both resists rationalized knowing under a scientific

gaze and reformulates the experience of self of those around her, whom she saturates with her strange presence, helps account for the narrative incommensurability of her chapter. It warps the narrative line, and narrating subjects, throughout.
This warp is the effect of an irrational, yet irrefutable, obligation to a dead person
that both is and is not the same as her dead body.

In the long interlude between her perishing and burial, Addie's entire family is
steeped in a strange metaphorical economy for understanding her absence, emotionally and imagistically substituting her with various object attachments—the
culmination of what André Bleikasten calls the novel's "demon of analogy."[66] The
most striking of these substitutions is the one-sentence chapter of Vardaman,
Addie's youngest child's: "My mother is a fish" (AILD 84). Faulkner is also explicit
about Vardaman's older brother Jewel: "Jewel's mother is a horse" (AILD 101).
Cash, the carpenter of the family, has implicitly replaced Addie with the coffin he
makes as she dies, and at the end of the novel, on the very day of Addie's burial,
her husband marries the woman from whom he borrows the shovel to dig Addie's
grave. Each character has "a shape to fill a lack" (Addie's own phrase), as if providing a collective analogical restitution for her absence (AILD 172). Faulkner depicts
a communal dynamic in which the quasi-absence of an unburied corpse generates a surplus of metaphorical presences, the exchange and negotiation of which
constitute a collective process of mourning. We might call this form of mourning for Addie defensive: it is an effacement of her, a dissolution of her absence
in a chain of whatever is available, translating her charismatic nonpresence into
positive terms that will not threaten the exchange values that give a community its
economic coherence.[67]

Faulkner more starkly introduces the tension between economic logic and ethical obligation before Addie dies, when Darl (another son) and Jewel must decide
whether to leave Addie's bedside for a day to take a three-dollar job hauling wood.
It is an undecidable situation ("I mislike undecision as much as ere a man," Anse
says about it). Darl is certain that they will miss Addie's death if they go, and this
will be painful for the family, including Addie ("'But if she dont last until you get
back,' he says. 'She will be disappointed'"). Yet Darl is equally certain that they
need the money to make the burial journey (AILD 17). With this decision between
making money and tending to or attending the death of the other, Faulkner is
not simply opposing marketplace value to ethical value; he is imagining their
co-implication, the way we might fund one with the other or, put more extremely,
the way ethics exists for the very purpose of being strategically sacrificed to the
marketplace. This situation embeds the question about the relation between marketplace and ethical values in a question about the value of time. While labor time

is a rationally valued commodity, the value of the moment of a person's death cannot be rationally calculated, cannot be given an exchange value for the market. This is the moment that is at stake. Faulkner registers the market irrationality of this moment of death in the chapter's irrational narrative structure. When Darl, far distant from Addie's deathbed, perceives and narrates the scene, it is as if the unique quality of this time collapses space. He narrates as someone present at or involved in the fatal moment: "She looks at Vardaman; her eyes, the life in them, rushing suddenly upon them; the two flames glare up for a steady instant. Then they go out as though someone had leaned down and blown upon them" (*AILD* 48). Darl's impossible access to the death of his mother is a violation of the novel's narrative economy, a warping of narrative logic under the irrational pressure of an ethical obligation to the dead that cannot be translated into economic terms.

Darl shows the outer limit of these financial and metaphorical economies around the death of the other, the point at which a more severe demand interrupts these processes of substitution and exchange. In a crucial passage that I also discuss at the beginning of this book, he participates in these processes to the point of his own psychic unraveling, collapsing the metaphorical and the real in a barely intelligible attempt to apply them to the experiences of being and nothingness:

> In a strange room you must empty yourself for sleep. And before you are emptied for sleep, what are you. And when you are emptied for sleep, you are not. And when you are filled with sleep, you never were. I dont know what I am. I dont know if I am or not. Jewel knows he is, because he does not know that he does not know whether he is or not. He cannot empty himself for sleep because he is not what he is and he is what he is not. Beyond the unlamped wall I can hear the rain shaping the wagon that is ours, the load that is no longer theirs that felled and sawed it nor yet theirs that bought it and which is not ours either, lie on our wagon though it does, since only the wind and the rain shape it only to Jewel and me, that are not asleep. And since sleep is is-not and rain and wind are *was*, it is not. Yet the wagon *is*, because when the wagon is *was*, Addie Bundren will not be. And Jewel *is*, so Addie Bundren must be. And then I must be, or I could not empty myself for sleep in a strange room. And so if I am not emptied yet, I am *is*.
>
> How often have I lain beneath rain on a strange roof, thinking of home. (*AILD* 80–81)

Buried in these contorted conjugations of being and time, in this simultaneous amplification and disintegration of a subjectivity, is a fantasy of the circuits of exchange of being itself, of some ontological transmission across a family or community, each member confirming or canceling the others in a sustained and traceable network of presence and absence. In this ontological co-implication, in which being is not immanent within the individual subject but shifts among subjects ek-centrically and ek-statically, Faulkner conjugates being out of the Heideggerian formulation that frames *Being and Time*:

> The being whose analysis our task is, is always we ourselves. The being of this being is always *mine*. In the being of this being it is related to its being. As the being of this being, it is entrusted to its own being. It is being about which this being is concerned.[68]

Heidegger conceives of Dasein "in accordance with the character of *always-being-my-own-being* [*Jemeinigkeit*]," ontologically self-contained as a discrete, autonomous instance of being.[69] It is a powerful idea for the way it gives us a dramatic relation to the simple fact of our own essential and nameless presence, and to the defining finitude of that presence, but it comes at the expense of recognition of the essential and nameless presence of the other, of being as it also is in alterity. Faulkner in his rough way opens this ontological closure, giving Darl the language to imagine being as it might be held in common, held without attachment or containment, held only as one fails to hold water.

The thirst for being is not simply one's own thirst:

> When I was a boy I first learned how much better water tastes when it has set for a while in a cedar bucket.... And at night it is better still. I used to lie on the pallet in the hall, waiting until I could hear them all asleep, so I could get up and go back to the bucket. It would be black, the shelf black, the still surface of the water a round orifice in nothingness, where before I stirred it awake with the dipper I could see maybe a star or two in the bucket, and maybe in the dipper a star or two before I drank. After that I was bigger, older. Then I would wait until they all went to sleep so I could lie with my shirt-tail up, hearing them asleep, feeling myself without touching myself, feeling the cool silence blowing upon my parts and wondering if Cash was yonder in the darkness doing it too, and been doing it perhaps for the last two years before I could have wanted to or could have. (*AILD* 11)

Darl's sexual awakening is folded into a more elusive prior one, into his intuition of the obscure fact of being itself: the elemental fullness of the black night, the silent stirring of light on water evokes the restless knowledge of one's own finitude and creates what I imagine as the conceptual space where ontology can emerge in thought. But even this Heideggerian ontology registers an excess, a complication

in the being it claims. Darl hears in the night's silence the other silence of the sleeping bodies, and his darkness is not so private as to exclude the possibility that Cash
shares it. He is stirred by an ontological awakening to others as well as to himself,
a way of inhabiting being that opens the possibility of community.

Community and Mortal Obligation

If it sees its fellow-being die, a living being can only exist outside itself.
—Georges Bataille, *Oeuvres Complètes*[70]

Faulkner tests the modern burial plot through an elusive idea of community in the face of modernity's atomization of life into individual claims of
self-possession. This investigation of modern community depends upon an
ability to vividly imagine a complex ontology of self that exceeds itself by gathering its ability to die from those with whom one achieves a life. If Joyce complicates the ontology of the living by affiliating it with a sense of contingency
among the dead and never-born, Faulkner complicates it with a sense of its
communality, by which one's dying is not simply one's own, and by which the
death of the other is a foundational experience of the self. (In my discussion of
Barnes, I will argue that she takes up this importance of the other's mortality
to the self in terms of non-normative sexuality.) More than an exploration of
the sociological intuition that a social group, if it is to be coherent, must share
deathways—although it is also this—Faulkner's most consequential exploration
is into Françoise Dastur's philosophical speculation that "we are open to the
world only because we have a relatedness to that nothing which is death."[71] If we
are to think our openness to the world, to the horizon of others in which we are
intelligible as a self, through our mortality, then our mortality becomes an element in the circuits of exchange that Darl imagines in a strange room, beneath
a strange roof. One's body is mortal, not before itself but before others. Butler
writes about how our "passion and grief and rage, all of which tear us from ourselves, bind us to others, transport us, undo us, implicate us in lives that are not
our own, irreversibly, if not fatally. . . . This disposition of ourselves outside ourselves seems to follow from bodily life, from its vulnerability and its exposure."[72]
The dying and dead body, not for-itself but a question or demand for every
other self around it, must be touched, tended, held, carried; other bodies must
give this failing or failed one whatever its culture will allow it to retain of its
presence. A corpse is a communal refraction of being, to the extent that genuine

community is still a possible way of being together. For Faulkner, the corpse in its strangeness is the sign of this ontological surplus, this out-branching and entanglement of mortal being across a community. In a series of crucial insights into Addie's death, Eric Sundquist explains that

> it is important here to distinguish literal from figurative death, for the book's title—its adverb capable of being construed as *while, how,* or even *as if*—endorses the fact that Addie's death as it is experienced (one might speak of the phenomenology of her death) occurs over the course of the book and in relation to each character, thus rendering the distinction both necessary and hazardous. The title contains this possibility, moreover, by intimating an elegiac past tense where the collected acts of individual memory (the speaking "I" of each narrator) are disembodied and merged with the dying "I" of the mother, and by playing on the colloquial use of *lay* as an intransitive verb, so as to blur further the distinction between past and present events, a blurring sanctioned and exacerbated by the mixing of narrative tenses among the book's fifty-nine chapters. The action of the book occurs, that is, as Addie *lies* dying and as she *lay* dying, with each narrative "I" participating in the dissolution of her "I" by reflecting and partially embodying it.[73]

Her death is shared and scattered, which Faulkner represents through the narrative fragmentation of time and perspective in a burial plot about an "I" that lies dying across a community. Narrating this radically communal way of dying is the purpose of Faulkner's formal innovations. Sundquist claims, in fact, that the novel's form embodies this mortal experience, that "*As I Lay Dying* is best understood...as a book in which death is the story and the story is a death, a book in which the authorial 'I' also lies dying"—a claim that Edwards echoes by describing Faulkner's writing as "possessed by something of a 'becoming-corpse,' which can be understood neither as an absence nor as a predictable decomposition."[74] And Sundquist correlates the novel's radical form to this dispersed, saturated communality of dying:

> It is in the action of grief, the refusal to let go those connections that once formed an integral self, that most painfully attests to the illusion of identity upon which our notions of self are founded. The "I" that lies dying, then, is the "I" of Addie and it is not; it is the "I" of each family member and it is not.... These paradoxes have their perfect analogous expression in the narrative form of the book, which both insists upon and yet prohibits our

imagining that the fragmentary, disembodied episodes are—or to be more exact, *were once*—connected to the body or self of a story presented by a single controlling narrator.[75]

Faulkner crafts a literary correlate to the dying-with that, in a line of thought that cuts against the social logic of markets and liberal individualism, constitutes community as the organization of the ontological surplus of the corpse. Edwards observes this literary correlation at the level of novelistic character: *As I Lay Dying* "insists on the discreteness of character in assigning each section to a different speaker, even as the unity of characterological body as a reliable 'container' of subjectivity is continually undone."[76] This undoing of a naturalized autonomy of discrete selves is the beginning of community.

Jean-Luc Nancy investigates the possibility of this thought in *The Inoperative Community*, in which he conceptualizes community as something other than a gathering of discrete individuals in "inconsequential atomism" sustained by "the metaphysics of the absolute for-itself," that is, by the logic "of being as ab-solute, as perfectly detached, distinct, and closed: being without relation" (*IC* 4). Nancy shows that the idea of absolute, self-contained, unrelated being is incoherent: the absolutely separate must somehow also contain its separation; the "separation itself must be enclosed," "the closure must not only close around a territory...but also, in order to complete the absoluteness of the separation, around the enclosure itself" (*IC* 4). He claims that ontological self-possession is undercut by the very seam of self-enclosure, which, at its outer edge, remains exposed to the other. Any ontological self-enclosure that is alongside others is not absolutely alone: "To be absolutely alone, it is not enough that I be so; I must be alone being alone—and this of course is contradictory" (*IC* 4). Nancy claims that it is impossible to be alone being alone because one is only alone in relation to some other from whom one is separated. This relation, even as a relation by and in separation, makes an absolute for-itself impossible; it "tears and forces open...the 'without relation' from which the absolute would constitute itself" (*IC* 4).

Nancy finds in this rupturing of the subject's immanence, in its irreducible ontological relationality, the definition of community. Community, for Nancy, is the undoing of absolute immanence, "*the being-ecstatic of Being itself*" (*IC* 6). This "being-ecstatic" is not ecstasy in its most common sense, not "effusion, and even less some form of effervescent illumination," but ecstasy in the sense of the Greek *ekstasis*, "standing outside oneself" (*IC* 6). Nancy's concept of community does not refer to a collection of individuals bound by social contracts—community is not society—but to a more radical condition of originary "sharing" that presents "to me my birth and my death," and therefore "my existence outside myself" (*IC* 26). In other words, community

> is constituted not only by a fair distribution of tasks and goods, or by a happy equilibrium of forces and authorities: it is made up principally of the sharing, diffusion, or impregnation of an identity by a plurality wherein each member identifies himself only through the supplementary mediation of his identification with the living body of the community. (*IC* 9)

This idea of the self's supplementary mediation by every other self—a mediation by which birth and death do not simply happen but are given to the self from beyond it—is fragile, difficult; community "has still not been thought" and involves "an experience—not perhaps, an experience that we have, *but an experience that makes us be*" (*IC* 26). The recalcitrance of this idea of community to thought and experience, Nancy suggests, gives it part of its power. By resisting us, it summons a move outside of the self and, in this passage, into knowledge of the self's finitude.

Community is where this knowledge is shared and where it "shares us," where death is not self-contained or individual; it is "a place from which to surmount the unraveling that occurs with the death of each of us—that death that, when no longer anything more than the death of the individual, carries an unbearable burden and collapses into insignificance" (*IC* 26, 1). The individual's death, in Nancy's idea of community, is not simply the cessation of the individual. Nor is it the transcendence of individual death in some sublation of the individual into the ongoing collective. Rather, the death of the individual brings everyone to death, exposing our shared finitude in "the presentation to its members of their mortal truth" (*IC* 15). We are in community to the degree that we die *along with* the dead. As Sundquist suggests above, this is one way to understand the indeterminacy of the "I" of the novel's title, a word occupied by fifteen different narrators, as an indetermination of the locus of dying.[77] Sundquist captures how "each of the Bundrens participates in the journey as he or she participates in the dying of Addie; each journeys and each dies, and in doing so testifies to the continued integrity of the dead mother, memorializing the passing of the body by expressing the emotional ties that continue to compose the self."[78] This indetermination, or communal dispersal, is also a way to understand Darl's condition by the novel's end. He eventually finds his family's system of metaphorical substitution, with which Addie's absence is absorbed into a chain of equivalences, intolerable enough to burn down the barn where her coffin is being kept one night; his resistance to this play of metaphorical substitution is why he says, after she dies, "I cannot love my mother because I have no mother" (*AILD* 95). Her corpse is saved, retained as a part of the economy he has come to dread, and he is taken to an asylum. One of his last thoughts is a wish for release from this communal system of exchange of and around the dead: "If you could just ravel out into time. That would be nice. It would be nice if you could just ravel out into time" (*AILD* 208). It is a wish for self-dissolution in the presence of the death of the other, a desire for a radically communal response to the dead that would not be assimilated to the immanence or economies of the living.

Time and the Death of the Other

Faulkner works through the idea that ritualized attention to the dead, in the extremities of obligation, disorients modern temporality. Victor Turner, in his anthropological study of the liminal, describes how "we are presented, in such rites, with a 'moment in and out of time,' and in and out of secular social structure, which reveals, however fleetingly, some recognition (in symbol if not always in language) of a generalized social bond that has ceased to be and has simultaneously yet to be fragmented into a multiplicity of structural ties."[79] Faulkner's narrative renders being as it is both in and out of time and, like Darl, seems to want to temporally unravel time's modern ideological form as a quantifiable, linear sequence through clearly demarcated and causally linked past, present, and future. It seeps into other dimensions of experience, as when Darl describes the cart's movement toward a junction in the road: "We go on, with a motion so soporific, so dreamlike as to be uninferant of progress, as though time and not space were decreasing between us and it" (*AILD* 107–108). This substitution of time for space further confuses the spatial collapsing, described earlier, in the narration of Addie's death-moment. The confusion between time and space in these passages is a slippage between the subject's interiority and exteriority: Darl's private sense of time, suddenly externalized as publicly perceivable, suggests the precarious boundaries of his subjectivity, the fluid limits of his interiority. We can consider this precariousness as an effect of the unburied corpse's proximity and its demands upon the living—not simply a demand for burial, as a practical action, but a demand that the living achieve some new experience of selfhood that accounts for the radical alterity of the dead. It is a demand for a restructuring of sovereign self-identity as an ethical subjectivity bound to others and forged in difference. In this sense, raveling out into time would be the ethical subject's phenomenological experience of the death of the other.[80] We can feel this estrangement of the subject's temporality, as if under an untranslatable demand from the dead other, in Dewey Dell's unraveling thought: "I heard that my mother is dead. I wish I had time to let her die. I wish I had time to wish I had. It is because in the wild and outraged earth too soon too soon too soon. It's not that I wouldn't and will not it's that it is too soon too soon too soon" (*AILD* 120).

Faulkner more clearly associates ethical responsiveness with such a disruption to standardized time when the family comes to a flooded river after the bridges have all washed away and must cross with cart and coffin. It is one of the novel's strangest images, which Darl narrates:

> The river itself is not a hundred yards across, and pa and Vernon and Vardaman and Dewey Dell are the only things in sight not of that single monotony of desolation leaning with that terrific quality a little from right to left, as though we had reached the place where the motion of the wasted world accelerates just before the final precipice. Yet they appear dwarfed. It is as though the space between us were time: an irrevocable quality. It is as though time, no longer running straight before us in a diminishing line, now runs parallel between us like a looping string, the distance being the doubling accretion of the thread and not the interval between. (*AILD* 146)

Imagine time not as a line but as a spiral looping outward: it approaches Nietzsche's idea of eternal recurrence or Yeats's images of history's gyres, endless repetition ahead of what is endlessly behind. "Every pain and every joy and every thought and sigh and everything unspeakably small or great in your life must return to you, all in the same succession and sequence—even this spider and this moonlight between the trees, and even this moment and I myself."[81] Faulkner's subtle, but crucial, difference in his rendering of this idea of repetition is to make it an issue not of Nietzschean will and vitality but of an ethical stance toward the dead: by carrying Addie through this river, the family inscribes mourning and mortal obligation into the idea of eternal recurrence and opens within it a pointedly anti-Nietzschean ethical dimension. Tull notices, a few minutes before, "When we were on the bridge Anse kept on looking back, like he thought maybe, once he was outen the wagon, the whole thing would kind of blow up and he would find himself back yonder in the field again and her laying up there in the house, waiting to die and it to do all over again" (*AILD* 137). It is the eternal recurrence of our encounter with the unburied, waiting corpse, and the endless re-enactment of our dissolution before it.

Modernism is a site of this impossible, endless re-enactment. Now that we have carted even our dead into modernity, this writing is one of the few realms in which they can still lay claim to our impatient, distractible fidelity. This claim is based on our shared finitude, on the dying-with that is made possible within

Nancy's community, and here the one bearing mortal obligation answers to the other with his or her own life as time falls in moments without duration, exterior to every sequence. The immanence of Heideggerian ontology and the temporal closure of Nietzschean eternal return are both distorted in the material presence of the unburied corpse: these thinkers cannot contain the ethical obligation to the corpse in their economies of being and power. The corpse can be buried but not contained. Faulkner insists that we are still a part of its death because it cannot bury itself.

3. The Erotics of Mortal Obligation in Eliot and Barnes

> Nothing can make us certain that we are in fact loved, since we cannot live in the minds of others as they feel towards us. Like the belief in love, the belief in death is a fiction that we learn to trust, and in this sense our deaths and our mortality are premised on our trust, on our ability to inhabit fictions as realities, on our faculty of intense and detailed unreality, on our capacity to exist in nonexistence. Death limits our fictions, but only because it is generated by them. It is a product of a more fundamental aspect of our nature—our ability to live what is not. And we live that which is not through other people. Fiction is shared.
>
> —Jonathan Strauss, "After Death"

Sexual reproduction and erotic pleasure have been latent concerns of earlier chapters, particularly in discussions of biopolitics and the pleasure of narrative suspense. These discussions at times implied what I argue here, that the modernization of the body's mortality is implicated in modern categories of sexuality. T. S. Eliot and Djuna Barnes—whose unlikely friendship has been underappreciated in modernist literary history—imagine in unprecedented ways the speculative terrain where twentieth-century experiences of mortality meet sexuality, a terrain crossed at awkward angles by philosophy, psychoanalysis, and queer theory. Eliot and Barnes met (as I discuss below) when Eliot edited and published *Nightwood* with Faber and Faber. Even as a part of a personally asymmetrical editorial transaction, itself taking place within a generally male-dominated social order, Barnes established herself as a significant figure in Eliot's literary, and even personal, life. Their frequent letters over many years were uncharacteristically affectionate. She sent him food packages from New York while he endured postwar rations in 1940s London. He paid the storage fees for things she had left there, and her photograph was displayed prominently in his office next to those of his wife, Yeats, Valéry, and Groucho Marx.[1] If she abdicated significant editorial control of *Nightwood* to him in 1936, he nevertheless embraced her as a potent figure within the contemporary landscape of experimental writing; he calls her, in his letter of July 23, 1945, the greatest living genius.[2] This may sound like a friend's attempt at flattery, but it also suggests that he found something, in certain moods, so preternaturally beautiful in *Nightwood* that he considered it a defining limit point for the possibilities of modern literature. Andrew Field also reports that "immediately after *Nightwood*, Barnes began to write poetry. Eliot told her that he wished he could write prose as well as she and gently threatened to give her a black eye if she persisted in writing poetry."[3] I claim that in their writing they do indeed fall into an argument, even if they share a sense that mortal obligation in the modern world is a queer enterprise.

I describe this argument between them in what are probably the most speculative or theoretically ambitious readings of this book; my difficulty in understanding how sex and death interact in some ethically consequential way has driven my interpretations into strange rooms. I try to show how Eliot and Barnes meet on ground where questions of existential obligation and erotic desire make sense of one another as equally vital aspects of the human and equally volatile aspects of the modern. In this encounter, Eliot and Barnes suggest, sex and death radicalize one another in ways that put familiar social forms and identities at risk. It is a risk that has to do with both radical ethical responsiveness and *jouissance*, Levinas and Lacan, and that which is at risk is the subject at home in the sexual and ethical norms of modernizing cultures. If Eliot is seeking to establish this home, one with enough rooms for both one's lovers and one's dead, Barnes insists on the impossibility of this project and condemns it—the social assimilation of modernity's dying and dead—as an illusion undermined by its own ineradicable queerness. This chapter, ultimately, is about how the problem of the other's death is an erotic problem. Eliot and Barnes imagine mortal obligation at the heart of desire, and as the principle of its queering.

The Future of Death in the Present of Love

We have at every moment the potential to die and, culminating with Heidegger's *Being and Time*, this potential has frequently been conceived in the West's philosophical tradition as that which individualizes and authenticates a human life, the single potential that no interpersonal relation can complicate or dissolve, since no other person can fulfill this potential on our behalf. Only I can fulfill my immanent potential to die, the one potential that, because it irrefutably thwarts all my projects and ways of being-in-the-world, forces me to cultivate meanings for my acts, in more or less anxiety, with an awareness of their inevitable futility.[4] This immanent and constitutive self-thwarting, this negation that is precisely of and within oneself, this complex involvement in one's own mortality—who would deny, once in the sway of this philosophical tradition, that this is a ground for human being, for the full formation and experience of self? Who in the lineage of this thought would deny that dying, which is underway in every moment of living, is the untrackable destiny of a life, the unnarratable epic of being-there, and that it is in our unique consciousness of mortality that we can come to feel the strange unlikeliness of the positing of our presence at all? Who would leave mortality— despite its recalcitrance to thought, because of its recalcitrance to thought—out of a fundamental account of human subjectivity?

Yet this thought of my death is not enough. The strangeness of my being, as mine, is not exhausted by my own dying. Other people die prior to me; others are mortal alongside me. My deepest involvement with others exposes to me their potential to die in every moment, and it may help us conceptualize the relationality of mortality, the uncontainable surplus of this fundamental potential, by considering human death as a dying-*at* and dying-*toward*, a finitude in others that is given to them and animated as theirs by my soliciting presence. We bear the other's dying before we bear our own, as a way to bear our own. Heidegger is of course right to say that nobody can die for me, but my mortal self-possession— what Strauss calls "the coercive ideology of mortal self-identity"—is derived from an originary transaction with the mortal other, with dying in its alterity.[5] The epic of human finitude begins in the terrain of the other's dying, which I traverse before I can know my own. We only "encounter" our own death because, as Levinas writes, "we encounter death in the face of the other."[6]

And yet this shift to the mortality of the other, in the wake of Levinas's ethical critique of Heideggerian ontology, is still not enough to describe how we are involved in one another's dying. The pitch of modernist formal experiment and ethical interrogation that concerns me in this chapter goes through and beyond Levinas's characteristic range, into the problematic of erotic desire. In the epigraph above, Strauss approaches the unknowability of death through the mystery of the other's love, an analogy based on the way each demands that we inhabit our fundamentally enabling fictions with others. In this chapter, I examine the other side of this dynamic, reversing its terms: the way we gain access to love, as a uniquely bracing desire, by engaging the mystery of the other's death, and how this access was imagined at a moment when the social experience of mortality was being fundamentally reorganized. "It is a point of resemblance between love and death, far more striking than those which are usually pointed out, that they make us probe deeper, in the fear that its reality may elude us, into the mystery of personality" Proust writes in *Swann's Way*, overlaying the other's death on our desire, and complicating the mystery of other minds with that of the other's death. Baudelaire makes the association more visceral in "Carrion" by graphically describing a corpse found by two lovers, causing the speaker to exclaim, "You will come to this, my queen, / after the sacraments, / when you rot underground among / the bones already there," so that her death is inscribed in their erotic bond.[7] After many incarnations, the perennial association of eros and thanatos takes on yet another meaning as death is modernized around the turn of the twentieth century.[8] Eliot, in *The Waste Land*, and Barnes, in *Nightwood*, represent the ethical stakes of the West's modernization of deathways in terms of the erotics of mortal obligation, the implication of another's dying in one's ability to desire, to lust, to sexually want or need. A sense of mortality as an organizing principle of sexuality and an element of erotic relation will reveal, as we read, the way in which an ultimate commitment to the other in his or her dying, to the dying of the other, is that which structures a libidinal network that resists the modern effacement of the dead from our lifeworlds. Death, as we know, is the whispered implication of sexual processes. We have at every moment the potential to die, and culminating in the antic, spellbinding rhetoric of *Nightwood*, which we will approach through *The Waste Land* as the text that it takes up and completes, this constitutive potential expresses itself as the erotic affirmation of another's immanent self-negation.

Levinas tentatively approaches this thought of the encounter with the other's mortality as an erotic affirmation, a desiring response to the other's potential to die: the self emerges in its singularity in ethical response to "the nakedness of the face" of the other "and its mortality. It is there," in the other's mortal nakedness, "that the concern for the other's death is realized, and that 'dying for him' 'dying his death' takes priority over 'authentic' death. This future of death in the present of love is probably one of the original secrets of temporality itself and beyond all metaphor."[9] This radical binding to another—this "present of love"—falls beyond even metaphorical representation and animates with its vanishing the enigma of time because it is ultimately a binding to a lack, to a dying, to no future whatsoever: the "future of death" is not a positive possibility for the relation but the possibility of negating the relation itself. It is the possibility of the other's impossibility, to adapt Heidegger's terms for authenticity to Levinas's for alterity. Levinas suggests a phenomenology of love based on the affirmation of the other as one exposed in mortality, a vertiginous encounter in the present with the other's death in the future, and in this sense of vertigo it is an encounter temporalized beyond the eternal present tense of an isolate first person.[10] Eliot and Barnes help us understand this vertigo—of temporality, of being in its metonymic chain toward death—as the mobile pulsion and frisson of desire. They seek in their innovations of technique to remap the currents of erotic pulsion across their modern worlds, as if desire had grown weightless that did not carry as its ultimate referent the dying, the corpse, immanent in any binding to another.

Lacan can also help us begin to track this thought of the erotics of mortal obligation, which he approaches from the other side, as it were, beginning not with the obligations of ethics but the fact of desire. Engaging with desire is at the heart of any philosophy of the good, for Lacan; in his seminar of 1959–1960, *The Ethics of Psychoanalysis*, he describes ethics not as the pursuit through moral reason of a sovereign and ideal good, which is in the Freudian scenario a function of the redirecting of libido into the superego's punitive authority, but the pursuit of the Real as it is the barred object of desire. Lacanian ethics, in other words, involves "an erotics that is above a morality" and entrance "into the zone in which [one] pursues his desire." Lacanian ethics is ultimately based on the question: "Have you acted in conformity with the desire that is in you?" (*EP* 84, 304, 314). He goes on to write, "From an analytical point of view, the only thing of which one can be guilty is of having given ground relative to one's desire," and this is why "the whole analytical experience is no more than an invitation to the revelation of his desire" (*EP* 319, 221). Turning the universal law of Kantian ethics on its head, and swerving from a Levinasian transcendence of ego in response to the exposure of the other, Lacan approaches obligation as a disquieting engagement with the alterity of one's drives, with the force of one's animating and unrepresentable desires, at the cost of the subject's stable identifications and commitments. Lacanian ethics pursues desire not for the sake of its satisfaction in a state of "psychological normalization" and "harmonization" but for the cultivation of a nonsatisfactory experience of the mobility of a desire that never rests in any final signifier and therefore never betrays its vital connection to the unsymbolizable Real (*EP* 302). The subject's duty is not to acknowledge desires in order to satisfy them but to live them as the movement of an inner alterity, means without ends, interrogations of its claim to being.

Desire is in this recalcitrant symbolization affiliated with death, the final term for its movement beyond pleasure. Lacan, mapping the deathward valence of *jouissance*, is influenced by Heidegger as well as Freud to the extent that the demand to engage the alterity of desire becomes a demand to know one's ongoing dying. "The function of desire must remain in a fundamental relationship to death. The question I ask is this: shouldn't the true termination of an analysis...in the end confront the one who undergoes it with the reality of the human condition?" (*EP* 303). The aspiration of psychoanalysis is to achieve "the state in which man is in that relationship to himself which is his own death" (*EP* 304). At issue, beyond the phenomenology of desire, is the enigma of the death drive, one of the most opaque and contested concepts in psychoanalysis. For Lacan, this drive is a function of the subject's existence in a world of signifiers and concomitant death of the Thing that results from the transformation of being into signification.[11] The Lacanian subject, structured by the negation of the Real that produces the symbolic field, desires limitlessly and beyond pleasure to its own negation; the emergence of the death drive as an aspect of the symbolic generates "a fundamental discordance of forms,...an abyss or...fault that prevents any centering of the ego in an imaginary unity."[12] It is the ethical project of psychoanalysis to know this discordance at the heart of the self's libidinal network, the negation of life and time that is held perpetually in abeyance by the symbolic apparatus.

I argue that Barnes tells neither Lacan's nor Levinas's story about ethical responses to mortality, simply, but complicates each with the other: not the force of the self's death drive, but a drive involving the other's death; not ethical responsibility for the mortal other, in a pious wish, but an erotic response to the other's mortality. Barnes represents desire as the phenomenological register of mortal obligation, the felt experience of being bound to the other in his and her dying, which becomes a dying at and toward the ethico-erotic subject, who solicits and receives it. The dead, increasingly excluded from modernized social practices and relations, are made ethically consequential for Barnes in the undercurrents of our libidinal networks, which find erotic forms for binding to the mortal other. In "Function and Field of Speech and Language," Lacan begins to shape this thought of desire as a recognition of the other in the context of death: "It is in effect as a desire for death that he affirms himself for others; if he identifies himself with the other, it is by fixing him solidly in the metamorphosis of his essential image, and no being is ever evoked by him except among the shadows of death."[13] It is a psychoanalytic approach to this thought of obligation to another's dying: the evocation of the other depends upon an erotic attunement to a shared mortality.

Eliot and Barnes provide competing visions of the political function and social legibility of these erotic forms that bind us to one another's mortality, and as ethical thinkers we need to commit to one or the other. *The Waste Land* is a poem about the arduous recuperation of the dead for a world in which they are becoming aesthetically obsolete, religiously impotent, culturally irrelevant; *Nightwood* is about the volatile excess of mortal experience and obligation to the modern social and political forms that would use them, and therefore about the ways that a legitimate ethics of mortality renders phenomenologies and social articulations of self formally incoherent, socially dangerous, and politically obscure. The dead, and the mortality that makes us dead, can be modernized as productive elements of the emerging social order, or not. Either prospect is terrifying. The social effacement of mortality is a fundamental repression, a painful exclusion of a defining dimension of human being, yet the accommodation of death to the modern social sphere—as an efficient byway for capital, the state, and medical authorities—can be considered an even worse violation of what it is to be human. Adorno takes the latter stance, describing the modernization of death as its degradation: death's "dignity used to resemble that of the individual....Death was the absolute price of absolute value. Now it shares the ruin of the socially defunct individual." Which is to say, our modern dying shares the marketized alienation of our living, so that the "radical replaceability of the individual makes his death practically—and in utter contempt—revocable."[14] Adorno's point is that it is exchangeable, replaceable, and, in terms of its social meaning, indifferent, "no more than the exit of a living creature from the social combine," a confirmation of "the absolute irrelevance of the natural organism in face of the social absolute."[15] This idea of a new quality of mortality, which Adorno identifies as already causing anxiety at the beginning of the century in the works of Kafka and Rilke, trivializes the force of death, reducing its power to fit the exchangeability and quantification of the market: "If the individual whom death annihilates is himself nothing, bereft of self-command and of his own being, then the annihilating power becomes also nothing, as if in a facetious application of Heidegger's formula of the nothing that nihilates."[16] Barnes, responding to this stark assessment, writes death as an impasse in representation, an instability in value, unintelligibility and rupture at the level of the social, and irony at the level of rhetoric, conceptualizing death as that which—if it is to be a force in our lives at all—must not be a recognizable part of modernity's homogenization and instrumentalization of life. It is death in the shadows, opaque to the meanings by which we come to organize our common worlds. Unlike *The Waste Land*, Barnes's novel refuses broad principles of social inclusion and reform for the radical possibility of death itself, death without norms, and the ethical force mobilized by mortality to disorient the homogenization and alienation of death in a normative order.

Normative mortality, non-normative mortality: these are semantic echoes of sexual categories, which allow us to hear the debate between Eliot and Barnes as one about the queer nature of death obligations, about the queerness of the erotic forms for this binding to the death of the other. In response to a fundamental sexual ambiguity in Eliot's poem, Barnes represents the dead and dying as the queer element—the unintelligible remainder, the energy askew—of the economies of desire that sequester the dead from the living in modern lifeworlds. The association of queerness with mortal obligation in these texts is very different from a traditional, homophobic association of homosexuality with death as simple negation of life;[17] to say that ethical responsiveness to the mortality of the other takes erotic forms, and specifically queer erotic forms, is to say that these ethical relations are non-normative in a modernizing world, and that queer subjectivity is a structure of self involved ethically with alterity. In their different ethics of representation and social inclusion, Barnes and Eliot anticipate a debate within queer theory about the accommodations of queerness to the norms that grant social intelligibility. *Nightwood*'s forbidding, recalcitrant rhetoric registers modern obligations at the limit of ethics: these obligations, felt profoundly enough, are an ethical abyss, without content or substance, a refusal of all positive social meanings. For Barnes, mortality is the uncontainable irony of modern social being, meaningless and disruptive of all projects. It is not her point in *Nightwood* to integrate the dead with the living or even to lament that this is nearly impossible—Eliot's two goals—but to work through the way that a commitment to the dying of the other violently ruptures the symbolic field. If, for Eliot, the dead are cultural orphans that need to be repatriated in order to relieve us of our own historical orphanhood, for Barnes our most ambitious ethics is to refuse the potentially instrumental violence of this repatriation, the potentially belittling domestication of this homecoming. For Barnes, in other words, the dead are modernity's futureless orphans, and in our dying so are we.[18]

Flaming Tongues

In late May 1936, as he was in the process of shepherding *Nightwood* through a difficult editing and publication process at Faber and Faber, Eliot visited Little Gidding, the site of a historically significant Anglican church that had been home to a devout religious community in the seventeenth century. Eliot had formally converted to Anglicanism almost ten years prior; his influential introduction to Barnes's novel, which he would write in the months following his visit to the church,[19] approved of her depiction of suffering with a theological suggestiveness, attuned in particular to its quality of deathliness: "All of us, so far as we attach ourselves to created objects and surrender our wills to temporal ends, are eaten by the same worm" (xv).[20] In section V of "Little Gidding," the long poem he later composed that makes up the last of his *Four Quartets* and which explores the meaning of this unique religious site that he had visited while dealing with Barnes, Eliot explores the life of the dead and the dying of the living:

> Every phrase and every sentence is an end and a beginning,
> Every poem an epitaph. And any action
> Is a step to the block, to the fire, down a sea's throat
> Or to an illegible stone: and that is where we start.
> We die with the dying:
> See, they depart, and we go with them.
> We are born with the dead:
> See, they return, and bring us with them. (*CP*, 208)

Eliot describes an ontological Möbius strip, a seamless and ongoing passage between lives which have always already died and the dead which, through the sheer force of double negation, birth life. Everything in our life is inscribed with our death, Eliot suggests, since dying is not an event but a basic condition. At the same time the dead cannot remain dead for the reanimating germ that they bear in an ongoing deliverance of new life. Each is replete with the other and achieved through the other, dialectically, so that the difference between them is merely the provisional one between stages of a cycle or formal one between the hours that pass during day and night. The living die, the dead live, and what first matters is the sense of reclamation and return between the two states, which disarticulates our individual identities and gathers us into a community across mortal lines.

The community has a sort of language, but one that is irreducible to the symbolic, outside the phenomenological theater of meaning. Earlier in "Little Gidding," Eliot writes:

> What the dead had no speech for, when living,
> They can tell you, being dead: the communication
> Of the dead is tongued with fire beyond the language of the living. (*CP*, 201)

Eliot conceives of life as the period of rhetorical frustration before the eloquence of death, an eloquence that has passed through the symbolic and been transmuted into a second order of unmediated contact with the Real, of a nonsymbolic fire-intensity, but one that encompasses both a first simplicity of infantile nonlanguage and its symbolic mediation. The eloquence of the dead, Eliot suggests, unifies the symbolic and Real, or makes the symbolic an immediately material, corporeal experience; it is language that speaks being without speaking about it. He evokes a sense of this achieved interpenetration in the final lines of "Little Gidding," with a return to the same flaming tongues:

> And all shall be well and
> All manner of thing shall be well
> When the tongues of flame are in-folded
> Into the crowned knot of fire
> And the fire and the rose are one. (*CP*, 209)

In the stripped-down, repetitive self-gathering of these final words, which settle into themselves as a tautology that finally reaches its own premise, we can think of the unification of fire and rose as that of language and Thing, the symbolic and the Real. It corresponds for Eliot to the interpenetration of the living and dead, as if the Thing had been resurrected by and within the symbolic function that murdered it. Eliot's flaming tongues speak the eloquence of language that has recuperated its origins in human mortality; we are eloquent because we die—we can be especially eloquent about this fact, as if this mattered—and relate to death as humans because of our faculty for language, itself a kind of death. Lacan proposes "a profound relationship uniting the notion of the death instinct to the problems of speech": that which is "before the serial articulations of speech" and "primordial to the birth of symbols," he writes, is "in death, from which ... existence takes on all the meaning it has." Language, the symbol which "manifests itself first of all as the murder of the thing," carries this negation within it, the sign of which is "the eternalization of [the subject's] desire."[21] Donna Bentolila López explains that "the meaning of death in psychoanalysis is inextricably bound to the human servitude to the world of language," a servitude by which the subject, according to Shoshana Felman, incorporates "death in language, *in order to survive*" as a linguistic subject.[22] Eliot imagines (as Lacan does not) a postmortem, postsymbolic "language" that brings the symbolic field out of its differential logic, its constitution in lack, to a condition of metaphysical plenitude and perfection, replete with final presences, self-imbued and total. It is a language not as meaningful but as metaphysically saturating, no longer in time or a function of death because it has been subsumed by grace. It is the structural irony of Eliot's poem—its motivating frustration—that it must use mortal language to evoke a language so beyond it. Only the language of the living can tell the living about the inflamed eloquence of the dead.[23]

Barnes uses her own image of a flaming tongue to suggest a different nexus of death and language. At the end of *Ladies Almanack* (1928), a gleeful satire of lesbian culture in Paris in the 1920s that preceded "Little Gidding" by fourteen years, she depicts the cremation and final rites of her widely mourned protagonist, Dame Musset:

> And when they came to the ash that was left of her, all had burned but the Tongue, and this flamed, and would not suffer Ash, and it played about upon the handful that had been she indeed. And seeing this, there was a great Commotion, and the sound of Skirts swirled in haste, and the Patter of much running in feet, but Señorita Fly-About came down upon that Urn first, and beatitude played and flickered upon her Face, and from under her Skirts a slow Smoke issued, though no thing burned, and the Mourners barked about her covetously, and all Night through, it was bruited abroad that the barking continued, like the mournful baying of Hounds in the Hills, though by Dawn there was no sound, And as the day came some hundred Women were seen bent in Prayer.[24]

Barnes gathers ritual death practice, linguistic contact with the dead, and the erotic under a queer sign; she ends *Ladies Almanack* with the idea that the dead are good sex, a site of intense pleasure as an alterity that can be engaged in the social and political margins of queerness. Not only does queerness survive death, but in doing so becomes the ironic slippage of death back into life, giving the very orgasmic thrill of life to the living. ("We die with the dying: / See, they depart, and we go with them," Eliot writes. According to Barnes, first we come with them.) Modernism is made strange by the possibility it intuits of an erotic form for a recuperative attunement to the ongoing dying of the other and the lingering eloquence of the dead; and the erotic form for doing so is queer. Dame Musset's tongue burns with a crematory fire that does not consume it: this is a figure for an articulation that does not finish a process of accruing to meaning, never sheds its captivating sensuousness for captive sense, and this power to hold the semantic and social order in abeyance for such an affective intensity queers the modern meaning of mortality. The dead, queered, are the uncontainable irony of the lifeworld that would master them, disruptive of the entirety of the social, so that even a group of women bent in prayer are in the same moment both religious and profane, sexual profanation doubled precisely as a sacred gathering.[25]

The Waste Land, I: Deathways in Linguistic Refraction

The Waste Land, a profane world on the verge of abandoning its search for the sacred, is also a burial ground with erotically fraught relations between the living and dead. It is a burial ground in the sense of its archival function, as a citational repository for the literary corpus of the West, and more explicitly in its scattered imagery of dead bodies, as if these were another order of allusions, not to the literary history we still possess but to its sites of exposed decay after our failures to tend to it properly. It is in this unsettled and unsettling distribution of corpses across the poem's fragmented grounds that the viability of knowing the sacred is at stake. The secularization of the West has correlated with the modernization of its deathways more than has been acknowledged—the institutionalization and medicalization of dying; the simultaneous privatization and state regulation of corpses, with the resulting technical specialization of the labor of caring for them; the appropriation of corpses for medical training and scientific research; the de-ritualization of mourning. To claim that a decisive trajectory of Western secularization lay along the rationalization and disenchantment of dying and corpse disposal is to imply a crucial function for literature, in its stance of cultural critique and ethical resistance: that it develop new forms, compelling in a secular age, for the traditional cultural authority and affective charisma of the corpse; and that it reimagine, in immanent and material terms, an economy of obligation between the living and dead. Eliot takes this up in *The Waste Land* as a project of recuperating the eloquence of our dying in the language that binds us, anticipating the inarticulable eloquence that he later imagines for the dead in "Little Gidding." Early interpretations of *The Waste Land*, guided by Eliot's own notes to it, explained its allusions to ancient fertility and rebirth rituals embodied in the grail legend and fisher king, themes explicitly involving resurrection of the dead (and typically read in terms of the "spiritual death" of Western civilization, even as Eliot himself rejected this reading). But *The Waste Land* is also an attempt to encounter dead people in the materiality of their deaths, not to resurrect them but to make death itself intelligible in cultural spheres that had increasingly effaced dying and dead bodies—and thereby a definitive ethical dimension—from social relations and practices. Christine Froula has observed, "If we can extrapolate from some of its contemporary reviewers, *The Waste Land*'s early audience would seem in fact to have recognized and instituted the poem as a monument in part out of a need to mark the real graves of real bodies."[26] As I discuss in Chapter One, those real bodies killed in the war had not come home. Eliot's poem grasps for them.

In the way that the poem seeks to reintegrate a mortal, or postmortem, eloquence beyond the language of the living into the wastage of the modern world, it is something like Walter Benjamin's concept of translation. Benjamin suggests that the task of the translator is not to replicate a text's meaning in one's own language but to find in the text to be translated an element of "pure language," language which in its alignment with the sacred "no longer means or expresses anything but is, as expressionless and creative Word, that which is meant in all languages"—and, therefore, akin to Eliot's "communication / Of the dead" that is "tongued with fire beyond the language of the living."[27] Benjamin's figure of the translator seeks to complement this refracted instance of pure language in the text by creating another one, refracted in turn by one's own language and fitting with the original "as fragments of a greater language, just as fragments are part of a vessel."[28] The fragmentary structure of Eliot's poem—what Denis Donoghue describes as its "cry for form" that manifests "not [as] form but the desperate analogy of form, tokens of a virtual form which would still be valid if there were such a thing"—stages the process of rejoining the multilingual shards around him into, if not unity, at least coherence: "These fragments I have shored against my ruin," to the degree that they are complementary refractions of an inarticulable original Word (*TWL* l. 433).[29]

Benjamin writes that the task of gathering these refractions estranges our language from itself, for it is the translator's purpose "to release in his own language that pure language which is exiled among alien tongues" and "for the sake of the pure language" to "break through decayed barriers of his own language."[30] He quotes Rudolf Pannwitz on the emergence of this native strangeness:

> The basic error of the translator is that he preserves the state in which his own language happens to be instead of allowing his language to be powerfully affected by the foreign tongue. Particularly when translating from a language very remote from his own, he must go back to the primal elements of language itself and penetrate to the point where work, image, and tone converge. He must expand and deepen his language by means of the foreign language.[31]

The hallucinatory strangeness of many of Eliot's passages in *The Waste Land* evokes this sense of inhabitation or possession by an alien intelligence sounding its uncanny music inside Eliot's English, an uncanniness that Eliot associates with death:

> A woman drew her long black hair out tight
> And fiddled whisper music on those strings
> And bats with baby faces in the violet light
> Whistled, and beat their wings
> And crawled head downward down a blackened wall
> And upside down in air were towers
> Tolling reminiscent bells, that kept the hours
> And voices singing out of empty cisterns and exhausted wells.

In this decayed hole among the mountains
In the faint moonlight, the grass is singing
Over the tumbled graves, about the chapel
There is the empty chapel, only the wind's home.
It has no windows, and the door swings,
Dry bones can harm no one. (*TWL* ll. 378–391)

We can think of this dreamlike scene of obscure bodies and mortal echoes, as disorganized in its spatial reversals as in its paratactic temporality, as an imagistic refraction of deathways into its component parts: night's finality, mournful song, gravesite, bodily remains, the abstracted process of decay itself. Distorted, these have no clear logic or agent. In its initial image, the woman transforming her hair into a fiddle to play "whisper music," we have the same dynamic that Owen creates at the end of "Anthem for Doomed Youth": the inscription of public and shared expressions onto a solitary private body (see Chapter One). The inhuman, dislocated sense of voice throughout—from the "empty cisterns and exhausted wells," singing grass, reminiscent bells, wind—pressures the idea of human speech with another order of articulation across mortal distinctions; the eloquence of the dead haunts the language of the living (which is why language itself can be thought of as a graveyard, a repository, a living history of the dead),[32] and why Eliot earlier uses a speech metaphor to describe the drowned corpse of Phlebas the Phoenician, for whom a "current under sea / Picked his bones in whispers" (*TWL* ll. 315–316). Eliot's English is made strange, in part, because it undertakes the task of translating what has become a foreign eloquence, the obsolete grammars of dying.

Eliot begins *The Waste Land* with the section "The Burial of the Dead" as if to announce that the poem will rewrite this grammar, these modern structures of thought and feeling, to accommodate the intimacies of mortal obligation and to return the dead to the symbolic weave of the world of the living. At the end of the section, we come to the poem's most explicit burial image:

Unreal City
Under the brown fog of a winter dawn,
A crowd flowed over London Bridge, so many,
I had not thought death had undone so many.
Sighs, short and infrequent, were exhaled,
And each man fixed his eyes before his feet.
Flowed up the hill and down King William Street,
To where Saint Mary Woolnoth kept the hours

With a dead sound on the final stroke of nine.
There I saw one I knew, and stopped him, crying 'Stetson!
'You who were with me in the ships at Mylae!
'That corpse you planted last year in your garden,
'Has it begun to sprout? Will it bloom this year?
'Or has the sudden frost disturbed its bed?
'Oh keep the dog far hence, that's friend to men,
'Or with his nails he'll dig it up again!
'You! hypocrite lecteur!—mon semblable—mon frère!' (*TWL* ll. 60–76)

This anonymous mass, for whom existential passage has been reduced to commuting, die silently and alone in a parody of circulation in public space. In the first half of this verse paragraph, Eliot's language itself moves posthumously, nearly every word a single syllable to match the plodding steps of the crowd, its meter indifferent to starts and stops, its assonance generally low, a soft background groan. The speaker's anxiety about the potential fertility of the corpse in Stetson's garden is, meta-poetically, an anxiety about its literary fertility, as a source of creative generation within the poem itself, which in its posthumous state needs it, and which uses the corpse buried within it to regenerate the lines from Webster's *White Devil* (altered) and Baudelaire's "To the Reader" in *Les Fleurs de Mal*—the fragrant harvest, as it were, of this corpse's fertilization. As Michael Levenson has argued, the "opening of the poem can be seen precisely as the sprouting of a corpse."[33] The garden-corpse is the poem's own fecund ground and therefore a refusal of what Lacan calls the second death beyond the biological one, death as total disruption of regeneration because it is hostage to a death drive that is "a direct will to destruction," a drive to "death insofar as it is regarded as the point at which the very cycles of the transformations of nature are annihilated," rather than an instinct for equilibrium (*EP* 212, 248). As Barnes will not, Eliot evades this destiny of desire to "direct us to a point lying beyond every possible meaning and experience. Only this second death can rightly be called, in the most literal sense, 'ob-scene'" "insofar as it is directly attached to language itself."[34] In contrast, this corpse is still potentially fertile.[35] And beyond its function as evidence that *The Waste Land* has been fertilized by the corpses of past poems that it can claim as its authority, Baudelaire's line creates a different kind of textual slippage, not into itself but across the reader. This second-person address, the final line of "Burial of the Dead," is an aggressive interpellation of the reader into the poem's climate of ambiguous guilt and despair. We are suddenly hailed at this textual gravesite and identified with the speaker himself as someone who needs and uses what is buried there. We are hypocritical, it seems, because we have tried to deny this need.

Earlier in "The Burial of the Dead," we come to a passage of biblical tones and images, a prophetic utterance also addressed in an interpellating second person:

> What are the roots that clutch, what branches grow
> Out of this stony rubbish? Son of man,
> You cannot say, or guess, for you know only
> A heap of broken images, where the sun beats,
> And the dead tree gives no shelter, the cricket no relief,
> And the dry stone no sound of water. Only
> There is shadow under this red rock,
> (Come in under the shadow of this red rock),
> And I will show you something different from either
> Your shadow at morning striding behind you
> Or your shadow at evening rising to meet you;
> I will show you fear in a handful of dust. (*TWL* ll. 19–30)

This voice, which in its austerity seems less a product of human thought than an emanation of the empty landscape, speaks to us with an uncanny authority of our own state of knowledge: initially, of our ignorance of the roots and branches that somehow, beyond our perception, grow there; subsequently, of the brokenness and desiccation that we do know. We are not invited to ask which among these things actually exists, or how this content of our mind is delivered to us from the outside, but merely to follow the voice's subtle movements of accusation and invitation, threat and consolation, thirst and relief. Throughout, the lines feel like a promise or threat to tell us something essential about death—about our own death—that we do not yet know. Aware of this, we are subject to the simultaneously distant and intimate authority of this voice, in the sense that this voice is authoring our subjectivity, which gives us externalized images of our internal depletion: beating sun, dead tree, dry stone. If we are made thirsty by the exterior landscape, it is ultimately an interior thirst for something like a self, a certified locus of feeling and self-regard, an "I" that can gather around the mortal lament of the name "son of man." Instead of this reliable self, the speaker offers a set of shifting shadows—the shadow under the rock becoming our own shadows at the beginning and end of day—which are images of absence begetting absence, a proliferation of negative spaces. Finally, we are offered the uneasy revelation or ambiguous corroboration of the announcement: "I will show you fear in a handful of dust." In this, we are ostensibly shown an image of our mortality but, more importantly, we are shown the fragility of this kind of exteriorization or objectification of our potential to die in every moment: the image is paltry and incoherent, since the subjective experience of fear cannot reside in the parsimonious and unconscious materiality of dust. The dust can only dissipate, a metaphor for our mortal knowledge undone before our eyes. It is an image, most fundamentally, of rhetorical breakdown in the proximity of death, a breakdown that leaves us knowing only the incommunicability of our dying self, that it cannot be intelligibly represented to us. The mortality which in these lines mobilizes us as a subject cannot be a part of our subjective experience or, therefore, ethical agency. Eliot seeks to correct this, to replenish this representational system.

In the meantime, these lines provide an initial sense of a breakdown, at the level of image and trope, of the social organization of mortality. Though far less emphasized in contemporary theoretical work on the politics of embodiment, the place of mortality and mortal remains in a social order is as culturally complex and politically charged as issues involving sexuality and reproduction. That we become corpses confuses the very notion of self-possession that underwrites social identity: after death our bodies are and are not ours, are and are not us. This ambiguity shows something of the fictionality of legal definitions of identity and property. Mortality, like sexuality and the ability to reproduce, gathers discourses of moral propriety and medical expertise into their highest regulatory efficiencies. And all these bodily situations or capacities make language fraught, for they continually unsettle the discursive practices that objectify and demarcate them as a way of producing their cultural coherence. By posing the cultural intelligibility of mortality as a problem, *The Waste Land* can be read as a response to the breakdown of discursive and ritual practices around deathways in the wake of mass war, particularly, a revelation that our dying is somewhere beyond what we can now say to one another. We have lost the words for our dying, themselves lost in a kind of discursive death: "Death has become *unnamable*. Everything henceforth goes on as if neither I nor those who are dear to me are any longer mortal."[36] Amid institutional silence and the paucity of modern discourse, "the subject especially seeks to *say* death," de Certeau writes, to utter "a *speech* that articulates, on the collapse of possessions and representations, the question: 'What does it mean to *be*?' ... This is speech that *has* nothing other than the loss out of which saying is formed."[37] In modern cultures, those in which the dying one "enters a region of meaninglessness," de Certeau observes, "the dying person is prevented from saying this nothing that he is becoming."[38] The end of this exclusionary logic, a logic underway at the beginning of the twentieth century that would fully unfold after the Second World War, is an imposed silence and stillness on the final, useless, mortal nakedness of one no longer available for a productive role in a medical regime: "It is *necessary* that the dying man remain *calm* and *rest*. Beyond the care and sedatives required by the sick man, this order appeals to the [hospital] staff's inability to *bear* the uttering of anguish, despair, or pain: it must not be *said*."[39]

Toward the beginning of the twentieth century, when this mortal language (in both senses of the phrase) is still falling away, when we can begin to say with de Certeau that "death is an elsewhere," Eliot tries to register the disorienting consequences for our dying and involvement with the mortality and remains of others.[40] If death is in its unknowability a shared fiction that we have come to trust as we do those we love (as Strauss persuasively describes it), then the poem is an expression of an ethical anxiety about the trustworthiness of our shared existential fictions involving both death and the desire that animates love. This is not simply an anxiety about our own dying, but about our role in the way others die, which is a function of the erotic. Eliot, a few lines after the preceding passage, comes to another unidentifiable speaker:

> "You gave me hyacinths first a year ago;
> They called me the hyacinth girl."
> —Yet when we came back, late, from the Hyacinth garden,
> Your arms full, and your hair wet, I could not
> Speak, and my eyes failed, I was neither
> Living nor dead, and I knew nothing,
> Looking into the heart of light, the silence. (*TWL* ll. 35–41)

Between death and life, bereft in his speechlessness of any eloquence shared by the living or dead, the speaker falls out of both sexual and mortal relation. The sexual relation is a mortal relation; we ache with mortality as we ache with desire, in a struggle to articulate them with eloquence until we have spent the power of eloquence that we have struggled to gather around a sense of self. The speaker in these lines has lived through the death of his desire and is now a posthumous self, but he is unfinished in his dying because he can neither say the words for it nor hear them from another. His desire is now toward death, but he cannot desire it without another—the hyacinth girl—returned to the circuit of his desire; he needs someone else to desire him as a mortal being, which will allow him to desire his own death enough to achieve it. In this overdetermined idea of self-alienation, from both sexual and mortal desire, the other is essential in one's own dying because it is the other toward whom one dies, in a transitive sense of mortality. Eliot opens *The Waste Land*, in his epigraph, with an encounter between one who cannot finish dying and someone who has arrived as if to receive it. Translated from Petronius's

Greek and Latin in the *Satyricon*: "For on one occasion I myself saw, with my own eyes, the Cumaean Sibyl hanging in the cage, and when some boys said to her, 'Sibyl, what do you want?' she replied, 'I want to die.'" She has been granted immortality without eternal youth, an endless deterioration. Her announcement of this fatal desire is not simply suicidal—not simply the expression of a thwarted death drive—but part of an encounter and exchange with those around her, an attempt to say her dying, and it is the point of the poem that follows to receive it and discover a modern idiom for saying it back.

In his meditation on modernized deathways, de Certeau suggests the role of desire in this mortal discourse, the way an involvement with the other's mortality manifests as a nearly erotic attunement:

> To be simply *called*: "Lazarus!"—and traced by his proper name in the language of another desire, without anything proper to him, in his death as at his birth, gives him the right to it: this would be a kind of communication beyond mere exchange. In it the necessary connection of desire with what it cannot have, with a loss, could be acknowledged. To be called in that way would be to "symbolize" death, to find words (that convey no informational content) for it, to open within the language of interlocution a resurrection that does not restore to life.[41]

To be given the right to one's death in an age of its alienation: this is the function of a hailing language that, beyond anything it says, performs a symbolic inclusion of the other's mortality, acknowledging the other's dying without recompense or utility, the loss at the heart of desire. How to hail, to call into language, the other as the dying one who, as immanent loss, can respond to one's desire only in dying? *The Waste Land* develops an erotics of mortal obligation through its struggle with language and poetic form, a struggle to make modern poetry sound the depths of ethical relation into the region where mortality and sexuality are not distinct, where desire for the other is also an involvement with his and her dying. Eliot continues the unfinished business with the hyacinth girl in the poem's second section, "A Game of Chess," where we come to another couple—or the same one, years later—similarly troubled by a discursive breakdown in the shadow of death, and coming once again to the point of knowing nothing:

> "My nerves are bad to-night. Yes, bad. Stay with me.
> Speak to me. Why do you never speak? Speak.
>   What are you thinking of? What thinking? What?
> I never know what you are thinking. Think."

> I think we are in rats' alley
> Where the dead men lost their bones.
>
>   "What is that noise?"
>   The wind under the door.
>   "What is that noise now? What is the wind doing?"
>   Nothing again nothing.
>   "Do
> You know nothing? Do you see nothing? Do you remember
> Nothing?"
>
> I remember
> Those are pearls that were his eyes. (*TWL* ll. 111–125)

The bones lie at the center of this jagged conversation as a barely articulated demand for meaning and value, for translation from their simple materiality into the cultural field, and Eliot lets them linger there, surrounded by the wind and thoughts of nothing, as a kind of negation of culture. Absent other traces in the world, these bones now function, tautologically, as the traces of their own deaths; their remains are the only reference to their remains; or, more anxiously for Eliot, they are the ossified remains of the literary corpus that it is the purpose of his poem to tend to, a poetic citation decayed beyond his powers of resurrection and therefore an expression of the uncertainty that Eliot feels about his own allusive poetic procedure. The voice must finally, almost mechanically, summon Shakespeare's line from *The Tempest* to cover them with something like a poetic shroud, and such an overt exercise in high-cultural shrouding is essentially an announcement that the dead are not indigenous to the modernized world. Eliot frequently enlists Shakespeare—as if cultural capital could supplant the emergent financialization and commodification of deathways—as the great conscriptive agent for the modern dead back into cultural legibility:

> A rat crept softly through the vegetation
> Dragging its slimy belly on the bank
> While I was fishing in the dull canal
> On a winter evening round behind the gashouse
> Musing upon the king my brother's wreck
> And on the king my father's death before him.
> White bodies naked on the low damp ground
> And bones cast in a little white garret,
> Rattled by the rat's foot only, year to year. (*TWL* ll. 187–195)

Eliot's Shakespeare—his note here points back to *The Tempest* 1.2—is a force of aesthetic redemption for neglected corpses, a nostalgic evocation of a long cultural history of the imaginative acts of responsibility that have been taken on behalf of them. But *The Tempest* is hardly a play about responsibility to the dead, and the bones in these lines, as in the ones above, can articulate nothing but their eerie, exposed neglect. It is as if all their aesthetic and ethical trappings, all the figural embellishments that have been applied to corpses over so many centuries in order to give them a value in our economies of obligation, had been gnawed away by the poem's infestation of rats. *The Waste Land* stages, as complementary crises in the modernization of the West, the isolated unspeakability of one's dying and the unmeaning, tautological nakedness of human remains. These symbolic crises of mortality coincide, for Eliot, with a crisis of heterosexuality, a form of desire that forecloses ethical response to the potential of the other in every moment to die, to the corpse immanent in the other.

The Waste Land, II: Nuptials for the Dead

The sexual relation is a mortal relation: our desire can become an index of our proximity to the other's dying, so that the social organization of sexuality and mortality are correlated. Both, in Eliot's era, were undergoing a modernization easy to describe as a liberalization, a relaxing of social norms. Eliot has Tiresias, the poem's closest approximation to a governing intelligence, narrate the scene of modern sex between the typist and "young man carbuncular," with all its distraction and anomie, in a way that evokes as a kind of counterpoint an image of death in antiquity: "(And I Tiresias have foresuffered all / Enacted on this same divan or bed; / I who have sat by Thebes below the wall / And walked among the lowest of the dead)" (*TWL* ll. 243–246). This sounds something like a claim for existential authenticity, if not moral authority, reminiscent of Owen's poetry directed at civilians from the war's trenches; but here Eliot depicts a massive chronological and diegetic as well as geographical gap between the living and the dead, as if modern sex so removed from its mortal context must lose its desire and be reduced to mechanical reproduction. Tiresias summons the ancient dead as an image of what exceeds this mechanization, an auratic presence in an age of mechanical sexual reproduction that provides an alibi not just for Tiresias's privileged status within the poem but for Eliot's ambitious poem as a whole, in what he imagines as a strange quid pro quo: in exchange for representation, corpses can certify the eloquence of modern writing, granting it its superiority over mass culture. Tiresias's

Theban dead continue the work of literary fertilization begun with the corpse in Stetson's garden.

In the poem's third section, "The Fire Sermon," Eliot describes the modern world's depletion of the dead in a way that reads like a farewell to a new class of exiles or emigrants, encoding within it an erotic frustration:

> The river's tent is broken: the last fingers of leaf
> Clutch and sink into the wet bank. The wind
> Crosses the brown land, unheard. The nymphs are departed.
> Sweet Thames, run softly, till I end my song.
> The river bears no empty bottles, sandwich papers,
> Silk handkerchiefs, cardboard boxes, cigarette ends
> Or other testimony of summer nights. The nymphs are departed.
> And their friends, the loitering heirs of city directors;
> Departed, have left no addresses. (*TWL* ll. 173–181)

Spenser's refrain to the Thames in "Prothamalion," a pastoral celebration of an approaching "Brydale day," is repeated here with an antithetical meaning, as a lament that the river has lost the material traces of those who have passed, that their lives have left no legible remains for the living to re-read. Eliot shows in these lines—a catalogue of lost traces that recalls Stephen Dedalus's list of his dead mother's remaining objects: "old featherfans, tasselled dancecards, powdered with musk, a gaud of amber beads in her locked drawer"—the disintegration of the symbolic location of the dead in our lifeworlds (*U* 1.255–1.256). We should think of this homelessness of the dead as a defining quality of the modernizing West—as a crucial part of a definition of its cultural modernity—to the extent that the forwarding addresses that the dead have not left for us are still desired, sought, imagined, and forged by those at the edges of this loss, which is to say, all of us at some time or another.[42] *The Waste Land* is a reimagining of these lines of attachment within their attenuation, an attempt to re-eroticize the dead as the nymphs that once generated cultural fertility and guaranteed, for Eliot, the high-cultural aesthetic value of poetry.

Within a few lines of this dissipation of the heterosexual desire of a pastoral "Brydale day," which coincides with the disappearance of the dead, Eliot's speaker elaborates the early image of rats' alley, quoted above, where the dead men lost their bones.

> But at my back in a cold blast I hear
> The rattle of the bones, and chuckle spread from ear to ear. (*TWL* ll. 185–186)

As with his reversal of the sense of Spenser's refrain, these lines rewrite the seduc-
tive pleasure of Marvell's "To His Coy Mistress" ("But, at my back, I always hear /
Time's wingèd chariot hurrying near") into a mingling of desire and death where
Marvell had efficiently segregated the two ("The grave's a fine and private place, /
But none, I think, do there embrace").[43] Eliot rewrites Marvell to introduce the
dead into the sexual economy of the living. The recurring rats that scamper
through the poem's scattered bones take on another meaning, then, or at least can
be understood as producing another important effect. These images of rats among
the dead are appalling for the way they intimately mingle inanimate with animate
bodies, an animal quickness with a corpse's uncanny immobility, in violation of
our instinctive need (from fear of pollution, from anxieties about retribution) to
keep them separate. In his long study of Nicolas Poussin's *Landscape with a Man
Killed by a Snake*, T. J. Clark considers the similar effect of an image of a snake
twined about a corpse, its "disgusting, erotic symbiosis" that causes another in the
painting to flee in panic: "What is it that the running...man recoils...from? Not
from death pure and simple, I would say, and not just from the snake's endless,
formless liveliness, but from the obscene mixture of the two—from the way one
state feeds on the other."[44] Shifting the discomfort from sight to sound, Eliot produces a similar effect with his rats, a queasy sense of impurity or contamination,
as well as a revulsion against the appetite that binds them. But instead of fleeing,
Eliot's speakers return again and again to these rats among the dead, this morbid turbulence, and in the context of his erotic citations and allusions throughout
these lines we can consider this an erotic turbulence as well. The typical disgust
that one might feel at the thought of rats and corpses is here a poetic symptom of
an anxious desire—a desire that brings the lines to acute discomfort, as they try
so hard, amid the collapse of heterosexual norms about them,[45] not to go queer.

Recent critical assessments of representations of sexuality in Eliot's work have
emphasized the way its queer shapes and trajectories are in tension with Eliot's own
self-presentation. Colleen Lamos claims that "T. S. Eliot presents the dilemma of
an avowedly heterosexual, homophobic writer whose work is obliquely yet significantly marked by homoerotic investments."[46] Biographers—unapologetically in
opposition to Eliot's impersonal theory of poetry—have argued about the sexual
relationships he cultivated in his personal life,[47] but the more consequential discussions have been textual exegeses of the sexual imaginary in his poetry, primarily,
and letters and essays, secondarily.[48] However, in one particular case biography and
poetic imagination seem to come into close contact, a case that is also at the nexus
of sexuality and death. When Eliot studied in Paris from 1910–1911, he lived in a
pension with Jean Verdenal, a medical student with a strong interest in literature

and philosophy. Verdenal's surviving letters to Eliot, written after Eliot left Paris, reveal their affection for one another.⁴⁹ After Verdenal was killed in the war, at the Dardanelles on May 2, 1915, Eliot dedicated his first volume of poetry to "Jean Verdenal *mort aux Dardanelles.*"⁵⁰ In a short essay in *Criterion* in 1934, Eliot nostalgically revisits his time in Paris twenty-three years earlier with an effusive image of his friend: "I am willing to admit that my own retrospect is touched by a sentimental sunset, the memory of a friend coming across the Luxembourg Gardens in the late afternoon, waving a branch of lilac, a friend who was later (so far as I could find out) to be mixed with the mud of Gallipoli."⁵¹ Several critics have suggested that Verdenal's textual presence in Eliot's oeuvre extends into *The Waste Land*, and that the poem can be read as an extended elegy to his dead friend.⁵² But it is in particular the erotics of this elegiac impulse that concern us. Wayne Koestenbaum puts this in especially pointed terms: "According to Freud and Breuer, 'hysterics suffer mainly from reminiscences'; *The Waste Land* suffers from reminiscences of Jean Verdenal...There is a link between the poem's homosexual conception (Pound's sperm, Eliot's 'arse') and the poem's mourning for a dead man. The 'nuptials' of Eliot and Pound act out the poem's secret love for Verdenal." He continues: "Memories of beloved dead men induce the poem's forgetful and hysterical weaving from plot to plot and voice to voice." ⁵³ Less biographically ("We may never know if Eliot loved Jean Verdenal, nor need we"), Lamos traces the "melancholic homoeroticism" or "homo-elegiac" texture of Eliot's early poetry, which "commemorates a love for the dead"; she writes elsewhere that "homoeroticism in Eliot's poetry invariably takes the form of necrophilia, not only because it is safer that way but because homosexuality is itself seemingly fatal."⁵⁴ Consider Mr. Eugenides and the homosexual possibility he represents in "The Fire Sermon," when he, "with a pocket full of currants," proposes a weekend affair to the speaker: what precisely is the whisper we hear when we come to "Death by Water"?

> Phlebas the Phoenician, a fortnight dead,
> Forgot the cry of gulls, and the deep sea swell
> And the profit and loss.
> A current under sea
> Picked his bones in whispers. (*TWL* ll. 312–316)

An awkward echo of an insignificant word, a trace refraction, a minor linguistic gesture—but enough so that we are interpellated into at least the ruins of the poem's structure of elegiac desire: "O you who turn the wheel and look to windward, / consider Phlebas, who was once handsome and tall as you" (*TWL* ll. 320–321).⁵⁵

Eliot's interweaving of the elegiac and homoerotic, more than a sign of his sexual discomfort or association of homosexuality with death, constructs queerness as an acknowledgement of the value of dying and dead bodies in an age of their obsolescence and sequestration. Eliot's poem expresses mortal obligation in and as queer desire. This complication, or liberalization, of erotic networks to include the excluded objects of ethical attachment gives an ethical valence to the very field of the erotic; the marginalized obligations that significant strains of modernism sought to value are inseparable from their innovative representations of sexuality. Joseph Allen Boone, although without analyzing *The Waste Land*, has described in significant scope and detail the complex libidinal currents of modernism, the "perverse narrative trajectories" that "dissolve distinctions of 'inner' and 'outer'—and, along with them, the normalizing sexual categories that...this binary maintains."[56] In this textual non-normativity of desire, Boone writes, modernist texts embody a "polymorphously labile sexuality whose expressions may run in any of several directions," within "a deliberately perverse textual circuitry within whose spaces something akin to queer desire is produced and circulated."[57] To approach modernism so comprehensively as a queering of desire, as a pervasive complication and overrunning of the basic social categories that organize legitimate sexuality, is to describe resonant political meanings in the era's aesthetic innovations. These texts, Boone writes, transform "narrative form into a material embodiment of the sexually dissident, queer communities that these texts struggle to usher into the field of representation."[58] But modernism becomes strange, in part, because its dynamic erotic imaginary is also an interrogation of the processes by which deathways were being modernized, a sexual critique of this new bodily alienation from its own and others' dying. Eliot's poem dramatizes the struggle to, in Boone's phrase, usher into the field of representation our dying and involvement with the dying of others, even though this struggle is fundamentally distinct from campaigns for other forms of social freedom, recognition, and equality. The struggle for agency in deathways—the struggle to become an agent of one's own ethicality, to be subject to existential obligation—touches at crucial points the struggle to be the agent of one's own desires, but also diverges from this, even if Lacan would have us collapse the two by conceptualizing ethics as a fidelity to the irreducible mobility of one's own desire. There are non-normative forms of desire, Eliot and Barnes help us speculate, that can express fidelity to the mortality of the other. Thus, the libidinal currents that we map across the social world can recuperate our primordial ethical relations, our tending to the dead without their expropriation.

Nightwood, Eliot, and the Roaming Signifier

Barnes's *Nightwood* radicalizes, to a point of ethical extremity, Eliot's response to this potential expropriation. The novel is about the various people who fall in love with Robin Vote, an American whom we first encounter in Paris. All of the lovers are in one way or another outside the social mainstream. Early in the novel, Robin marries Felix Volkbein, descendant of an Austrian mother and Italian Jewish father, and gives birth to their child Guido. She soon leaves them for Nora Flood, whom she meets at the circus and lives with in Paris for several years, and it is this relationship that is at the heart of the novel. Despite their passionate bond, Robin has a series of affairs with other women, leaves Nora for Jenny Petherbridge, and soon leaves Jenny too. Felix, Nora, and Jenny, who remain painfully in love with her, never understand her discontent or motivation. Unfocalized by the novel's heterodiegetic narrator, she is opaque to us as well. If Robin is the unspeaking, unexplained center of the novel's action,[59] the character at the center of its discourse is Dr. Matthew O'Connor, whose voracious and often drunk speeches to and about these characters are a dizzying combination of gossip, metaphysical and theological speculation, ribald joking, implausible historical anecdote, and personal memory.[60] His large and pervasive voice, by turns mesmerizing and baffling, approximates the consciousness of the novel's world itself, and this inebriate quasi-omniscience combined with his gender ambiguity has led various critics to associate him with Tiresias in *The Waste Land*.[61] It is not surprising, then, that O'Connor is the character that Eliot most extensively discusses in his introduction to the novel. Its eight chapters take place principally in Paris, but also in Berlin, Vienna, and New York, apparently over several years in the 1920s (Barnes wrote it from 1931–1936; her relationship with Thelma Wood, on which the novel is based, was primarily in the early-mid 1920s, although she saw Thelma also during the years she was writing the novel). In her editing process, Barnes rearranged the order of the chapters several times; they hold together at only the most oblique causal and temporal axes.[62]

Eliot, as Barnes's editor, significantly affected the novel. While not the most extreme editor of her drafts—her friend Emily Coleman was that—Eliot cut about thirteen pages (about fifteen thousand words) from the final typescript that Barnes (with Coleman as energetic go-between) had submitted to Faber and Faber in 1935. In addition to these pages he deleted many other words and phrases relating to sexuality and religion.[63] Monika Faltejskova attributes many of these suppressions, which were not explicable by standard editorial procedures or fear of the censor, to "the guilt Eliot experienced as a result of his own sexual ambiguity" which caused him to be "over-sensitive to passages with homosexual content."[64] This claim, which resonates with the now established, if contested, body of commentary on Eliot's personal sexuality, is especially interesting for the way it echoes claims about Ezra Pound's similar purgation of homosexuality from *The Waste Land* about fourteen years earlier.[65] With *The Waste Land* and *Nightwood*, we have two highly articulated performances of modernist difficulty originally published only after an editorial scrubbing of socially unacceptable sexual desires, only to be republished after each author's death in their earlier drafts—Valerie Eliot's 1971 publication of *The Waste Land: A Facsimile and Transcript of the Original Drafts* (including Ezra Pound's and Vivienne Eliot's margin notes) and Cheryl Plumb's 1995 edition of *Nightwood: The Original Version and Related Drafts*. Although similar, these two cases of a return of the editorially repressed have a decisive difference in their dynamics of editorial authority, a difference that allows us to take Barnes's earlier version as a crucial object of analysis while taking Eliot's as a superseded background. While Pound was an influential personality for Eliot, he dealt with him as a friend rather than an agent of an institution. On the other hand, Eliot was was a senior editor at a major publishing house when dealing with Barnes's manuscript. Moreover, he was a formidable presence in the official literary world, a high-cultural celebrity with great critical influence, and the power of this prestige would have been nearly irresistible to Barnes. By this point, *Nightwood* had already been rejected by many publishers over several years—"no standard publishing house could take it," a Simon and Schuster editor had recently written her—and Barnes was desperate enough for publication to agree to Eliot's deletions and other suggestions.[66] Coleman recorded in her diary Barnes's description of her meeting with Eliot at which she told him "I'll take anything from you, Mr. Eliot."[67] It is safe to say that the cuts she made with Eliot were (as Plumb puts it) those of acquiescence rather than intention, so that the earlier draft more clearly shows her interest in the difficult interrogation of modern mortality and sexuality that Eliot begins in *The Waste Land*.[68]

Nightwood appealed to Eliot in the first place for its style: "The novel is so good a novel that only sensibilities trained on poetry can wholly appreciate it" because of its "great achievement of a style, the beauty of [its] phrasing."[69] While her prose is another creature than the poetry that Eliot suggests it to be, it is the meaning of Barnes's elusive, complex rhetorical technique, alarming readers sentence by sentence with their analogical, imagistic, and syntactic acrobatics, that critics have grappled with since its publication. It is not too much to say that Barnes invented a narrative rhetoric—with its signifiers roaming like Robin through the

Paris night—as much as Eliot reformed modern lyric. Karen Kaivola claims that Barnes seeks "a language capable of breaking through to the other side of culture, to its destruction."[70] Focusing more specifically on Barnes's analogies, Alide Cagidemetrio describes the novel's "continual metaphorical osmosis, a dilating of meaning through equivalences," a quality that Daniela Caselli identifies as the way "the literal refuses to work as such in *Nightwood*, which speaks in similes and 'in metaphors' because its density allows no transparency."[71] Caselli elaborates: "Critics have commented on the dizzying metaphorical substitution at work in *Nightwood*, but in the novel there is no opposition between literal and figurative meaning; the figurative…invests everything: all needs to be made sense of, nothing simply *is*."[72] It is Barnes's tendency toward profligate, ornate figuration— analogies generating analogies, nearly to this point of dissolving the ontology of the literal—that registers something inhuman, hyperbolically driven from beyond consciousness, in her language. The novel's first two sentences:

> Early in 1880, in spite of a well-founded suspicion as to the advisability of perpetuating that race which has the sanction of the Lord and the disapproval of the people, Hedvig Volkbein, a Viennese woman of great strength and military beauty, lying upon a canopied bed, of a rich spectacular crimson, the valance stamped with the bifurcated wings of the House of Hapsburg, the feather coverlet an envelope of satin on which, in massive and tarnished gold threads, stood the Volkbein arms,—gave birth, at the age of forty-five, to an only child, a son, seven days after her physician predicted that she would be taken.
>
> Turning upon this field, which shook to the clatter of morning horses in the street beyond, with the gross splendour of a general saluting the flag, she named him Felix, thrust him from her, and died. (*N* 3)

It is hard to know if this overloaded syntax is laboring to birth, as a rhetorical parallel to Hedvig's labor, or struggling to contain the metaphor that emerges late in the first sentence—"the feather coverlet an envelope of satin"—but in either case an irresistible urge-to-metaphor in this writing announces itself immediately. The metaphor itself is as slight as the newborn Felix and as gratuitous as he will prove to be in his plotless drifting; it is metaphor for the sake of nothing but the pleasure of it. Hedvig's death in birthing Felix, after thrusting him into the world where his father has also already died, is the death of descriptive literalism and novelistic realism for an orphan style.[73] The novel begins by making death simultaneous with birth, mortality an equivalent narrative principle as sexuality and reproduction, so that the novel is saturated with orphanhood at the level of both plot and style.

Boone reads *Nightwood*'s orphaned style as an expression of queer sexuality, correlating the "permanent isolation" and "outcast state" of its queer characters to "the tendency of signifiers in the novel to divorce themselves from their signifieds and become 'linguistic orphans' thrust out into a sea of uncertainty where other equally homeless, 'lost' words drift in search of an anchoring meaning."[74] More recently, Teresa de Lauretis has read *Nightwood*'s "terror of uncertain signs" (a phrase she takes from Barthes) as its inscription of sexuality as a drive indistinguishable from the death drive. Along with Caselli's attention to the novel's Gothic qualities and Erin Carlston's to its Decadent influence,[75] de Lauretis's is one of very few recognitions of the novel's stark preoccupation with mortality as a bodily capacity that shapes subjectivity. Without connecting mortality to queerness specifically, she traces "*the figural inscription of sexuality as drive,*" "a psychic force that is at once sexual drive and death drive" in *Nightwood*. Her psychoanalytic approach to "the figural weave of the text" reveals "the disturbing, spectral presence of something silent, uncanny, unrepresentable, and yet figured," a "textual inscription" of the death drive that contorts the literal in Barnes's writing into rhetorical forms that obliquely say, even as they hide, their origin in dying.[76] (And so the doctor asks, "Must I, perchance like careful writers, guard myself against the conclusions of my readers? [*N* 80].)" What Boone sees as the radical uncertainty of signifiers in the novel, as a kind of linguistic queerness, becomes for de Lauretis a radical power of reference, the rhetorical refracting and echoing of a drive both constitutive of and excluded from subjectivity.

The argument I want to make reconfigures Boone's and de Lauretis's separate insights into queer sexuality and death, which *Nightwood* asks us to conceptualize in their relation to one another, in a way that responds to the social reorganization of mortality over the first part of the twentieth century. More emphatically than Eliot, Barnes imagines queer forms for the erotics of mortal obligation while simultaneously imagining the social and psychic volatility of these obligations to modern worlds with a growing cultural illiteracy in mortality. Where *The Waste Land* undertakes repatriating the dead as an alibi for modern aesthetic and spiritual legitimacy, Barnes embraces an ethics of mortality for its delegitimating powers, for the ways it casts into doubt every social identity and relation. In this argument about the recalcitrance of mortal obligation to social meaning, I am drawing from the concept of the death drive its unsymbolizable force and affective excess, but applying it to death in its alterity, to our implication in another's dying. In this sense, we must think the obscure animation of the Lacanian death drive, as that which haunts our inhabitation of a symbolic world, alongside Levinas's concept of originary ethical binding, also as a priori to subjectivization and as non-intentional as a drive, and also that which disturbs a normative social order with an irrational demand on the subject.[77] Following Lacan's philosophy of the drive, and as a way to read Barnes, we can think of Levinas's ethical responsiveness to the other as that primordial binding which must be excluded from social relations for sociality to be possible.

Nightwood and the Curve of Dying-with

Death is *Nightwood*'s climate, the atmospheric precondition of its style, the condition that the doctor recognizes in Felix's son Guido for whom "death in the weather is a tonic to him" (*N* 107).[78] The doctor in many of his monologues is a kind of philosopher of death—"'Jehovah, Sabaoth, Elohim, Eloi, Helion, Jodhevah, Shaddai! May God give us to die in our own way!'" he pronounces, as a kind of principle of differentiation—and this is why Nora tells him, "You know what none of us know until we have died. You were dead in the beginning" (*N* 77, 125–126). Many of his reflections on death are prompted by what he observes between Robin and her different lovers. He tells Nora that "'to our friends...we die every day, but to ourselves we die only at the end. We do not know death, or how often it has essayed our most vital spirit. While we are in the parlour it is visiting in the pantry....But what of our own death—permit us to reproach the night, wherein we die manifold alone'" (*N* 82). We die alone, but our friends know our mortality better than we do; because it is a visitor we never receive properly, others help us receive it, what Derrida calls the gift of death.[79] The doctor later admonishes Nora again, even more cryptically: "'And death—have you thought of death? What risk do you take? Do you know which dies first, you or she? And which is the sorrier part, head or feet? I say, with that good Sir Don, the feet. Any man can look upon the head in death, but no man can look upon the feet. They are most awfully tipped up from the earth. I've thought of that also'" (*N* 127). It is not clear who dies first, you or she, because these deaths are intertwined, and it may be that the corpse's feet are sorrier to look upon because they are the more animal, more a piece of body without a self, and so a more troubling reminder that our love attaches to mortal flesh. Felix is also audience to the doctor's pronouncements about the mortality of what we love: "'Man is born as he dies, rebuking cleanliness, and there is a middle condition, the slovenliness that is usually an accompaniment of the 'attractive' body, a sort of earth on which love feeds'" (*N* 100). Even in its span of liveliness the body is a metonym for its own burial. It is always already dead, the doctor suggests, and love is essentially preparation for burial:

We are but skin about a wind, with muscles clenched against mortality. We sleep in a long reproachful dust against ourselves. We are full to the gorge with our own names for misery. Life, the pastures in which the night feeds and prunes the cud that nourishes us to despair. Life, the permission to know death. We were created that the earth might be made sensible of her inhuman taste; and love that the body might be so dear that even the earth should roar with it. (*N* 72)

Our lives are small instances of the earth's coming-to-consciousness, the momentary subjectivization and eroticization of the elements, which are returned in death to the earth so that it too can know what it is to be subject to the inhuman power of a drive. The doctor later makes explicit where this erotics of mortal obligation tends all along: " 'I put it in Taylor's words, "Did not *Periander* think fit to lie with his wife *Melissa* after she had already gone hent to heaven?" Is this not night work of another order also, but night work still?' " (*N* 87).[80] And this barely suppressed necrophilia is why the narrator associates Robin, the novel's center of erotic attraction, with a corpse: "The perfume that her body exhaled was of the quality of that earth-flesh, fungi"; "We feel that we could eat her, she who is eaten death returning" (*N* 34, 36).

The question Barnes poses is about the sexually queer nature of dying-with, of a night work we undertake around one another's potential to die in every moment. Death is the central term of the erotic bond between Nora and Robin: "In death Robin would belong to her. Death went with them, together and alone" (*N* 52). Nora describes her desire for Robin in mortal terms, connoting social impossibility: " 'Love is death, come upon with passion; I know, that is why love is wisdom. I love her as one condemned to it' "; " 'Robin's love and mine was always impossible, and loving each other, we no longer love. Yet we love each other like death' " (*N* 115, 116). As Robin inexplicably begins to drift from Nora, more and more frequently leaving their home for others, the narrator provides an astonishing image for the structure of Nora's feelings:

Love becomes the deposit of the heart, analogous in all degrees to the "findings" in a tomb. As in one will be charted the taken place of the body, the raiment, the utensils necessary to its other life, so in the heart of the lover will be traced, as an indelible shadow, that which he loves. In Nora's heart lay the fossil of Robin, intaglio of her identity, and about it for its maintenance ran Nora's blood. Thus the body of Robin could never be unloved, corrupt or put away. Robin was now beyond timely changes, except in the blood that animated her. That she could be spilled of this, fixed the

walking image of Robin in an appalling apprehension on Nora's mind,—
Robin alone, crossing streets, in danger. Her mind became so transfixed
that, by the agency of her fear, Robin seemed enormous and polarized; all
catastrophes ran toward her, the magnetized predicament; and crying out,
Nora would wake from sleep, going back through the tide of dreams into
which her anxiety had thrown her, taking the body of Robin down with her
into it, as the ground things take the corpse, with minute persistence, down
into the earth, leaving a pattern of it on the grass, as if they stitched as they
descended. (*N* 50–51)

Love in the first two sentences is a funerary process in which the loved one undergoes a kind of psychic burial within the self. In the third sentence, love becomes
a version of gestation: Nora maintains Robin, after this mortal introjection, with
her own blood, which because of its circulation in another circulates the other's
mortality back through the self.[81] The other's life, introjected, is also the introjection of the other's dying. Robin becomes a paradox of corpse and fetus, dead
yet precariously alive, an ambiguous figure for embodiment at the limit points
of its becoming and passing away, and this instability in Robin's being becomes
the first truth—the "intaglio," the engraved signature—of Nora's identity. In this
sense, Barnes is not interested in the Heideggerian authenticity of being-toward-
death or in its psychoanalytic cousin, the death drive, but in the possibility of an
identity formed around the dying of the other to whom one is erotically bound. In
his 1975–1976 seminar *Death and Time*, Levinas says that "it is not my nonbeing
that causes anxiety, but that of the loved one or of the other, more beloved than
my being. What we call, by a somewhat corrupted term, love, is *par excellence* the
fact that the death of the other affects me more than my own. The love of the other
is the emotion of the other's death."[82] And Barnes suggests that this love of the
other in the shadow of his or her mortality, a mortal riveting, can express itself in
an age of mortality's sequestration as a queerness able to resist this sequestration.
Nora's metaphorical transformation, by the end of this paragraph, into Robin's
burial agent and ground is also the transformation of the materiality of corpses
and burial into a purely psychic dynamic, a reimagining of subjectivity as a site for
symbolic performances of alienated material practices. As Nora later tells the doctor about Robin, "'It is only through me that she will die over and over'" (*N* 124).
As a psychic absorption of the materiality of another's dying, this image is also an
allegory for the sublimation of the deathways fading from social experience to a
purely textual level, its evaporation from the knowable world and condensation in
and as literature.

It is important to notice that, in these analogies of love with the findings of a tomb and final pattern on the grass of a grave, Barnes does not base emotional relation on a responsibility to bear memory or witness to another's life. She imagines a more obscure dynamic: Nora maintains Robin not as a life lived but *as one who is to die.* She maintains her as and in her potential vanishing, so that if there is any element of memorialization or witness here it is of the bare fact of Robin's mortality that precedes any particular experience. As I mention in Chapter One, Geoff Dyer (writing about the culture of memory and monuments after the First World War), describes a similar tensing of death in relation to soldiers on their much larger and more public scale: "*They are going to have died*: this is the tense not only of the poems of Owen (who carried photos of the dead and mutilated in his wallet) but also of photographs from the war. Although he was thinking only of photographs, both are, in Roland Barthes's phrase [in *Camera Lucida*], 'prophecies in reverse.'"[83] The difference, of course, between Robin and the soldiers, one who is to die and they who are going to have died, is the actual realization of the event of death as a present tense somewhere in this narrative. Robin, the novel's foremost death-figure, is alive throughout. Yet she is steeped in her own, and everyone else's, mortality. This potential in every moment to die is outside biography proper, unclaimable as an experience because it is the precondition of experience, equivalent to the founding negation at the origin of the Lacanian symbolic and, in another sense, to what D. A. Miller calls the nonnarratable aspect of a story: a simple equilibrium regained in death, an "incapacity to generate a story" from a lack of any lack to propel the narrative forward.[84] *Nightwood* attends to this unnarratable and nonnarratable core in characters' attempts to account for themselves. The doctor tells Nora, "I have a narrative, but you will be hard put to it to find it," and Jenny experiences a narrative blindness in relation to her own stories, which "were humorous, well told. She would smile, toss her hands up, widen her eyes; immediately everyone in the room had a certain feeling of something lost, sensing that there was one person who was missing the importance of the moment, who had not heard the story—the teller herself" (*N* 82, 59). The doctor has earlier told his listeners at a party that "death is like taking your thumb out of a bowl of soup; it *has* to leave a hole, but it doesn't," and this non-space of death (which *has* to be there, but is not) is what the narrative wraps around and must avoid to keep going (*N* 23).[85] The circumstances of someone's perishing are narratable; the mere fact of someone's mortality is too banal to be narrated; but our dying-with, the introjection of the other's death in the self as an erotic knowledge, generates narrative by quietly eluding it and driving it askew.

Barnes figures this structuring nonpresence of the other's mortality in stranger ways, at the limits of her narrative technique. The doctor tells Nora: " 'Once in the war I saw a dead horse that had been lying long against the ground. Time and the birds, and its own last concentration had removed the body a great way from the head. As I looked upon that head, my memory weighed for the lost body; and because of that missing quantity even heavier hung that head along the ground. So love, when it has gone, taking time with it, leaves a memory of its weight' " (*N* 107–108). He seems to be saying that there is a physical weight to love-memory, or that love can be felt in memory as one somehow feels the loss of one's body after death, or perhaps that our sexual memories are themselves corpselike remainders of our love in need of burial. But the point of this grotesque image is to confuse the very terms of sexuality and mortality, to drag a carcass into our thoughts of love, their suppressed referent. In their last conversation, Nora confesses to the doctor a disturbed thought she had about Robin before finally losing her: " 'Then I kissed her, holding her cold hands and feet and I said: "Die now, so you will be quiet, so you will not be touched again by dirty hands; so you will not take my heart and your body and let them be nosed by dogs—die now, then you will be mine forever." (What right has anyone to that?)' " (*N* 120). This thought of one's death as a kind of possession exchangeable between intimates—but a possession that only exists in such an exchange, never as simply one's own, a possession realized in its dispossession—takes on a similar form with Felix and his sickly young son Guido ("mentally deficient, and emotionally excessive, an addict to death") in the years after Robin has abandoned them (*N* 90). Felix confesses his mortal thoughts: " 'Do you know, doctor, I find the thought of my son's possible death at an early age a sort of dire happiness, because his death is the most awful, the most fearful thing that could befall me. The unendurable is the beginning of the curve of joy. I have become entangled in the shadow of a vast apprehension, which is my son; he is the central point toward which life and death are spinning, the meeting of which my final design will be composed' " (*N* 99). It is one thing to naively claim that after the worst, everything else veers upward, joyward, better by comparison; but it is very different to say, as Felix does, that the worst causes or structures the very possibility of joy. The death of his son is a "dire happiness," the curve of his joy, because it gives him the catastrophic destiny that his contingent life has lacked. He goes on to tell the doctor that Robin, Guido's mother, " 'is with me in Guido, they are inseparable.' " Nora and Felix wrap their lives around Robin's death, that is, around the negation of her narrative future, constructing narratives that exist to generate their own negation. This is a desperate formal response to the cultural negation of the negation that is death, a third turn of the screw: negation upon negation upon negation.

Tracking the deathward curve of joy that Felix describes, Lacan asks, "Does life have anything to do with death? Can one say that the relationship to death supports or subtends, as the string does the bow, the curve of the rise and fall of life?" (*EP* 294).[86] Barnes asks us to take this thought further, not simply that life has a fundamental orientation toward death, in the form of a drive constituted by the negation of the Real in the symbolic, but that one's life is in formative tension with the mortality of the other, and that this tension is sexual. Lacan approaches this ontological curving, or queering, again: "The drive represents...the curve of fulfillment of sexuality in the living being. Is it surprising that its final term should be death, when the presence of sex in the living being is bound up with death?"[87] Lacan is asking about the death drive of the individuated subject, but the erotic energy of this drive registers the presence of another, a partner in the circuit of desire. Is there a drive to die with the other, a fantasmatic ethical excess that haunts the clarifying, normative aspiration of ethics? Barnes, following through with an ethical possibility glimpsed by Eliot, represents this non-normative erotic attunement to the mortality of the other as the precariousness of ethics itself, a breakdown at the level of ethical binding that makes narrative curve toward its own negation.

Nightwood and the Suicide of Obligation

While de Lauretis does not make an explicit connection between *Nightwood*'s figuration of the death drive and its rhetorical and thematic queerness, Lee Edelman suggests in *No Future: Queer Theory and the Death Drive* the critical incentive for doing so.[88] In his powerful investigation into queerness as the ironic narrative thwarting of all political ideologies oriented toward the child-bearing meaning of the future, and so an investigation into queerness as the embodiment of "the social order's death drive," Edelman shows us how to read for the textual panic of our encounters with *jouissance*, "movement beyond the pleasure principle, beyond the distinctions of pleasure and pain, a violent passage beyond the bounds of identity, meaning, and law," and so into the realm of death.[89] Edelman, analyzing the ideological coercion of the figure of the Child as the sign for a "familiar familial narrativity of reproductive futurism" and its demand for social meaning and functionality in sexuality, asks if it is possible for queerness to "redefine such notions as 'civil order' through a rupturing of our foundational faith in the reproduction of futurity."[90] His vigorous linking of queerness to the social order's death drive—that is, to the revelation of "the constancy, the inescapability, of...access to jouissance in the social order itself, even if that order can access its constant access to jouissance only in the process of abjecting that constancy of access onto the queer"—is especially striking for *Nightwood*.[91] As has often been noted, its plot, similar to that implied in the fragments of *The Waste Land*, is rife with reproductive refusal and breakdown, so that Barnes's inscription of the death drive figures not only in the work's rhetorical complexity but also in its narrative structure. Boone, for example, argues that "the overall shape of *Nightwood*...—disavowing the dynamics of narrative succession—is radically nongenerative and, by implication, productively queer....Complementing this wholesale repudiation of children are all the non-reproductive adults who populate the text," which are "the absolute devaluation of the monogamous (and heterosexual) couple as the desired 'end' of love (or, for that matter, the ending of a novel)." Anticipating (without his Lacanian framework) Edelman's argument about the function of the queer, as a site of rupture by the unsymbolizable drive at the heart of the symbolic, to disrupt every social meaning and identity, Boone claims that *Nightwood* "thwarts any 'sense of an ending' that would impose final meaning on the queer desires of the sexually disenfranchised." [92] It is clear that the novel's circulation of desire baffles any social plot of reproductive futurism, just as it relishes at the stylistic level a rhetorical excess that refuses acts of socially significant discourse, but what is not yet clear is how these refusals say something about the modern subject's attenuated obligations to dying and dead bodies. What does the affiliation of queerness with the radical nonsignification and antisociality of the death drive have to do with the modernization of deathways, with the circulation of actual corpses?

There is a reading of Levinas I have avoided throughout this book—a reading I had to avoid if I was to establish anything like a coherent ethics of modernism—that takes his concepts of ethical subjectivity and primordial responsiveness to the other into the realm of the death drive, as something like a suicidal urge. Until now—until Barnes—I have approached modernism as an attempt to recuperate the value of the dead for modern economies of obligation, to rearrange cultural authority around new symbolic representations of the dead, to reanimate affective and ethical agency as it confronts the mortality of the other. And I have found this compatible with Levinas. But Barnes's novel is so inordinately strange in part because it ultimately turns against this project, refusing to make the dead modern, and in a sense refusing the equilibrium of modern subjectivity altogether. For Barnes, mortal obligation cannot be a properly *social* practice at all, but only a disruption of the social, what Edelman would call the queer refusal to reiterate the

structure of social normalization for "the ambit of future meaning" even the buried corpse needs to survive in the cultural worlds of the living.[93] There is a reading
of Levinas, in other words, in which we can conceive of the mortal relation as no
relation whatsoever, along the lines of Lacan's insistence that, in the abyss of the
signifier, there is no sexual relation. If the sexual relation is a mortal relation, then
at their ethical extremes these relations entail asymptotic dissolutions of social
meaning and the symbolic function, signs that the death of the other is nothing for
the self but a hallucination, a fetish.

Toward the end of the novel, in another startling meditation, Barnes has the
doctor proclaim to Nora, who is still struggling to endure Robin's departure, this
impossibility of relation:

> Because the lesson we learn is always by giving death and a sword to our
> lover. You are full to the brim with pride but I am an empty pot going for-
> ward, saying my prayers in a dark place; because I know no one loves, I least
> of all, and that no one loves me, and that's what makes most people so pas-
> sionate and bright, because they want to love and be loved, when there is
> only a bit of lying in the ear to make the ear forget what time is compiling.
> So I, Dr. O'Connor, say, creep by, softly, and don't learn anything, because
> it's always learned of another person's body; take action in your heart and
> be careful whom you love—for a lover who dies, no matter how forgotten,
> will take somewhat of you to the grave. Be humble like the dust, as God
> intended, and crawl, and finally you'll crawl to the end of the gutter and not
> be missed and not much remembered. (N 122)

The doctor makes abjection itself an eloquence in his unforgiving model of erotic
binding by which even a lover who has been forgotten retains a part of you as she
dies, far away and long after the sex, dispersing your ontology across the world in
a kind of mortal promiscuity. It is a more elaborately sexual version of the mortal
co-implication that Nora describes in another way: "For all of us die over again in
somebody's sleep" (N 124). We die out and about, through others, just as they die
through us, as if mutually impregnated with one another's deaths. Nora elaborates
the doctor's thought a few pages later, telling him about a time she, while search-
ing the streets of Marseilles for Robin, "stood in the centre of eroticism and death,
death that makes the dead smaller, as a lover we are beginning to forget dwindles
and wastes; for love and life are a bulk of which the body and heart can be drained"
(N 130). It is her point that our forgetting a lover slowly kills her, precisely because
we have loved her, and the implication is that every erotic encounter, save one that
never ends, begins the death of the erotic partner. But they all end. This mortal

valence of desire becomes even more complicated because, in the doctor's thought, the lover who kills you does so in a kind of mediated suicide—you have provided the sword with which to do it. This rendering of pain is a cruelty but also, in a psychoanalytic line of thought, an unnamable satisfaction. Lacan discusses Freud's horror at the golden rule, to love your neighbor as yourself, as a horror at the way it is actually a satisfaction in the cruelty involved in eros, "the fact that my neighbor's *jouissance*, his harmful, malignant *jouissance*, is that which poses a problem for my love" (*EP* 187). Imagining St. Martin offering his cloak out of neighborly love to a beggar, Lacan follows this love to its root in the drives where it responds to the other's unspoken desires: "Perhaps over and above the need to be clothed, he was begging for something else, namely, that saint Martin either kill him or fuck him" (*EP* 186). The doctor, talking to Nora, works through this difficult interpretation of the golden rule in a way that seems similarly attentive to the dangerous psychic forces lurking behind altruism, but with a crucial difference:

> Ah yes—I love my neighbour. Like a rotten apple to a rotten apple's breast affixed we go down together, nor is there a hesitation in that decay, for when I sense such, there I apply the breast the firmer, that he may rot as quickly as I, in which he stands in dire need or I miscalculate the cry. I, who am done sooner than any fruit! The heat of his suppuration has mingled his core with mine, and wrought my own to the zenith before its time. The encumbrance of myself I threw away long ago, that breast to breast I might go with my failing friends. (*N* 127)

He is not describing a drive hiding behind altruism to kill and fuck, a stark pre-social aggression, but a drive to embrace another's dying flesh with one's own and coax it along, another version of social nihilism that changes one's subject position from a site of self-possession to the site of the other's dispossession. This combination of desire and dying may be the sense of Lacan's cryptic claim for the power of "the genital act": "It is doubtless possible to achieve for a single moment in this act something which enables one human being to be for another in the place that is both living and dead of the Thing. In this act and only at this moment, he may simulate with his flesh the consummation of what he is not under any circumstances" (*EP* 300).

Is the doctor's drive to accomplish the dying of these others—not to kill them, nor to make them kill him, but to realize their being by erotically experiencing its passing—an ethics? It is worth rereading his remarkable last sentence: "The encumbrance of myself I threw away long ago, that breast to breast I might go with my failing friends." Barnes does not leave us in the realm of any socially recognizable ethics of obligation or responsibility, but in the realm of selfhood that seeks, with an erotic hunger, its dying from others. If it is something like a death drive, it is one of another sort than Freud's and Lacan's: not empty repetition, but an empty and unending guilt poured into the irreducible space between self and other, a collapse of the self into an ethical abyss. Reading Levinas closely, Simon Critchley is finally compelled to ask:

> Might one not wonder whether Levinas's ethics condemn us to a lifetime of trauma and lacerating guilt that cannot—and moreover, should not—be worked through? Doesn't Levinas leave us in a situation of sheer ethical overload where I must be responsible even for my persecutor, and where the more that I am just the more I am guilty. If so, then such a position risks amounting to nothing less than a rather long philosophical suicide note or at the very least an invitation to some fairly brutal moral masochism.[94]

Levinas's ethical temptation—obligation without object or meaning, a total eclipse of the subject by the mortality of the other—makes any practical thinking about suffering difficult. His thought reduces the self, in David Wood's phrase, to "a guilty monad scurrying out to carry out his infinite obligations, then scurrying back."[95] Furthermore, under certain lights Levinas's thought seems so extreme as to defeat its own purpose by foreclosing not just the self but the other as a real presence or person with any kind of ethical agency of his or her own. In this manner of endless dying-with, ethics as will-to-suicide, the other becomes an opportunity for self-mortification rather than a viable term in a mutual relation, the creation of which we might hold to be the most important ethical, or at least social, task. Wood asks:

> If we understand the ethical relation to the other as purely asymmetri-cal, we are establishing this relation on the same grounds, with a reversed valence, as those that allow the greatest violence. Asymmetry is just what characterizes the relation between overwhelming power and victimhood. And what worries me here is that focusing on the relation of asymmetry will distract us from thinking about those *complex forms of mutual depen-dency and interaction* which would block a simple reversal of the valence of the relation. The idea that the obligation is all mine (and mine more than others) is clearly meant to define the nature and purity of obligation. But can this not be taken to deprive the other of all capacity for moral agency? Or magnanimity? Or generosity?[96]

Levinas risks effacing the other in his claims for a pure and infinite obligation that the self bears alone.

But the extremity of Levinas's ethical vertigo, in which responsibility to the other is infinite and prior to every experience of the self because it is this being-hostage to the other which appoints the self to itself, offers the possibility—as does no other line of thought—of recognizing the force of the other's death within the economy of the subject. Our relations to the dying and dead are, of course, ruthlessly asymmetrical. For Levinas, at least, the other's death is not finally nothing, not a nothingness, which it is even if it causes us to go through a process of mourning as psychic self-reconstruction: in this economics of de- and re-cathexis, the dead other is simply a lost object to be replaced in our affective economy. Ethical subjectivity for Levinas is ethical precisely for its approach to the self as a form of valuation of the other, even in death, without translation or liquidation into other values. Barnes explores this possibility of untranslatable relation—another version of a breakdown in relation, the Levinasian relation without relation—and the damage it entails. The doctor, speaking to Nora, offers a set of images for this damage in what is probably the most bizarre extended metaphor of the novel:

> So, I say, what of the night, the terrible night? The darkness is the closet in which your lover roosts her heart, and that night-fowl that caws against her spirit and yours, dropping between you and her the awful estrangement of his bowels. The drip of your tears is his implacable pulse. Night people do not bury their dead, but on the neck of you, their beloved and waking, sling the creature, husked of its gestures. And where you go, it goes, the two of you, your living and her dead, that will not die; to daylight, to life, to grief, until both are carrion. (N 76)

These are barely readable sentences, simultaneously obscene and oracular, a kind of night algebra of the psyche's darkest mechanics. It may be worth paraphrasing their logic, as much as possible: 1) the night is a closet your lover's heart inhabits as a roosting bird, cawing and leaving droppings, in the space between you and her; 2) your tears provide the pulse, or heartbeat, of this bird, which is metaphorically your lover's heart; 3) night people sling their dead on your neck; 4) the dead one, which will not die, goes with you wherever you go until you are both carrion. There are several crucially ambiguous words in these sentences, and entire statements that make no sense, even if they make no sense in compelling ways. What does it mean that the night-fowl, the lover's heart, "caws against her spirit and yours"? What is the "estrangement of his bowels"? Who are the night people— you and the lover? Others on the margins of society? What does it mean that a corpse is "husked of its gestures" and that it will not die? The asymmetry between the reader and text—we are inordinately responsible for bringing to meaning a passage that is vulnerable to an eclipse of all meaning—mirrors the extremity of the erotic relation it evokes of one to the other's death.

Aside from Levinas's baring of the ethical import of the death of the other, Barnes confronts us with another issue. With these opacities, the unnerving effect of these sentences in their contorted affiliation of loving with dying is to make death seem both more intensely real and, at the same time, less intelligible, both more suffocating and less sensible: death becomes, in her writing, a saturating presence but a purely rhetorical construction; every life is revealed to be as much in its process of dying as it is subject to desire, but this dying is perceived to be the effect of an antic language wrought before us at its logical and analogical limits. These sentences, and so many like them throughout the novel, absorb death into the state of a hyperbolic rhetorical performance, realizing it and derealizing it in the same act, as if the social-realist or empirical experience of death had been evacuated to this experimental literary realm, its last sanctuary. In other words, Barnes's language, in its rhetorical and imagistic involutions—what Boone calls its queerness—does not represent death in some kind of referential transaction but assimilates the burden of death into itself, a language now bearing in its alienated strangeness our knowledge of mortality for us. This knowledge is no longer subjective but linguistic, a textual effect. Her language reconstructs death again and again with such an anxious erotic energy because this mode of language is the only remaining place where mortality is claimable, even if it is not claimable between subjects outside of language. The suicidal nature of ethical response to another's dying for Levinas correlates, ultimately, to an effacement of subjectivity from Barnes's amplification of the rhetorical machinery that comes to contain death on its own, the elsewhere of modern death.

If *The Waste Land* is an attempt to translate the purity of the eloquence of the dead into linguistic fragments still gatherable for use by ethical subjects in the social world they would reform, *Nightwood* is an acknowledgement that there can be no translation of the purity of the dead into the world of the living. There can only be its increasingly ornate facsimile, an entirely linguistic claim to another's mortality which is itself an entirely linguistic construction. If we imagine with Eliot the eloquence of the dead as Benjamin's "pure language," which human languages piece together fragment by fragment, we must also consider with Barnes what de Man, in his interpretation of Benjamin's essay, describes as the impossibility of translation. It is impossible, for de Man, not because of some aspect of reality that is too subtle or complex for representation in language, but because translation—like critical philosophy and literary theory—is a purely intralinguistic act that has no final reference to an "extralinguistic correlate" (which is why my paraphrase of Barnes's passage, above, is such ineffective reading, an avoidance of reading).[97] As a linguistic response to what within language is derived from the "pure language" without meaning, translation in this ideal sense undoes any meaning or reference sensible in the world beyond language in its isolation and autonomy. De Man writes that, in Benjamin's thought, intralinguistic acts like translation

> disarticulate, they undo the original, they reveal that the original was always disarticulated. They reveal that their failure, which seems to be due to the fact that they are secondary in relation to the original, reveals an essential failure, an essential disarticulation which was already there in the original. They kill the original, by discovering that the original was already dead. They read the original from the perspective of a pure language (*reine Sprache*), a language that would be entirely freed of the illusion of meaning—pure form if you want; and in so doing they bring to light a dismembrance, a de-canonization which was already there in the original from the beginning.[98]

Barnes's absorption of mortality into an entirely rhetorical dimension of being is a disarticulation of anything like mortality "itself," a revelation that our dying is not available to us beyond our stylizations of it. Eliot would have these stylizations recanonize the dead, reauthenticate origins and originality; for Barnes, these stylizations reveal that the dead no longer have a social existence with any meaning and that dying no longer takes place outside of this literary compensation, where its non-normative erotic dimension can be named.

Literature, for Barnes, is dying: not because it is perishing, but because in its modern forms it can be a sustained mode of dying, the displaced site of this bodily capacity, absorbed by this language as the social and psychic space for it diminishes in modern worlds. The literary has become, for Barnes, a place where dying lives on in a form untranslatable to other realms. It also comes at the price of this one. While Barnes and Eliot agree about a purpose of the modernist experiment—that it make us anxious about the rationalization and sequestration of death—we can also see their fundamental difference. For Barnes, this absorption of death into the literary is so complete as to thwart its generative place in a literary lineage. Where Eliot discerns an unfolding tradition and seeks to retrieve its neglected dead for his age, Barnes writes *Nightwood* as and about the end of literary tradition and the history of influence. If she takes up and completes Eliot's poem, it is in order to bring this generational dynamic to an end.

The End of Literary Inheritance

Barnes undermines the business of receiving and bequeathing, not just in her plot against reproductive futurism but in her philosophy of aesthetic tradition and creation. As is well known, Eliot in "Tradition and the Individual Talent" proposes a model of artistic creation based on a "historical sense" in which "not only the best, but the most individual parts of [the poet's] work may be those in which the dead poets, his ancestors, assert their immortality most vigorously."[99] He conceptualizes the genuinely new as the resurrection of what remains vital in the old, so that the individual or original is such only in a tradition of individuality or originality, a repeating and interconnected series of literary instances of unique contemporaneity. It is for this reason, that the dead of the tradition are the essential material that the poet knows, that Eliot admonishes the writer to "write not only with his own generation in his bones, but with a feeling that the whole of the literature of Europe from Homer and within the whole of the literature of his own country has a simultaneous existence and composes a simultaneous order."[100] In this simultaneity of literary history, the genuinely new poem reaches back to inflect the tradition that motivates it, a retroactive shaping of the literary past. The poet works to carry the dead—Stetson's ambiguously fertile corpse, Phlebas adrift in the sea—in order to write individually in the present of the living and thereby bring the present into simultaneity with the past it is retrieving.

This temporal paradox in Eliot's idea of creativity, and the challenge it sets up of achieving the stature of one's precedents and progenitors, has itself become an inevitable part of the critical tradition and intellectual history, widely influential and reiterated in, for example, Bloom's theory of influence anxiety.[101] This temporal aspect of Eliot's essay has proven particularly compelling to readers in two ways: it gives the writer the possibility of retroactively affecting a source tradition by adding a strong poem to it and it allows readers to imagine literary history as a coherent and organized field, dynamic but totalizable. These seductions fail with Barnes. Her first resistance to the idea of a creative economy of influence and originality, in which the present intensifies its experience of itself by passing through whatever remains alive of the past, is that it resembles a kind of structuralism, a systematic determination of each of its elements in relation to one another. She seeks an intensification of another sort. In his essay on tradition, Eliot writes that "no poet, no artist of any art, has his complete meaning alone. His significance, his appreciation is the appreciation of his relation to the dead poets and artists. You cannot value him alone; you must set him, for contrast and comparison, among the dead."[102] This evaluative gathering is at the same time a reduction of the writer to the function of literary relations. As Paul Morrison argues, Eliot's essay bears a "family resemblance" to structural linguistics in that it "reduces all concrete human utterances to the manifestation of possibilities already latent in an 'ideal' structural paradigm. Structure is 'complete' before the 'supervention of novelty'" and therefore "works toward the 'conformity' that is the assimilation of the new to the structural determinants of an 'ideal' order."[103] If Eliot's model of the new within a tradition organizes the intelligibility of literary merit with a nearly architectural grace, it does so at the expense of a certain kind of integrity of what might not be relative to other elements in a structure; he has no way in this essay (as Christian theology will later provide him) of describing the intelligibility of a value or quality that is absolute, a fact in and of itself. Further, he has no way of considering what might be distinct about the final iteration of a series, the moment that brings a tradition to the crisis of its finality. Barnes complicates Eliot's thought with both possibilities.[104]

In the first place, she describes Nora in terms of a quality beyond comparison, an intensity outside of any system of mutually defining intensities, a singular self-manifestation:

> She was the only woman of the last century who could go up a hill with the Seventh Day Adventists and confound the seventh day,—with a muscle in her heart so passionate that she made the seventh day immediate. Her fellow worshippers believed in that day and the end of the world out of a bewildered entanglement with the six days preceding it; Nora believed for the beauty of that day alone. She was by fate one of those people who are born unprovided for except in the provision of herself. (*N* 48)

To imagine the *absolutely* seventh day, isolated from all others and not needing six previous days for its identity, is to imagine the sudden rupture of the unconditioned within the sequential and causal, but a rupture that must awkwardly retain the name of one in the sequence. If Eliot suggests that the arrival of the seventh day retroactively constructs the previous six days as parts of a week, Barnes argues that the arrival of the seventh day negates the earlier days altogether to make itself the only genuine day that has happened, even if its name contradicts this premise and seeks to resignify itself. This force of absolute arrival is in Nora's heart, the apocalypse of her passion. She is a figure for socially unmediated desire, the transcendence of desire in its mimetic and derived social allocations that René Girard so thoroughly describes as the background for influential literature: "The great novelists reveal the imitative nature of desire. In our days its nature is hard to perceive because the most fervent imitation is the one most vigorously denied.... The romantic *vaniteux* does not want to be anyone's disciple. He convinces himself that he is thoroughly *original*," which is to say, he convinces himself that he desires without influence by others even though such influence is determining.[105] Girard's description of the "true hierarchy of desire" in which "an ego [is] powerless to desire by itself" within its system of mediations, reflections, and influences is homologous to Eliot's structuralist model of aesthetic creation, in which each creative act is a function of the relations among those already existing.[106] Barnes is equally discontent with both claims; she has the doctor criticize Jenny, Nora's opportunistic usurper for Robin's affection, as a figure for this model of relational identity and derivative desire: "'Having a conviction that she is somehow reduced, she sets about collecting a destiny—and for her, the sole destiny is love, anyone's love and so her own. So only someone's love is her love. The cock crew and she was laid—her present is always someone else's past, jerked out and dangling'" (*N* 83). The narrator corroborates: "Her walls, her cupboards, her bureaux, were teeming with second-hand dealings with life.... Someone else's marriage ring was on her finger; the photograph taken of Robin for Nora sat upon her table. The books in her library were other people's selections"; "The words that fell from her mouth seemed to have been lent to her"; "When she fell in love it was with a perfect fury of accumulated dishonesty; she became instantly a dealer in second-hand and therefore incalculable emotions" (*N* 58–59, 60).

In her critique of the structuralist problematic of inheritance, tradition, and influence, Barnes is not turning to a naïve originalism or ideology of self-determination. She imagines the heart's passion as a nonrelative quality, absolute and without determining context, because its non-normative involvement in the other's death is not a function of any system of social identities, responsibilities, or tasks. Even if the erotic response to the mortality of the other has nothing to do with a claim to self-authorship in one's desires or creative acts, it is still unconditioned by precedent or expectation. If anything, it is conditioned by a vivid intuition of the mortality of the other, an intuition foreclosed from normative social relations in modern deathways. Barnes suggests that it is the other in his and her dying who authors this nonrelative, nonderivative quality of a heart's desire that, in an antinomian breach of social order, "makes the seventh day immediate." In the long passage discussed above, in which "love becomes the deposit of the heart, analogous in all degrees to the 'findings' in a tomb," Barnes makes the heart a figure for this involvement with the death of the other, and she frequently elaborates this figure of the heart as the sign of that which is not determined by any system in its proximity. In addition to being a philosopher of death, the doctor is a theorist of this antinomian organ: "'The modern child has nothing left to hold to, or to put it better, he has nothing to hold with. We are adhering to life now with our last muscle—the heart'" (*N* 38). It is the self's last remainder because it is of a different order than the rest of us, irreducible to a general bodily system. He later promises: "'What an autopsy I'll make, with everything all which ways in my bowels!... [M]y heart that will be weeping still when they find my eyes cold'" (*N* 85). The heart, as our point of contact with the mortality of the other, is a mournful truth outside of a tradition, a radicalization of truth, more force than knowledge. The doctor, after one of his stories, offers a moral: "I tell you, Madame, if one gave birth to a heart on a plate, it would say 'Love,' and twitch like the lopped leg of a frog" (*N* 22–23). It would say love at the pitch of the antinomian grotesque, the heart gone too queer for social assimilation. Desperate for Robin to return home from her night wanderings, Nora seeks to compel her "by the very velocity of the beating of her heart," the incommensurate aspect of herself that can claim erotic knowledge of Robin's mortality (*N* 54). The heart, as strange in Barnes's thought as death because of its non-adequation to any set of determinants that would explain it, is not the function of an individual talent arriving through a tradition, but an aberration and violence, the sign of an unrepeatable and uninfluenced dying-with. The most potent aspect of the individual—the nexus of sex and death, desire as it wraps around mortality—is not derived from tradition and does not add to it.

Barnes uses Felix as a figure for adherence to tradition, and we can read him as a subtle parody of Eliot's system for historically constructing cultural value. Felix has an "obsession for what he termed 'Old Europe': aristocracy, nobility, royalty," largely because of his exclusion from it, so that "he hunted down his own disqualification, re-articulating the bones of the Imperial Courts long forgotten... He felt that the great past might mend a little if he bowed low enough, if he succumbed and gave homage" (*N* 9). "'To pay homage to our past is the only gesture that also includes the future,'" Felix tells the doctor, who later elaborates it with a sense of historical disjunction and absurdity: "'In the old days I was possibly a girl in Marseilles thumping the dock with a sailor, and perhaps it's that memory that haunts me. The wise men say that the remembrance of things past is all that we have for a future, and am I to blame if I've turned up this time as I shouldn't have been?'" (*N* 38, 77). Felix—who takes his rooms "because a Bourbon had been carried from them to death," as if inhabiting the death rooms of the aristocracy leant one their prestige—wants a son from Robin to continue the line, but their son Guido is born ill and can provide no generational future (*N* 9). When he is an infant, Robin nearly murders him: "One night, Felix, having come in unheard, found her standing in the center of the floor, holding the child high in her hand as if she were about to dash it down, but she brought it down gently" (*N* 44). When she repeats this gesture of generational cessation with the doll that Nora gives her, it is more strange, a repetition of a refusal to repeat. Nora tells the doctor: "'She picked up the doll and hurled it to the floor and put her foot on it, crushing her heel into it; and then, as I came crying behind her, she kicked it, its china head all in dust, its skirt shivering and stiff, whirling over and over across the floor'" (*N* 122–123). Barnes makes the form and content of the repetition contradict each other, a desire to end generation and inheritance itself generating a series of acts.

Barnes has us think about the end of lineage, the negation of the future by a refusal to fold death into life's productive forms for it, as the collapse of repetition. The novel allegorizes the end of its narrative energies by coming to various versions of a final instance or iteration of an action that has exhausted its motivating desire. Toward the novel's beginning, before Felix meets Robin, he meets the doctor at a party given by Count Altamonte. The count suddenly throws out everyone except for the woman by his side and, after the guests leave, the doctor explains that "'Count Onatorio Altamonte,—may the name eventually roll over the Ponte Vecchio and into the Arno,—suspected that he had come upon his last erection'" (*N* 21). What is the status of one's last erection, when one knows it as such? If virginity—being the first—is a traditional excitement, Barnes proposes the stranger desire of being the last to have a particular lover as an even more decisive act of sexual possession of someone into his dying. Elaborating this idea of a mortal finality, of an end to repetition, embedded in sexual pleasure, the doctor later imagines the lower class of prostitute, the "'ladies of the *haute* sewer taking their last stroll, sauntering on their last Rotten Row, going slowly along in the dark, holding up their badgered flounces, or standing still, letting you do it, silent and indifferent as the dead, as if they were thinking of better days, or waiting for something that they had been promised when they were little girls'" (*N* 110). The first time, with its promise of beginnings, is not the point; it is the last time, reeking of mortality at the end of desire, that reveals the lie at the heart of the structure of inheritance. Robin, as desiderata, becomes a figure not of desire's endless return but of its cancellation:

> The Marchesa remarked that everyone in the room had been going on from interminable sources since the world began, and would continue to reappear, but that there was one person who had come to the end of her existence and would return no more. As she spoke, she looked slyly at Robin, who was standing by the piano speaking to the child in an undertone; and at the Marchesa's words Jenny began to tremble slightly, so that every point of her upstanding hair—it stood about her head in a bush, virile and unlovely—quivered. (*N* 62)

Robin will not return because Barnes uses her to imagine the collapse of time's extension as a tradition or lineage into an absolute dying, culturally irretrievable and socially unusable. Robin marks the place of Lacan's second death; she is analogous in Lacan's thought to Antigone, who "pushes to the limit the realization of something that might be called the pure and simple desire of death as such. She incarnates that desire" (*EP* 282). Nora, who despite everything cannot not desire her, explains her suffering to the doctor: " 'Every hour is my last, and,' she said desperately, 'one can't live one's last hour all one's life!' " (*N* 113). Every hour is her last because, if our role in the dying of the other is not to be nothing, hour does not bequeath hour, the past does not generate a future. In Barnes's stark scenario, we do not inherit from the dead but die with them—we inherit only their dying, an erotic transaction subversive to the normative relations that would structure time into meaning and sexuality into reproduction. When Robin, in her ongoing betrayal, returns home in the first light of dawn with another woman, Nora realizes this immanent finality, this cancellation of seriality: "As she closed her eyes, Nora said 'Ah!' with the intolerable automatism of the last 'Ah!' in a body struck at the moment of its final breath" (*N* 57). That she lives on in an empirical sense does not detract from this moment's refusal to be subsumed in a mutually supporting network of relations that can be called time's passage and the accumulation of eros into a history. Death is no longer assimilable to this history, and in its space apart draws eros in its wake. There is no social relation or symbolic form for our helplessness in the face of the other's mortality. This helplessness is, in Henry Staten's phrase, "the pouring-out or gashing-open of the self that is caught in the rapture of the beloved's allure." Staten asks if it is "really unthinkable...to pour out all one's being toward merely mortal objects precisely as mortal," to love "what is mortal precisely *as* mortal and because it is mortal." "Would such a love as this set off unbearable grief, a despair that would...unsettle the very grounds of possibility of rationality and of a community based on rationality?"[107] Yes, Barnes answers, it is unthinkable to love the mortality of the other, but it is as necessary as it is unthinkable. It comes with threat of rupture to the social and symbolic fields, scrubbed of the signs of their dead. In a world that no longer says its dying, this erotic language at its outskirts says it for us.

Coda

Williams and Stevens, Inventing Farewell

The world, somebody wrote, is the place we prove real by dying in it.

—Salman Rushdie, *Satanic Verses*

My goal throughout this book has been to show that if corpses are an embarrassment for modernizing societies, they are in their strangeness a potent aesthetic resource for modern literature. New cultural tensions around dying and dead bodies—this phrase is redundant if we feel as Barnes does that all bodies are one or the other—demanded in the twentieth century a literary practice with uniquely ethical ambitions toward the dead. Modernism can be read as an imaginative, speculative expression of obligations to the dead in a moment in which familiar cultural terms for these obligations were falling apart. In preceding chapters, I have approached ideas of mortal obligation that emerged in modernism as articulations of resistance to several modernizing pressures: to the state's nationalist appropriation of the corpses it produces in war, to the rationalization of time into forms that exclude the slow plots of the dead in their liminality, and to the social coercion of erotic desire to produce futurity. I have conceptualized modernism's representations of mortal obligation primarily as various kinds of extremity and complexity in what it is to be a subject involved in others' deaths, a subject structured, even, by others' capacity to die. In this sense, mortal obligation is a principle that contradicts models of self based on instrumental rationality, economic self-interest, nationalist identification, self-propriety, and other rubrics of psychic autonomy and coherence. How modern people, in the tangles of secularism, obligate themselves to those who die is incoherent, and modernism imagined this incoherence as something it could organize as the beginning of new ethical commitments. These beginnings took many forms: Owen's voice of pained witnessing and synecdochic amplification of the self; Woolf's narrative rendering of an unknowable subject in intimate exile from the social gallery of identity; Joyce's subject in a narrative struggle against burial incompetence, and his dispersal of the self's actuality in its contingency; Faulkner's communal, multiply inhabited dying "I," endlessly unraveling in time; Eliot's voices fragmented by elegiac, homoerotic desire; and Barnes's lovers erotically attuned to one another's mortality at the outskirts of both rhetorical and social intelligibility. Imagining these desires, responsibilities, and identities demanded modernism's new ways of making novels and poems.

Yet it is not clear that any of this imagining mattered, or matters, to the West's death practices. This would be the most ambitious claim for the social consequences of this writing (as it would be for any aesthetic practice): that its powers of symbolic play and resolution carried powers of social causation as well, that its imaginative and aesthetic work was socially embedded in such a way that it actually changed what people thought and did in social situations not directly related to literary practices and institutions. How would it make sense to claim that writing, publishing, and distributing modernist texts were a kind of death practice, a social action involving the material fact of corpses? It was not. It was a literary practice involving relevant themes. And it knew its own inconsequential standing. But by way of this coda, in a short discussion of an interconnected set of poems by William Carlos Williams and Wallace Stevens, I want to show the ambivalence of this resignation, the way it was in tension with a pragmatic, pedagogical desire to provoke its readers into becoming agents of their own ethical capacities in relation to the dead. Williams affirms the ground for these relations, insisting that it is solid and beneath our feet, while Stevens develops elegiac images of an ungrounding, a final deterritorialization of our corpses. In these two poets, an argument: modernism matters because it persuasively voices possibility, or it matters because it eloquently works through our resignation. In a basic way, this is an argument that we might find throughout modernism about a wide range of issues. I believe that the creative social movements around deathways in the latter twentieth century[1] support the former stance, modernism's sense of possibility, but I recognize that this claim to resistance means nothing without Stevens's remarkable sense of the symbolic depletion and ethical alienation that forced social actors to recreate their forms of agency from (as it were) the ground up. Whether or not Williams's provocations caused anything to happen, they gave a compelling shape to the possibilities of ethical thought and feeling that others exploited after them, and that people still struggle to exploit by creating new death practices, with new significances, today. Even if modernism never made anything new happen, it revealed that something could.

Yet even this proposition is steeped in various ironies from the outset. At his funeral service in 1963, Williams's friends and family declined to do what he clearly prescribes in his funeral-poem "Tract," even as they planned to read it at his graveside. He published "Tract," a kind of funeral manifesto, in 1916 and again, revised, in his 1917 volume *Al Que Quiere!* The poem exhorts readers to bury their dead without pretense. This idea, that we might will ourselves into emotional honesty and simplicity as we bury the dead, is itself a pretense; "Tract" has been described as an openly sentimental poem, and Williams himself in an interview decades later dismissed it as "hackneyed."[2] Yet, despite the poem's pretense that we might bury the dead without pretense, it vividly asserts a kind of corpse-pedagogy by insisting that we correct and recreate our burial practices. This process begins with a stripping away, an incremental process of symbolic attrition, and ends with an undefined sense of new practical possibilities. This sense of practical possibility for bearing the modernized dead is what I want to better understand. Whoever it is that speaks to us in this poem seems to do so with such an understanding:

> I will teach you my townspeople
> how to perform a funeral—
> for you have it over a troop
> of artists—
> unless one should scour the world—
> you have the ground sense necessary.

> See! the hearse leads.
> I begin with the design for a hearse.
> For Christ's sake not black—
> nor white either—and not polished!
> Let it be weathered—like a farm wagon—
> with gilt wheels (this could be
> applied fresh at small expense)
> or no wheels at all:
> a rough dray to drag over the ground.

> Knock the glass out!
> My God—glass, my townspeople!

For what purpose? Is it for the dead
to look out or for us to see
how well he is housed or to see
the flowers or the lack of them—
or what?
To keep the rain and snow from him?
He will have heavier rain soon:
pebbles and dirt and what not.
Let there be no glass—
and no upholstery, phew!
and no little brass rollers
and small easy wheels on the bottom—
my townspeople what are you thinking of?

A rough plain hearse then
with gilt wheels and no top at all.
On this the coffin lies
by its own weight.

            No wreathes please—
especially no hot house flowers.
Some common memento is better,
something he prized and is known by:
his old clothes—a few books perhaps—
God knows what! You realize
how we are about these things
my townspeople—
something will be found—anything
even flowers if he had come to that.
So much for the hearse.

For heaven's sake though see to the driver!
Take off the silk hat! In fact
that's no place at all for him—
up there unceremoniously
dragging our friend out to his own dignity!
Bring him down—bring him down!
Low and inconspicuous! I'd not have him ride
on the wagon at all—damn him—

the undertaker's understrapper!
Let him hold the reins
and walk at the side
and inconspicuously too!

Then briefly as to yourselves:
Walk behind—as they do in France,
seventh class, or if you ride
Hell take curtains! Go with some show
of inconvenience; sit openly—
to the weather as to grief.
Or do you think you can shut grief in?
What—from us? We who have perhaps
nothing to lose? Share with us
share with us—it will be money
in your pockets.
              Go now
I think you are ready.[3]

If we are now ready to go forth and bury, it is because we are willing to abandon our familiar ways of doing so; the work of re-enchanting relations to the dead, and to the object of the corpse itself, begins with stripping away the ritual practices and familiar paraphernalia that we use at another's death. The poem is about taking care of another's corpse better by taking care of it less, with less elegance and hierarchy, by giving it less shelter, by wrapping it in a thinner set of conventions—much of this, simply to say, by spending less cash to get it into the ground. Indeed, Williams suggests precisely this symbolic strategy of generating collective meaning out of an intentional minimalism or non-commodification, as if this would be the first step in establishing an honest and unmediated performance of one's obligation to a corpse. Keeping it real, in this line of thought, is keeping it cheap: the dead do not want our money but our grief, our time, our exposure to the elements, and, implicated in all these, our creative making. It is a tract against our passivity. Williams's strategy of re-enchantment by attrition is one that demands the active creation of a new aesthetic practice, the expense of composing some hitherto unknown kind of collective, ritual satisfaction. Such a practice, he tells us, "will be money / in [our] pockets" because it will involve us in an alternate system of exchange across mortal lines, an economy of obligation through which our labor for the dead is returned in the form of the new imaginative powers derived from them.

This tract is therefore part of modernism's negotiation with its literary predecessors for its own status, the poem's corpse a rough allegory for modernism's forebears.[4] The burial party we are meant to join carries something of an Imagist spareness, as a figure for Williams's association with that movement. To bury right is to get one's place in poetic history right. Put otherwise, Williams uses the scene of mortal obligation to generate modernism's new aesthetic possibilities from old ones. This function of modernist corpses, in which the bodies that need to be both abandoned and preserved are the bodies of the literary past, becomes even more evident a few years later with the most infamous corpse in modernist poetry, the one buried in Stetson's garden in the first section of *The Waste Land* (which I discuss in Chapter Three). Williams offers us a less anxious, more pragmatic, and more apparently democratic vision of meaningful social action in the context of death's modernization.[5] Williams's pedagogical, hortatory version of modernism claims its relevance as a significant cultural force, a claim based on its ability to resignify death practices for the social collective. The fact that those attending his own funeral service, where "Tract" was read, decided to drive instead of walk to the cemetery does not negate the poem's pedagogical dimension. It just shows us that this remaking of corpse disposal must be subtle, nonprogrammatic, free from even literary prescription. His funeral party worried that walking would have seemed pretentious.[6]

Within a year of the publicatoin of "Tract," Stevens rehearses a similar deritualization and symbolic stripping of the unburied dead, an explicit response to the war. "The Death of a Soldier," from 1918, sounds like a rewriting of "Tract" once the towspeople have wandered off and left the corpse alone under an empty horizon:

> Life contracts and death is expected,
> As in a season of autumn.
> The soldier falls.
>
> He does not become a three-days personage,
> Imposing his separation,
> Calling for pomp.
>
> Death is absolute and without memorial,
> As in a season of autumn,
> When the wind stops,
>
> When the wind stops and, over the heavens,
> The clouds go, nevertheless,
> In their direction.[7]

There is no pedagogy in this poem, no exhortation to learn an alternative to exhausted pomposity, for there is no alternative to be learned or because we are no longer agents able to do so. Stevens imagines, with a kind of pleasure, the breakdown of every ritual and symbolic measure so that only a vast emptiness remains. For Stevens the point is to sound this emptiness rather than develop new collective practices for filling it. The wind stops as the body's breath stops at dying, yet the clouds continue moving as if even in the spareness of this death there remained some other volition or task. It is the detached volition of a mind thinking and imagining, in quintessential Stevens fashion, a volition with little sociality, as tautological and redundant to material bodies on the ground as the poem's final tautological and redundant line: the clouds go "in their direction." The poem does not seek to motivate social action by having us imagine what it would be like to refashion our material practices, as Williams's does, but simply, quietly, has us think death as absolute, in its mere nonbeing, a test of our ability to locate ourselves and our dead in social emptiness and emotional abstraction. This symbolic deflation is also the final effect of "The Emperor of Ice-Cream" (1922), in which the speaker, like the one in "Tract," carefully instructs us in what to do with a corpse: "Take from the dresser of deal, / Lacking the three glass knobs, that sheet / On which she embroidered fantails once / And spread it so as to cover her face."[8] This act of covering the mere thingliness of her corpse with her own aesthetic creation— much like reading Williams's poem at his own funeral—may be emotionally satisfying for her survivors, yet for Stevens it is as tautological and redundant as the windless clouds passing away from the soldier, an insufficient gesture that leaves her feet exposed and postmortem presence mute. The nature of such a modernist project in these poems is not pragmatic, toward another possibility, but about our resignation. Or, if we want to think of it as pedagogical, it is for the way it teaches us to reconcile ourselves to the increasingly mediated, abstract nature of relations between the living and dead in aggressively modernizing cultures.

At the end of the modernist era, Stevens provides as no one else an elaborate statement about the exhaustion of cultural resources for articulating mortal obligations. "The Owl in the Sarcophagus," written and published in 1947, is one of his most opaque elegies, a severe test of just how far one's material, socially legible obligations to the corpses in one's midst can be absorbed into the private obscurity of the imagination. If the corpse is abstracted into the impersonality of wind and sky by the end of "The Death of a Soldier," it scarcely appears at all in "The Owl in the Sarcophagus"; from the beginning, we are in the world of Stevens's most hieratic allegorical displacements. He wrote the elegy for his friend Henry Church, as he acknowledges in a letter to Church's wife, but this is not evident in the poem itself, and this imprecision extends the elegy's scope of concern to the larger population of dead that inhabit the poem.[9] The first of the poem's six long sections reads:

> Two forms move among the dead, high sleep
> Who by his highness quiets them, high peace
> Upon whose shoulders even the heavens rest,
>
> Two brothers. And a third form, she that says
> Good-by in the darkness, speaking quietly there,
> To those that cannot say good-by themselves.
>
> These forms are visible to the eye that needs,
> Needs out of the whole necessity of sight.
> The third form speaks, because the ear repeats,
>
> Without a voice, inventions of farewell.
> These forms are not abortive figures, rocks,
> Impenetrable symbols, motionless. They move
>
> About the night. They live without our light,
> In an element not the heaviness of time,
> In which reality is prodigy.
>
> There sleep the brother is the father, too,
> And peace is cousin by a hundred names
> And she that in the syllable between life
>
> And death cries quickly, in a flash of voice,
> Keep you, keep you, I am gone, oh keep you as
> My memory, is the mother of us all,
>
> The earthly mother and the mother of
> The dead. Only the thought of those dark three
> Is dark, thought of the forms of dark desire.[10]

These forms that tend to our dead are of another order of being that live without time and without our light, that is, without our ways of feeling or knowing. They are human inventions that no longer carry human meanings or refer to human intentions. The mother bids farewell without a voice, using the inaudible syllable that comes between life and death, an articulation that we cannot hear of the vanishing moment of transition. These three figures are forms without describable content, or, at most, a content of something like empty atmosphere—sleep, peace, a blank sovereignty over all. Joan Melville describes this estranged tone as the product of "a quiet, insulated environment that evokes the feeling of a hospital ward or a nursery. In response to the initial shock, the poet's desire is for anesthetizing reassurance."[11] This institutional, anesthetized atmosphere around mortal tending and ethical desire correlates precisely to what was happening to cultural practices around the dead during these years, the economic abstraction, legal codification, bureaucratic regulation, and medicalization of obligations to dying and dead bodies—that is, processes that neutered their social power and ritual density. It is surely awkward to so closely associate Stevens's subtle lyricism with these crude social facts, but the point of this association is to better describe the bizarre effects of these social facts on modern consciousness. It is a form of consciousness for which the mother's unheard "inventions of farewell" are new ways of articulating one's alienation from the dead, of naming the silence between them and us.

The mother, the figure that binds the living and the dead, is also the site of Stevens's negotiation with poetic tradition. I am compelled by these literary historical resonances because they show modernism's awareness of aesthetic obligations even as it has readers imagine an ethical one. While "The Owl in the Sarcophagus" has often been associated with Whitman's "When Lilacs Last in the Dooryard Bloom'd," the figure of the mother of the dead is more elaborate in one of Whitman's Civil War poems, "Pensive on Her Dead Gazing," a powerful invention of farewell from an earlier era. The poem begins:

> Pensive on her dead gazing I heard the Mother of All,
> Desperate on the torn bodies, on the forms covering the battle-fields gazing,
> (As the last gun ceased, but the scent of the powder-smoke linger'd,)
> As she call'd to her earth with mournful voice while she stalk'd,
> Absorb them well O my earth, she cried, I charge you lose not my sons, lose
>   not an atom,
> And you streams absorb them well, taking their dear blood,
> And you local spots, and you airs that swim above lightly impalpable,
> And all you essences of soil and growth, and you my rivers' depths,
> And you mountain sides, and the woods where my dear children's blood
>   trickling redden'd
> And you trees down in your roots to bequeath to all future trees,
> My dead absorb or South or North—[12]

This plea for the dead, for their full physical absorption into the natural world, is also the humanization of that world, a mapping of ethical significance across the

land and its wildlife. It is at the same time a claim to the fundamental, natural quality of this ethical desire: caring for dead bodies, as an ethical act, is in this vision an
elemental process of the earth and its nonhuman forms of life, part of their vitality. Whitman composes a plea able to collapse the distinction between nature and
culture at this scene of mass slaughter, a plea with the memorable rhetorical force
to reconcile the material and symbolic dimensions of human corpses at the very
point that this reconciliation is in acute historical crisis. For the Mother of All, the
innumerable dead require the entire world's conversion into a burial ground—
an endless accommodation. Whitman uses her as a figure for the viability of this
summons to the earth for its total conversion.

Stevens returns to this figure in 1947 to suggest that such a summons on behalf
of the mass war dead has been exhausted, as has the earth to which this summons
is directed. Stevens rewrites Whitman's gesture of world-making in reverse, as its
undoing, in an effort to have us imagine the dead without a world. All that is left
for Stevens, confronted with the worldless dead, is the cultural memory of this
world-making. It is memory on the verge of nostalgia. In section four, he provides
an image of this memory in another embroidery, a stitched cloth worn by the
brother called "peace" and "peace after death":

> Adorned with cryptic stones and sliding shines,
> An immaculate personage in nothingness,
> With the whole spirit sparkling in its cloth,
>
> Generations of the imagination piled
> In the manner of its stitchings, of its thread,
> In the weaving round the wonder of its need,
>
> And the first flowers upon it, an alphabet
> By which to spell out holy doom and end,
> A bee for the remembering of happiness.[13]

These lines are complex because Stevens imagines the gathering of human imagining of death as that which clothes death. It is an elegiac *mise en abyme*, mourning's
involution, the poem's own slippage into the garment it describes. By having a figure of death wear the accumulated history of its imagined forms, and by suggesting that this continuous cultural embroidering is all that death finally is, Stevens
denaturalizes death and obligations to the dead, depicting the artifice behind their
natural status that Whitman so eloquently constructs. This deconstruction is no
less eloquent, but it poses a distinctive problem. In this reabsorption of death

practices out of the earth and into the immateriality of the human imagination—a realm he invokes in section three as being as impalpable as "water of an afternoon in the wind / After the wind has passed"—Stevens radically diminishes the power of death practices to bind people to one another as a consequential fact of the world.[14] In this aesthetic retrenchment—following Barnes's in *Nightwood*—the modern world, to paraphrase Rushdie, is not the place we can prove real by dying in it; modernized cultures are those which have tended to dissolve material obligations and ritual improvisations around others' dying. "This is the mythology of modern death / And these, in their mufflings, monsters of elegy, / Of their own marvel made," Stevens writes at the end of the poem: perhaps there is something to marvel at about the end of mortal obligation.[15]

This difficult poem goes on (it goes, opaquely, "in its direction"). As others continue to interpret it, I hope that the historical question of what another's death requires of those who survive, and what resources are available for acting on obligations to dead bodies, will be a part of the critical discussion. Even when voicing a kind of exhaustion, modernism investigates with an inexhaustible energy possibilities for transacting with the dead. These transactions, no matter how abstract or aestheticized they become, begin with the material facts of their flesh and blood, their decaying tissues and alarming smells, the elaborate muteness of their unmoving proximity, all the ways they make the rooms they inhabit stranger. Modernism attempted to know and value this strangeness. It told us that we need it to remain plausibly human, creatures for whom a dead body has difficult meanings it is a duty to understand.

Notes

Introduction

1. My desire to harness, as a critical starting point, the sheer otherness of modernist writing to established knowledge and familiar ways of feeling owes a debt to Marianne DeKoven, who powerfully invokes this quality in a different kind of study but also with an implicit interest in the enigma of mortality. I like to think that my opening thoughts at least distantly echo hers:

> Modernist writing *is* "rich and strange": its greatness lies in its density and its estranging dislocations. The sea-change of the early twentieth-century, as represented in modernism, is, like the phrase "rich and strange" itself, irresolvably ambiguous. It encompasses at once death, suffering ("suffer a sea-change"), horror (the skeleton bones stripped bare to become coral, the gelatinous eyes themselves congealing into pearl), and at the same time a redemptive transformation not merely into coral and pearls, but "into something rich and strange," with its connotations on the one hand of fascination, luxury, indulgence ("jouissance"), and on the other of excess, transgression, and the bizarre. Arielian sea-change is different from the death and resurrection cycle of myth and religion, because it rewrites simple dualistic ("self-other") valorization, where death and suffering are the entirely negative price paid for an entirely positive redemption and rebirth. In Ariel's song, death and transfiguration are both, simultaneously, with irreducible self-contradiction, terrible and wonderful." (DeKoven, *Rich and Strange*, 3–4)

DeKoven's suggestion that modernism takes death as more than mere negation, but as a complex and recalcitrant realm of meaning, points us toward the substantial, material presence of the corpse, which is emphatically not a negation, and with which this book is concerned. Michael Mendelson suggests another way to think about the strangeness of this material presence in the rooms of modern culture: "We do not need to know who, nor do we even need to know how. We need only be told that there is a body in the next room and suddenly all is transfigured. It is almost as if such circumstances were governed by a strange physics all their own. Dead bodies, we know, cannot move, as least not in the customary ways. And yet, having been told of its proximity, it is as if we instantly felt a presence of sorts intrude itself among us" (Mendelson, "The Body in the Next Room," 186). How modernism captures a sense of this intrusion as an ethical intuition is my concern.

2. Proust, *Remembrance of Things Past* v. 1, 720–721.

3. Faulkner, *As I Lay Dying*, 80–81.

4. Adorno, *Minima Moralia*, 231; Freud, "Thoughts for the Times on War and Death," 292. This historicism and cultural relativism toward death is even less characteristic of Derrida, who acknowledges that "one no longer speaks the same death where one no longer speaks the same language. The relation to death is not the same on this side of the Pyrenees as it is on the other side.... Every culture is characterized by its way of apprehending, dealing with, and, one could say, 'living' death as a trespass. Every culture has its own funerary rites, its representations of dying, its ways of mourning or burying, and its own evaluation of the price of existence, of collective as well as individual life. Furthermore, this culture of death can be transformed even within what we believe we can identify as a single culture, sometimes as a single nation, a single language, or a single religion...One can speak of a history of death, and, as you now, it has been done, for the West at least" (Derrida, *Aporias*, 24). But he goes on to argue that this "anthropologico-historical" approach to death is limited by its failure to ask fundamental philosophical questions about dying: "The historian knows, thinks he knows, or grants to himself the unquestioned knowledge of what death is, of what being-dead means; consequently, he grants to himself all the criteriology that will allow him to identify, recognize, select, or delimit the objects of his inquiry or the thematic field of his anthropologico-historical knowledge. The question of the meaning of death and of the word 'death,' the question 'What is death in general?' or 'What is the experience of death?' and the question of knowing *if* death 'is'—and *what* death 'is'—all remain radically absent *as questions*" (Ibid., 25). I'm interested in a similar tension between the historical and the transhistorical, not in mortality per se, as an abstract or latent capacity to die, but in the material fact of corpses that people tend to.

5. Yeats, "Death," *Collected Poems*, 234.

6. Said, *Beginnings*, xiii.

7. Friedman, *Fictional Death and the Modernist Enterprise*, 18.

8. Friedman characterizes these representational problems in several ways: "Modernists elide the dying process (Woolf, Forster); refract it through untrustworthy memory (Marlow in *Heart of Darkness*, Stephen in *Ulysses*); base it in materiality (*Women in Love*, *As I Lay Dying*, "Snows of Kilimanjaro"); or foreground the complementarity of eros and thanatos (Lawrence's "The Woman Who Rode Away" and *The Man Who Died*; the "Hades" chapter of *Ulysses*)" (ibid., 18–19).

9. Pound, *Lustra*, 43.

10. Freud, "Thoughts for the Times on War and Death," 291.

11. Gourgouris, *Does Literature Think?*, 341.

12. Kristeva, *Powers of Horror*, 3.

13. Moretti, *Modern Epic*, 6.

14. Hartman, *Lose Your Mother*, 18.

15. Kristeva, *Powers of Horror*, 3; Strauss, *Human Remains*, 273.

16. Brown, *The Reaper's Garden*, 261.

17. Rilke, *The Notebooks of Malte Laurids Brigge*, 13.

18. Woolf, *Roger Fry*, 278.

19. For recent modernist scholarship about these issues, see Ramazani, *Poetry of Mourning*; Spargo, *The Ethics of Mourning*; Gilbert, *Death's Door*; Rae, ed., *Modernism and Mourning*; Moglen, *Mourning Modernity*; Kalaidjian, *The Edge of Modernism*; Watkin, *On Mourning*; Ricciardi, *The Ends of Mourning*; Eng and Kazanjian, eds., *Loss*; Detloff, *The Persistence of Modernism*; and Forter, *Gender, Race, and Mourning in American Modernism*.

20. Pascal Boyer describes the strangeness of the corpse from an evolutionary biological and cognitive perspective: corpses "create the kind of dissociation that in other contexts we see in people with brain damage or other forms of cognitive impairment" because they engage contradictory categories with which we make inferences about, or interpretations of, our surroundings (Boyer, *Religion Explained*, 222).

21. Serres, *Conversations on Science, Culture, and Time*, 138. Serres seems to be channeling an early twentieth-century ethos in this claim. Jewel Spears Brooker surveys a list of reconstructions of human origins in the later nineteenth and early twentieth centuries, from Darwin's to Frazer's, and concludes, "What T. S. Eliot said of *The Golden Bough* can be said of all these works: they should be read 'as a revelation of that vanished mind of which our own is a continuation'" (Eliot, "London Letter," *Dial* 71.4 (October 1923) 353. Quoted in Brooker, "Mimetic Desire and the Return to Origins in *The Waste Land*," 130).

22. Leroi-Gourhan, "The Flowers Found with Shanidar IV, a Neanderthal Burial in Iraq," 564; Stewart, "The Neanderthal Skeletal Remains from Shanidar Cave, Iraq," 164; Solecki, "Shanidar IV, a Neanderthal Flower Burial in Northern Iraq," 880; Riel-Salvatore and Clark, "Grave Markers," 449. Theya Molleson describes other kinds of evidence: burial "appears to have been initiated by the neandertals of north-west Europe about 70,000 years ago. At Le Moustier in France the burial of a child was found in a cave associated with tools of Mousterian type. A similar burial in a cave at Teshik Tash, Uzbekistan, also features a child. The body was surrounded by mountain goat horns, particularly large ones, held in place by stones and the whole covered over with earth. Finally a small fire was burned near the burial spot...It is possible to infer from the nature of the burial that it was accompanied by some form of ceremony in which a number of people took part" (Molleson, "The Archeology and Anthropology of Death," 16–17). See also Movius, "The Mousterian Cave of Teshik Tash, South Eastern Uzbekistan, Central Asia."

23. Archeologists and anthropologists sometimes add toolmaking to the list: "Along with large brains, toolmaking and language, the deliberate inhumation of the dead is a unique human characteristic. Badgers are known to earth up the part of a sett where a badger has died; other animals will remove dead bodies from their immediate living area but these activities hardly constitute the ceremonial associated with human death" (Molleson, "The Archeology and Anthropology of Death," 15). That

intentional corpse disposal is unique to humans is significant, but my point—that it is pervasive among humans—is slightly different.

24. Harrison, *Dominion of the Dead*, xi.

25. Foltyn, "Dead Beauty," 76. Baudrillard suggests that the point of this aestheticizing strategy is to prevent the symbolic decomposition of the social group faced with the decaying corpse: "Every society has always...staved off the abjection of natural death, the *social* abjection of decomposition which voids the corpse of its signs and its social force of signification, leaving it as nothing more than a substance, and by the same token, precipitating the group into the terror of its own symbolic decomposition. It is necessary to ward off death, to smother it in artificiality in order to evade the unbearable moment when flesh becomes nothing but flesh, and ceases to be a sign" (Baudrillard, *Symbolic Exchange and Death*, 180). Even if he thinks aestheticizing the corpse is a decisive part of every society, he criticizes a contemporary tendency in theUnited States to deny the perceptibility of death altogether by creating corpses with an artificial "naturalness" that are mere simulacra of the living (ibid., 181). For a sociological analysis of this representation of the dead as alive in the United States, and how it contrasts with British practices, see Davis, "Dirt, Death, Decay and Dissimulation."

26. Malinowski, *Magic, Science, Religion and Other Essays*, 47; Durkheim, *The Elementary Forms of Religious Life*, 51; Boyer, *Religion Explained*, 228. This similar claim that Boyer rejects, a kind existential cousin, that one's anticipatory anxieties about dying are the primary motivation for symbolic making and cultural expression, including religion, is common. Zygmaut Bauman is exemplary: "The fact of human mortality, and the necessity to live with the constant awareness of that fact, go a long way toward accounting for many a crucial aspect of social and cultural organization of all known societies"; "The horror of death is the horror of the void, of the ultimate absence, of 'non-being'. The conscience of death is, and bound to remain, *traumatic*" (Bauman, *Mortality, Immortality, and Other Life Strategies*, 9, 13). This emphasis on the unknowability of the void of death, as pure negation, disregards entirely the concrete presence of the other's dead body as it waits before us for care. It is only in a highly modernized society that the idea of death, as existential imperative, could so thoroughly supplant attention to actual dead people; in this sense, Bauman symptomizes the condition I take as the context for this study. This is why Boyer claims that "religion may well be much less about death than about dead bodies" (Boyer, *Religion Explained*, 228). Jonathan Strauss vividly contrasts the affective and sensory differences between death in the abstract and actual dead bodies: "Death is clean and annihilating; it converts concrete reality into concepts and has no odor, since it is the absence of sensation. The dead, in contrast, are filthy and foul-smelling leftovers. Death elicits terror, the affect of sublimity...The dead, on the other hand, fill us with horror, a queasy mix of disgust and fear, the anxiety that the corruptible material world could penetrate through our senses to infect our insubstantial being" (Strauss, *Human Remains*, 268).

27. Vico, *The New Science*, §13, 531, 12, 537; cf. 333. Harrison comments extensively on Vico throughout *The Dominion of the Dead*. Regarding Vico's three universal institutions, Harrison claims that marriage and religion are more likely to die out than

burial (xi). On Harrison's elaboration of these ideas of burial, place, and dwelling, see in particular chapters two and three.

28. Levinas, *Is It Righteous To Be?*, 124.

29. For this sense of "collective symbolic formations" we could also use the phrase "collective representations," following Robert Hertz's influential 1907 anthropological study, "A Contribution to the Study of the Collective Representation of Death," where he argues that "death has a specific meaning for the social consciousness; it is the object of a collective representation" (Hertz, *Death & The Right Hand*, 28).

30. However, in his anthropological survey of traditional death practices, Maurice Bloch refers to "those societies which seem almost to ignore the dead, abandon them and do nothing much about them. Examples of such societies are the Siriono and the Hadza...where there is no authority except of men over women and where there is therefore no symbolic representation of permanent structures. This means that in those societies, discontinuity and individuality is no threat but only an irrelevance. In these cases there is practically no reason for elaborate funerary rituals. When someone dies one leaves the corpse with as little fuss as possible and then moves on" (Bloch, "Death, Women and Power," 230). But this lack of fuss, that is, of elaborate ritualization of continuity and community, should not be confused with a nonsymbolic relation to the corpse or a situation in which human remains do not have consequential collective meanings attached to them. The Hadza, the hunting and gathering tribe of Northern Tanzania that Bloch mentions, for example, assign the responsibility for burying their dead to specific categories of people, lay a Hadza corpse on its left side facing Mt. Hanang, harden the soil of the burial site to prevent it from being disturbed by animals, and organize a session of wailing and lamentation (Woodburn, "Social dimensions of death in four African hunting and gathering societies," 189–190). This is hardly ignoring the dead.

31. Harrison, *Dominion of the Dead*, xi. Several scholars have pursued this claim that human culture as such originates in awareness of the dead and mortuary practices. Eelco Runia argues that marking the remains of the dead enables historicist thought: "By burying the dead—or, as in southeast Asia, by burning them—humankind may well have created a prime condition for traditions, for stability, for transcendence, for religion, for, in one word, culture.... Burying the dead is a means to take leave of the deceased without giving them up. It's an evolutionarily advantageous practice because it enables humans to bring much more to bear on the present than what their consciousness can contain" (Runia, "Burying the Dead, Creating the Past," 324). Paul Ricoeur makes a similar connection, claiming that "the historiographical operation" is "the equivalent of the social ritual of entombment, of the act of sepulcher"; "It is this act of sepulcher that historiography transforms into writing" (Ricoeur, *Memory, History, Forgetting*, 365–366). Françoise Dastur, in *Death: An Essay on Finitude*, makes a broader claim about mourning as the foundation of culture: "For man is a political animal, as Aristotle's well-known definition has it, only because he lives in society not merely with his 'contemporaries' but also—and perhaps more so—with those who have gone before.... That human life is a life 'with' the dead is perhaps what truly distinguishes human existence from purely animal life...In fact there is no culture except where a certain mastery over

the irreversible flow of time is assured, and this implies the bringing into play of a multitude of techniques aimed at alleviating the pain of absence. The absence *par excellence* is the absence of the dead.... This is why it is not illegitimate to see in mourning, understood broadly as coming to terms with an absence, the origin of culture itself" (Dastur, *Death*, 8–9).

32. Stevens, *The Palm at the End of the Mind*, 127; Joyce, *Ulysses*, 3.479–3.480.

33. Lacan, "Function and Field of Speech and Language," 104.

34. Rose, *Mourning Becomes the Law*, 132.

35. Harrison, *Dominion of the Dead*, 20.

36. This question about corpse disposal sounds like Barthes's about narrative: "Caring nothing for the division between good and bad literature, narrative is international, transhistorical, transcultural: it is simply there, like life itself. Must we conclude from this universality that narrative is insignificant? Is it so general that we can have nothing to say about it except for the modest description of a few highly individualized varieties, something literary history occasionally undertakes?" (Barthes, *Image-Music-Text*, 79). I bring these matters together in Chapter Two in a discussion of how modern death obligations are narrated.

37. Rosen, *Dignity*, 138.

38. Ibid., 142.

39. Ibid., 140.

40. Ibid., 142.

41. Ibid., 157.

42. Freud, "Thoughts for the Times on War and Death," 295. Freud continues his thought with a description of our ambivalence toward the dead: this prohibition "was acquired in relation to dead people who were loved, as a reaction against the satisfaction of the hatred hidden behind the grief for them; and it was gradually extended to strangers who were not loved, and finally even to enemies" (ibid.). He elaborates this idea in chapter two of *Totem and Taboo*, for example, "The taboo upon the dead arises, like the others, from the contrast between conscious pain and unconscious satisfaction over the death that has occurred. Since such is the origin the ghost's resentment, it follows naturally that the survivors who have the most to fear will be those who were formerly its nearest and dearest.... The fact that a dead man is helpless is bound to act as an encouragement to the survivor to give free rein to his hostile passions, and that temptation must be countered by a prohibition" (Freud, *Totem and Taboo*, 61). Thomas Mann makes a version of this forbidding claim, that our ethical response to the dead disguises our hate for them, in *The Magic Mountain*: "What we call mourning for our dead is perhaps not so much grief at not being able to call them back as it is grief at not being able to want to do so" (Mann, *The Magic Mountain*, 675). I am interested in an alternative idea, that we respond to the dead with ethical desire that gives us a more basic satisfaction than any resentment we might be guarding against. Which is why I turn to Levinas, below.

43. Levinas, *Difficult Freedom*, 100.

44. Levinas, *Is It Righteous To Be?*, 124.

45. Levinas, *Totality and Infinity*, 179.

46. Levinas, *Entre-nous*, 131, 145.

47. Levinas, *God, Death, and Time*, 39.
48. Levinas, *Is It Righteous To Be?*, 126.
49. Levinas, *God, Death, and Time*, 83. Levinas's sense of the power of bodily remains extends into one of his commentaries on Hebrew Biblical narrative: "It is recounted how at the moment when the people left Egypt, Moses looked for the bones of Joseph to bring them back to the Holy Land. Has this narrative no signification beyond the Jews? Does not Joseph represent a certain moment of exile and the wisdom of an ingenious economic administration which nevertheless remains faithful to the Promised Land where one must transport his bones?" (Levinas, *Is It Righteous To Be?*, 76).
50. Vico, *The New Science*, §337.
51. Despite his ongoing descriptions of sudden, mass death throughout London, Defoe's narrator frequently, and at times defensively, insists that the city competently managed its corpses: "But the Magistrates cannot be enough commended in this, that they kept such good Order for the burying of the Dead, that as fast as any of those they employ'd to carry off, and bury the dead, fell sick or dy'd, as was many Times the Case, they immediately supply'd the places with others; which by reason of the great Number of Poor that was left out of Business... was not hard to do: This occasion'd, that notwithstanding the infinite Number of People which dy'd, and were sick almost all together, yet, there were always clear'd away, and carry'd off every Night; so that it was never to be said of *London*, that the living were not able to bury the Dead" (Defoe, *A Journal of the Plague Year*, 85; cf. 138, 143, 147, 180–182). In contrast, the twentieth-century novels I mention frequently let them pile up, more obviously symptoms of civic and cultural breakdown.
52. Camus, *The Plague*, 176.
53. Vico, *The New Science*, §333.
54. Conrad, *Heart of Darkness*, 83–84.
55. For one of Conrad's variations on this scene, see his story "An Outpost of Progress," in which the disgraced corpses are white, suggesting that the logic of colonial domination will eventually extend itself to any body it can.
56. Levi, *The Drowned and the Saved*, 123–124. Jonathan Glover further considers the relations among humiliated or degraded humanity, disrespect for the remains of the dead, and political oppression in the context of Nazi concentration camps:

> When victims are seen as less than human, the murderers find it hard to treat their remains with respect.... When the thousandth corpse was cremated, one of the Nazi staff dressed as a clergyman and gave a parody of a funeral address. Any serious funeral would have been a reminder of the victims' humanity.
>
> The Nazis carried dehumanizing to relentless extremes after death. Women's hair from Auschwitz was sold for making mattresses. Recognizable human ashes from the crematoria, often containing teeth or vertebrae, were used as thermal insulation between wooden walls, as fertilizer, and instead of gravel for the paths of the nearby SS village. It is hard to believe the main motive was economic. (Glover, *Humanity: A Moral History of the Twentieth Century*, 341)

In a similar line of thought, Luc Capdevila and Danièle Voldman observe that in the "mass murder planned and carried out by Nazi ideologues, one cannot separate the methods of execution and what happened to bodies" (Capdevila and Voldman, *War Dead*, 104). For an extensive, thorough series of articles on Nazi anatomy practices, see the special 2012 issue dedicated to the topic: Hildebrandt and Redies, eds., *Annals of Anatomy*. For an extensive discussion of the relation between the traumas of colonialism and the Second World War's extermination camps, but without an emphasis on corpses, see Rothberg, *Multidimensional Memory*.

57. Sappho, *The Poetry of Sappho*, 18.

58. This is the politics of the dead inaugurated by Walter Benjamin's essay "On the Concept of History" (Benjamin, *Selected Writings*, v. 4) For an astonishing elaboration of Benjamin's philosophy of history in relation to the unclaimed corpses of the 1781 Zong slaveship massacre, and therefore relevant to Conrad's interest in the transatlantic construction of race, see Baucom, *Spectres of the Atlantic*. For a powerful poetic response to the dead of this massacre, with an eloquent essay on the arduous poetics of such memorial work, see Philip and Boateng, *Zong!* In *Precarious Life*, Judith Butler approaches this sense of the politics of the dead from another angle, with a focus on the political meaning of grief: "The question that preoccupies me in the light of recent global violence is, Who counts as a human? Whose lives count as lives? And, finally, *What makes for a grievable life?*" (Butler, *Precarious Life*, 20).

59. Although he doesn't formulate it as such, Gary Lederman alerts us to a paradox: "control of the dead carries significant social weight," yet "anthropologists and ethnographers provide numerous accounts of corpse-handlers who are social outcasts and occupy a marginal place in the social order" (Lederman, *Rest in Peace*, xvii). This social authority over corpses often involves wielding it from a physical distance and the delegation of corpse preparation to others.

60. Jessica Mitford's 1963 *The American Way of Death* is the classic, groundbreaking examination of the funeral industry's economic manipulation of the bereaved; this was updated in 1998 as *The American Way of Death Revisited* with additional chapters, and a particularly important one ("A Global Village of the Dead") on new monopolies by multinational corporations in the death care industry.

61. Blanchot, *The Space of Literature*, 256.

62. Strauss, *Human Remains*, 271.

63. Lawrence, *The Prussian Officer and Other Stories*, 196.

64. Blanchot, *The Space of Literature*, 257.

65. Lawrence, *The Prussian Officer and Other Stories*, 198.

66. Strauss, *Human Remains*, 271.

67. Lawrence, *The Prussian Officer and Other Stories*, 199.

68. Strauss, *Human Remains*, 273.

69. Rilke, *Selected Poetry*, 63.

70. Blanchot, *The Space of Literature*, 258.

71. This is following Harrison's thought that "to be human means to translate our mortality into history" (Harrison, *Dominion of the Dead*, 2).

72. For this term, see Krüger-Kahloula, "On the Wrong Side of the Fence." For a relevant study on the racial politics of a cemetery in Georgia, and how this relates to documentary projects more generally, see Auslander, "Saying Something Now." And for a far-reaching study on the mortuary politics in Haiti under slavery, see Brown's *The Reaper's Garden*.

73. For an analysis of the legal and ethical idea of "posthumous interests" in terms of a dead person's body, reputation, and estate, see Sperling's *Posthumous Interests*. He develops "an interest theory of rights" for the dead, arguing that it is more useful and logical to consider the interests, rather than the rights, of the recently dead, because a consideration of the interests of the deceased can be used to build a more robust concept of the deceased's ability to make claims on others (Sperling, *Posthumous Interests*, 3).

74. For further discussions of contentious social histories around modern corpses see, as exemplary, Richardson, *Death, Dissection, and the Destitute* (on Victorian England) and Sappol, *A Traffic of Dead Bodies* (on nineteenth-century United States). For analyses of literary responses to Victorian social conflicts over the dead, see Hotz, *Literary Remains*, and Marshall, *Murdering to Dissect*.

75. Thomas, "Funeral Rites," 3236. Jonathan Strauss develops this idea of the corpse's speech, or language, in a vivid meditation on rotting tissue. As Thomas does not, he offers an image of the abject itself speaking: "The corpse oozes: it must have been a familiar experience during a period when vigils were held at home and the body washed by members of the family. There would have been an intimacy with the dead, with how they leak and fall apart and yet retain the name and semblance of a friend, with how they write their nonsense across the blank sheets in which the living wrap them. And yet, for all its impenetrable mystery, theirs still seems to be a language. It is scrawled on the shroud by a subject beyond meaning: that subject without subjectivity that can be glimpsed in the fantasmatics of the corpse, that flows like the gases and fluids seeping from its body, that collects like a miasma.... The language of the corpse is the specificity of a certain stain or smear" (Strauss, *Human Remains*, 272).

76. Faulkner, *Absalom, Absalom!*, 71.

77. Foucault traces, without anything like nostalgia, precisely this conceptual shift in eighteenth-century medical discourse that culminates with Bichat: "Death is therefore multiple, and dispersed in time: it is not that absolute, privileged point at which time stops and moves back; like disease itself, it has a teeming presence that analysis may divide into time and space; gradually, here and there, each of the knots breaks, until organic life ceases, at least in its major forms, since long after the death of the individual, miniscule, partial deaths continue to dissociate the islets of life that still subsist"; "Bichat relativized the concept of death, bringing it down from that absolute in which it appeared as an indivisible, decisive, irrecoverable event: he volatized it, distributed it throughout life in the form of separate, partial, progressive deaths, deaths that are so slow in occurring that they extend even beyond death itself" (Foucault, *The Birth of the Clinic*, 142, 144). As Foucault does not, Ariès describes this relativization or dispersal of dying as a problem in obliquely humanist or existentialist terms: "Death has been dissected, cut to bits by a series of little steps, which finally make it impossible to know which step was the real death, the one in which consciousness was lost, or the one in which breathing stopped. All these little silent deaths have replaced and erased the great dramatic act of death, and no one any longer has the strength or patience to wait over a period of weeks for a moment which has lost a part of its meaning" (Ariès, *Western Attitudes toward Death*, 88–89). Foucault does not posit a "real" death.

78. Péguy, *Men and Saints*, 99.

79. Ariès, *Western Attitudes toward Death*, 25, 13.

80. Jahan Ramazani makes a somewhat similar, and widely influential, claim about the self-reflexive and melancholic nature of modern elegy: in recent generations, he writes, "every elegy is an elegy for elegy—a poem that mourns the diminished efficacy and legitimacy of poetic mourning" (Ramazani, *Poetry of Mourning*, 8).

81. Gorer, *Death, Grief, and Mourning in Contemporary Britain*, 173. This argument about a cultural reversal between sex and death after the Victorian age tempted Norbert Elias as well (Elias, *The Loneliness of the Dying*, 43–44). But David Cannadine specifically rejects the kind of historical accounts given by Gorer, Elias, and Ariès: "The conventional picture of death in the nineteenth century is excessively romanticized and insufficiently nuanced" because, among other things, "it is arguable that the Victorian celebration of death was not so much a golden age of effective psychological support as a bonanza in commercial exploitation" (Cannadine, "War and Death, Grief and Mourning in Modern Britain," 188, 191). Nor, he argues, was death banished from twentieth-century cultural life so thoroughly as has been claimed: he acknowledges "the massive, all-pervasive pall of death which hung over Britain in the years between 1914 and 1939, and also the inventiveness with which the grief-stricken responded to their bereavement" (ibid., 230). My argument is that modernism is a part of this inventiveness. Similarly, Oliver Leaman writes that "one wonders how deep the consolation apparently afforded by religion in the past really extended.... We just do not know, and our predecessors seemed just as eager to continue to live as is the case with contemporary agents" (Leaman, "Secularization," 400). In a different complication of this picture, Tony Walter contrasts commercial, municipal, and religious structures of authority in death practices among Westernized countries in the twentieth and twenty-first centuries; modern death at the institutional level is itself far from uniform (Walter, "Three Ways to Arrange a Funeral").

82. Weber, *From Max Weber*, 140.

83. Jameson, *The Political Unconscious*, 261. Anthony Giddens comes close to this point in *Modernity and Self-Identity*, positing a transcendental experience with finitude but not necessarily with a Kierkegaardian or Heideggerian anxiety or anguish, with their focus on individual authenticity (Giddens, *Modernity and Self-Identity*, 48–50). Chris Shilling rejects even a basic transcendental model of mortal self-awareness in a more extensive critique of existentialist panic, "locating the contemporary 'problem' of death within the historically developed orientations that people have adopted towards their bodies. Consequently, I view death as having become a particular existential problem for people as a result of modern forms of embodiment, rather than being a universal problem for human beings which assumes the same form irrespective of time and place" (Shilling, *The Body and Social Theory*, 176–177; cf. 177–188). It seems that, in his comment, Jameson falls somewhere between the two.

84. Ariès, *The Hour of Our Death*, 15, 19.

85. Jameson develops the concept of the ideologeme as discursive units which can "manifest either as a pseudoidea—a conceptual or belief system, an abstract value, an opinion or prejudice—or as a protonarrative, a kind of ultimate class fantasy about the 'collective characters' which are the classes in opposition" (Jameson,

The Political Unconscious, 87). Their location and recuperation are complex: an ideologeme "exists nowhere as such: part of the 'objective spirit' or the cultural Symbolic order of its period, it vanishes into the past along with the latter, leaving only its traces—material signifiers, lexemes, enigmatic words and phrases—behind it" (ibid., 201). My point is that the recurring thought that dying was once a generally satisfying experience, saturated in cultural authenticity, is this kind of pervasive, variably instantiated fantasy.

86. For analyses of the correlation between death and individual authenticity in Western thought, see Marcuse, "The Ideology of Death" and Strauss, "After Death." For a discussion of Woolf's reckoning with this ideology in *To the Lighthouse*, in the spirit of these analyses, see my "A Plot Unraveling into Ethics."

87. On the displacement of women by men in the modernization of death practices, associated with the displacement of midwives at births, see Richardson, *Death, Dissection, and the Destitute*, 17, 19, 21; Sappol, *A Traffic in Dead Bodies*, 60–63; and Bloch, "Death, Women and Power."

88. Jalland, *Death in War and Peace*, 2. For a description of changes tending toward the dead's segregation in the eighteenth century, particularly at the level of city planning, see Roach, *Cities of the Dead*, 47–55.

89. Rugg, "From Reason to Regulation," 202; Strange, *Death, Grief and Poverty in Britain, 1870–1914*, 30.

90. Davies, *The Law of Burial, Cremation and Exhumation*, 61.

91. Pinfold, "The Green Ground," 86–87. The overcrowding of London's burial grounds became a sensational issue over the 1830s and 40s, provoked by the press and George Alfred Walker's dramatic exposé *Gatherings from Graveyards* (1839), all of which culminated in Edwin Chadwick's 1843 government report on urban interment. For a detailed cultural history of the eviction of the dead from Paris around the turn of the nineteenth century, see Strauss, *Human Remains*. Ambrose Bierce's definition: "**Cemetery**, *n.* An isolated suburban spot where mourners match lies, poets write at a target and stone-cutters spell for a wager" (Bierce, *The Devil's Dictionary*, 15). More of Bierce's definitions in the footnotes that follow. Bierce wrote his dictionary between 1881–1906; it was first published in 1911.

92. Jalland, "Victorian Death and its Decline," 248; Jalland, *Death in War and Peace*, 5.

93. Laderman, *Rest in Peace*, 2.

94. Rugg, "From Reason to Regulation," 221. For a detailed discussion of the cemetery financing and development during this period, see Arnold, *Necropolis*, chapter eight.

95. Rugg, "The Origins and Progress of Cemetery Establishment in Britain," 105.

96. Jupp, *From Dust to Ashes*, 16, 62–63.

97. Jalland, *Death in War and Peace*, 100, cf. 105–118.

98. Jupp, *From Dust to Ashes*, 93, 98, ix. In a vivid image of the association between cremation and secularization in the West, Prothero reports that "during the first years of the French Republic, revolutionaries attempted to dechristianize funeral rites by promoting cremation. In 1794, the corpse of Beauvais, a physician and member of the National Assembly, was cremated and his ashes deposited in an urn in the national archives; and in 1799 the Seine Department passed legislation favoring cremation" (Prothero, *Purified by Fire*, 8–9). This literal archiving of a corpse is one of the strangest innovations in corpse disposal that I know about.

99. Prothero, *Purified by Fire*, 20–21, 56 ff.

100. Farrell, *Inventing the American Way of Death*, 164; NFDA, "Cremation Facts." For a comparative analysis of British cremation and US embalming, see Davies, "Dirt, Death, Decay and Dissolution."

101. Laderman, *Rest in Peace*, 8. Bierce's definition: "**Embalm**, *v.t.* To cheat vegetation by locking up the gases upon which it feeds. By embalming their dead and thereby deranging the natural balance between animal and vegetable life, the Egyptians made their once fertile and populous country barren and incapable of supporting more than a meagre crew. The modern metallic burial casket is a step in the same direction, and many a dead man who ought now to be ornamenting his neighbor's lawn as a tree, or enriching his table as a bunch of radishes, is doomed to a long inutility. We shall get him after awhile if we are spared, but in the meantime the violet and rose are languishing for a nibble at his *gluteus maximus*" (Bierce, *The Devil's Dictionary*, 30).

102. Farrell, *Inventing the American Way of Death*, 146, 156, 152, 158–159.

103. Quigley, *Modern Mummies*, 6.

104. Laderman, *Rest in Peace*, 4.

105. Ibid., 6, 8, 19.

106. Faust, *This Republic of Suffering*, 96; cf. 92–101.

107. Moller, *Confronting Death*, 86.

108. Cather, *O Pioneers!*, 72.

109. Farrell, *Inventing the American Way of Death*, 178, 181. Bierce's definition: "**Funeral**, *n.* A pageant whereby we attest our respect for the dead by enriching the undertaker, and strengthen our grief by an expenditure that deepens our groans and doubles our tears" (Bierce, *The Devil's Dictionary*, 40).

110. Habestein and Lamers, *The History of American Funeral Directing*, 245, 251. Habestein and Labers also describe experiments in these years with municipal funeral trains, but the "cortege or funeral procession seemingly lost some of its dignity as iron wheels creaked and screeched on turns and rumbled over intersections, and the public seemed unable to repress a feeling of repugnance at the spectacle of a funeral 'shooting through the streets at a high rate of speed'" (Habestein and Lamers, *The History of American Funeral Directing*, 245). As I discuss in Chapter Two, Bloom in *Ulysses* suggests precisely this innovation to others during Dignam's funeral (Joyce, *Ulysses*, 6.405-6.408). Bierce's definition: "**Hearse**, *n.* Death's baby-carriage" (Bierce, *The Devil's Dictionary*, 49).

111. Faulkner, *Collected Stories*, 797.

112. Rosenberg, "Community and Communities," 8, 11.

113. Rosenberg, "Community and Communities," 4, 9; Vogel, *The Invention of the Modern Hospital*, 1.

114. Vogel, "Introduction," ii; Howell, "Machines and Medicine," 110.

115. Rosenberg, "Community and Communities," 12.

116. Laderman, *Rest in Peace*, 3.

117. Vogel, "Introduction," ii-iii; Rosenberg, "Community and Communities," 13.

118. Rilke, *The Notebooks of Malte Laurids Brigge*, 8–9.

119. Ariès, *Western Attitudes toward Death*, 88.

120. Sappol, *A Traffic in Dead Bodies*, 95.

121. Smith, "The Autopsy in Private Practice," 575–576; Krumbhaar, "The Need for Postmortem Examinations and Methods of Securing Them," 1682–1683.

122. Lynch, "Better Autopsies and More of Them," 576. Bierce's definitions: "**Grave**, *n*. A place in which the dead are laid to await the coming of the medical student"; "**Body-snatcher**, *n*. A robber of grave-worms. One who supplies the young physicians with that which the old physicians have supplied the undertaker" (Bierce, *The Devil's Dictionary*, 44, 12).

123. Sappol, *A Traffic in Dead Bodies*, 106.

124. Smith, "The Autopsy in Private Practice," 576.

125. Williams, *The Doctor Stories*, 75–76.

126. Karsner, "The Autopsy," 1369, 1372. In a reflection on his hospital administrative experience in a 1922 issue of *Modern Hospital*, E. M. Bluestone takes this principle seriously: "Broadly speaking, no hospital is larger than its pathological laboratory," so that, after a year with a 56 percent autopsy rate, "we were unable to explain 44 per cent of our deaths except by indirect evidence. This figure represents our scientific deficit for the year" (quoted in Karsner, "The Autopsy," 1371).

127. Suiter, "On the Disposal of the Dead, with Special Reference to the Prevalent Practice of Embalming," 1037.

128. Roach, *Cities of the Dead*, 48.

129. Singer, "The First Mortality Follow-up Study," 306; Rugg, "From Reason to Regulation," 216. Singer describes how "the Registration Act of 1836 established a network of local registration offices to record all births, marriages, and deaths. Previous records had been incomplete because, since 1538, births, marriages, and burials (not deaths) had been recorded in parishes of the Anglican Church. Some cities published weekly bills of mortality, but these were not complete. The civilian registration system was essential for the national vital statistics now kept by the GRO" (Singer, "The First Mortality Follow-up Study," 306).

130. Prior, "Actuarial Visions of Death," 182.

131. Farr, *Fifth Annual Report of the Registrar General*, quoted in Singer, "The First Mortality Follow-up Study," 307.

132. Prior, *The Social Organisation of Death*, 7; Prior, "Actuarial Visions of Death," 180, 183.

133. Hacking, "How Should We Do the History of Statistics?," 185.

134. Prior, *The Social Organisation of Death*, 8.

135. Ewald, "Insurance and Risk," 209.

136. The Business Historical Society, Inc., *History of the Foundation of the Actuarial Society of America*, 50–51.

137. Thomas, "Funeral Rites," 3241.

138. Ibid.

139. Shilling, *The Body and Social Theory*, 192; Giddens, *Modernity and Self-Identity*, 203.

140. Lash, *Another Modernity, A Different Rationality*, 10.

141. Taylor, *A Secular Age*, 540. Taylor is particularly interested in Freud as a thinker of the self as the endless mystery that supplants the mystery of the cosmos, and so it is fitting that Lacan also describes this interiorization, which he similarly attributes to Freud: "It is obvious that, even if one once located them there, there is no point now in seeking the phallus or the anal ring in the starry sky; they have been definitely

expelled. For a long time even in scientific thinking, men seemed to inhabit cosmological projections. For a long time a world soul existed, and thought could comfort itself with the idea that there was a deep connection between our images and the world that surrounds us. This is a point whose importance does not seem to have been noticed, namely, that the Freudian project has caused the whole world to reenter us, has definitely put it back in its place, that is to say, in our body, and nowhere else" (Lacan, *EP*, 92).

142. Woolf, *The Waves*, 153.

143. Baudrillard, *Symbolic Exchange and Death*, 126, 134.

144. Ibid., 131.

145. Canetti, *Crowds and Power*, 78, 47.

146. Harrison, *The Dominion of the Dead*, 84.

147. Canetti, *Crowds and Power*, 77.

148. Williams, *Paterson*, 143–144.

149. For a theorization of agency in contemporary corpses, see Harper, "The Social Agency of Dead Bodies."

150. Berger, *Hold Everything Dear*, 3–5.

151. Baudrillard, *Symbolic Exchange and Death*, 132.

152. Stevens, *The Palm at the End of the Mind*, 7. However, Marcel Mauss shows us that the surplus power of the dead is traditionally recruited for magic, not art (Mauss, *A General Theory of Magic*, 101–102). This makes it possible for us to think of the more recent category of the aesthetic as the modernization of magic.

153. Many have examined how experiments with time (narrative, memory, the new) were central to modernism. See Schleifer, *Modernism and Time*; Berman, *Preface to Modernism*; Kern, *The Culture of Time and Space 1880–1918*; Harvey, *The Condition of Postmodernity*, chapter two. As both an analysis and symptom of this phenomenon, see Habermas, *The Philosophical Discourse of Modernity*, chapter one, which traces back to Hegel the philosophical consciousness of history as a problem of the ever-emerging New in its alienation from the past. In a similar vein, Peter Osborne writes that "modernity is a culture of time of which nineteenth- and twentieth-century European philosophy has been a crucial constituent part. Whether one is, like Baudelaire, 'weighed down, every moment, by the conception and sensation of time,' or, like the Surrealists, energized and uplifted by its transformative power, it has become increasingly hard to be indifferent to either its simple passage or sudden ruptural force. Time imposes itself as a problem within nineteenth and twentieth century European philosophy, in a qualitatively different way from that in which it previously appeared as a paradigmatic example of the unchanging character of philosophical questions" (Osborne, *The Politics of Time*, x).

154. Lash, *Another Modernity, A Different Rationality*, 294.

155. Baudrillard, *Symbolic Exchange and Death*, 158–159.

Chapter 1

1. Bourke, *Dismembering the Male*, 210.

2. Strange, *Death, Grief and Poverty in Britain 1870–1914*, 266.

3. See Richardson, *Death, Dissection, and the Destitute* for a detailed and influential analysis of this legislation. For discussion of a complementary set of political issues in the United States, see Sappol, *A Traffic in Dead Bodies*. See Hotz, *Literary Remains* for an examination of literary responses to Victorian social conflicts over the dead, including the Anatomy Act. Without discussing the Anatomy Act but in a discussion closely related to the class conflict at its heart, Strange argues that there "are parallels... between working-class cultures of death before the war and rituals developed in wartime to deal with the circumstances of large numbers of deaths in brutal contexts and foreign spaces: the network of support and notions of 'adoptive kinship,' the improvisation of commemorative ritual, and the development of psychological strategies to manage grief where symbolic of verbal forums for expression were compromised. The most striking parallel between bereavement before and during the war, however, is with reference to the pauper or common grave" (Strange, *Death, Grief and Poverty in Britain 1870–1914*, 266). Similarly, Bourke compares workhouse and war corpses, both of which were buried by the state (Bourke, *Dismembering the Male*, 215).

4. See Scarry, *The Body in Pain*, chapter two, and particularly section I, for a robust meditation on how the central purpose of war is to injure bodies and how this fact is obfuscated.

5. See Winter, *Sites of Memory, Sites of Mourning*, 23–27, for a discussion of this policy in England and France. After long refusing a return of the dead from war zones, in September 1920 the French government yielded to strong political pressure and reversed its stance, allowing their exhumation and return.

6. Bloch and Parry, "Introduction," 41.

7. Taylor, "Introduction," 149.

8. Foucault, *The Birth of Biopolitics*, 4.

9. Brown, *The Reaper's Garden*, 258.

10. Hemingway, *Death in the Afternoon*, 133–134.

11. Beckett, *The Great War 1914–1918*, 438.

12. This figure comes from J. M. Winter's *The Great War and the British People* (67). Using different sources, he calculates the figure to be 722,785 (71). See his chapter 3, "The Lost Generation," 65–99, for a thorough discussion of the statistical difficulties in calculating British war casualties. Ian Beckett puts the number at 722,000 (*The Great War 1914–1918*, 440).

13. For a discussion of these programs, see DeGroot, *Blighty*. He writes: "Beginning in 1920, pilgrimages to the graveyards in France and Belgium were organised. The word 'pilgrimage' (as they were officially called) was particularly apt. The visits proved very popular; cemeteries became, as they were intended, shrines of remembrance. The first to organise trips was the Young Men's Christian Association (YMCA), followed soon after by the British Legion, Red Cross and other charitable groups. The cost—£6 in 1920—was kept as low as possible, but still ruled out the very poor. Before long, sensing a market, the travel agent Thomas Cook began to organise tours and advise on suitable hotel accommodation. Cars could be rented at railway stations and maps to cemeteries supplied. French and Belgian entrepreneurs conducted tours of battlefields, complete with real trenches" (DeGroot, *Blighty*, 286). See also Jalland, *Death in War and Peace*, 63–82.

14. Hemingway, *Death in the Afternoon*, 134.
15. Booth, *Postcards from the Trenches*, 53, 50.
16. Blunden, *Undertones of War*, 131.
17. Clarke, 'Memoir,' 6. Quoted in Bourke, *Dismembering the Male*, 77.
18. Cloete, *A Victorian Son*, 231.
19. Fussell, *The Great War and Modern Memory*, 49.
20. Owen, *Collected Letters*, 429.
21. Dyer, *The Missing of the Somme*, 12. Bourke also refers to this phenomenon of soldiers digging graves in advance and attributes it, at least in part, to an official order of the 47th Division, from M. Alexander, May 22, 1917 (Bourke, *Dismembering the Male*, 214).
22. Cloete, *A Victorian Son*, 227.
23. West, *The Diary of a Dead Officer*, 82–83.
24. Leed, *No Man's Land*, 21.
25. Winter, *The Great War and the British People*, 305.
26. Keegan, *The First World War*, 421–422.
27. Cloete, *A Victorian Son*, 236–237.
28. Read, *Naked Warriors*, 17.
29. Booth, *Postcards from the Trenches*, 51.
30. West, *The Diary of a Dead Officer*, 65–66.
31. The war recreated and exacerbated a familiar Victorian anxiety about accidentally being buried alive. Terror of being buried alive was so pervasive among soldiers that, as Eric Leed writes, "hysterical paralysis as a result of premature burial earned its own pathological category as 'burial alive neurosis.'" In this scenario, dying "was given not just to those who appeared in the mortality statistics but also to those who were forced to remain in the expanding moment between the extinction of all choice and the extinction of life" (Leed, *No Man's Land*, 23).
32. MacGill, *The Great Push*, 248–249.
33. Boyd-Orr, *As I Recall*, 71.
34. Borden, *The Forbidden Zone*, 181–182.
35. Winter, "Some Paradoxes of the First World War," 9.
36. Beckett, *The Great War 1914–1918*, 349.
37. Bourke, *Dismembering the Male*, 211. In an important literary study, Sandra Gilbert renders this amplification of state power over soldiers in symbolic terms: "Helplessly entrenched on the edge of No Man's Land, [a] faceless [soldier] saw that the desert between him and his so-called enemy was not just a metaphor for the technology of death and the death dealt by technology, it was also a symbol for the state, whose nihilistic machinery he was powerless to control or protest. Fearfully assaulted by a deadly bureaucracy on the one side and a deadly technocracy on the other, he was No Man, an inhabitant of the inhumane new era and a citizen of the unpromising new land into which this war of wars had led him" (Gilbert, "Soldier's Heart," 198).
38. Longworth, *The Unending Vigil*, 28.
39. Winter, *Sites of Memory, Sites of Mourning*, 23.
40. Longworth, *The Unending Vigil*, 23.

41. Ibid., 56

42. Bourke, *Dismembering the Male*, 235.

43. Winter, *Sites of Memory, Sites of Mourning*, 23; Longworth, *The Unending Vigil*, 56–57.

44. Eksteins, *Rites of Spring*, 255; Dyer, *The Missing of the Somme*, 14.

45. Faust, *This Republic of Suffering*, 268.

46. Quoted in Longworth, *The Unending Vigil*, 33.

47. Bourke, *Dismembering the Male*, 225–226.

48. December 18, 1920, 15, 18. Quoted in Bourke, *Dismembering the Male*, 226.

49. Williamson, *The Wet Flanders Plain*, 130–131. Quoted in Bourke, *Dismembering the Male*, 225.

50. Scarry, *The Body in Pain*, 127.

51. Ibid., 118–119.

52. Booth, *Postcards from the Trenches*, 21.

53. Ibid., 23.

54. Macherey, *A Theory of Literary Production*, 113.

55. Robb, *British Culture and the First World War*, 111, 121.

56. Ibid., 97.

57. Deer, *Culture in Camouflage*, 35; Robb, *British Culture and the First World War*, 121.

58. Robb, *British Culture and the First World War*, 119–120.

59. Gough, *A Terrible Beauty*, 23.

60. Ibid., 22–23.

61. Cork, *A Bitter Truth*, 125.

62. *Illustrated London News*, September 4, 1915, and May 15, 1915; Gough, *A Terrible Beauty*, 43.

63. *Daily Mirror*, November 22, 1916. Quoted in Walsh, *C. R. W. Nevinson*, 177.

64. However, Bourke mentions that, "despite censorship regulations, photographs of dead soldiers were widely circulated," and shows an example, but does not provide further information about how or where these photographs were circulated (Bourke *Dismembering the Male*, 211).

65. Cork, *A Bitter Truth*, 125.

66. Gough, *A Terrible Beauty*, 46, 51.

67. Bone, *The Western Front* v.1, LXXII.

68. Bone, *The Western Front* v. 2, XX.

69. Ibid., XLVII.

70. Owen, *Collected Letters*, 429.

71. Gough, *A Terrible Beauty*, 38.

72. The ideological acceptance of such a painting brings to mind a passage in Blunden's memoir, in which he recalls "a shell-hole...used by us as a latrine, with those two flattened German bodies in it, tallow-faced and dirty-stubbled, one spectacled, with fingers hooking the handle of a bomb" (Blunden, *Undertones of War*, 128). This close attention to the German dead, like Orpen's, registers a displaced desire to look closely at the British dead too.

73. Brown, *The Imperial War Museum Book of the First World War*, 236; Simmonds, *Britain and World War One*, 243. Subsequent War Office films were less successful with the public, so "in February 1918 the ministry attempted to stimulate public interest in official films by launching 'cine-motor' tours, where free film

shows would be projected from the backs of specially adapted lorries, either onto a 25-foot screen or the gable ends of houses. The initial experiment in Wales proved enough of a success to persuade propagandists that the idea was viable, and two major tours were undertaken in April and May, and September and October, 1918, attracting audiences averaging 163,000—a far cry from the millions who paid to watch *Battle of the Somme* just two years earlier" (Simmonds, *Britain and World War One*, 244).

74. Haste, *Keep the Home Fires Burning*, 90–91; Robb, *British Culture and the First World War*, 119. In 1925, Brigadier General John Charteris, speaking at the National Arts Club in New York, admitted that when he was head of intelligence services for the British army during the war he had helped produce the story of the corpse factory as propaganda to turn China against the Germans. For an extensive discussion of this entire affair, see Rubinshtain, *German Atrocity or British Propaganda*.

75. Sassoon, *Collected Poems*, 27.

76. Gough, *A Terrible Beauty*, 171.

77. Heard, *William Roberts*, 45–46, 51.

78. Gough, *A Terrible Beauty*, 290.

79. Clark, *The Sight of Death*, 236.

80. I have not been able to discover if Williamson was left-handed. Williamson's background note to the painting describes the attack it was based on:

> Before dawn, an intensive bombardment of our lines opened up, and was maintained for a couple of hours. In the gloom and rain the storm troops then came over, and smashed through our first two lines. The picture shows them moving with exact discipline and just appearing to the few men in reserve. The shell holes in the foreground show the accuracy of the preceding bombardment. The British are hopelessly outnumbered, but training and discipline keep them going, without thought of retirement. Two men are firing a Lewis gun. The wounded man has a poor chance of getting away; he must cross much open country swept by enemy fire, and go through a heavy barrage. At the last the few left were surrounded, but fought their way out, some wounded, some being taken prisoner. (Quoted in Gough, *A Terrible Beauty*, 292)

81. "No purpose could be served, from the official point of view, by stressing the obscenity of war. Orpen's attempts to acknowledge the conflict's worst aspects counted against him in political circles" (Cork, *A Bitter Truth*, 195).

82. Gough, *A Terrible Beauty*, 130–150.

83. Cork, *A Bitter Truth*, 195–196.

84. Gough, *A Terrible Beauty*, 38.

85. Gough, *A Terrible Beauty*, 38; Walsh, *C. R. W. Nevinson*, 202–203.

86. Walsh, *C. R. W. Nevinson*, 160–161.

87. Ibid., 176–178.

88. Ibid., 178.

89. Quoted in Walsh, *C. R. W. Nevinson*, 178.

90. This biographical summary is based on Hibberd, *Wilfred Owen* and Jon Stallworthy's timeline in Owen, *The complete poems and fragments* v. 1, xiii-xix.

91. Dyer, *The Missing of the Somme*, 30.

92. Das, *Touch and Intimacy in First World War Literature*, 141–142. Das's investigation into literary responses to the war's tactile experiences, and particularly the tactility between soldiers' bodies, approaches death as the loss of touch and war poetry as its symbolic compensation: "Trench poetry might be seen as a phantasmatic space within which the returned soldier-poets would continue to reach out to their dead comrades, infusing them with the warmth they had once known" (Iibid., 28). This is a helpful way for thinking about the final line of "Greater Love," cited below.

93. Sarah Cole analyzes "Greater Love" in detail, focusing on its dynamics of male intimacy in the context of violence. In particular, she comments on lines in which "Owen stresses that the pathos of the physical body reaches its apex neither in heterosexual conventions nor in the spirit of comradeship, but at the moment of dismemberment and death" (Cole, *Modernism, Male Friendship, and the First World War*, 161).

94. Cole, *At the Violet Hour*, 39.

95. Ibid., 44.

96. Dugmore, *When the Somme Ran Red*, xi–xiii, xiv.

97. Brooke, *The Collected Poems*, 115.

98. Deer, *Culture in Camouflage*, 26; cf. 27.

99. Woolf, *Mrs. Dalloway*, 180–181.

100. Forster, *Abinger Harvest* and *England's Pleasant Land*, 31.

101. Ibid., 31–32.

102. Read, *Naked Warriors*, 34.

103. Whitman, *Leaves of Grass and Other Writings*, 255–256.

104. Harrison, *Dominion of the Dead*, 20.

105. Others have provided different kinds of insight about this poem. Jay Winter considers "Parable" in the context of two other notable war poems about the binding of Isaac, also from 1918: Osbert Sitwell's "The Modern Abraham" and "The Next War" (Winter, *Sites of Memory, Sites of Mourning*, 220). Douglas Kerr considers a biographical contradiction embedded within the poem: "As a soldier he described himself ruefully as 'a conscientious objector with a very seared conscience'(*CL* 461), but as an officer he was more than that—he was the voice and instrument of an authority whose words could have terrible meanings for the people in his charge. The secret irony of 'The Parable of the Old Man and the Young'...was that Owen himself was cast as Abram, the patriarch commissioned to execute an order by a higher command whose word he could not question....Owen's rank put him among the patriarchs and the crucifiers" (Kerr, *Wilfred Owen's Voices*, 221–222).

106. Ramazani, *Poetry of Mourning*, 69.

107. Capdevila and Voldman, *War Dead*, 38.

108. Ibid., 46, 58, 52, 42. For details about the system of identity discs used to identify and account for soldiers, see van Emden, *The Quick and the Dead*, 136. For a detailed discussion of corpse logistics during the U. S. Civil War, see Faust, *This Republic of*

Suffering, chapter three. For further discussion of changes in war death in the West, and particularly in memorialization, see Ariès, *The Hour of Our Death*, 547–551.

109. Dyer, *The Missing of the Somme*, 27.

110. Gilbert, *The First World War*, xv.

111. Foucault, "'Omnes et Singulatim,'" 325.

112. Foucault, *Security, Territory, Population*, 1.

113. Ibid., 122.

114. Foucault, *The History of Sexuality* v. 1, 145–146.

115. Ibid., 144.

116. Ibid., 138.

117. Ibid., 103.

118. Ibid., 137.

119. Stathis Gourgouris speculates on the implication of biopolitics in violent death in the contemporary world in a critique of capitalism. He seems to approach biopolitics through Adorno's thought, that is, with a concern for how capitalism cultivates not simply life but damaged life: "Life is valued, protected, and produced everywhere it is devalued, incapacitated, and abused. If capitalism can claim to be immortal, that is precisely because it has managed to make profitable technologies of both death and birth.... Great is the irony that shows an alleged politics of life (the humanitarian impulse) rising out of the industry of death, a skill at which so-called civilizing governments are particularly adept" (Gourgouris, *Does Literature Think?*, 341–342).

120. Winter, "Some Paradoxes of the First World War," 10.

121. Ibid., 12.

122. Soloway, "Eugenics and Pronatalism in Wartime Britain," 373. For an analysis of pronatalism during the War in France, see Huss, "Pronatalism and the Popular Ideology of the Child in Wartime France"; in Germany, see Usborne, "'Pregnancy is the Woman's Active Service.'"

123. Foucault, *The History of Sexuality* v. 1, 136.

124. Agamben, *Homo Sacer*, 122.

125. England and France both selected their corpses by lot, but France ritualized its selection process more than the British.

> The British selection was made without publicity: six unidentified bodies were dug from sites of battle in France and Belgium, sealed in coffins and driven in six motor ambulances to an army hut near Ypres, where an officer was blindfolded and led until his hand touched one of the coffins. The French procedure was thoroughly public, making the selection itself the beginning of the ritual. The choice was entrusted not to an officer but to a newly conscripted corporal whose father was among the Missing; the eight coffins were borne to no mere hut but to an underground citadel at Verdun, where Corporal Auguste Tain placed on one of them a bouquet of flowers picked from the battlefield. The ceremony of choosing was itself an episode in the sacralization of Verdun as a holy place of the Third Republic. (Inglis, "Entombing Unknown Warriors," 11)

For a slightly different account of France's process, see Mosse, *Fallen Soldiers*, 94–95.

126. Bourke, *Dismembering the Male*, 237; Dyer, *The Missing of the Somme*, 22. In Paris, the coffin of the unknown French soldier "was accompanied throughout the day by

a fictitious family: a war widow, a mother and father who had lost a son and a child who had lost his father"; "the ceremonies of 11 November 1920 brought to the streets of Paris hundreds of thousands of people in tears, convinced they were seeing their lost relative go by" (Audoin-Rouzeau and Becker, *14–18*, 199).

127. Mosse, *Fallen Soldiers*, 94.

128. van Emden, *The Quick and the Dead*, 264–265.

129. Cannadine, "War and Death, Grief and Mourning in Modern Britain," 223.

130. Gregory, *The Silence of Memory*, 26; Cannadine, "War and Death, Grief and Mourning in Modern Britain," 223.

131. Gregory, *The Silence of Memory*, 26–27.

132. Blythe, *The Age of Illusion*, 10.

133. November 11, 1920. Quoted in Bourke, *Dismembering the Male*, 250; quoted in Watkins, *The Undiscovered Country*, 240.

134. Laqueur, "Names, Bodies, and the Anxiety of Erasure," 126.

135. Cole, *Modernism, Male Friendship, and the First World War*, 152.

136. Verdery, *The Political Lives of Dead Bodies*, 50.

137. Italy, Belgium, Portugal, and the United States performed the ceremony in 1921, Czechoslovakia and Yugoslavia in 1922, Romania and Bulgaria in 1923; by 1930 it had also been performed by Austria, Hungary, Poland, and Greece, while the Canadians and Australians "were content to have the body in Westminster Abbey defined as representing the whole empire" (Inglis, "Entombing Unknown Soldiers," 7). However, this ceremony did not succeed in Germany. John Keegan describes the debacle, which revealed the volatile emotional power of this appropriation of corpses in the context of war, and particularly the volatility of relations between anonymous corpses and the state:

> When the Germans attempted to create a national memorial to their dead in 1924… the unveiling broke down into a welter of political protest. The speech made by President Ebert, who had lost two sons, was heard out. The two minutes of silence that was supposed to follow was interrupted by the shouting of pro-war and anti-war slogans, which precipitated a riot that lasted all day. The agony of a lost war continued to divide Germany, as it would until the coming of Hitler nine years later. Soon after his assumption of the Chancellorship, Nazi writers began to represent Hitler, the "unknown corporal," as a living embodiment of the "unknown soldier" Weimar Germany had failed as a state to honour. It was not long before Hitler, in his speeches as *Fürhere* of the German nation, began to refer to himself as "an unknown soldier of the world war." He was sowing the seed that would reap another four million German corpses. (Keegan, *The First World War*, 6)

138. Inglis, "Entombing Unknown Soldiers," 17–18. John Dos Passos's enthralling last chapter in *Nineteen Nineteen* traces the course of the U.S. unknown before being buried in Arlington National Cemetery. It is not all satirical, but it ends with a satire of this practice of awarding military decorations to unknowns:

> Where his chest ought to have been they pinned
> the Congressional Medal, the D.S.C., the Mèdaille Militaire, the Belgian Croix de Guerre, the Italian gold medal, the Vitutea Militara sent by Queen Marie of

Rumania, the Czechoslovak War Cross, the Virtuti Militari of the Poles, a wreath sent by Hamilton Fish, Jr., of New York, and a little wampum presented by a deputation of Arizona redskins in warpaint and feathers. All the Washingtonians brought flowers.

Woodrow Wilson brought a bouquet of poppies. (Dos Passos, *Nineteen Nineteen*, 412)

W. H. Auden also slyly satirizes reverence toward these unknowns in the dedication to *Poems* (1930): "*Let us honour if we can / The vertical man / Though we value none / But the horizontal one*" (Auden, *The English Auden*, 19). This satirizing of collective adherence to an unknown corpse continues in his 1939 poem "The Unknown Citizen."

139. Verdery, *The Political Lives of Dead Bodies*, 28, 29. Scarry discusses the referential instability of war casualties in *The Body in Pain*, 116–117.

140. Anderson's insight is into both the quintessential modernity of the tomb and its necessarily nationalist structure:

> No more arresting emblems of the modern culture of nationalism exist than cenotaphs and tombs of Unknown Soldiers.... [T]hey are... saturated with ghostly *national* imaginings. (This is why so many different nations have such tombs without feeling any need to specify the nationality of their absent occupants. What else could they be *but* Germans, Americans, Argentinians... ?)
>
> The cultural significance of such monuments becomes even clearer if one tries to imagine, say, a Tomb of the Unknown Marxist or a cenotaph for fallen Liberals. Is a sense of absurdity avoidable? The reason is that neither Marxism nor Liberalism are much concerned with death and immortality. If the nationalist imagining is so concerned, this suggests a strong affinity with religious imaginings. (Anderson, *Imagined Communities*, 9-10)

The nearly devotional response to the tomb certainly supports this association. Inglis describes in detail ways in which unknowns were enlisted for nationalist causes, typically by conservative political parties, in "Entombing Unknown Warriors," 18–19.

141. Dyer, *The Missing of the Somme*, 29.

142. Woolf, *The Common Reader*, 34. This sounds less like disparagement when compared to Yeats, who in his later role of anthologizer explains Owen's exclusion from the 1936 *Oxford Book of Modern Verse* by saying, in its introduction, that "passive suffering is not a theme for poetry" (Yeats, "Introduction," xxxiv). Woolf also discusses Owen in *Three Guineas*, where she finds him a rare example of a man against the militarization of culture (Woolf, *Three Guineas*, 8).

143. Woolf, *To the Lighthouse*, 146.

144. In *Mrs. Dalloway*, Ms. Kilman passes through Westminster Abbey where, "as people gazed round and shuffled past the tomb of the Unknown Warrior, still she barred her eyes with her fingers and tried in this double darkness, for the light in the Abbey was bodiless, to aspire above the vanities, the commodities, to rid herself both of hatred and love" (Woolf, *Mrs. Dalloway*, 133–134).

145. London, "Posthumous Was a Woman," 50. For other essays on Woolf's reaction to the postwar culture of public memorialization, see McVicker, "'Six Essays on London Life'" and Bradshaw, "'Vanished Like Leaves.'"

146. Dyer, *The Missing of the Somme*, 35.
147. Schleifer, *Modernism and Time*, 126.
148. Woolf, *Mrs. Dalloway*, 9, 153; c.f. 138, 182.
149. Jameson, "Cognitive Mapping," 353.
150. And, at the end of Woolf's British museum passage, who is this woman yelling in the street, demanding access, but the displaced women who once held sovereignty over the bodies and rituals of the dead, displaced from corpses just as they were from births over the nineteenth and twentieth centuries? In his history of the War Graves Commission, Longworth describes how, at its first meeting in November 1917, the question was raised about the absence of women, despite the fact that women's organizations had pressed for representation: "Gosling later raised the question at a Commission meeting but others hinted at female inefficiency and the matter went no further. Most of the Commissioners were imbued with Victorian attitudes that had no doubt been hardened by recollections of suffragette activities before the war" (*The Unending Vigil*, 29).
151. In a compelling analysis, Allyson Booth reads this image of tombstones in transit as a subversion of the basic signifying apparatus around the dead: "Woolf...presents us with mobile stones that point to a corpse in Putney without actually marking it. Subverting our implicit trust in the durability of the materials marking graves and their ability to ensure permanence of epitaph, Woolf evokes smoke rather than granite to make a grave, as we see when bits of the Cornish coastline prompt the narrator to think of buried corpses...In other words, the painstaking effort of the War Graves Commission accurately and permanently to mark the graves of as many dead soldiers as possible...are disregarded by a narrator who imagines a grave in the sea (indicated by the swoop of a gull), a gravestone on a truck (in London, with its fleeting salute to a corpse buried in Putney)" (Booth, *Postcards from the Trenches*, 45).
152. Inglis, "Entombing Unknown Warriors," 13.
153. Smythe, "Woolf's Elegiac Enterprise," 70.
154. Booth, *Postcards from the Trenches*, 46.
155. Woolf describes a curious moment at the Cenotaph in her diary entry for December 12, 1920: "I forget my first view of Molly [Hamilton], going down the Strand the night of the Cenotaph; such a lurid scene, like one in Hell. A soundless street; no traffic; but people marching. Clear, cold, & windless. A bright light in the Strand; women crying Remember the Glorious Dead, & holding out chrysanthemums. Always the sound of feet on the pavement. Faces bright & lurid—poor M.'s worn enough by that illumination. I touched her arm; whereupon she jumped, like some one woken. A ghastly procession of people in their sleep" (Woolf, *Diary* v. 2, 79–80).
156. Agamben, *Homo Sacer*, 119.
157. Woolf, *To the Lighthouse*, 160.
158. The widespread interest in spiritualism and séances after the war was a crucial part of this phenomenon. David Cannadine reports, for example, that there were 309 societies associated with the Spritualists National Union by 1919, up from 125 in 1902, the year of its founding, and up from 141 in 1914. By the mid-1930s, there were over two thousand local spiritualist societies, involving a quarter of a million people

(Cannadine, "War and Death, Grief and Mourning in Modern Britain," 227–229). See also Watkins, *The Undiscovered Country*, 246–252.

159. Woolf, *Mrs. Dalloway*, 51.

Chapter 2

1. There is a wide range of commentary relevant to the term *burial plot*. Peter Brooks considers this double sense, both spatial and temporal, of *plot* (although without considering burial plots specifically): "There may be a subterranean logic connecting these heterogeneous meanings. Common to the original sense of the word is the idea of boundedness, demarcation, the drawing of lines to mark off and order. This easily extends to the chart or diagram of the demarcated area, which in turn modulates to the outline of the literary work. From the organized space, plot becomes the organizing line, demarcating and diagramming that which was previously undifferentiated. We might think here of the geometrical expression, plotting points, or curves, on a graph by means of coordinates, as a way of locating something, perhaps oneself (Brooks, *Reading for the Plot*, 12). Lisa K. Perdigao has also used the phrase "Modernist Burial Plot" in her discussion of Brooks in *From Modernist Entombment to Postmodern Exhumation*, 13 ff. In *Narrative Bodies*, Daniel Punday writes that "one of the essential conditions for meaningful narrative is to sort bodies from nonbodies" and observes that "in contrast to the importance given a dead body in a play like Sophocles's *Antigone*—where a dead body continues to be a *body* endowed with cultural and familial significance—we might note the complete lack of interest in such bodies in most contemporary popular action films and adventure stories, where the bodies of the dead antagonists are rarely accorded significant attention. In these narratives bodies are inanimate and thus, narratively at least, no longer bodies at all" (Punday, *Narrative Bodies*, 58–59).

2. Harrison, *Dominion of the Dead*, 143.

3. In this distinct temporality, the burial plot complements the elegy; it elaborates the traditional (if often superseded) "plot" of elegiac lyric, in which a more or less discrete subjectivity recuperates itself from intense grief, by using a longer narrative form to tell a communal story about the logistics for transporting and burying the dead. We might think of this logistical plot as the social correlative for the elegy's psychic one, and that what is at stake in this objectification or externalization of private grief is the community's role in tending to the dead. I take up the idea of community in my discussion of Faulkner.

4. Humphreys, "Death and Time," 263.

5. Kermode, *The Sense of an Ending*, 45.

6. "Decay is the justification for all funeral rites. Everything is brought into play in order to tame it (display of the corpse), hide it (winding-sheets, the sarcophagus), forbid it absolutely (embalming and mummification, incineration, cannibalistic ingestion), retard it (corporal attentions), or accelerate it (towers of silence...). A profound need underlies all these approaches to decay: to stabilize the deceased in an indestructible medium—a stage marking the reconciliation of the community with his death. These remains—mummy, relic, ashes, or bones—all civilizations, without exception, persist in preserving" (Thomas, "Funeral Rites," 3238).

7. Arnold van Gennup introduced the concept of liminality in 1904 in *Les rites de passage* with close attention to death rituals, and was surprised by the way in which the corpse's transitional phase dominated its initial separation from or final incorporation into other states: "On first considering funeral ceremonies, one expects rites of separation to be their most prominent component, in contrast to rites of transition and rites of incorporation, which should be only slightly elaborated. A study of the data, however, reveals that the rites of separation are few in number and very simple, while the transition rites have a duration and complexity sometimes so great that they must be granted a sort of autonomy" (van Gennup, *The Rites of Passage*, 146). This "sort of autonomy" of the corpse's time of transition is what interests me. Victor Turner's resuscitation of the concept of the liminal in the latter 1960s gives us further language for the quality of the undisposed corpse: "During the intervening 'liminal' period, the characteristics of the ritual subject (the 'passenger') are ambiguous; he passes through a cultural realm that has few or none of the attributes of the past or coming state"; "Liminal entities are neither here nor there; they are betwixt and between the positions assigned and arrayed by law, custom, convention, and ceremonial"; "the most characteristic midliminal symbolism is that of paradox, or being *both* this *and* that" (Turner, *The Ritual Process*, 94; Turner, "Variations on a Theme of Liminality," 37).

8. Heidegger, *Being and Time*, 221–222.

9. Harrison, *Dominion of the Dead*, 147.

10. Fynsk, "Crossing the Threshold, on 'Literature and the Right to Death,'" 75.

11. Ray, "From Remote Times to the Bronze Age," 14.

12. Boyer, *Religion Explained*, 209.

13. Blotner, "Line and Page Notes to *As I Lay Dying*," 266.

14. Homer, *The Iliad*, ll. 5–6. Harrison even suggests that "the underlying 'matter' of the epic as a whole" is the "dreaded fate" of a corpse not receiving ceremonial disposal (Harrison, *Dominion of the Dead*, 146). As I suggest in the introduction, I think this is also an apt description of the underlying matter for a few modern novels of quasi-epic ambition: Cormac McCarthy's *Blood Meridian*, Albert Camus's *The Plague*, and José Saramago's *Blindness*. While not plotted according to burial obligations, their worlds are covered with corpses that need burial, and these corpses take on increasing significance as the novels go on.

15. For a discussion of modernism's treatment of the related tradition of katabasis, descending to the underworld to speak with the dead in the fashion of Odysseus, see Lewis, *Religious Experience and the Modernist Novel*, 170–177.

16. Even in an article focused entirely on "Hades," Terrinoni initially approaches the chapter as a kind of a warm up for "Circe," important for how it anticipates the later chapter's descent into something like the underworld. (He goes on to interpret the chapter in terms of Swedenborg and Jung) (Terrinoni, "Hades"). R. M. Adams takes a similar, slightly disappointed, stance: "The real *descensus Averni* of Joyce's book…is reserved for the chapter known as 'Circe'; there we see a really haunting vision of Bloom's psychic underworld, compared with which 'Hades', though overcast and perhaps obsessed, is essentially a daylight chapter" (Adams, "Hades," 92). He goes on, perhaps protesting too much, to assure us that "[t]his is said, not to

diminish the episode, simply to define its quality" (ibid.). Maria Tymoczko insists on the same comparison: "There is no heroic crisis for Bloom in 'Hades': he escapes 'back to the world again' (6.995), but he returns relatively unchanged. The personal crisis and integration characteristic of the hero's incursion to the otherworld are reserved for the adventure in Nighttown" (Tymoczko, *The Irish Ulysses*, 201). This comparison distracts from the unique narrative task that Joyce sets for himself in "Hades," not to get Bloom to the underworld, but to settle someone else (Dignam / Elpenor) there. Tymoczko goes on to say that "Joyce used the motif of the ordinary funeral to a variety of good ends" in "Hades," but doesn't elaborate (ibid.). For an exception to this dismissive tendency, and for an elaborate, impressive reading of the chapter's dynamics of visibility and the implications of death for the gender-ing of labor, see Devlin, "Visible Shades and Shades of Visibility." Among all the episodes, Woolf singles out "Hades" for praise in "Modern Fiction" (Woolf, *The Common Reader*, 151).

17. Lewis, *Religious Experience and the Modernist Novel*, 187.

18. Adams, "Hades," 93. Adams describes Joyce's biographical background for the chapter as primarily the burial of his friend Matthew Kane in Glasnevin on July 13, 1904, although conflated with the funerals of his mother (August 1903) and brother George (March 1902), at the same cemetery. He also refers to elements of "Hades" that occur in *Stephen Hero* as Isabel Dedalus's funeral (Adams, "Hades," 92–94, 107–108).

19. Humphreys, "Death and Time," 274; Ellman, *James Joyce*, 244. Sebastian Knowles elaborates this point about rampant resurrections: "Everywhere in Joyce characters are being raised from the dead, from 'The Ballad of Joking Jesus'—'*And tell Tom, Dick and Harry I rose from the dead*' (19)—to Lazarus, losing his job (105), and back to Michael Furey, who is reincarnated in 'The Dead' as a spectral image from the past, to be reburied not in earth but in the snow that falls faintly over all the living and the dead. The return of Stephen's mother and the reawakening of Finnegan are only the first places to start in Joyce, for an eternity of being dead is Joyce's greatest preoccupation. Bloom is a posthumous child in 'Circe' (494) and a grass widow dan-dles a post mortem child in 'Eumaeus' (624), before which the curse '*Mortacci sui!*' (621) suggests the rotting of the dead. Dignam returns, ghouleaten, as a lugubrious beagle (472), and in the final pandemonium of 'Circe' the earth trembles, a chasm opens, and '*The dead of Dublin from Prospect and Mount Jerome in white sheepskin overcoats and black goatfell cloaks arise and appear to many*' (598)" (Knowles, *The Dublin Helix*, 49).

20. Gifford, Ulysses *Annotated*, 248.

21. As I discuss in the introduction, Vico thinks of burial in similar contract-theory terms: "With good reason burials were characterized by the sublime phrase 'com-pacts of the human race' (*foedera generis humani*), and with less grandeur were described by Tacitus as 'fellowships of humanity' (*humanitatis commercia*)" (Vico, *The New Science*, §337).

22. Joyce, *A Portrait of the Artist as a Young Man*, 135.

23. This follows Annette Weiner's anthropological argument: "The regulative force in the reproductive and regenerative cycles...occurs in death....Death, then, represents

an enormous loss, yet death constitutes the major regenerating mechanism within the system" (Weiner, "Reproduction," 81–82). Similarly, Thomas Louis-Vincent refers to funeral rites "as a theater of renewal" (Thomas, "Funeral Rites," 3234).

24. Barthes, *S/Z*, 76.

25. Bourdieu, *The Logic of Practice*, 106–107. With a similar evocation of the work of time, Baudrillard claims that "initiation is the accented beat of the operation of the symbolic. It aims neither to conjure death away, nor to 'overcome' it, but to articulate it socially" (Baudrillard, *Symbolic Exchange and Death*, 131).

26. Kenner, *Dublin's Joyce*, 225.

27. Wilson, *Axel's Castle*, 207, 209, 210.

28. Daiches, *The Novel and the Modern World*, 148–149.

29. Frank, *The Idea of Spatial Form*, 10, 21. On the other hand, Wyndham Lewis criticized Joyce, along with others, for being part of the "Time School" and celebrating the "time-mind" in contrast to his own spatially inflected "position of the plastic and visual intelligence" (Lewis, *Time and the Western Man*, xix).

30. For some of these connections, see Gordon, "Phantom Ship."

31. Moretti, *Modern Epic*, 153.

32. Bourdieu, *The Logic of Practice*, 98, 99.

33. And not just Milan: the Brookwood Necropolis Railway, a dedicated cemetery line, had been running from London since November 1854. See Clarke, *The Brookwood Necropolis Railway*.

34. Adorno, *Minima Moralia*, 232. Baudrillard describes an even more pernicious role for death in capitalism: "Labour power is instituted on death. A man must die to become labour power. He converts this death into a wage.... The very possibility of quantitative equivalence presupposes death. This is generally understood in the sense of physical exhaustion. But it must be understood in another sense. Labour is not opposed like a sort of death, to the 'fulfilment of life', which is the idealist view; labour is opposed *as a slow death* to a violent death.... Labour therefore everywhere draws its inspiration from deferred death.... Whoever works *has not been put to death*, he is refused this honour. And labour is first of all the signs of being judged worthy only of life. Does capital exploit the workers to death? Paradoxically, the worst it inflicts on them is refusing them death" (Baudrillard, *Symbolic Exchange and Death*, 39). This refusal of actual death for the slow death of compelled labor is why "the only effective reply to power is to give back what it gives you, and this is only symbolically possible by means of death"; in other words, "since [the state] thrives on my slow death, I will oppose it with my violent death" (ibid., 43).

35. Following Alex Woloch, we might also think of this tension between diachrony and synchrony, or the diachronic bulge of Dignam's burial within the novel's governing rhetorical system, as a strange version of the competition between protagonists and minor characters for narrative space and readerly attention. Woloch's analysis of "how the discrete representation of any specific individual is intertwined with the narrative's continual apportioning of attention to different characters who jostle for limited space within the same fictive universe" applies to the question of the attention demanded by Dignam in his coffin (Woloch, *The One vs. The Many*, 13). The strange twist is that Dignam, as a corpse, and the corpse by all accounts of an

unremarkable person, makes his minor claim for attention without any personality whatsoever to fascinate us, with no power of reference to an individual human life. He gathers far more attention dead than he would have alive, as if being dead distorted the "distributional matrix" of narrative reading (ibid.). (It would have been interesting had Woloch's incisive reading of *The Iliad* (1–11) been extended to Elpenor in *The Odyssey*.)

36. Brooks, *Reading for the Plot*, xv.

37. Ibid., 10.

38. Brooks, Reading for the Plot, 22; Benjamin, *Selected Writings* v. 3, 151.

39. Brooks, *Reading for the Plot*, 323. For his extensive discussion of the relation between narrative and the body, see Brooks, *Body Work*.

40. Gifford, Ulysses *Annotated*, 480.

41. In *Hamlet in Purgatory*, Stephen Greenblatt examines a very different but conceptually relevant shift in the social forms available for transactions between the living and dead. He describes the effect on Shakespeare's drama of the doctrinal rejection of Purgatory in England in the mid-fifteenth century, a purging of a realm in which a "large group of the dead...continued to exist in time and to need something that they could get only from the living, something that would enable them to escape from the hideous, dark prison in which they were trapped" (Greenblatt, *Hamlet in Purgatory*, 17). These dead, no longer able to be assisted through the purchase of suffrages, were left on their own. But they haunted the cultural landscape: "The ghosts who cry out desperately in the pages of More's *Supplication*, for fear that they are being forgotten, the ghosts who are consigned to oblivion by skeptics and reassigned to Hell in the writings of the triumphant Protestants, the ghosts who are increasingly labeled as fictions of the mind— these do not altogether vanish in the sixteenth century. Instead they turn up onstage" (ibid., 151). This struggle of the dead to reappear in human time after their doctrinal scrubbing, as with the ghost of Hamlet's father, continues in the twentieth century, and my broad point throughout this discussion is that Joyce shows how this struggle becomes more difficult.

42. Baudrillard, *Symbolic Exchange and Death*, 164.

43. *Tanakh*, 54.

44. Kenner, *"Ulysses,"* 81.

45. Ibid. Kenner also discusses this issue in an earlier book, in which he comments on Bloom's thoughts about chance in "Nausicaa": " 'Chance' is a node of intersecting themes; Bloom's continual inability to decide which events have an intelligible pattern in them and which have not is at the root of much of his pathos. He plays with ideas of chance and destiny, the fortuitous and the ineluctable, as his mood dictates; the scholastic definition of chance...controls many of the ironies of Bloomsday" (Kenner, *Dublin's Joyce*, 203).

46. Attridge, "The Postmodernity of Joyce: Chance, Coincidence, and the Reader," 14.

47. Ibid., 14–15.

48. What, for example, do we do with the recurrence of "three pounds, thirteen and six" being the same payment both to the writer of "Matcham's Masterstroke" in *Titbits* and that which Bloom imagines for a corpse sold as fertilizer: "carcass of William Wilkinson, auditor and accountant, lately deceased, three pounds thirteen and six.

With thanks" (*U* 4.505, 6.772–775; Osteen, *The Economy of* Ulysses, 56)? Like so much else in the novel, it is merely a coincidence until there is a reader for whom it is not. To me, as I discuss below, the association of the dead with an experience of contingent meaning is itself significant.

49. Bloom's question is the one that Kierkegaard criticizes as the sign of despair: "Imagine a self (and next to God there is nothing as eternal as a self), and then imagine that it suddenly occurs to a self that it might become someone other—than itself. And yet one in despair in this way, whose sole desire is the most lunatic of lunatic metamorphoses, is infatuated with the illusion that this change can be accomplished as easily as one changes clothes" (Kierkegaard, *The Sickness Unto Death*, 53). I don't think Joyce makes Bloom's thought an element of despair, and that this approach to the radical possibilities of contingency is a part of Joyce's exploration of the most exciting possibilities of the secular.

50. Gifford notes that, according to available records, the Prince of Wales did not in fact visit Gibraltar in 1870, the year of Molly's birth, but did in 1859 and 1876 (Gifford, Ulysses *Annotated*, 616).

51. Franco Moretti reads these effects in *Ulysses* as an expression of an emerging consumerist ideology of endless possibility:

> In the universe of consumption, this term means something very simple: it is a desire, a wish for new things. In the literature of the twentieth century, a very strong sense of *multiplicity* is added to this first meaning. Freedom no longer to do *something*, but rather *anything*: the idea that human beings are plural, indeterminate, realities: an intersection of existences, all equally possible.... With the appearance of this stream of consciousness, contact between the two worlds begins to fail; and the possible leads an independent life, alien and indeed hostile to any form of realization. Because realization is always renunciation: by confirming one possibility, it excludes all others. And so, instead of turning into action, the stream of consciousness finds itself *competing* with it and growing at its expense... For every narrative imposes choices, or exclusions—while the stream of consciousness seeks to keep the field of the possible wide open. And so, instead of a well developed fantasy, it gives us four drafts of ten words... They are, precisely, possibilities in the pure state: to be enjoyed as such, without any further consequence. (Moretti, *Modern Epic*, 145–147)

52. Discussing *Ulysses*, Wolfgang Iser has described this self-estrangement in contingency as the reduction of one's life to "mere curiosity": "If what happened did not happen inevitably, then the real is nothing but a chance track left by the possible. And if reality is nothing but one chance track, then it pales to insignificance beside the vast number of unseen and unfulfilled possibilities; it shrinks to the dimensions of a mere curiosity" (Iser, *The Implied Reader*, 206).

53. Beckett, *Collected Shorter Prose 1945–1980*, 101.

54. This is the "moral sentiment" that Adam Smith eloquently describes in a long, surprising passage toward the beginning of his systematic theory of sympathy: "It is miserable, we think, to be deprived of the light of the sun; to be shut out from life and conversation; to be laid in the cold grave, a prey to corruption and the reptiles of the earth; to be no more thought of in this world, but to be obliterated, in a little

time, from the affections, and almost from the memory, of their dearest friends and relations. Surely, we imagine, we can never feel too much for those who have suffered so dreadful a calamity....It is from this very illusion of the imagination, that the foresight of our own dissolution is so terrible to us, and that the idea of those circumstances, which undoubtedly can give us no pain when we are dead, makes us miserable while we are alive" (Smith, *The Theory of Moral Sentiments*, 12–13).

55. Derrida also imagines this unfinished task by affiliating the dead with the never-born, and by imagining this affiliation as a demand for justice that unhinges the present from itself: "No justice...seems possible or thinkable without the principle of some *responsibility*, beyond all living present, within that which disjoints the living present, before the ghosts of those who are not yet born or who are already dead...Without this *non-contemporaneity with itself of the living present*, without that which secretly unhinges it, without this responsibility and this respect for justice concerning those who *are not there*, of those who are no longer or who are not yet *present and living*, what sense would there be to ask the question 'where?' 'where tomorrow?' 'whither?'" (Derrida, *Spectres of Marx*, xix).

56. Berger, Berger, and Keller, *The Homeless Mind*, 9.

57. Critical approaches to the corpse in *As I Lay Dying* have varied widely, from questions of material culture and its role in nation-building to questions of textuality and "paginal form." For the former, see Baldanzi and Schlabach, "What Remains?" For the latter, see Kaufmann, "The Textual Coffin and the Narrative Corpse of *As I Lay Dying*." For a Foucauldian and Deleuzean-Guattarian approach to the novel's corpse, that seeks to avoid both materialist and textual reductions, see Edwards, "Extremities of the Body," which I discuss in more detail below.

58. While this doesn't particularly affect my argument, I want to mention a point that I haven't seen made elsewhere about Addie's request to be buried with her family of origin. Krüger-Kahloula, in an extensive survey of discrimination in burial policies and the racial politics of "necrogeographic mapping," includes a relevant description of African American burial practices in coastal Georgia. She quotes from page 213 of Margaret Davis Cate's and Orrin Sage Wightman's *Early Days of Coastal Georgia* (New York, 1955): "In some Sea Island communities, ancestry outweighs matrimony. The belief is strong among the Negroes that our body must lie with those your ancestors. Sometimes this meant that a husband and wife were buried in different cemeteries, the woman being buried by her parents in one burying ground while the husband was laid with his family in another. Even today when Negroes die elsewhere their bodies are brought back from great distances that they may rest with their own people" (quoted in Krüger-Kahloula, "On the Wrong Side of the Fence," 139). The association of Addie with African American deathways intensifies questions about how class and race relate in Faulkner's thought.

59. Nietzsche speculates about the role of the divine in the relation between the living and the dead (without discussing corpses as such) in his genealogy of the modern subject's capacity for a bad conscience: "There is a prevailing conviction that the tribe *exists* only because of the sacrifices and deeds of the forefathers,—and that these have to be *paid back* with sacrifices and deeds: people recognize an *indebtedness* [Schuld], which continually increases because these ancestors continue to exist as mighty spirits....The ancestors of the *most powerful* tribes just have grown to an

immense stature and must have been pushed into the obscurity of divine mystery and transcendence:—inevitably the ancestor himself is finally transfigured into a *god*" (Nietzsche, *On the Genealogy of Morality*, 65–66). His idea that the concept of the divine is *generated* by our guilty or indebted confrontation with the dead turns on its head the idea that the gods command us to tend to the dead: this ethical obligation is not commanded of us by the gods, but helps us create them.

60. *Tanakh*, 453.

61. *The New Oxford Annotated Bible*, 116 NT.

62. Sundquist, *Faulkner,* 42.

63. The primary Anglo-American legal manifestation of this fictionality and ambiguity is in the corpse's legal status as "quasi-property," involving custodianship and certain possessory rights, including the right to damages on behalf of the corpse before its disposal, but not full property rights, including the right to sell. Percival Jackson writes in *The Law of Cadavers and of Burial and Burial Places* that "questions which relate to the custody and disposal of the remains of the dead do not depend upon the principles which regulate the possession and ownership of property" (quoted in Sperling, *Posthumous Interests*, 142). The complex history of the concept of quasi-property has involved bodies, body parts, and bodily products throughout. Corpses have remained an especially fraught issue in this area of law. Daniel Sperling asks: "Is there something inherent in the law itself that does not make it possible to overcome people's fear of death? Historical review of the regulation of the dead suggests that the law has always suffered from low confidence in its treatment of the dead, characterized by shaky responses ranging from irrational assertiveness to complete emotionalism" (ibid., 5).

64. Nietzsche, *The Gay Science*, 110.

65. Edwards, "Extremities of the Body," 743.

66. Quoted in Sundquist, *Faulkner*, 39.

67. For an extended discussion of this network of psychic substitutions, within the context of commodity culture, see Clewell, *Mourning, Modernism, Postmodernism*, 58–74, where she argues that "compensatory substitution emerges as an absurdity" and that "the novel insists that any mourning that finds its substitutions is no mourning at all" (Clewell, *Mourning, Modernism, Postmodernism*, 66, 67). See also Edwards, "Extremities of the Body," 758. Freud describes an interesting ambivalence in traditional societies toward the dead, relevant for our purposes: while they often have rigid taboos against contact with the corpse or with anyone who has handled the corpse, suggesting a kind of hostility towards the dead, they also resist the temptation to efface its presence: "A man who has lost his wife must resist a desire to find a substitute for her…Substitutive satisfactions of such a kind run counter to the sense of mourning and they inevitably kindle the ghost's wrath" (Freud, *Totem and Taboo*, 68).

68. Heidegger, *Being and Time*, 39.

69. Ibid., 40.

70. Nancy's *The Inoperative Community*, which I discuss in detail below, is an extended commentary on Bataille's thought about community; this sentence is quoted in *The Inoperative Community*, 15.

71. Dastur, *Death*, 81.

72. Butler, *Precarious Life*, 25.
73. Sundquist, *Faulkner*, 30.
74. Sundquist, *Faulkner*, 39–40; Edwards, "Extremities of the Body," 759.
75. Sundquist, *Faulkner*, 33–34.
76. Edwards, "Extremities of the Body," 743.
77. For further discussion of the function of the title's pronoun, see Mortimer, *Faulkner's Rhetoric of Loss*, 15.
78. Sundquist, *Faulkner*, 41–42.
79. Turner, *The Ritual Process*, 96.
80. Levinas thematizes time extensively as a way to describe the self's ethical obligations to the other. His concept of diachrony, which emerges piecemeal throughout his major works, refers to a temporality beyond the totalized, immanent subject, a temporality involving a primordial and unrepresentable past that was never a present, and a prophetic future that will never arrive.
81. Nietzsche, *The Gay Science*, 194.

Chapter 3

1. Ackroyd, *T. S. Eliot*, 223; Field, *Djuna*, 219; Faltejskova, *Djuna Barnes, T. S. Eliot and the Gender Dynamics of Modernism*, 113; Herring, *Djuna*, 234.
2. Field, *Djuna*, 219.
3. Ibid., 214.
4. Strauss discusses the nineteenth-century precedents and twentieth-century legacies of this "value of absolute mortality as an individualizing principle" that culminates so prominently in *Being and Time* (Heidegger is, according to Strauss, "undoubtedly the preeminent philosopher of death in the last two hundred years") (Strauss, "After Death," 90, 97). Strauss reads so carefully into this tradition which reflects "a kind of subjectivity that is unique to the last two hundred years" that he articulates its fundamental limitation, a critique that I have tried to elaborate throughout this book: "The whole great tradition of a selfhood based on mortality is a misconstruction, an ideological subterfuge that distracts us from our relations to living people" (ibid., 90, 103). For further analysis of this death-based model of subjectivity, see also Strauss, *Subjects of Terror*, 23–73, 269–287.
5. Strauss, "After Death," 100.
6. Levinas, *God, Death, and Time*, 105.
7. Proust, *Remembrance of Things Past* v. 1, 336; Baudelaire, *Les Fleurs du Mal*, 36.
8. Ariès describes the European history of this association:

> At the end of the fifteenth century, we see the themes concerning death begin to take on an erotic meaning. In the oldest dances of death, Death scarcely touched the living to warn him and designate him. In the new iconography of the sixteenth century, Death raped the living. From the sixteenth to the eighteenth centuries, countless scenes of motifs in art and in literature associate death with love, Thanatos with Eros. These are erotico-macabre themes, or simply morbid ones, which reveal extreme complaisance before the spectacles of death, suffering, and torture....
>
> Like the sexual act, death was henceforth increasingly thought of as a transgression which tears man from his daily life, from rational society, from his

monotonous work, in order to make him undergo a paroxysm, plunging him into an irrational, violent, and beautiful world. Like the sexual act death for the Marquis de Sade is a break, a rupture. This idea of rupture is something completely new. Until this point the stress had been on the familiarity with death and with the dead.... This notion of a break was born and developed in the world of erotic phantasms. (Ariès, *Western Attitudes toward Death*, 55–58)

9. Levinas, *Entre Nous*, 217.

10. Henry Staten establishes a similar line of thought as a fundamental one: "As soon as desire is felt by a mortal being for a mortal being, eros (as desire-in-general) will always be to some degree agitated by the anticipation of loss—an anticipation that operates even with regard to what is not yet possessed" (Staten, *Eros in Mourning*, xi). Levinas conceives of love as a love for and through this anticipated loss, in what can only be seen psychoanalytically as a pathological or irrational expenditure in a psychic economy; the agitation at the anticipated loss of the other is inseparable from the love itself. Staten describes the tension between loving one who will die and a long idealizing, transcendental tradition in Platonism and Christianity that admonishes us to love only what is immortal. Jacque Lynn Foltyn approaches the relation between mourning and eros from the other direction, not through the mortality of the desired one but the beautification and erotic power of corpses: she argues that "cross-culturally, the corpse body is marked for passage into another world and transformed into the cultural body, aesthetically displaying a group's common values, customs, social roles and social relations"; as a consequence of this aestheticization of the corpse, which "can appear mask-like and even more beautiful in death than in life, it too, may be viewed as erotic" (Foltyn, "Dead Beauty," 74, 78). She describes throughout how "we aesthetically transform the dead into memory and ourselves into mourners, and so transgress, if you will, the boundary of death itself" by conjoining "the pain of grief and the pleasures of beauty" (ibid., 72, 78). Georges Bataille undertakes a quasi-anthropological exploration of the relation between the erotic and mortality throughout *Erotism: Death and Sensuality*.

11. For Lacan, unlike Freud, the death drive is not biological. He addresses the death drive—elaborating Freud's biological concept into one that accounts for the symbolic—most extensively in Seminar II, *The Ego in Freud's Theory and in the Technique of Psychoanalysis*, as well as in Seminar VII, *The Ethics of Psychoanalysis*. Donna Bentolila López: "Since Lacan's rereading of the fort-da experience, one could say that the subject has no way of coming into being save at the price of a certain 'death,' taken over so to speak, by the symbol, which manifests itself first of all as the murder of the thing. This injects, from the very start, a negativity essential to the constitution of the psychic apparatus. In this way, one could argue that the subject only comes alive and enters into life at the price of a certain 'mortification,' and he will forever be in need of the symbol" (López, "The Enigma of the Death Drive," 13).

12. López, "The Enigma of the Death Drive," 12.

13. Lacan, "Function and Field of Speech and Language," 105.

14. Adorno, *Minima Moralia*, 231–232.

15. Ibid., 232.

16. Ibid. Guy Debord takes up Adorno's line of thought in terms of the more radically vacated ontology of postmodernism: today, he writes, "spectator's consciousness,

immobilized in the falsified center of the movement of its world, no longer experiences itself as a passage toward self-realization and toward death. One who has renounced using his life can no longer admit his death....This social absence of death is identical to the social absence of life" (Debord, *Society of the the Spectacle*, sec. 160).

17. See Watney, *Policing Desire*, and Bersani, "Is the Rectum a Grave?," a discussion in part of "heterosexual association of anal sex with a self-annihilation originally and primarily identified with fantasmatic mystery of an insatiable, unstoppable female sexuality" (Bersani, *Is the Rectum a Grave?*, 29).

18. Harrison develops the striking claim that informs my language here: "Everywhere one looks across the spectrum of human cultures one finds the foundational authority of the predecessor. Nonhuman species obey only the law of vitality, but humanity in its distinctive features is through and through necrocratic. Whether we are conscious of it or not we do the will of our ancestors: our commandments come to us from their realm; their precedents are our law; we submit to the dictates, even when we rebel against them.... Why this servitude? We have no choice. Only the dead can grant us legitimacy. Left to ourselves we are all bastards" (Harrison, *Dominion of the Dead*, ix–x). This thought is in the tradition of Eliot's, particularly in "Tradition and the Individual Talent," in the sense that both take the relation to the dead as an agonistic starting point, a debtor's struggle, for artistic agency. As I discuss at the end of this chapter, Barnes will reject this model of inheritance and influence.

19. Plumb, "Introduction," xxii–xxv; Faltejskova, *Djuna Barnes, T. S. Eliot and the Gender Dynamics of Modernism*, 72–113; Ackroyd, *T. S. Eliot*, 239, 263; Sharpe, *T. S. Eliot*, 159. According to Plumb and Faltejskova, Eliot had first seen excerpts in fall 1935 from Barnes's friend Emily Coleman; received the whole thing shortly thereafter; expressed a willingness to publish it by January 26, 1936; and on April 27, 1936, wrote to Coleman that "I really believe that we are now getting to the point at which something can be done about 'Nightwood.' I should like very much to see you and have a talk with you about the book and about Miss Barnes" (quoted in Plumb, "Introduction," xxii). Eliot and Barnes met for editorial discussions on June 3 and around June 12 and before June 23, 1936. Faber and Faber published the book in October 1936. Sometime before December, Eliot wrote his introduction, which first appeared in the American edition published by Harcourt Brace in March 1937.

20. Eliot's thought here follows Augustine in the *Confessions*, where he approaches the relation between desire and mortality that concerns both Eliot and Barnes: "I was in misery, and misery is the state of every soul overcome by friendship with mortal things and lacerated when they are lost" (Augustine, *Confessions*, 4.6). Henry Staten discusses Augustine's passage as exemplary of the idealizing tradition that avoids loving what is mortal (Staten, *Eros in Mourning*, 2). Staten goes on to discern this idealizing tendency in Lacan, who also approaches worldly attachments as constitutively flawed, albeit in different terms: "The *objet a* is readily translatable into Christian language: 'the religious tradition,' Lacan tells us in his reading of Hamlet, calls the *objet a* a "*vanitas.*" 'This is how all objects are presented, all the stakes in the world of human desire—the *objets a*'" (Quoted in Staten, *Eros in Mourning*, 167). I am interested in Lacan's ambivalence about libidinal attachments to the mortal

other, about how he also approaches involvement with the other's mortality as constitutive of love.

21. Lacan, "Function and Field of Speech and Language," 101, 105, 104. Blanchot, following Hegel in a way that reveals Lacan's similar debt to him, meditates on this idea of the murder of the thing in language in relevant terms, although without Lacan's focus on the desire that results: "When I say, 'This woman,' real death has been announced and is already present in my language; my language means that this person, who is here right now, can be detached from herself, removed from her existence and presence, and suddenly plunged into a nothingness in which there is no existence or presence" (Blanchot, *The Work of Fire*, 323). He returns to this thought again and again: "In speech what dies is what gives life to speech; speech is the life of that death"; "language is *the life that endures death and maintains itself in it*" (ibid., 327, 336). Following Blanchot, and thinking as well of Lacan, Strauss writes that "the cadaver is the figure of linguistic desire" and that the "corpse is malodorous and repellent and yet we long for it with every word we speak" (Strauss, *Human Remains*, 268, 264; cf. 259–270).

22. López, The Enigma of the Death Drive," 13; Felman, *Jacques Lacan and the Adventure of Insight*, 134. Many have attempted to conceptualize language in terms of death, even if Lacan is distinct from most of these with his focus on desire. Agamben takes up this question—of the way humans "appear as both *mortal* and *speaking*"; of the way humans "possess the 'faculty' for language...and the 'faculty' for death"—in a very different way from Lacan, with a rigorous metaphysical analysis, following Hegel and Heidegger, of Voice (Agamben, *Language and Death*, xii). He traces its articulation of the negative: "The essential relationship between language and death takes place—for metaphysics—in Voice. *Death and Voice have the same negative structure and they are metaphysically inseparable.*" This is why "*thinking death is simply thinking the voice....*Just as, for Hegel, the animal finds its voice in violent death, so Dasein, in its authentic Being toward death, finds a Voice" (ibid., 86, 60). Blanchot also describes this relation between death and voice: "I say my name, and it is as though I were chanting my own dirge: I separate myself from myself, I am no longer either my presence or my reality, but an objective, impersonal presence, the presence of my name, which goes beyond me and whose stonelike immobility performs exactly the same function for me as a tombstone weighing on the void" (Blanchot, *The Work of Fire*, 324). Similarly, in his exploration of the nature of historiography, Michel de Certeau asserts that "our relation with language is always a relation with death" (de Certeau, *The Writing of History*, 102). Heidegger, of course, participates in this conversation: "Mortals are they who can experience death as death. Animals cannot do this. But animals cannot speak either. The essential relation between death and language flashes up before us, but remains still unthought" (Heidegger, *On the Way to Language*, 107).

23. Eliot in a sense relied on precisely this poetic limitation, because it leaves the essential truth and compensatory task to religion, his privileged field. Paul Morrison contrasts Eliot to Pound in this regard: "Pound is committed to the fascist city of man; Eliot awaits the coming City of God. (Hence he rejects all terrestrial fulfillments, fascist or communist.) The most poetry can hope to accomplish is to lead us, as

Beatrice led Dante, to a place where something that is not poetry can be revealed. Words toward the Word, but a crucial synapse separates the two" (Morrison, *The Poetics of Fascism*, 10). It is the point of Eliot's lines about the eloquence of the dead, then, to make us desire more than what they can offer—to make us desire the dead, in terms of their redemption from the degradation of human life.

24. Barnes, *Ladies Almanack*, 84.

25. Susan Lanser interprets this scene as a transformation of "death [in]to sexual resurrection," a reclaiming of "the positivity of the female body and the lesbian experience" in and for a reclaimed female voice, a reading that emphasizes sexual and gender politics rather than the politics or ethics of deathways (Lanser, "Speaking in Tongues," 164). As I hope I have done, Lanser also shows the ironic powers of this passage, noting that its irony also extends inward, in its subtle powers of metacommentary: "No finale could be more appropriate for the intricate discourse of *Ladies Almanack*, a text that speaks in tongues" (Lanser, "Introduction," xli); "this verbal play is metaplay: the Tongue—and Text—outlives the flesh" (Lanser, "Speaking in Tongues," 164).

26. Froula, "Corpse, Monument, Hypocrite Lecteur," 305.

27. Benjamin, *Selected Writings* v. 1, 261.

28. Ibid., 260.

29. Donoghue, *Words Alone*, 118, 117. Although he does not refer to him here, Donoghue further brings out the Benjamin in Eliot, essentially elaborating Benjamin's ideas about translation as a re-assembly of a fragmented ideal unity in terms of poetic form: "This is the work of 'The Waste Land,' 'Ash-Wednesday,' and *Four Quartets*: to establish the Word that is true because it is not our invention, against the reduction of Logos to Lexis that has been effected upon the sole authority of the human will" (ibid., 131). And, following Simmel's meditations on the aesthetics of ruins in landscape: "The ruin in language presents a different case. These fragments are broken from an original transparent language, the language before Babel destroyed its empire and established the thousand nationalisms of speech.... So the impression of peace in a ruin in landscape is replaced, so far as the ruin in language is in question, by an impression of guilt, frustration, and pathos. The only release from this impression is the partial consolation of seeing words aspire beyond their condition to create the very form by which their fragmentary state is judged" (ibid., 137).

30. Benjamin, *Selected Writings* v. 1, 261.

31. Quoted in Benjamin, *Selected Writings* v. 1, 262.

32. Throughout chapter five of *Dominion of the Dead*, Harrison examines this fact that, "regardless of our dialect, we speak with the words of the dead. That, in a special sense, is how and why we speak at all." Words, he writes with an image that also informed Eliot's construction of *The Waste Land*, "contain within them humic underworlds where the dead hold sway over the very means of speech. To descend into those depths philologists need a golden bough" (Harrison, *Dominion of the Dead*, 72). In his claim that "we are thrown into the history as well as historicity of the word," and that "in the age of the new barbarism words lose their moral memory," Harrison's thought helps us see language itself as a fertile burial ground echoing with the meaning of the lives that have passed through it (ibid., 86).

33. Levenson, *A Genealogy of Modernism*, 172–173.

34. Van Haute, "Death and Sublimation in Lacan's Reading of *Antigone*," 109; Lacan, *EP*, 285. To illustrate this idea of the second death, a function of the unappeasable desire inhering in the symbolic and therefore beyond ecological equilibrium, Lacan quotes an exemplary passage from de Sade's *System of Pope Pius VI*: "Nature wants atrocities and magnitude in crimes; the more our destructions are of this type, the more they will be agreeable to it. To be of even greater service to nature, one should seek to prevent the regeneration of the body that we bury. Murder only takes the first life of the individual whom we strike down; we should also seek to take his second life, if we are to be even more useful to nature. For nature wants annihilation; it is beyond our capacity to achieve the scale of destruction it desires" (quoted in Lacan, *EP*, 211).

35. For a detailed discussion of the ambivalent way, between enchantment and disenchantment, that "the materiality of rotting corpses permeates the poem" with reference to the war, see Cole, *At the Violet Hour*, 68–73 (68).

36. Ariès, *Western Attitudes toward Death*, 106.

37. de Certeau, *The Practice of Everyday Life*, 192, 193.

38. Ibid., 190, 193. Baudrillard's concept of symbolic exchange and death, which I discuss in the introduction, is another description of the exclusion and silence that de Certeau describes. Baudrillard writes that "the most serious danger the sick man represents, and by reason of which he is genuinely asocial and like a dangerous madman, is his profound demand to be recognised as such and to *exchange his disease*. It is an aberrant and inadmissible demand from the sick (and the dying) to base an exchange on this difference, not in order to be cared for and recover, but to *give* his disease so that it might be *received*, and therefore symbolically recognised and exchanged, instead of being neutralised in the techniques of clinical death and the strictly functional survival called health and curing" (Baudrillard, *Symbolic Exchange and Death*, 183–184).

39. Ibid., 190.

40. Ibid., 192.

41. Ibid., 193.

42. In a manuscript of what will apparently become "What the Thunder Said," Eliot has a dead person accuse the modern world of just this kind of confusion and bad faith:

> [impulses
> My feverish [impulsions gathered head
> A man lay flat upon his back, and ~~said~~/cried
> "It seems that I have been a long time dead:
> Do not report the me to the established world
>   It
> ~~The world~~ has seen strange [revolutions since I died".
>   [catalepsies
>   [I abide
> It has seen strange [revolutions: [let me abide". (Eliot, *The Waste Land: A Facsimile and Transcript of the Original Drafts*, 113)

"Do not report me to the established world": that is, the world established for the modern lives of the living, purged (in a kind cultural revolutionary program) of the dead. Although suggestive, Eliot, I believe, had to cut this section because of the way the dead man too glibly shares our language, a loss of his alterity.

43. Marvell, *The Complete Poems*, 50.

44. Clark, *The Sight of Death*, 236.

45. It is curious to note that this collapse was beginning to become apparent in Eliot's own life. Donoghue claims that "the poem issued, however circuitously, from the unhappiness of Eliot's first marriage" rather than from a Spenglerian despair for Western civilization. By 1921, as he was writing it, the couple was dealing with "money troubles, interminable illnesses of husband and wife, bad nerves in both, exhaustion, Vivienne's affair with the goatish Bertrand Russell—even though Eliot may have been party to it in the beginning and in any case was too much of a gentleman to object or to remove the tempter" (Donoghue, *Words Alone*, 110, 132).

46. Lamos, "The Love Song," 23.

47. Caroline Seymour-Jones claims that Eliot's friendship with his friend Jean Verdenal was a "revelation. Full of conflict, ascetic, yet deeply sensual as his poetry reveals, Eliot discovered that his new-found intimacy with Verdenal crystallized the struggle between his instinctive sexual orientation, which seemed predominantly homosexual at the time, and the dictates of tradition and conscience" (Seymour-Jones, *Painted Shadows*, 53). She adds that while theirs was a "gay relationship" it was "unlikely to have been a physical one," unlike those she claims he had with several young men years later (ibid., 53, 359–363). James E. Miller similarly interprets an erotic desire and intimacy between Verdenal and Eliot in their letters and Eliot's drafts of *The Waste Land* (Miller, *T. S. Eliot*, 123, 128). Gabrielle McIntire also refers to Eliot's "homosexual predilections," but Lyndall Gordon examines the relationship between the two men and asks, "Who can now determine the exact ways people of the past bent their inclinations in order to construct gender according to absurd models of masculinity and femininity?" (McIntire, *Modernism, Memory, and Desire*, 219, n. 45; Gordon, *T. S. Eliot*, 53). John Worthen dismisses these biographical claims altogether: "At the heart of all the arguments I have seen for Eliot's homosexuality lies a series of fabrications, half-truths and suppositions. He may have been attracted to men when young; he may even have found when he got married that he was not entirely heterosexual, though I suspect that exactly the opposite was the case: that he discovered just how startlingly heterosexual he was" (Worthen, *T. S. Eliot*, 140).

48. Wayne Koestenbaum's close reading of the correspondence between Eliot and Pound about *The Waste Land* is exemplary. He analyzes its highly developed figurative language, in all its ribaldry and innuendo, to the effect that Pound, as Eliot's editor, impregnated Eliot in anal sex with *The Waste Land*, and then served as midwife for it: "Eliot and his friends were conscious of the male anus as a tender and charged site where metaphors of reproduction and creativity intersect. The male modernist anus, a barren, intrinsically unprocreative zone, achieves a weird flowering—lilacs out of the dead land—when men collaborate; Pound penetrates Eliot's waste land, and fills the hollow man with child" (Koestenbaum, *Double Talk*, 123). Reading the cancelled lines "Fresca was baptized in a soapy sea / Of Symonds—Walter Pater—Vernon Lee" in *The Waste Land* drafts, Koestenbaum argues that Eliot eventually had to suppress this list of homosexual writers in order to keep the poem's fragile heteronormativity at least partly intact (Eliot, *The Waste Land: A Facsimile and*

Transcript of the Original Drafts, 41; Koestenbaum, *Double Talk*, 125). Koestenbaum also argues, following Barbara Everett, that Pound's margin note "Marianne" in response to the hyacinth girl passages refers to Pierre Marivaux's novel *La vie de Marianne*, and that in this French context the hyacinths "signified homosexuality" (ibid.).

49. After moving into Eliot's old room at the pension, for example, Verdenal writes in February 1912, "My dear friend, we are not so very far, you and I, from the point beyond which people lose that indefinable influence and emotional power over each other, which is reborn when they come together again." He requests that Eliot "send me news of yourself with suggestive details, you know the sort of thing; shake off your elegant nonchalance and spare me a little time stolen from your studies—however unworthy of it I am" (quoted in Seymour-Jones, *Painted Shadows*, 51).

50. Gordon, *T. S. Eliot*, 137.

51. Eliot, "A Commentary," 452. Quoted in Miller, *T. S. Eliot*, 116.

52. I review this commentary in detail because it paints a consistent and compelling picture. Robert Sencourt writes from his personal acquaintance with Eliot that "Jean Verdenal, as Phlebas the Phoenician, has left a profound imprint on *The Waste Land*" (Sencourt, *T. S. Eliot*, 243 n. 7). Stephen Spender also speaks from his personal acquaintance with him when he writes that "Eliot once referred to *The Waste Land* as an elegy. Whose elegy? His father's? Jean Verdenal's—mort aux Dardanelles in the war?" (Spender, *T. S. Eliot*, 111). John Peter was the first to publicize this argument about the importance of Verdenal to *The Waste Land* in a July 1952 essay that Eliot suppressed by threat of lawsuit, but which was republished in 1969 (albeit with an apologetic afterward); he describes "the love he [the speaker] feels for a dead man" as an issue throughout the poem, and in section four in particular: "He sees the friend upon whom his love was centred not only as someone who has been reft from him but also as someone already acclimatised to the kingdom of Death and perhaps unconscious of the yearning to which his death has given rise....The speaker's love is unrequited now, Death having made it so" (Peter, "A New Interpretation of *The Waste Land*," 156, 159–160). In his 1969 afterward, he elaborates: "Anyone reading Eliot with real attentiveness today, I think, can hardly avoid the conclusion that in his own youth he had a close romantic attachment to another young man," and goes on to cite Eliot's dedication to Verdenal in *Prufrock and Other Observations* in 1917. James E. Miller notes that Eliot began writing *The Waste Land* a few weeks after returning to the pension in December 1920 where he had first befriended Verdenal ten years prior; his January 22, 1921, letter to his mother says: "I stayed at my old pension Casaubon, you know the old people are all dead, and the grandson is now the proprietor....If I had not met such a number of new people there Paris would be desolate for me with pre-war memories of Jean Verdenal and the others" (quoted in Miller, *T. S. Eliot*, 133; cf. 365). Before this biography, Miller wrote an entire book on Verdenal and Eliot's poetry; see Miller, *T. S. Eliot's Personal Waste Land*. Sandra Gilbert, in an essay on the anti-pastoral elegy in modernism after the war, writes that in *The Waste Land* "the poet himself plunged into the muck of a 'rats' alley' where 'the dead men lost their bones,' and a waste land at whose center his dead friend is buried" (Gilbert, "Rats' Alley," 193, c.f. 196).

53. Koestenbaum, *Double Talk*, 123, 133.

54. Lamos, "The Love Song," 38, 28; Lamos, *Deviant Modernism*, 114.

55. For further discussion of this pun, see Frye, *T. S. Eliot*, 67, and Morrison, *Poetics of Fascism*, 67.

56. Boone, *Libidinal Currents*, 9.

57. Ibid., 209, 211.

58. Ibid., 220.

59. Kenneth Burke describes her "as a kind of 'unmoved mover' (the term that Aristotle applies to God)" (Burke, *Language as Symbolic Action*, 242).

60. "At first we only hear the doctor talking; we do not understand why he talks," Eliot writes in the introduction, and elaborates: "Most of the time he is talking to drown the still small wailing and whining of humanity, to make more supportable its shame and less ignoble its misery" (Eliot, "Introduction," xii, xiv). This description gives a sense of the barely categorizable vitality of the doctor's voice.

61. Joseph Frank catalogues their "probably not accidental" similarities in detail: "Like the man-woman Tiresias, symbol of the universal experience, the doctor has homosexual inclinations; like Tiresias he has 'fore-suffered all' by apparently being immortal (he claims to have a 'prehistoric memory,' and is always talking as if he existed in other historical periods). Like Tiresias again, who 'walked among the lowest of the dead,' the doctor is father confessor to the creatures of the night world who inhabit the novel as well as being an inhabitant of that world himself. And in his role of commentator, the doctor 'perceived the scene, and foretold the rest'" (Frank, *The Widening Gyre*, 43). These are useful connections, but Frank seems to confuse Tiresias's genders and sexualities: according to the tradition, the complexity of his identity does not seem to include same-sex relationships, as the doctor's does.

62. This non-sequential quality is what prompted Joseph Frank to include *Nightwood* in his influential 1945 essay "Spatial Form in Modern Literature" (republished in 1963 in *The Widening Gyre: Crisis and Mastery in Modern Literature*): "The eight chapters of *Nightwood* are like searchlights, probing the darkness from a different direction yet ultimately illuminating the same entanglement of the human spirit"; "these chapters are knit together, not by the progress of any action—either narrative action or, as in a stream-of-consciousness novel, the flow of experience—but by continual reference and cross reference of images and symbols that must be referred to each other spatially throughout the time-act of reading" (Frank, *The Widening Gyre*, 31–32). Frank and Burke exemplify the first wave of literary scholarship on *Nightwood*, new critical readings of its style, with some attention to its theological motifs. By the 1980s and 1990s, these readings were superseded by feminist and queer readings that placed less emphasis on *Nightwood* as a high modernist text, and these more political approaches have until only recently largely defined the critical conversation around Barnes. More recent scholarship has taken up race, philosophy of history, nationalism, and animality.

63. Plumb, "Introduction," xxiii; Faltejskova, *Djuna Barnes, T. S. Eliot and the Gender Dynamics of Modernism*, 189, n. 5. See note 19, above, for details of their editorial and publication timeline. Before Plumb's research into this editorial history and the publication of Phillip Herring's biography in the mid-1990s, scholars had often believed Eliot to be responsible for far more extensive cuts; Plumb writes that, even

with his concerns about censorship, "the editorial hand was light...Eliot blurred sexual, particularly homosexual, references and a few points that put religion in an unsavory light. However, meaning was not changed substantially" (Plumb, "Introduction," xxiii). Yet recent research also reveals that Eliot made his changes, as Faltejskova describes it, with a "tactic of carefully planned evasion," so that Barnes had no time to respond to them before the book's publication (Faltejskova, *Djuna Barnes, T. S. Eliot and the Gender Dynamics of Modernism*, 91). In other words, even if his changes were not nearly as extensive as once believed, he still "ensured his control over the text" (ibid., 91; c.f. 72–74 for a detailed discussion of the critical history of Eliot's editorial involvement in *Nightwood*).

64. Faltejskova, *Djuna Barnes, T. S. Eliot and the Gender Dynamics of Modernism*, 104.

65. See Koestenbaum, *Double Talk*, 112–139.

66. Quoted in Plumb, "Introduction," xvi. This same editor, Clifton Hadiman, would write an enthusiastic review of *Nightwood* about two years later in *The New Yorker*, after several other very favorable reviews had been published: "My hunch is that 'Nightwood', if not a work of genius throughout, has genius in it. That is rare enough....Miss Barnes is master of an English style all her own—sombre, not elegant; elliptical, not neat" (quoted in Faltejskova, *Djuna Barnes, T. S. Eliot and the Gender Dynamics of Modernism*, 6). Faltejskova discusses these contradictory responses in terms of the general dismissal of women's writing as serious literature of the time.

67. Quoted in Plumb, "Introduction," xxii.

68. Plumb, "Textual Apparatus," 144.

69. Eliot, "Introduction," xii, xvi.

70. Kaivola, *All Contraries Confounded*, 100. Her claim is complicated by its corollary that Barnes's subversive, destructive language at the same time "reinscribes key components of fascistic discourses. The text's language seems at once subversive and complicit, comic and tragic, sexist and feminist, racist and not racist, ahistorical and historical," a set of oppositions that produces "a fearful force of unusual intensity" (ibid., 60). Kaivola's entire approach is rejected by Susana S. Martins, who argues that "Barnes is too sophisticated a thinker not to recognize that 'the other side of culture' is still culture, an imaginary Other necessary for cultural self-definition. Her goal is not the destruction of culture, an impossibility in any case, but the examination of how and why culture posits something known as nature or the primitive. *Nightwood* is closer to a study of how culture is served by the production of the Other" (Martins, "Gender Trouble and Lesbian Desire in Djuna Barnes's *Nightwood*," 115).

71. Quoted in Caselli, *Improper Modernism*, 158; Caselli, *Improper Modernism*, 158.

72. Ibid., 163.

73. I realize that this claim—that Hedvig's death in the plot is the death of literalism and realism at the level of the novel's style and rhetoric—is itself a purely metaphorical one. I make it in part because of Hedvig's characterization as severe, large, materially imposing: "When she danced, a little heady with wine, the dance floor had become a tactical manoeuvre; her heels came down staccato and trained, her shoulders as conscious at the tips as those which carry the braid and tassels of promotion; the turn of her head held the cold vigilance of a sentry whose rounds are not without

apprehension" (*N* 5–6). She seems like a force for unforgiving literalism. For better or for worse, I think such a critical-metaphorical urge responds to Barnes's own urge-to-metaphor.

74. Boone, *Libidinal Currents*, 238.

75. Caselli writes, for example, that the love between Robin and Nora "is baroquely emblazoned with the stillness of death, the geology of stratification, and the 'umbra' of resurrection" (Caselli, *Improper Modernism*, 177). Erin G. Carlston argues that Barnes's "central preoccupation…, an emphasis on suffering and death," is derived from the Decadence movement of previous decades, with its baroque and morbid aestheticism. She recalls Arthur Symons definition of it in 1897 as an apt description of Barnes's writing: "that learned corruption of language by which style ceases to be organic, and becomes, in the pursuit of some new expressiveness or beauty, deliberately abnormal" (Carlston, *Thinking Fascism*, 51; quoted in Carlston, *Thinking Fascism*, 50).

76. de Lauretis, "*Nightwood* and the 'Terror of Uncertain Signs,'" 127, 129. Her reading elaborates others' insights about both Barnes's and Eliot's writing as capturing something like a preconscious or unconscious movement of mind before it has become reified as thought proper, explicable and accountable. Louis Kannenstine shows how Barnes's novel "snatch[es] the *sensation* of a thought out of the conscious thought process that would normally erase it" (*The Art of Djuna Barnes*, 90). Denis Donoghue reflects on the strangeness of the fiddle and bat passage in *The Waste Land*, discussed above: "If the whole passage sounds like a dream, it is because dreams consist of unofficial impulses active at a stage long before their official reception as thoughts, emotions, ideas. In normal usage language intervenes in the process of feeling too late to do anything more than apply to the aged thing called a thought its official label, so that it may be easily transported from one place to another. At that stage most of the damage to feeling has been done, and the rest is done by assimilating these thoughts to the public structure of attitude and convention which constitutes that 'life' to which the poet's spirit can only oppose itself" (*Words Alone*, 135). De Lauretis's invocation of the death drive allows us to name these as-yet-unthought thoughts as the stirrings of unthinkable thoughts of death, or, as I'm arguing, of the self's non-intentional responsiveness to the mortality of the other.

77. For various commentaries that compare Levinas to Lacan, or to psychoanalysis more broadly, but without a focus on mortality or death obligations, see Critchley, *Ethics—Politics—Subjectivity*, chapters 8 and 9; Critchley, *Infinitely Demanding*; Harasym, ed., *Levinas and Lacan*; Bergo, "Levinasian Responsibility and Freudian Analysis"; Atterton, "'The Talking Cure.'"

78. It is worth mentioning the prominence of the theme of death in Barnes' s youthful writing. Much of her very early poetry is about death; see in particular the first section, "Early Published Poems, 1911–1929," of her *Collected Poems*; the corpse-poem "Suicide" in her 1915 *Book of Repulsive Women*; and her short play "The Death of Life," first published in *The New York Telegraph Sunday Magazine*, December 17, 1916, also essentially a piece of juvenilia, which indicates an initial exploration of death's implication in love. One exemplary exchange:

> [TORO]: Life is different for folks only in where they meet their loves and where they bury them.

[RAGNA]: I haven't met my love yet.

[TORO]: [*emptying his cup*] It's only a corpse that can be standard and it's only the morgue where equal attention fills the requirements of all. (Barnes, *At the Roots of the Stars*, 16)

After Ragna kills herself, another character says, to end the play: "We will bury her deep beneath our hearts, yours and mine—for her soul is a flower, and that we may not touch; bur her spirit is wine, and that we may drink, that she may have her shroud" (ibid., 24). This suggestion of an incorporation of the another's death anticipates images I trace in *Nightwood*.

79. See Derrida, *The Gift of Death*, chapter two.

80. Barnes, comically, has the doctor change the sense of a Christian sermon on marriage in this reference to the seventh century B. C. Greek emperor Periander. Bishop Jeremy Taylor's sermon XVII, "The Marriage Ring; or, the Mysteriousness and Duties of Marriage," was originally published in *Twenty Five Sermons* in England in 1651 (the same year that he published *The Rule and Exercise of Holy Dying*). In his marriage sermon, Taylor entertains a fantasy of heterosexual harmony, including during sex: "He provides, and she dispenses; he gives commandments, and she rules by them; he rules her by authority, and she rules him by love; she ought by all means to please him, and he must by no means displease her. For as the heart is set in the midst of the body, and though it strikes to one side by the prerogative of nature, yet those throbs and constant motions are felt on the other side also, and the influence is equal to both: so it is in conjugal duties; some motions are to the one side more than to the other, but the interest is on both, and duty is equal in the several instances. If it be otherwise, the man enjoys a wife as Periander did his dead Melissa, by an unnatural union, neither pleasing nor holy, useless to all purposes of society, and dead to content" (Taylor, *The Whole Works of the Right Rev. Jeremy Taylor, D. D.*, 263). This rejection of sex "useless to all purposes of society" will be Edelman's concern, below.

81. For an analysis of Barnes's complex mother-child figurations, see Lee, "*Nightwood*, 'The Sweetest Lie.'"

82. Levinas, *God, Death, and Time*, 105.

83. Dyer, *The Missing of the Somme*, 35.

84. Miller, *Narrative and Its Discontents*, 5. Miller mentions that "there is a wide spectrum of ways in which a novel may characterize the function of the nonnarratable. In traditional fiction, marriage is a dominant form of this ne plus ultra, but death is another" (ibid., 3–4).

85. de Lauretis reads for the unnarratable in terms of sexual trauma and with a focus on Robin: "Robin, we might say, is the splinter in the skin of the text. Her enigma is insoluble just as the cause of sexual trauma is unrecoverable. The novel can only refer to it as it is refracted in the emotions, desires, or reminiscences she elicits in the other characters, evoking for them the feeling of a past 'not yet in history'" (de Lauretis, "*Nightwood* and the 'Terror of Uncertain Signs,'" 124).

86. This image echoes Heraclitus's aphorism: "For the bow the name is life, but its work is death" (Heraclitus, *Fragments*, LXVI). (His wisdom also includes: "Corpses are more worthless than excrement" [ibid., LXXXV]).

87. Lacan, *Four Fundamental Concepts*, 177.

88. In *Freud's Drive: Psychoanalysis, Literature and Film* (where she publishes an expanded version of her article about *Nightwood*), de Lauretis includes a chapter on "The Queer Space of the Drive," but acknowledges her difference from Edelman (87).

89. Edelman, *No Future*, 3, 25.

90. Ibid., 17.

91. Ibid., 5.

92. Boone, *Libidinal Currents*, 241, 242.

93. Edelman, *No Future*, 106.

94. Critchley, *Infinitely Demanding*, 67–68.

95. Wood, "Some Questions for My Levinasian Friends," 168.

96. Ibid., 167.

97. de Man, *The Resistance to Theory*, 84.

98. Ibid.

99. Eliot, *Selected Prose*, 38.

100. Ibid.

101. This seems hard to dispute, despite Bloom's denials. For an extensive discussion, see Fry, "How to Live with the Infinite Regress of Strong Misreading."

102. Eliot, *Selected Prose*, 38.

103. Morrison, *Poetics of Fascism*, 69, 74–75.

104. De Man complicates this thought, too, in his discussion in "Shelley Disfigured" of the bad faith construction of literary tradition. Analogizing canonization and burial, he argues that "what we have done with the dead Shelley, and with all the other dead bodies that appear in romantic literature...is simply to bury them, to bury them in their own texts made into epitaphs and monumental graves. They have been made into statues for the benefit of future archeologists 'digging in the grounds for the new foundations' of their own monuments. They have been transformed into historical and aesthetic objects. There are various and subtle strategies, much too numerous to enumerate, to accomplish this," with, for our purposes, Eliot's as a primary example (de Man, *The Rhetoric of Romanticism*, 121). He goes on, more emphatically, about Shelley's poem: "*The Triumph of Life* warns us that nothing, whether deed, word, thought, or text, ever happens in relation, positive or negative, to anything that precedes, follows, or exists elsewhere, but only as a random event whose power, like the power of death, is due to the randomness of its occurrence. It also warns us why and how these events then have to be reintegrated in a historical and aesthetic system of recuperation that repeats itself regardless of the exposure of its fallacy" (ibid.). I think all this of *Nightwood*, too, but with Barnes's revelation that this deconstruction of history and lineage involves a radical and deeply ironic ethical binding to another's mortality.

105. Girard, *Deceit, Desire, and the Novel*, 14–15.

106. Ibid., 15. For an analysis of *The Waste Land* in terms of Girard's concept of mimetic desire, see Brooker, "Mimetic desire and the return to origins in *The Waste Land*."

107. Staten, *Eros in Mourning*, xii.

Coda

1. The recent cultural history of these movements in the West, in all their exploratory and sometimes awkward forms, still needs to be written—the history of the creators

of ecological burial grounds; the artist communities who make of their dead collective, buriable, or combustible works of art; the individual families that parse their local legal requirements for withdrawing their dead from morgues and keeping them from funeral homes in order to prepare them for disposal without strangers, in home funerals (or "do-it-yourself" funerals); the young who learn ancient religious traditions by which one prepares dead bodies, hands on, for last rites; those anywhere who do not have their dead embalmed despite intense pressure from the funeral industry to do so; those who painstakingly make coffins and urns for their loved ones or themselves; those who invent, through sheer creativity and need and despite the risk of embarrassment, some collective ritual to perform as they bid their corpses farewell. All these efforts have proliferated in recent decades, but without the widespread acknowledgement they deserve.

2. Wallace, "An Interview with William Carlos Williams," 146.

3. Williams, *Collected Poems* v. 1, 72–74.

4. Malcuit, "The Poet's Place," 60.

5. Williams's narrator in the story "Mind and Body" finds a curious way to express this democratic, inclusive sense of death rituals: "It is good to feel a solidarity with a group but do not forget that that kindly old priest by telling you that there is just one way to be saved, by excluding all the other people of the earth represents a cruelty of the most inhuman sort. For myself, I went on, if I were dying in Africa and the chief of the tribe who was my friend asked the chief medicine man to do a ceremonial dance for me, with beating of tom toms to conduct me into the other world, I should feel a real comfort which I believe would be a greater solace to me than the formula of some kindly priest" (Williams, *Doctor Stories*, 7).

6. Reed, *William Carlos Williams, Poet from Jersey*, 350–353.

7. Stevens, *The Palm at the End of the Mind*, 35.

8. Ibid., 79. Both Jahan Ramazani and Eleanor Cook associate "Tract" and "Emperor" (Ramazani, *Poetry of Mourning*, 91; Cook, *A Reader's Guide to Wallace Stevens*, 60).

9. Stevens, *Letters of Wallace Stevens*, 566.

10. Stevens, *The Palm at the End of the Mind*, 302–303.

11. Melville, "Inventions of Farewell," 17 n. 2.

12. Whitman, *Leaves of Grass and Other Writings*, 417–418.

13. Stevens, *The Palm at the End of the Mind*, 305.

14. Ibid., 304.

15. Ibid., 306.

Bibliography

Ackroyd, Peter. *T. S. Eliot*. London: Hamish Hamilton, 1984.

Adams, R. M. "Hades." *James Joyce's Ulysses: Critical Essays*. Edited by Clive Hart and David Hayman. Berkeley: University of California Press, 1974. 91–114.

Adorno, Theodor. *Minima Moralia*. Translated by E. F. N. Jephcott. London: Verso, 1978.

Agamben, Giorgio. *Homo Sacer: Sovereign Power and Bare Life*. Stanford, CA: Stanford University Press, 1998.

Agamben, Giogio. *Language and Death: The Place of Negativity*. Translated by Karen E. Pinkus with Michael Hardt. Minneapolis: University of Minnesota Press, 1991.

Anderson, Benedict. *Imagined Communities: Reflections on the Origins and Spread of Nationalism*. Revised edition. New York: Verso, 1991.

Ariès, Philippe. *The Hour of Our Death*. Translated by Helen Weaver. New York: Alfred A. Knopf, 1981.

Ariès, Philippe. *Western Attitudes toward Death: From the Middle Ages to the Present*. Translated by Patricia M. Ranum. Baltimore: Johns Hopkins University Press, 1974.

Arnold, Catherine. *Necropolis: London and Its Dead*. London: Simon and Schuster, 2006.

Atterton, Peter. "'The Talking Cure': The Ethics of Psychoanalysis." *Radicalizing Levinas*. Edited by. Peter Atterton and Matthew Calarco. Albany: State University of New York Press, 2010. 185–203.

Attridge, Derek. "The Postmodernity of Joyce: Chance, Coincidence, and the Reader." *Joyce Studies Annual* 6 (Summer 1995): 10–18.

Auden, W. H. *The English Auden: Poems, Essays and Dramatic Writings 1927–1939*. Edited by Edward Mendelson. London: Faber and Faber, 1977.

Audoin-Rouzeau, Stéphane and Annette Becker. *14–18: Understanding the Great War*. Translated by Catherine Temerson. New York: Hill and Wang, 2000.

Augustine. *Confessions*. Translated by Henry Chadwick. New York: Oxford University Press, 1991.

Auslander, Mark. "Saying Something Now: Documentary Work and the Voices of the Dead." *Michigan Quarterly Review* 44.4 (Fall 2005): 685–703.

Baldanzi, Jessica, and Kyle Schlabach. "What Remains? (De)composing and (Re)covering American Identity in *As I Lay Dying* and the Georgia Crematory Scandal." *Journal of the Midwest Modern Language Association* 36.1 (2003): 38–55.

Barnes, Djuna. *At the Roots of the Stars: The Short Plays*. Edited by Douglas Messerli. Los Angeles: Sun & Moon Press, 1995.

Barnes, Djuna. *Book of Repulsive Women: 8 Rhythms and 5 Drawings*. Los Angeles: Sun & Moon Press, 1996.

Barnes, Djuna. *Collected Poems, with Notes toward the Memoirs*. Edited by Phillip Herring and Osías Stutman. Madison: University of Wisconsin Press, 2005.

Barnes, Djuna. *Ladies Almanack*. Normal, IL: Dalkey Archive Press, 1992.

Barnes, Djuna. *Nightwood: The Original Version and Related Drafts*. Edited by Cheryl J. Plumb. Normal, IL: Dalkey Archive Press, 1995.

Barthes, Roland. *Image—Music—Text*. Translated by Stephen Heath. New York: The Noonday Press, 1977.

Barthes, Roland. *S/Z*. Translated by Richard Miller. New York: Farrar, Straus and Giroux, 1974.

Bataille, Georges. *Erotism: Death and Sensuality*. Translated by Mary Dalwood. San Francisco: City Lights, 1986.

Baucom, Ian. *Spectres of the Atlantic: Finance Capital, Slavery, and the Philosophy of History* Durham, NC: Duke University Press, 2005.

Baudelaire, Charles. *Les Fleurs du Mal*. Translated by Richard Howard. Boston: David R. Gordine, 1982.

Baudrillard, Jean. *Symbolic Exchange and Death*. Translated by Iain Hamilton Grant. London: Sage Publications, 1993.

Bauman, Zygmunt. *Mortality, Immortality, and Other Life Strategies*. Stanford, CA: Stanford University Press, 1992.

Beckett, Ian F. W. *The Great War 1914–1918*. 2nd ed. New York: Pearson Longman, 2007.

Beckett, Samuel. *Collected Shorter Prose 1945–1980*. London: John Calder, 1984.

Benjamin, Walter. *Selected Writings* v. 1, 3, 4. Translated by Edward Jephcott, Howard Eiland, and others. Edited by Howard Eiland and Michael W. Jennings. Cambridge, MA: Belknap Press, 1996–2003.

Berger, John. *Hold Everything Dear: Dispatches on Survival and Resistance*. New York: Pantheon Books, 2007.

Berger, Peter, Brigitte Berger, and Hansfried Keller. *The Homeless Mind: Modernization and Consciousness*. New York: Random, 1973.

Bergo, Bettina. "Levinasian Responsibility and Freudian Analysis: Is the Unthinkable an Un-Conscious?" *Addressing Levinas*. Edited by Eric Sean Nelson, Antje Kapust, and Kent Still. Evanston, IL: Northwestern University Press, 2005. 257–295.

Berman, Art. *Preface to Modernism*. Chicago: University of Illinois Press, 1994.

Bersani, Leo. *Is the Rectum a Grave? and Other Essays*. Chicago: University of Chicago Press, 2010.

Bierce, Ambrose. *The Devil's Dictionary*. New York: Dover, 1993.

Blanchot, Maurice. *The Space of Literature*. Translated by Ann Smock. Lincoln: University of Nebraska Press, 1982.

Blanchot, Maurice. *The Work of Fire*. Stanford: Stanford University Press, 1995.

Bloch, Maurice. "Death, Women and Power." *Death and the Regeneration of Life*. Edited by Maurice Bloch and Jonathan Parry. Cambridge: University of Cambridge Press, 1982. 211–230.

Bloch, Maurice, and Jonathan Parry. "Introduction: Death and the Regeneration of Life." *Death and the Regeneration of Life*. Edited by Maurice Bloch and Jonathan Parry. Cambridge: University of Cambridge Press, 1982. 1–44.

Blotner, Joseph. "Line and Page Notes to *As I Lay Dying*." *As I Lay Dying* by William Faulkner. NY: Vintage International, 1985.

Blunden, Edmund. *Undertones of War*. New York: Penguin, 1928.

Blythe, Ronald. *The Age of Illusion: England in the Twenties and Thirties, 1919–1940*. London: Hamish Hamilton, 1963.

Bone, Muirhead. *The Western Front* v. 1 and 2. London: Country Life, 1916–1917.

Boone, Joseph Allen. *Libidinal Currents: Sexuality and the Shaping of Modernism*. Chicago: University of Chicago Press, 1998.

Booth, Allyson. *Postcards from the Trenches: Negotiating the Space between Modernism and the First World War*. Oxford: Oxford University Press, 1996.

Borden, Mary. *The Forbidden Zone*. London: William Heinemann, 1929.

Bourdieu, Pierre. *The Logic of Practice*. Translated by Richard Nice. Stanford, CA: Stanford University Press, 1980.

Bourke, Joanna. *Dismembering the Male: Men's Bodies, Britain and the Great War*. Chicago: University of Chicago Press, 1996.

Boyd-Orr, Lord. *As I Recall*. London: Macibbon and Kee, 1966.

Boyer, Pascal. *Religion Explained: The Evolutionary Origins of Religious Thought*. New York: Basic Books, 2001.

Bradshaw, David. "'Vanished Like Leaves': The Military, Elegy and Italy in *Mrs. Dalloway*." *Woolf Studies Annual* 8 (2002): 107–125.

Brooke, Rupert. *The Collected Poems*. New York: Dodd, Mead and Co., 1935.

Brooker, Jewel Spears. "Mimetic Desire and the Return to Origins in *The Waste Land*." *Gender, Desire, and Sexuality in T. S. Eliot*. Edited by Cassandra Laity and Nancy K. Gish. Cambridge: Cambridge University Press, 2004. 130–149.

Brooks, Peter. *Body Work: Objects of Desire in Modern Narrative*. Cambridge, MA: Harvard University Press, 1993.

Brooks, Peter. *Reading for the Plot: Design and Intention in Narrative*. Cambridge, MA: Harvard University Press, 1992.

Brown, Malcolm. *The Imperial War Museum Book of The First World War*. London: Sidgwick & Jackson, 1991.

Brown, Vincent. *The Reaper's Garden: Death and Power in the World of Atlantic Slavery*. Cambridge, MA: Harvard University Press, 2008.

Burke, Kenneth. *Language as Symbolic Action: Essays on Life, Literature, and Method*. Berkeley: University of California Press, 1966.

The Business Historical Society, Inc. *History of the Foundation of the Actuarial Society of America*. New York: The James Kemptater Print, 1889. Online: http://books.google.com/books?id=IBwpAAAAYAAJ&printsec=frontcover&source=gbs_ViewAPI#v=onepage&q&f=false. Retrieved 6/18/12.

Butler, Judith. *Precarious Life: The Powers of Mourning and Violence*. New York: Verso, 2004.

Camus, Albert. *The Plague.* Translated by Stuart Gilbert. New York: Vintage International, 1991.

Canetti, Elias. *Crowds and Power.* Translated by Carol Stewart. Middlesex: Penguin, 1973.

Cannadine, David. "War and Death, Grief and Mourning in Modern Britain." *Mirrors of Mortality: Studies in the Social History of Death.* Edited by Joachim Whaley. New York: St. Martin's Press, 1981. 187–242.

Capdevila, Luc, and Danièle Voldman. *War Dead: Western Societies and the Casualties of War.* Translated by Richard Veasey. Edinburgh: Edinburgh University Press, 2006.

Carlston, Erin G. *Thinking Fascism: Sapphic Modernism and Fascist Modernity.* Stanford, CA: Stanford University Press, 1998.

Caselli, Daniela. *Improper Modernism: Djuna Barnes's Bewildering Corpus.* Burlington, VT: Ashgate Publishing, 2009.

Cather, Willa. *O Pioneers!* Boston: Houghton Mifflin, 1913.

Clarke, John M. *The Brookwood Necropolis Railway.* Abingdon, Oxfordshire: Oakwood Press, 1988.

Clark, T. J. *The Sight of Death: An Experiment in Art Writing.* New Haven, CT: Yale University Press, 2006.

Clewell, Tammy. *Mourning, Modernism, Postmodernism.* New York: Palgrave Macmillan, 2009.

Cloete, Stuart. *A Victorian Son: An Autobiography, 1897–1912.* London: William Collins & Sons, 1972.

Cole, Sarah. *At the Violet Hour: Modernism and Violence in England and Ireland.* Oxford: Oxford University Press, 2012.

Cole, Sarah. *Modernism, Male Friendship, and the First World War.* Cambridge: Cambridge University Press, 2003.

Conrad, Joseph. *Heart of Darkness and The Secret Sharer.* New York: Signet Classics, 1997.

Conrad, Joseph. "An Outpost of Progress." *The Portable Conrad.* Edited by Morton Dauwen Zabel. New York: The Viking Press, 1947. 459–489.

Cook, Eleanor. *A Reader's Guide to Wallace Stevens.* Princeton, NJ: Princeton University Press, 2007.

Cork, Richard. *A Bitter Truth: Avant-Garde Art and the Great War.* New Haven, CT: Yale University Press, 1994.

Critchley, Simon. *Ethics—Politics—Subjectivity: Essays on Derrida, Levinas and Contemporary French Thought.* New York: Verso, 1999.

Critchley, Simon. *Infinitely Demanding: Ethics of Commitment, Politics of Resistance.* New York: Verso, 2007.

Daiches, David. *The Novel and the Modern World.* Chicago: University of Chicago Press, 1939.

Das, Santanu. *Touch and Intimacy in First World War Literature.* Cambridge: Cambridge University Press, 2005.

Dastur, Françoise. *Death: An Essay on Finitude.* Translated by Jonn Llewelyn. London: Athlone Press, 1996.

Davis, Christie. "Dirt, Death, Decay and Dissimulation: American Denial and British Avoidance." *Contemporary Issues in the Sociology of Death, Dying, and Disposal.* Edited by Glennys Howarth and Peter C. Jupp. New York: St. Martin's Press, 1996. 60–71.

Davies, M. R. Russell. *The Law of Burial, Cremation and Exhumation.* 5th ed. London: Shaw & Sons, 1982.

Debord, Guy. *The Society of the Spectacle.* Translated by Donald Nicholson-Smith. New York: Zone Books, 1994.

de Certeau, Michel. *The Practice of Everyday Life.* Translated by Steven Rendall. Berkeley: University of California Press, 1984.

de Certeau, Michel. *The Writing of History.* New York: Columbia University Press, 1988.

Deer, Patrick. *Culture in Camouflage: War, Empire, and Modern British Literature.* Oxford: Oxford University Press, 2009.

Defoe, Daniel. *A Journal of the Plague Year.* Edited by Paula Backscheider. New York: W. W. Norton, 1992.

DeGroot, Gerard J. *Blighty: British Society in the Era of the Great War.* London: Longman, 1996.

DeKoven, Marianne. *Rich and Strange: Gender, History, Modernism.* Princeton, NJ: Princeton University Press, 1991.

de Lauretis, Teresa. *Freud's Drive: Psychoanalysis, Literature and Film.* New York: Palgrave Macmillan, 2008.

de Lauretis, Teresa. "*Nightwood* and the 'Terror of Uncertain Signs.'" *Critical Inquiry* 34.5 (Winter 2008): 117–129.

De Man, Paul. *The Resistance to Theory.* Minneapolis: University of Minnesota Press, 1986.

De Man, Paul. *The Rhetoric of Romanticism.* New York: Columbia University Press, 1984.

Derrida, Jacques. *Aporias.* Translated by Thomos Dutoit. Stanford: Stanford University Press, 1993.

Derrida, Jacques. *The Gift of Death*, 2nd ed. Translated by David Wills. Chicago: University of Chicago Press, 2008.

Derrida, Jacques. *Spectres of Marx: The State of the Debt, the Work of Mourning, and the New International.* Translated by Peggy Kamuf. New York: Routledge, 1994.

Detloff, Madelyn. *The Persistence of Modernism: Loss and Mourning in the Twentieth Century.* Cambridge: Cambridge University Press, 2009.

Devlin, Kimberly J. "Visible Shades and Shades of Invisibility: The En-Gendering of Death in 'Hades.'" *Ulysses—En-Gendered Perspectives: Eighteen New Essays on the Episodes.* Edited by Kimberly J. Devlin and Marilyn Reizbaum. Columbia: University of South Carolina Press, 1999. 67–85.

Donoghue, Denis. *Words Alone: The Poet T. S. Eliot.* New Haven, CT: Yale University Press, 2000.

Dos Passos, John. *Nineteen Nineteen. U. S. A.* Boston: Houghton Mifflin, 1930.

Durkheim, Emile. *The Elementary Forms of Religious Life.* Translated by Carol Cosman. Abridged Mark S. Cladis. Oxford: Oxford University Press, 2001.

Dugmore, A. Radclyffe. *When the Somme Ran Red.* New York: George H. Doran Co., 1918.

Dyer, Geoff. *The Missing of the Somme.* London: Hamish Hamilton, 1994.

Edelman, Lee. *No Future: Queer Theory and the Death Drive.* Durham, NC: Duke University Press, 2004.

Edwards, Erin E. "Extremities of the Body: The Anaptic Corporeality of *As I Lay Dying.*" *Modern Fiction Studies* 55.4 (Winter 2009): 739–764.

Eksteins, Modris. *Rites of Spring: The Great War and the Birth of the Modern Age.* Boston: Houghton Mifflin, 1989.

Elias, Norbert. *The Loneliness of the Dying*. Translated by Edmund Jephcott. Oxford: Basil Blackwell, 1985.

Eliot, T. S. *Collected Poems 1909–1962*. New York: Harcourt Brace, 1963.

Eliot, T. S. "Introduction." *Nightwood*. Djuna Barnes. New York: New Directions: 1937.

Eliot, T. S. *Selected Prose*. Edited by Frank Kermode. New York: Harcourt Brace / Farrar, Straus & Giroux, 1956.

Eliot, T. S. *The Waste Land: A Facsimile and Transcript of the Original Drafts*. New York: Harcourt Brace Janovitch, 1971.

Ellman, Richard. *James Joyce. A New and Revised Edition*. Oxford: Oxford University Press, 1982.

Eng, David and David Kazanjian, eds. *Loss: The Politics of Mourning*. Berkeley: University of California Press, 2003.

Ewald, François. "Insurance and Risk." *The Foucault Effect: Studies in Governmentality*. Chicago: University of Chicago Press, 1991. 197–210.

Faltejskova, Monika. *Djuna Barnes, T. S. Eliot and the Gender Dynamics of Modernism: Tracing Nightwood*. New York : Routledge, 2010.

Farrell, James J. *Inventing the American Way of Death, 1830–1920*. Philadelphia: Temple University Press, 1980.

Faulkner, William. *Absalom, Absalom!* New York: Vintage International, 1986.

Faulkner, William. *As I Lay Dying*. New York: Vintage International, 1990.

Faulkner, William. *Collected Stories*. New York: Vintage, 1977.

Faust, Drew Gilpin. *This Republic of Suffering: Death and the American Civil War*. New York: Vintage, 2008.

Felman, Shoshana. *Jacques Lacan and the Adventure of Insight*. Cambridge, MA: Harvard University Press, 1987.

Field, Andrew. *Djuna: The Formidable Miss Barnes*. Austin: University of Texas Press, 1983.

Foltyn, Jacque Lynn. "Dead Beauty: The Preservation, Memorialisation and Destruction of Beauty in Death." *Contemporary Issues in the Sociology of Death, Dying, and Disposal*. Edited by Glennys Howarth and Peter C. Jupp. New York: St. Martin's Press, 1996. 72–83.

Forster, E. M. *Abinger Harvest and England's Pleasant Land. The Abinger Edition of E. M. Forster* v. 10. Edited by Elizabeth Heine. London: André Deutsch, 1996.

Forter, Greg. *Gender, Race, and Mourning in American Modernism*. Cambridge: Cambridge University Press, 2011.

Foucault, Michel. *The Birth of Biopolitics: Lectures at the Collège de France 1978–1979*. Translated by Graham Burchell. Edited by Michel Senellart. New York: Picador, 2008.

Foucault, Michel. *The Birth of the Clinic: An Archeology of Medical Perception*. Translated by A. M. Sheridan Smith. New York: Vintage, 1975.

Foucault, Michel. *The History of Sexuality: An Introduction* v. 1. Translated by Robert Hurley. New York: Vintage, 1990.

Foucault, Michel. "'Omnes et Singulatim': Toward a Critique of Political Reason." *Power*. Translated by Robert Hurley and others. Edited by James D. Faubion. New York: The New Press, 2000. 298–325.

Foucault, Michel. *Security, Territory, Population: Lectures at the Collège de France 1977–78*. Translated by Graham Burchell. Edited by Michel Senellart. New York: Palgrave Macmillan, 2004.

Frank, Joseph. *The Idea of Spatial Form*. New Brunswick, NJ: Rutgers University Press, 1991.

Frank, Joseph. *The Widening Gyre: Crisis and Mastery in Modern Literature*. Bloomington: Indiana University Press, 1963.

Freud, Sigmund. "Thoughts for the Times on War and Death." *The Standard Edition of The Complete Psychological Works*. Volume XIV. Translated by James Strachey. London: Hogarth Press and the Institute of Psychoanalysis, 1957.

Freud, Sigmund. *Totem and Taboo. The Standard Edition of The Complete Psychological Works*. Volume XIII. Translated by James Strachey. London: Hogarth Press and the Institute of Psychoanalysis, 1955.

Friedman, Alan Warren. *Fictional Death and the Modernist Enterprise*. Cambridge: Cambridge University Press, 1995.

Froula, Christine. "Corpse, Monument, Hypocrite Lecteur: Text and Transference in the Reception of *The Waste Land*." *Text* 9 (1996): 297–314.

Fry, Paul. "How to Live with the Infinite Regress of Strong Misreading." *Modern Language Quarterly* 69.4 (December 2008): 437–459.

Frye, Northrop. *T. S. Eliot: An Introduction*. Chicago: University of Chicago Press, 1963.

Fussell, Paul. *The Great War and Modern Memory*. London: Oxford University Press, 1975.

Fynsk, Christopher. "Crossing the Threshold, on 'Literature and the Right to Death.'" *Maurice Blanchot: The Demand of Writing*. Edited by Carolyn Bailey Gill. London: Routledge, 1996. 70–90.

Giddens, Anthony. *Modernity and Self-Identity: Self and Society in the Late Modern Age*. Stanford, CA: Stanford University Press, 1991.

Gifford, Don. Ulysses *Annotated: Notes for James Joyce's* Ulysses. With Robert J. Seidman. 2nd edition. Berkeley: University of California Press, 1988.

Gilbert, Martin. *The First World War: A Complete History*. New York: Henry Holt and Co., 1994.

Gilbert, Sandra. *Death's Door: Modern Dying and the Ways We Grieve*. New York: W.W. Norton, 2006.

Gilbert, Sandra M. "Rats' Alley": The Great War, Modernism, and the (Anti) Pastoral Elegy." *New Literary History* 30.1 (Winter 1999): 179–201.

Gilbert, Sandra M. "Soldier's Heart: Literary Men, Literary Women, and the Great War." *Behind the Lines: Gender and the Two World Wars*. Edited by Margaret Randolf Higonnet et al. New Haven, CT: Yale University Press, 1987. 197–259.

Girard, René. *Deceit, Desire, and the Novel: Self and Other in Literary Structure*. Translated by Yvonne Freccero. Baltimore: Johns Hopkins University Press, 1965.

Glover, Jonathan. *Humanity: A Moral History of the Twentieth Century*. London: Jonathan Cape, 1999.

Gordon, John. "Phantom Ship." *James Joyce Quarterly* 44.4 (Summer 2007): 793–799.

Gordon, Lyndall. *T. S. Eliot: An Imperfect Life*. New York: W. W. Norton., 1998.

Gorer, Geoffrey. *Death, Grief, and Mourning in Contemporary Britain*. London: The Cresset Press, 1965.

Gough, Paul. *A Terrible Beauty: British Artists in the First World War*. Bristol: Sansom & Co., 2010.

Gourgouris, Stathis. *Does Literature Think? Literature as Theory for an Antimythical Era*. Stanford, CA: Stanford University Press, 2003.

Greenblatt, Stephen. *Hamlet in Purgatory*. Princeton, NJ: Princeton University Press, 2001.

Gregory, Adrian. *The Silence of Memory: Armistice Day 1919–1946*. Oxford: Berg, 1994.

Habermas, Jürgen. *The Philosophical Discourse of Modernity*. Translated by Frederick G. Lawrence. Cambridge, MA: MIT Press, 1990.

Habestein, Robert W., and William M. Lamers. *The History of American Funeral Directing*. 2nd revised edition. Milwaukee: National Funeral Directors Association of the United States, 1981.

Hacking, Ian. "How Should We Do the History of Statistics?" *The Foucault Effect: Studies in Governmentality*. Chicago: University of Chicago Press, 1991. 181–195.

Harasym, Sarah, ed. *Levinas and Lacan: The Missed Encounter*. Albany: State University of New York Press, 1998.

Harper, Sheila. "The Social Agency of Dead Bodies." *Mortality* 15.4 (November 2010): 308–322.

Harrison, Robert. *The Dominion of the Dead*. Chicago: University of Chicago Press, 2003.

Hartman, Saidiya. *Lose Your Mother: A Journey Along the Atlantic Slave Route*. New York: Farrar, Straus and Giroux, 2007.

Harvey, David. *The Condition of Postmodernity*. Cambridge: Blackwell, 1989.

Haste, Cate. *Keep the Home Fires Burning: Propaganda and the First World War*. London: Allen Lane, 1977.

Heard, Andrew. *William Roberts 1895-1980*. Newcastle: Hatton Gallery, University of Newcastle, 2004.

Heidegger, Martin. *Being and Time*. Translated by Joan Stambaugh. Albany: State University of New York Press, 1996.

Heidegger, Martin. *On the Way to Language*. Translated by Peter D. Hertz. New York: Harper, 1971.

Hemingway, Ernest. *Death in the Afternoon*. New York: Charles Scribner's Sons, 1932.

Heraclitus. *The Fragments of the Work of Heraclitus of Epheus on Nature*. Translated by G. T. W. Patrick. Baltimore: N. Murray, 1880.

Herring, Phillip. *Djuna: The Life and Work of Djuna Barnes*. New York: Viking, 1995.

Hertz, Robert. *Death & The Right Hand*. Translated by Rodney and Claudia Needham. Glencoe, IL: The Free Press, 1960.

Hibberd, Dominic. *Wilfred Owen: A New Biography*. Chicago: Ivan R. Dee, 2003.

Hildebrandt, Sabine and Christoph Redies, eds. *Annals of Anatomy. Special Issue: Anatomy in the Third Reich* 194 (2012).

Holme, Charles, ed. "The War Depicted by Distinguished British Artists." *The Studio*. London: 1918.

Homer. *The Iliad*. Translated by Richard Lattimore. Chicago: University of Chicago Press, 1951.

Homer. *The Odyssey*. Translated by Richard Lattimore. New York: HarperPerennial, 1967.

Hotz, Mary Elizabeth. *Literary Remains: Representations of Death and Burial in Victorian England*. Albany: State University of New York Press, 2009.

Howell, Joel D. "Machines and Medicine: Technology Transforms the American Hospital." *The American General Hosptial*. Edited by Dana Elizabeth Long and Janet Golden. Ithaca, NY: Cornell University Press, 1989. 109–134.

Humphreys, S. C. "Death and Time." *Mortality and Immortality: The Archeology and Anthropology of Death*. Edited by S. C. Humphreys and H. King. London: Academic Press, 1981. 261–283.

Huss, Marie-Monique. "Pronatalism and the Popular Ideology of the Child in Wartime France: The Evidence of the Picture Postcard." *The Upheaval of War: Family, Work and Welfare in Europe, 1914–1918.* Edited by Richard Wall and Jay Winter. Cambridge: Cambridge University Press, 1988. 329–367.

Inglis, K. S. "Entombing Unknown Soldiers: From London and Paris to Baghdad." *History and Memory* 5.2 (Fall/Winter 1993): 7–31.

Iser, Wolfgang. *The Implied Reader: Patterns of Communication in Prose Fiction from Bunyan to Beckett.* Baltimore: The Johns Hopkins University Press, 1974.

Jalland, Pat. *Death in War and Peace: Loss and Grief in England 1914–1970.* Oxford: Oxford University Press, 2010.

Jalland, Pat. "Victorian Death and Its Decline: 1850–1918." *Death in England: An Illustrated History.* Edited by Peter C. Jupp and Clare Gittings. New Brunswick, NJ: Rutgers University Press, 2000. 230–255.

Jameson, Fredric. "Cognitive Mapping." *Marxism and the Interpretation of Culture.* Edited by Cary Nelson. Chicago: University of Illinois Press, 1988. 347–357.

Jameson, Fredric. *The Political Unconscious: Narrative as a Socially Symbolic Act.* Ithaca, NY: Cornell University Press, 1981.

Joyce, James. *A Portrait of the Artist as a Young Man.* New York: Penguin, 1963.

Joyce, James. *Ulysses.* Edited by Hans Walter Gabler. New York: Vintage, 1993.

Jupp, Peter C. "Enon Chapel: No Way for the Dead." *The Changing Face of Death: Historical Accounts of Death and Disposal.* Edited by Peter C. Jupp and Glennys Howarth. London: Macmillan Press, 1997. 90–104.

Jupp, Peter C. *From Dust to Ashes: Cremation and the British Way of Dying.* New York: Palgrave MacMillan, 2006.

Kafka, Franz. "The Hunter Gracchus." *The Complete Stories.* Translated by Willa and Edwin Muir. Edited by Nahum N. Glatzer. New York: Schocken Books, 1971.

Kaivola, Karen. *All Contraries Confounded: The Lyrical Fiction of Virginia Woolf, Djuna Barnes, and Marguerite Duras.* Iowa City: University of Iowa Press, 1991.

Kalaidjian, Walter. *The Edge of Modernism: American Poetry and the Traumatic Past.* Baltimore: Johns Hopkins University Press, 2006.

Kannenstine, Louis. *The Art of Djuna Barnes: Duality and Damnation.* New York: New York University Press, 1977.

Karsner, Howard T. "The Autopsy." *The Journal of the American Medical Association* 88.18 (April 30, 1927): 1367–1373.

Kaufmann, Michael. "The Textual Coffin and the Narrative Corpse of *As I Lay Dying.*" *Arizona Quarterly* 49.1 (Spring 1993): 99–116.

Keegan, John. *The First World War.* New York: Knopf, 1999.

Kenner, Hugh. *Dublin's Joyce.* Boston: Beacon Press, 1956.

Kenner, Kenner. *"Ulysses."* London: George Allen & Unwin, 1980.

Kermode, Frank. *The Sense of an Ending: Studies in the Theory of Fiction.* London: Oxford University Press, 1967.

Kern, Stephen. *The Culture of Time and Space 1880–1918.* Cambridge, MA: Harvard University Press, 1983.

Kerr, Douglas. *Wilfred Owen's Voices: Language and Community.* Oxford: Clarendon Press, 1993.

Kierkegaard, Søren. *The Sickness unto Death: A Christian Psychological Exposition for Upbuilding and Awakening*. Translated by Howard V. Hong and Edna H. Hong. Princeton, NJ: Princeton University Press, 1980.

Knowles, Sebastian D. G. *The Dublin Helix: The Life of Language in Joyce's Ulysses*. Gainesville: University Press of Florida, 2001.

Kostenbaum, Wayne. *Double Talk: The Erotics of Male Literary Collaboration*. New York: Routledge, 1989.

Kristeva, Julia. *Powers of Horror: An Essay on Abjection*. Translated by Leon S. Roudiez. New York: Columbia University Press, 1982.

Krüger-Kahloula, Angelika. "On the Wrong Side of the Fence: Racial Segregation in American Cemeteries." *History and Memory in African-American Culture*. Edited by Geneviève Fabre and Robert O'Meally. Oxford: Oxford University Press, 1994. 130–149.

Krumbhaar, E. B. "The Need for Postmortem Examinations and Methods of Securing Them." *The Journal of the American Medical Association* 80.23 (June 9, 1923): 1682–1683.

Lacan, Jacques. *The Ethics of Psychoanalysis*. Translated by Dennis Porter. Edited by Jacques Alain-Miller. New York: W. W. Norton, 1992.

Lacan, Jacques. *The Four Fundamental Concepts of Psychoanalysis*. Translated by Alan Sheridan. Edited by Jacques Alain-Miller. New York: W. W. Norton, 1998.

Lacan, Jacques. "Function and Field of Speech and Language." *Écrits: A Selection*. Translated by Alan Sheridan. New York: W. W. Norton, 1977.

Laderman, Gary. *Rest in Peace: A Cultural History of Death and the Funeral Home in Twentieth-Century America*. Oxford: Oxford University Press, 2003.

Lamos, Colleen. *Deviant Modernism: Sexual and Textual Errancy in T. S. Eliot, James Joyce, and Marcel Proust*. Cambridge, Cambridge University Press, 1998.

Lamos, Colleen. "The Love Song of T. S. Eliot: Elegiac Homoeroticism in the Early Poetry." *Gender, Desire, and Sexuality in T. S. Eliot*. Edited by Cassandra Laity and Nancy K. Gish. Cambridge: Cambridge University Press, 2004. 23–42.

Lanser, Susan Sniader. "Introduction." *Ladies Almanack*. New York: New York University Press, 1992.

Lanser, Susan Sniader. "*Speaking in Tongues: Ladies Almanack* and the Discourse of Desire." *Silence and Power: A Reevalution of Djuna Barnes*. Edited by Mary Lynn Broe. Carbondale: Southern Illinois Press, 1991. 156–169.

Laqueur, Thomas W. "Names, Bodies, and the Anxiety of Erasure." *The Social and Political Body*. Edited by Theodore R. Schatzki and Wolfgang Natter. New York: The Guilford Press, 1996. 123–141.

Lash, Scott. *Another Modernity, a Different Rationality*. Oxford: Blackwell, 1999.

Lawrence, D. H. *The Prussian Officer and Other Stories*. Edited by John Worthen. Cambridge: Cambridge University Press, 1983.

Leaman, Oliver. "Secularization." *Encyclopedia of Death and Dying*. Edited by Glennys Howarth and Oliver Leaman. London: Routledge, 2001. 399–402.

Lee, Judith. "*Nightwood*, 'The Sweetest Lie.' " *Silence and Power: A Reevaluation of Djuna Barnes*. Edited by Mary Lynn Broe. Carbondale: Southern Illinois University Press, 1991. 207–218.

Leed, Eric. *No Man's Land: Combat and Identity in World War I*. London: Cambridge University Press, 1979.

Leroi-Gourhan, Arlette. "The Flowers Found with Shanidar IV, a Neanderthal Burial in Iraq." *Science*, New Series 190. 4214 (November 7, 1975): 562–564.

Levenson, Michael H. *A Genealogy of Modernism: A Study of English Literary Doctrine 1908–1922*. Cambridge: Cambridge University Press, 1984.

Levi, Primo. *The Drowned and the Saved*. Translated by Raymond Rosenthal. New York: Summit Books, 1986.

Levinas, Emmanuel. *Difficult Freedom: Essays on Judaism*. Translated by Seán Hand. Baltimore: Johns Hopkins University Press, 1997.

Levinas, Emmanuel. *Entre Nous: Thinking-of-the-Other*. Translated by Michael B. Smith and Barbara Harshav. New York: Columbia University Press, 1998.

Levinas, Emmanuel. *God, Death, and Time*. Translated by Bettina Bergo. Stanford, CA: Stanford University Press, 2000.

Levinas, Emmanuel. *Is It Righteous To Be? Interviews with Emmanuel Levinas*. Edited by Jill Robinson. Stanford, CA: Stanford University Press, 2001.

Levinas, Emmanuel. *Totality and Infinity: An Essay on Exteriority*. Translated by Alphonso Lingis. Pittsburgh, PA: Duquense University Press, 1969.

Lewis, Pericles. *Religious Experience and the Modernist Novel*. Cambridge: Cambridge University Press, 2010.

Lewis, Wyndham. *Time and Western Man*. New York: Harcourt Brace, 1928.

London, Bette. "Posthumous Was a Woman: World War I Memorials and Woolf's Dead Poet's Society." *Woolf Studies Annual* 16 (2010): 45–70.

Longworth, Philip. *The Unending Vigil: A History of the Commonwealth War Graves Commission 1917–1967*. London: Constable, 1967.

López, Donna Bentolila. "The Enigma of the Death Drive: A Revisiting." *Psychoanalysis and Contemporary Thought* 19 (1996): 3–27.

Lynch, Kenneth. "Better Autopsies, and More of Them." *The Journal of the American Medical Association* 89.8 (August 20, 1927): 576–578.

MacGill, Patrick. *The Great Push: An Episode of the Great War*. New York: George H. Doran Co., 1916.

Macherey, Pierre. *A Theory of Literary Production*. Translated by Geoffrey Wall. London: Routledge Classics, 2006.

Malcuit, William Q. "The Poet's Place: William Carlos Williams and the Production of an American Avant-Garde." *William Carlos Williams Review* 28.1–2 (Spring/Fall 2008): 55–77.

Malinowski, Bronislaw. *Magic, Science and Religion and Other Essays*. London: Souvenir Press, 1974.

Mann, Thomas. *The Magic Mountain*. Translated by H. T. Lowe-Porter. Vintage International, 1992.

Marcuse, Herbert. "The Ideology of Death." *The Meaning of Death*. Edited by Herman Feifel. New York: McGraw Hill, 1959. 64–76.

Marshall, Tim. *Murdering to Dissect: Grave-robbing, Frankenstein and the Anatomy Literature*. Manchester: Manchester University Press, 1995.

Martins, Susana S. "Gender Trouble and Lesbian Desire in Djuna Barnes's *Nightwood*." *Fronteirs: A Journal of Women Studies* 20.3 (1999): 108–126.

Marvell, Andrew. *The Complete Poems*. Edited by Elizabeth Story Donno. New York: Penguin, 1972.

Mauss, Marcel. *A General Theory of Magic*. Translated by Robert Brain. London: Routledge, 1972.

McIntire, Gabrielle. *Modernism, Memory, and Desire: T. S. Eliot and Virginia Woolf* Cambridge: Cambridge University Press, 2008.

McVicker, Jeanette. "'Six Essays on London Life': A History of Dispersal," Part II. *Woolf Studies Annual* 10 (2004): 141–172.

Melville, Joan. "'Inventions of Farewell': Wallace Stevens' 'The Owl in the Sarcophagus.'" *The Wallace Stevens Journal* 16.1 (Spring 1992): 3–21.

Mendelson, Michael. "The Body in the Next Room: Death as Differend." *Images of the Corpse: From the Renaissance to Cyberspace*. Edited by Elizabeth Klaver. Madison: University of Wisconsin Press, 2004. 186–205.

Miller, D. A. *Narrative and Its Discontents: Problems of Closure in the Traditional Novel*. Princeton, NJ: Princeton University Press, 1981.

Miller, James E. *T. S. Eliot: The Making of an American Poet, 1888–1922*. University Park: The Pennsylvania State University Press, 2005.

Miller, James E. *T. S. Eliot's Personal Waste Land: Exorcism of the Demons*. University Park: The Pennsylvania State University Press, 1977.

Mitford, Jessica. *The American Way of Death*. New York: Simon and Schuster, 1963.

Mitford, Jessica. *The American Way of Death Revisited*. New York: Alfred A. Knopf, 1998.

Moglen, Seth. *Mourning Modernity: Literary Modernism and the Injuries of American Capitalism*. Stanford, CA: Stanford University Press, 2007.

Moller, David Wendell. *Confronting Death: Values, Institutions, and Human Mortality*. New York: Oxford University Press, 1996.

Molleson, Theya. "The Archeology and Anthropology of Death: What the Bones Tell Us." *Mortality and Immortality: The Anthropology and Archeology of Death*. Edited by S. C. Humphreys and Helen King. London: Academic Press, 1981. 15–32.

Moretti, Franco. *Modern Epic: The World-System from Goethe to García Márquez*. Translated by Quintin Hoare. New York: Verso, 1996.

Morrison, Paul. *The Poetics of Fascism: Ezra Pound, T. S. Eliot, Paul de Man*. New York: Oxford University Press, 1996.

Mortimer, Gail L. *Faulkner's Rhetoric of Loss: A Study in Perception and Meaning*. Austin: University of Texas Press, 1983.

Mosse, George L. *Fallen Soldiers: Reshaping the Memory of the World Wars*. Oxford: Oxford University Press, 1990.

Movius, H. V. "The Mousterian Cave of Teshik Tash, South Eastern Uzbekistan, Central Asia." *Bulletin of the American School of Prehistoric Research* 17 (1953): 11–71.

Nancy, Jean-Luc. *The Inoperative Community*. Translated by Peter Connor, Lisa Garbus, Michael Holland, and Simona Sawhney. Edited by Peter Connor. Minneapolis: University of Minnesota Press, 1991.

The New Oxford Annotated Bible. 3rd edition. Edited by Michael Coogan. Oxford: Oxford University Press, 2001.

NFDA. "Cremation Facts." http://www.nfda.org/about-funeral-service-/trends-and-statistics.html#cfacts. Retrieved June 16, 2012.

Nietzsche, Friedrich. *The Gay Science, with a Prelude in German Rhymes and an Appendix of Songs*. Translated by Josefine Nauckhoff and Adrian Del Caro. Edited by Bernard Williams. Cambridge: University Press, 2001.

Nietzsche, Friedrich. *On the Genealogy of Morality*. Translated by Carol Diethe. Edited by Keith Ansell-Pearson. Cambridge: University Press, 1994.

Osborne, Peter. *The Politics of Time: Modernity and the Avant-Garde*. New York: Verso, 1995.

Osteen, Mark. *The Economy of Ulysses: Making Both Ends Meet*. Syracuse, NY: Syracuse University Press, 1995.

Owen, Wilfred. *Collected Letters*. Edited by Harold Owen and John Bell. London: Oxford University Press, 1967.

Owen, Wilfred. *The Complete Poems and Fragments*. Vol. 1. Edited by Jon Stallworthy. London: Chatto & Windus, The Hogarth Press, and Oxford University Press, 1983.

Péguy, Charles. *Men and Saints: Prose and Poetry*. Translated by Anne and Julilan Green. London: Kegan Paul, 1947.

Perdigao, Lisa K. *From Modernist Entombment to Postmodernist Exhumation: Dead Bodies in Twentieth-Century American Fiction*. Burlington, VT: Ashgate, 2010.

Peter, John. "A New Interpretation of *The Waste Land*." *Essays in Criticism* 19.2 (April 1969): 140–175.

Philip, M. NourbeSe, and Setaey Adamu Boateng. *Zong!* Middletown, CT: Wesleyan University Press, 2008.

Pinfold, John. "The Green Ground." *The Changing Face of Death: Historical Accounts of Death and Disposal*. Edited by Peter C. Jupp and Glennys Howarth. London: Macmillan Press, 1997. 76–89.

Plumb, Cheryl. "Introduction." *Nightwood: The Original Version and Related Drafts* by Djuna Barnes. Edited by Cheryl J. Plumb. Normal, IL: Dalkey Archive Press, 1995. vii–xxvi.

Plumb, Cheryl. "Textual Apparatus." *Nightwood: The Original Version and Related Drafts* by Djuna Barnes. Edited by Cheryl J. Plumb. Normal, IL: Dalkey Archive Press, 1995. 141–319.

Pound, Ezra. *Lustra*. New York: Alfred A. Knopf, 1917.

Prior, Lindsay. "Actuarial Visions of Death: Life, Death and Chance in the Modern World." *The Changing Face of Death: Historical Accounts of Death and Disposal*. Edited by Peter C. Jupp and Glennys Howarth. London: Macmillan Press, 1997. 177–193.

Prior, Lindsay. *The Social Organisation of Death: Medical Discourse and Social Practices in Belfast*. London: The MacMillan Press, 1989.

Prothero, Stephen. *Purified by Fire: A History of Cremation in America*. Berkeley: University of California Press, 2001.

Proust, Marcel. *Remembrance of Things Past* v. 1. Translated by C. K. Scott Moncrieff and Terence Kilmartin. New York: Vintage, 1981.

Punday, Daniel. *Narrative Bodies: Toward a Corporeal Narratology*. New York: Palgrave Macmillan, 2003.

Quigley, Christine. *Modern Mummies: The Preservation of the Human Body in the Twentieth Century*. London: McFarland & Company, 1998.

Rae, Patricia, ed. *Modernism and Mourning*. Lewisburg: Bucknell University Press, 2007.

Ramazani, Jahan. *Poetry of Mourning: The Modern Elegy from Hardy to Heaney*. Chicago: University of Chicago Press, 1994.

Ray, Keith. "From Remote Times to the Bronze Age: *c.* 500,000 B.C. to *c.* 600 B. C." *Death in England: An Illustrated History*. Edited by Peter C. Jupp and Clare Gittings. New Brunswick, NJ: Rutgers University Press, 2000. 11–39.

Read, Herbert. *Naked Warriors*. London: Art & Letters, 1919.

Ricciardi, Alessia. *The Ends of Mourning: Psychoanalysis, Literature, Film*. Stanford, CA: Stanford University Press, 2003.

Richardson, Ruth. *Death, Dissection, and the Destitute*. 2nd edition. Chicago: University of Chicago Press, 2000.

Ricoeur, Paul. *Memory, History, Forgetting*. Translated by Kathleen Blarney and David Pellauer. Chicago: University of Chicago Press, 2004.

Riel-Salvatore, Julien, and Geoffrey Clark, "Grave Markers: Middle and Early Upper Paleolithic Burials and the Use of Chronotypology in Contemporary Paleolithic Research." *Current Anthropology* 42.4 (August–October 2001): 449–479.

Rilke, Rainer Maria. *Selected Poetry*. Edited and translated by Stephen Mitchell. New York: Vintage Books, 1980.

Rilke, Rainer Maria. *The Notebooks of Malte Laurids Brigge*. Translated by Stephen Mitchell. New York: Vintage International, 1982.

Roach, Joseph. *Cities of the Dead: Circum-Atlantic Performance*. New York: Columbia University Press, 1996.

Robb, George. *British Culture and the First World War*. New York: Palgrave, 2002.

Rose, Gillian. *Mourning Becomes the Law: Philosophy and Representation*. Cambridge: Cambridge University Press, 1996.

Rosen, Michael. *Dignity: Its History and Meaning*. Cambridge, MA: Harvard University Press, 2012.

Rosenberg, Charles E. "Community and Communities: The Evolution of the American Hospital." *The American General Hosptial*. Edited by Dana Elizabeth Long and Janet Golden. Ithaca, NY: Cornell University Press, 1989. 3–17.

Rothberg, Michael. *Multidimensional Memory: Remembering the Holocaust in the Age of Decolonization*. Stanford, CA: Stanford University Press, 2009.

Rubinshtain, Shim'on. *German Atrocity or British Propaganda: The Seventieth Anniversary of A Scandal: German Corpse Utilization Establishments in the First World War*. Jerusalem: Acadamon, Hebrew University, 1987.

Rugg, Julie. "From Reason to Regulation: 1760–1850." *Death in England: An Illustrated History*. Edited by Peter C. Jupp and Clare Gittings. New Brunswick, NJ: Rutgers University Press, 2000. 202–229.

Rugg, Julie. "The Origins and Progress of Cemetery Establishment in Britain." *The Changing Face of Death: Historical Accounts of Death and Disposal*. Edited by Peter C. Jupp and Glennys Howarth. London: Macmillan Press, 1997. 105–119.

Runia, Eelco. "Burying the Dead, Creating the Past." *History and Theory* 46 (October 2007): 313–325.

Rushdie, Salman. *The Satanic Verses*. New York: Viking, 1988.

Said, Edward. *Beginnings: Intention and Method*. New York: Columbia University Press, 1975.

Sappho. *The Poetry of Sappho*. Translated by Jim Powell. Oxford: Oxford University Press, 2007.

Sappol, Michael. *A Traffic in Dead Bodies: Anatomy and Embodied Social Identity in Nineteenth-Century America*. Princeton, NJ: Princeton University Press, 2002.

Sassoon, Siegfried. *Collected Poems 1908–1956*. London: Faber and Faber, 1961.

Scarry, Elaine. *The Body in Pain: The Making and Unmaking of the World*. Oxford: Oxford University Press, 1985.

Schleifer, Ronald. *Modernism and Time: The Logic of Abundance in Literature, Science, and Culture, 1880–1930*. Cambridge: Cambridge University Press, 2000.

Sencourt, Robert. *T. S. Eliot: A Memoir*. Edited by Donald Adamson. New York: Dodd, Mead & Co., 1971.

Serres, Michel, with Bruno Latour. *Conversations on Science, Culture, and Time*. Translated by Roxanne Lapidus. Ann Arbor: University of Michigan Press, 1995.

Seymour-Jones, Caroline. *Painted Shadows: A Life of Vivienne Eliot*. London: Constable, 2001.

Shakespeare, William. *Hamlet*. Edited by Ann Thompson and Neil Taylor. London: Arden Shakespeare, 2006.

Sharpe, Tony. *T. S. Eliot: A Literary Life*. London: Macmillan, 1991.

Sherman, David. "A Plot Unraveling into Ethics: Woolf, Levinas, and 'Time Passes.'" *Woolf Studies Annual* 13 (2007): 159–179.

Shilling, Chris. *The Body and Social Theory*. London: Sage Publications, 1993.

Simmonds, Alan G. V. *Britain and World War One*. New York: Routledge, 2012.

Singer, Richard B. "The First Mortality Follow-up Study: The 1841 Report of William Farr (Physician) on the Mortality of Lunatics." *Journal of Insurance Medicine* 33 (2001): 298–309.

Smith, Adam. *The Theory of Moral Sentiments*. Edited by D. D. Raphael and A. L. Macfie. Indianapolis: Liberty Fund, 1982.

Smith, Frederick C. "The Autopsy in Private Practice." *The Journal of the American Medical Association* 89.8 (August 20, 1927): 575–576.

Smythe, Karen. "Virginia Woolf's Elegiac Enterprise." *NOVEL: A Forum on Fiction* 26.1 (Autumn 1992): 64–79.

Solecki, Ralph S. "Shanidar IV, a Neanderthal Flower Burial in Northern Iraq." *Science*, New Series 190.4217 (November 28, 1975): 880–881.

Soloway, Richard A. "Eugenics and Pronatalism in Wartime Britain." *The Upheaval of War: Family, Work and Welfare in Europe, 1914–1918*. Edited by Richard Wall and Jay Winter. Cambridge: Cambridge University Press, 1988. 369–388.

Spargo, R. Clifton. *The Ethics of Mourning: Grief and Responsibility in Elegiac Literature*. Baltimore: Johns Hopkins University Press, 2004.

Spender, Stephen. *T. S. Eliot*. Edited by Frank Kermode. New York: The Viking Press, 1975.

Sperling, Daniel. *Posthumous Interests: Legal and Ethical Perspectives*. Cambridge: Cambridge University Press, 2008.

Staten, Henry. *Eros in Mourning: Homer to Lacan*. Baltimore: Johns Hopkins University Press, 1995.

Stevens, Wallace. *Letters of Wallace Stevens*. Edited by Holly Stevens. New York: Alfred A. Knopf, 1970.

Stevens, Wallace. *The Palm at the End of the Mind*. Edited by Holly Stevens. New York: Vintage Books, 1967.

Stewart, T. D. "The Neanderthal Skeletal Remains from Shanidar Cave, Iraq: A Summary of Findings to Date." *Proceedings of the American Philosophical Society* 121.2 (April 29, 1977): 121–165.

Strange, Julie-Marie. *Death, Grief and Poverty in Britain, 1870–1914*. Cambridge: Cambridge University Press, 2005.

Strauss, Jonathan. "After Death." *Diacritics* 30.3 (Fall 2000): 90–104.

Strauss, Jonathan. *Human Remains: Medicine, Death, and Desire in Nineteenth-Century Paris*. New York: Fordham University Press, 2012.

Strauss, Jonathan. *Subjects of Terror: Nerval, Hegel, and the Modern Self*. Stanford, CA: Stanford University Press, 1998.

Suiter, A. Walter. "On the Disposal of the Dead, with Special Reference to the Prevalent Practice of Embalming." *Journal of the American Medical Association* XXV.24 (December 14, 1895): 1034–1038.

Sundquist, Eric J. *Faulkner: The House Divided*. Baltimore: Johns Hopkins University Press, 1983.

Tanakh. 2nd edition. Philadelphia: The Jewish Publication Society, 2000.

Taylor, Charles. *A Secular Age*. Cambridge, MA: Harvard University Press, 2007.

Taylor, Jeremy. *The Whole Works of the Right Rev. Jeremy Taylor, D. D.* Vol. 5. 3rd edition. London: James Moyes, 1839.

Taylor, Lawrence J. "Introduction: The Uses of Death in Europe." *Anthropological Quarterly* 62. 4 (October 1989): 149–154.

Terrinoni, Enrico. " 'Hades': The Unknown Country of *Ulysses*." *Studi Irlandesi*. Edited by Carlo Bigazzi. Rome: Yorick Libri, 2004.

Thomas, Louis-Vincent. "Funeral Rites: An Overview." *Encyclopedia of Religion*. Vol. 5, 2nd edition. Edited by Lindsay Jones. Detroit: Macmillan Reference, 2005. 3233–3241.

Turner, Victor W. *The Ritual Process: Structure and Anti-Structure*. Chicago: Aldine Publishing Company, 1969.

Turner, Victor. "Variations on a Theme of Liminality." *Secular Ritual*. Edited by Sally F. Moore and Barbara G. Myerhoff. Amsterdam: Van Corcum, 1977. 36–52.

Tymoczko, Maria. *The Irish Ulysses*. Berkeley: University of California Press, 1994.

Usborne, Cornelie. " 'Pregnancy is the Woman's Active Service.' Pronatalism in Germany during the First World War." *The Upheaval of War: Family, Work and Welfare in Europe, 1914–1918*. Edited by Richard Wall and Jay Winter. Cambridge: Cambridge University Press, 1988. 389–416.

van Emden, Richard. *The Quick and the Dead: Fallen Soldiers and Their Families in the Great War*. London: Bloomsbury, 2011.

van Gennup, Arnold. *The Rites of Passage*. Translated by Monika B. Vizedom and Gabrielle L. Caffee. London: Routledge, 2004.

Van Haute, Phillipe. "Death and Sublimation in Lacan's Reading of *Antigone*." *Levinas and Lacan: The Missed Encounter*. Edited by Sarah Harasym. Albany: State University of New York Press, 1998. 102–120.

Verdery, Katherine. *The Political Lives of Dead Bodies: Reburial and Postsocialist Change*. New York: Columbia University Press, 1999.

Vico, Giambattista. *The New Science*. Translated by Thomas Goddard Bergin and Max Harold Fisch. Ithaca, NY: Cornell University Press, 1968.

Vogel, Morris J. "Introduction." *On the Administrative Frontier of Medicine: The First Ten Years of the American Hospital Association, 1899–1908*. Edited by. Morris J. Vogel. New York: Garland Publishing, 1989. i–xii.

Vogel, Morris J. *The Invention of the Modern Hospital: Boston, 1870–1930*. Chicago: University of Chicago Press, 1980.

Wallace, Emily M., and William Carlos Williams. "An Interview with William Carlos Williams." *The Massachusetts Review* 14.1 (Winter 1973): 130–148.

Walsh, Michael J. *K. C. R. W. Nevinson: This Cult of Violence*. New Haven, CT: Yale University Press, 2002.

Walter, Tony. "Three Ways to Arrange a Funeral: Mortuary Variation in the Modern West." *Mortality* 10.3 (August 2005): 173–192.

Watkin, William. *On Mourning: Theories of Loss in Modern Literature*. Edinburgh: Edinburgh University Press, 2004.

Watkins, Carl. *The Undiscovered Country: Journeys Among the Dead*. London: Bodley Head, 2013.

Watney, Simon. *Policing Desire: Pornography, AIDS, and the Media*. Minneapolis: University of Minnesota Press, 1987.

Weber, Max. *From Max Weber: Essays in Sociology*. Translated by H. H. Gerth and C. Wright Mills. New York: Oxford University Press, 1946.

West, Arthur Graeme. *The Diary of a Dead Officer*. London: George Allen & Unwin, Ltd., 1918.

Weiner, Annette B. "Reproduction: A Replacement for Reciprocity." *American Ethnologist* 7.1 (February 1980): 71–85.

Whitman, Walt. *Leaves of Grass and Other Writings*. Edited by Michael Moon. New York: W. W. Norton, 2002.

Whittemore, Reed. *William Carlos Williams, Poet from Jersey*. Boston: Houghton Mifflin, 1975.

Williams, William Carlos. *The Collected Poems: Volume I, 1909–1939*. Edited by A. Walton Litz and Christopher MacGowan. New York: New Directions, 1986.

Williams, William Carlos. *The Doctor Stories*. New York: New Directions, 1984.

Williams, William Carlos. *Paterson*. Revised edition. New York: New Directions, 1992.

Wilson, Edmund. *Axel's Castle: A Study in the Imaginative Literature of 1870–1930*. New York: Charles Scribner's Sons, 1931.

Winter, J. M. *The Great War and the British People*. Cambridge, MA: Harvard University Press, 1986.

Winter, J. M. "Some Paradoxes of the First World War." *The Upheaval of War: Family, Work and Welfare in Europe, 1914–1918*. Edited by Richard Wall and Jay Winter. Cambridge: Cambridge University Press, 1988. 9–42

Winter, Jay. *Sites of Memory, Sites of Mourning: The Great War in European Cultural History*. Cambridge: Cambridge University Press, 1995.

Woloch, Alex. *The One vs. The Many: Minor Characters and the Space of the Protagonist in the Novel*. Princeton, NJ: Princeton University Press, 2003.

Wood, David. "Some Questions for My Levinasian Friends." *Addressing Levinas*. Edited by Eric Sean Nelson, Antje Kapust, and Kent Still. Evanston, IL: Northwestern University Press, 2005. 152–169.

Woodburn, James. "Social Dimensions of Death in Four African Hunting and Gathering Societies." *Death and the Regeneration of Life*. Edited by Maurice Bloch and Jonathan Parry. Cambridge: University of Cambridge Press, 1982. 187–210.

Woolf, Virginia. *The Common Reader*. New York: Harcourt, 1925.

Woolf, Virginia. *The Death of the Moth and Other Essays*. New York: Harcourt Brace Janovitch, 1942.

Woolf, Virginia. *Jacob's Room*. London: Penguin, 1992.

Woolf, Virginia. *Mrs. Dalloway*. London: Harcourt Brace, 1925.

Woolf, Virginia. *Roger Fry: A Biography*. London: Harcourt Brace, 1940.

Woolf, Virginia. *Three Guineas*. London: Harcourt, 1938.

Woolf, Virginia. *To the Lighthouse*. London: Penguin, 1992.

Woolf, Virginia. *The Waves*. London: Harcourt Brace, 1931.

Worthen, John. *T. S. Eliot: A Short Biography*. London: Haus, 2009.

Yeats, W. B. *Collected Poems*. Revised 2nd edition. Edited by Richard J. Finneran. New York: Scribner Paperback Poetry, 1983.

Yeats, W. B. "Introduction." *Oxford Book of Modern Verse*. Oxford: Oxford University Press, 1936.

Index

abjection, 6, 19, 20, 22, 35, 36, 47–48, 111, 182, 208n25, 213n75
Actuarial Society of America, 34–35
Adorno, Theodor, 3, 117, 118, 152
Agamben, Giorgio, 94–95, 105, 239n22
American Medical Association, 31–32
Anatomy Act (1832), 44
Anderson, Benedict, 97, 226n140
Ariès, Phillipe, 25–26, 213n77, 224n108, 236–237n8
Arnold, Catherine, 215n94
Attridge, Derek, 125
Auden, W. H., 226n138
Augustine, 238n20
Auslander, Mark, 212n72
autopsy. *See* dissection

Barnes, Djuna, 146–147
  early writing, 246–247n78
  Ladies Almanack, 155–156, 240n25
  Nightwood, 151–153, 171–193, 204, 238n19, 245–246n73
Barthes, Roland, 113–114, 174, 178, 210n36
Bataille, Georges, 237n10
Battle of the Somme, The (film), 64–66, 221–222n73
Baucom, Ian, 212n58
Baudelaire, Charles, 149
Baudrillard, Jean, 38–39, 123–124, 208n25, 231n25, 231n34, 241n38
Bauman, Zygmaut, 208n26
Beckett, Samuel, 128
Benjamin, Walter, 120, 129, 157–158, 186–187, 212n58, 240n29

Berger, John, 38
Bersani, Leo, 238n17
Bible, The, 132–133
Bierce, Ambrose, 215n91, 216n101, 216n109, 216n110, 217n122
biopolitics, 91–95
Blanchot, Maurice, 19, 20–21, 23–24, 239n21, 239n22
Bleikasten, André, 136
Bloch, Maurice, 45, 209n30, 215n87
Bloom, Harold, 188, 248n101
Blunden, Edmund, 47, 78, 221n72
Bone, Muirhead, 59–64
Boone, Joseph Allen, 170, 174, 181
Booth, Allyson, 47, 227n151
Bourdieu, Pierre, 114, 116
Borden, Mary, 52–53
Bourke, Joanna, 219n3, 220n21, 221n64
Boyd-Orr, Lord, 52
Boyer, Pascal, 10, 207n20, 208n26
British Artists at the Front, 72, 73
Brooke, Rupert, 81, 82
Brooker, Jewel Spears, 207n21, 249n106
Brooks, Peter, 120, 121, 228n1
Brookwood Necropolis Railway, 231n33
Brown, Vincent, 6, 46, 212n72
burial. *See* corpse, burial of *and* burial alive
burial alive, 52–53, 220n31
burial plot, 108–111, 131–133, 228n1
Burke, Kenneth, 244n59, 244n62
Butler, Judith, 129, 139, 212n58

Cagidemetrio, Alide, 173
Camus, Albert, 16, 229n14